Comedy and Trauma in Germany and Austria after 1945
The Inner Side of Mourning

LEGENDA

LEGENDA is the Modern Humanities Research Association's book imprint for new research in the Humanities. Founded in 1995 by Malcolm Bowie and others within the University of Oxford, Legenda has always been a collaborative publishing enterprise, directly governed by scholars. The Modern Humanities Research Association (MHRA) joined this collaboration in 1998, became half-owner in 2004, in partnership with Maney Publishing and then Routledge, and has since 2016 been sole owner. Titles range from medieval texts to contemporary cinema and form a widely comparative view of the modern humanities, including works on Arabic, Catalan, English, French, German, Greek, Italian, Portuguese, Russian, Spanish, and Yiddish literature. Editorial boards and committees of more than 60 leading academic specialists work in collaboration with bodies such as the Society for French Studies, the British Comparative Literature Association and the Association of Hispanists of Great Britain & Ireland.

The MHRA encourages and promotes advanced study and research in the field of the modern humanities, especially modern European languages and literature, including English, and also cinema. It aims to break down the barriers between scholars working in different disciplines and to maintain the unity of humanistic scholarship. The Association fulfils this purpose through the publication of journals, bibliographies, monographs, critical editions, and the MHRA Style Guide, and by making grants in support of research. Membership is open to all who work in the Humanities, whether independent or in a University post, and the participation of younger colleagues entering the field is especially welcomed.

ALSO PUBLISHED BY THE ASSOCIATION

Critical Texts
Tudor and Stuart Translations • New Translations • European Translations
MHRA Library of Medieval Welsh Literature

MHRA Bibliographies
Publications of the Modern Humanities Research Association

The Annual Bibliography of English Language & Literature
Austrian Studies
Modern Language Review
Portuguese Studies
The Slavonic and East European Review
Working Papers in the Humanities
The Yearbook of English Studies

www.mhra.org.uk
www.legendabooks.com

GERMANIC LITERATURES

Editorial Committee
Convenor: Professor Ritchie Robertson (University of Oxford)
Dr Barbara Burns (Glasgow University)
Professor Jane Fenoulhet (University College London)
Professor Anne Fuchs (University of Warwick)
Dr Jakob Stougaard-Nielsen (University College London)
Professor Annette Volfing (University of Oxford)
Professor Susanne Kord (University College London)
Professor John Zilcosky (University of Toronto)

Germanic Literatures includes monographs and essay collections on literature originally written not only in German, but also in Dutch and the Scandinavian languages. Within the German-speaking area, it seeks also to publish studies of other national literatures such as those of Austria and Switzerland. The chronological scope of the series extends from the early Middle Ages down to the present day.

APPEARING IN THIS SERIES

1. *Yvan Goll: The Thwarted Pursuit of the Whole*, by Robert Vilain
2. *Sebald's Bachelors: Queer Resistance and the Unconforming Life*, by Helen Finch
3. *Goethe's Visual World*, by Pamela Currie
4. *German Narratives of Belonging: Writing Generation and Place in the Twenty-First Century*, by Linda Shortt
5. *The Very Late Goethe: Self-Consciousness and the Art of Ageing*, by Charlotte Lee
6. *Women, Emancipation and the German Novel 1871-1910: Protest Fiction in its Cultural Context*, by Charlotte Woodford
7. *Goethe's Poetry and the Philosophy of Nature: Gott und Welt 1798–1827*, by Regina Sachers
8. *Fontane and Cultural Mediation: Translation and Reception in Nineteenth-Century German Literature*, edited by Ritchie Robertson and Michael White
9. *Metamorphosis in Modern German Literature: Transforming Bodies, Identities and Affects*, by Tara Beaney
10. *Comedy and Trauma in Germany and Austria after 1945: The Inner Side of Mourning*, by Stephanie Bird
11. *E.T.A. Hoffmann's Orient: Romantic Aesthetics and the German Imagination*, by Joanna Neilly
12. *Structures of Subjugation in Dutch Literature*, by Judit Gera

Managing Editor
Dr Graham Nelson, 41 Wellington Square, Oxford OX1 2JF, UK
www.legendabooks.com

Comedy and Trauma in Germany and Austria after 1945

The Inner Side of Mourning

STEPHANIE BIRD

Germanic Literatures 10
Modern Humanities Research Association
2016

Published by Legenda
an imprint of the Modern Humanities Research Association
Salisbury House, Station Road, Cambridge CB1 2LA

ISBN 978-1-909662-95-7 *(HB)*
ISBN 978-1-781883-12-9 *(PB)*

All rights reserved. No part of this publication may be reproduced or disseminated or transmitted in any form or by any means, electronic, mechanical, photocopying, recording or otherwise, or stored in any retrieval system, or otherwise used in any manner whatsoever without written permission of the copyright owner, except in accordance with the provisions of the Copyright, Designs and Patents Act 1988, or under the terms of a licence permitting restricted copying issued in the UK by the Copyright Licensing Agency Ltd, Saffron House, 6–10 Kirby Street, London EC1N 8TS, *England, or in the USA by the Copyright Clearance Center, 222 Rosewood Drive, Danvers MA 01923. Application for the written permission of the copyright owner to reproduce any part of this publication must be made by email to legenda@mhra.org.uk.*

Disclaimer: Statements of fact and opinion contained in this book are those of the author and not of the editors or the Modern Humanities Research Association. The publisher makes no representation, express or implied, in respect of the accuracy of the material in this book and cannot accept any legal responsibility or liability for any errors or omissions that may be made.

Trademark notice: Product or corporate names may be trademarks or registered trademarks, and are used only for identification and explanation without intent to infringe.

© *Modern Humanities Research Association 2016*

Copy-Editor: Charlotte Brown

CONTENTS

	Acknowledgments	ix
	Abbreviations	x
	Introduction: Comedy, Trauma, and the Ethics of Representation	1
1	Ingeborg Bachmann: Comedy and the Women's Weepie	31
2	Rainer Werner Fassbinder: Ludicrous Melodrama and Comic Double Vision	58
3	W. G. Sebald: Melancholy's Seduction and the Pleasures of Comedy	84
4	Volker Koepp and Reinhard Jirgl: Comedy and Monologic Histories	110
5	Ruth Klüger: Comedy and *Ressentiment*	144
6	Edgar Hilsenrath and Jonathan Littell: Perpetrators, Comedy, and the Fantasy of Justice	167
	Conclusion	199
	Bibliography	204
	Index	219

For my father

ACKNOWLEDGMENTS

I would like to thank the AHRC for its generous funding of the collaborative research project 'Reverberations of War in Germany and Europe since 1945' of which this book was a part.

I am indebted to Mary Fulbrook, Julia Wagner, Christiane Wienand, Alexandra Hills, Gaëlle Fisher, Richard Sheppard, Mererid Puw Davies, Helena Flam, and Erica Carter. Their insights and their comments have been valuable throughout my work on this project. I also thank the editorial team at Legenda, my editor and reader, whose suggestions were perceptive and crucial. I am grateful to Amalia Theodorakopoulos for her permission to reproduce 'In Wien wird weiter lustig durcheinanderregiert'. I am grateful too to my Dad who died this year, to my Mother and Mark, and to John. Most of all I thank Isaac and Simeon for their remarkable humour; and Miriam Bathsheba, who more than anyone proved to me the importance of comedy in the thick of it.

s.b., London, December 2015

ABBREVIATIONS

The following abbreviations are used throughout for references to primary works:

Fi	Imre Kertész, *Fiasco*, trans. by Tim Wilkinson (New York: Melville House, 2011)
F	Imre Kertész, *Fateless*, trans. by Tim Wilkinson (London: Vintage, 2006)
DK	Imre Kertész, *Dossier K.*, trans. by Tim Wilkinson (New York: Melville House, 2013)
M	Ingeborg Bachmann, *Malina*, in *'Todesarten'-Projekt*, ed. by Monika Albrecht and Dirk Göttsche, 4 vols (Munich: Piper, 1995), III.1
BS	Ingeborg Bachmann, 'Besichtigung einer alten Stadt', in *'Todesarten'-Projekt*, ed. by Albrecht and Göttsche, III.2
DBF	Ingeborg Bachmann, *Das Buch Franza*, in *'Todesarten'-Projekt*, ed. by Albrecht and Göttsche, II
GR	Ingeborg Bachmann, *Goldmann/Rottwitz-Roman*, in *'Todesarten'-Projekt*, ed. by Albrecht and Göttsche, I
S	Ingeborg Bachmann, *Simultan*, in *'Todesarten'-Projekt*, ed. by Albrecht and Göttsche, IV
A	W. G. Sebald, *Austerlitz* (Munich: Süddeutsche Zeitung/Bibliothek, 2008)
AusE	W. G. Sebald, *Austerlitz*, trans. by Anthea Bell (London: Hamish Hamilton, 2001)
DA	W. G. Sebald, *Die Ausgewanderten* (Frankfurt a.M.: Fischer, 2008)
TE	W. G. Sebald, *The Emigrants*, trans. by Michael Hulse (London: Harvill, 1997)
RS	W. G. Sebald, *Die Ringe des Saturn* (Frankfurt a.M.: Fischer, 2007)
Rings	W. G. Sebald, *The Rings of Saturn*, trans. by Michael Hulse (London: Harvill, 1998)
SG	W. G. Sebald, *Schwindel. Gefühle.* (Frankfurt a.M.: Fischer, 2009)
V	W. G. Sebald, *Vertigo*, trans. by Michael Hulse (London: Vintage, 2002)
B-S	Volker Koepp, *Berlin — Stettin* (Edition Salzgeber, 2010)
HZuFZ	Volker Koepp, *Herr Zwilling und Frau Zuckermann* (Edition Salzgeber, 2010)
U	Volker Koepp, *Uckermark* (Edition Salzgeber, 2010)
DJiC	Volker Koepp, *Dieses Jahr in Czernowitz* (Edition Salzgeber, 2010)
P	Volker Koepp, *Pommerland* (Edition Salzgeber, 2010)
Me	Volker Koepp, *Memelland* (Edition Salzgeber, 2010)
H	Volker Koepp, *Holunderblüte* (Edition Salzgeber, 2008)
KN	Volker Koepp, *Kurische Nehrung* (Edition Salzgeber, 2010)
St	Reinhard Jirgl, *Die Stille* (Munich: DTV, 2009)
Fla	Ruth Klüger, *Frauen lesen anders* (Munich: DTV, 1997)
GW	Ruth Klüger, *Gelesene Wirklichkeit: Fakten und Fiktionen in der Literatur* (Göttingen: Wallstein, 2006)
K	Ruth Klüger, *Katastrophen: Über deutsche Literatur* (Göttingen: Wallstein, 2009)
LoM	Ruth Klüger, *Landscapes of Memory: A Holocaust Girlhood Remembered* (London: Bloomsbury, 2004)
uv	Ruth Klüger, *unterwegs verloren: Erinnerungen* (Munich: DTV, 2008)
wl	Ruth Klüger, *weiter Leben: Eine Jugend* (Munich: DTV, 1999)
DNuDF	Edgar Hilsenrath, *Der Nazi und der Friseur* (Munich: DTV, 2010)
TKO	Jonathan Littell, *The Kindly Ones*, trans. by Charlotte Mandell (London: Vintage, 2010)

INTRODUCTION

Comedy, Trauma, and the Ethics of Representation

'Sheer Impudence'

'We consider that your way of giving artistic expression to the material of your experiences does not come off, whereas the subject itself is horrific and shocking'.[1] These are the criticisms with which a publisher rejects the manuscript that the old boy, the protagonist of Imre Kertész's novel *Fiasco*, has submitted for consideration. The old boy's novel depicts his experience as a fourteen-year old Hungarian Jewish boy of being deported to Auschwitz. The publisher's disquiet over the old boy's unusual representation of a horrific and shocking subject stems from the fact that the 'protagonist's, to put it mildly, odd reactions' (*Fi*, 56) fail to transform the concentration camp experience into a shattering experience for the reader. The protagonist's 'gauche comments' and 'lack of compassion' function to 'repel and offend the reader' (*Fi*, 57). Prime examples of what is offensive are the protagonist's first impression of the shaven prisoners as 'suspect', and that he feels their 'jug ears, prominent noses, sunken, beady eyes with a crafty gleam' make them seem 'Quite like Jews in every respect'. And, shockingly, the crematoria elicit in him a feeling of '"a sense of a certain joke, a kind of student jape"' (*Fi*, 56). As though this is not enough, the style of the novel is 'clumsy' and 'tortuous' (*Fi*, 57).

On the penultimate page of the novel we learn that the old boy's novel was, after its initial rejection, published after all. This is actually no surprise, since the reader suspects all along that the novel is, in a complex interweaving of fact and fiction, Kertész's own first novel, *Fateless*. Indeed the reader can cross-reference the publisher's quotation from the old boy's novel with the point in Kertész's *Fateless* where the protagonist, György Köves, does refer to his 'sense of certain jokes, a kind of student prank'.[2] György's sense of a joke is provoked by the incompatibility of murder and civility that he observes upon arrival at Auschwitz-Birkenau, the way in which everyone is 'swaddling them with solicitude and loving-kindness' (*F*, 110), and the fact that the place where they are gassed is surrounded by lawns, trees, and flower beds. Despite feeling increasingly queasy, for he is aware of the outcome of the procedure, György nevertheless has the impression of a stunt: gentlemen in imposing suits, smoking cigars, who must have come up with a string of ideas, first of the gas, then of the bathhouse, next the soap, the flower beds, 'and so on' (*F*, 111), jumping up and slapping palms when they conjured up a good one.

The publisher's response in *Fiasco*, as well as the letter's ambiguous status between fact and fiction, both articulates and raises a range of concerns that remain central to debates around representations of atrocity and the Holocaust. The publisher's dismissal of György's responses as 'odd' complements his assumption that a horrific subject should produce a shattering experience for the reader. Thus he not only prescribes how someone ought to react to a horrific situation, but anticipates that the representation of horror should be translated into the reader's ability to feel that horror through emotional identification. György's lack of compassion (as the publisher sees it) for other victims, and his unsympathetic description of them, disqualifies him from making moral judgements, again implying that emotional identification with victims is the necessary heart of a moral response. It follows from the publisher's expectations that he should be offended that the extermination process could be figured as a joke. In *Dossier K.*, Kertész ascribes the rejection of *Fateless* to the artistic challenge it represented to the authority of the Hungarian dictatorship, which controlled the publishing house. He cites its 'sheer impudence [...], its style, its independence; a sarcasm inherent in its language that strains permitted bounds and dismisses the craven submissiveness that all dictatorships ordain for recognition and art'.[3] Yet the offence of coupling Auschwitz and a joke extends beyond the desire of a dictatorship for submissiveness. It also strains the expectation that Holocaust representation should remain uncoupled from the joke, and, more widely, from the comic.

It is such an expectation that this study seeks to challenge by drawing critical attention to the comic aesthetic at play in the work of key authors and directors. The book analyzes the intersection of comedy and suffering in selected German language novels and films that respond to the legacy of the Second World War and the Holocaust. It focuses on the work of Ingeborg Bachmann, Rainer Werner Fassbinder, W. G. Sebald, Volker Koepp, Reinhard Jirgl, and Ruth Klüger. Furthermore, it offers a comparison of Edgar Hilsenrath's and Jonathan Littell's treatment of perpetrator suffering. The texts and films have been selected for their explicit concern with suffering, and their engagement with the question of how suffering and trauma can be represented, but where their comic dimension has not been explored or centrally analyzed as part of interpretations of the work as a whole. My understanding of comedy is intentionally broad and is designed to encompass those aspects of the texts that challenge what Michael Mulkay refers to as 'serious discourse' by ignoring its demand for congruity. These aspects range from irony, through what is amusing or funny, to what in some cases is ludicrous, all of which open a space in which the celebration of 'interpretative duality' is key.[4]

Interpretative duality is central to the provocation of *Fateless*, for it undermines unambiguous moral distinctions. Primo Levi too invokes the notion of a joke in relation to Auschwitz. The prisoners, who have had nothing to drink for four days, are put into a room with a tap and a card that forbids drinking the water because it is dirty: 'Nonsense. It seems obvious that the card is a joke, "they" know that we are dying of thirst and they put us in a room, and there is a tap, and *Wassertrinken Verboten*'.[5] For both Kertész and Levi the joke arises from the incongruities of camp life, the absurdity of warning prisoners of the dangers of lice, or of the need to wash their hands, an absurdity intensified by its being expressed in kitsch rhyme: '*Nach dem Abort, vor dem Essen* | *Hände waschen, nicht vergessen*' [After the latrines, before eating | wash your hands, no forgetting].[6] In Levi's example the relationship of mocked and mocker is clear, but Kertész's text disturbs this moral polarity chiefly, as he himself identifies, by the narrative tone.

György consistently maintains a distanced gaze on his experiences, his observations not only sarcastic but also peculiarly detached and understated even when he describes his torment. At the end of his first day in Auschwitz he is 'tired out by the host of new events, experiences, and impressions, and moreover drowsy' (F, 116), as though he has been sightseeing. He admits: 'the meal system in Auschwitz, I have to say, was most peculiar' (F, 119), and his own associations too add to the sense of peculiarity. The tightly and ruthlessly controlled column of marching prisoners at Buchenwald, of which he is part, reminds him 'of those caterpillars in a matchbox that as a child I had guided with the aid of slips of paper and prods, all of which somehow slightly intoxicated, even utterly fascinated, me' (F, 122). The physical and mental degradation of the prisoners and the collapse of friendships are registered by György when he nearly fails to recognize one of the boys he was deported with. The once dapper Fancyman is now a 'strange creature [...] his face all sunken, pinched, and peaky' (F, 154), who shuffles past unable even to respond to György's greeting: 'and I thought to myself: Can you beat that! Who'd have thought it!' (F, 155).

In *Fateless*, the absurdity of the camps is never absent from the combination of the narrator's distance with his scrupulous search for accuracy. The sense of a joke is not limited to muddying the clear moral distinction between perpetrator and victim, but manifests itself too in György's startling, even funny, observations and remarks. In their 'impudence', these at times seem to intimate a joke, played on any reader who, like the publisher, and like the journalist who questions György upon his return to Budapest, anticipates reading about 'the hell of the camps' (F, 248). But, as he says, 'I had nothing at all to say about that as I was not acquainted with hell and couldn't even imagine what that was like' (F, 248). For him the experience of Auschwitz is not exactly described by 'ghastly' (F, 117) but by 'boredom, together with that strange anticipation' of waiting for 'nothing to happen' (F, 119). Hell, in contrast, would be a 'place where it is impossible to become bored' (F, 249). Expectations of Holocaust representation are strained to the limit when György's account culminates in a moment of 'sharp, painful, futile longing' for the camp: he feels 'nostalgia, homesickness' for, 'in a certain sense, life there had been clearer and simpler' (F, 261). In the face of those who ask only about the 'atrocities', the most memorable experience for him is that 'even there, next to the chimneys, in the intervals between the torments, there was something that resembled happiness' (F, 262).

The narrator laconically observes the torment of the camps, at the same time remaining fascinated by their absurdity and building a sense of the absurd into his narrative style. This layering of the absurd is typical of Kertész's comic aesthetic more generally, which emerges from the way he holds together so many aspects: the complex emotional responses to his camp experiences, explicit concerns about how to represent those experiences aesthetically, and the position of writing for himself and for an audience. In *Fiasco*, the old boy's notes describe the ambiguous pleasure of remembering the camps, the 'strange ecstasy' and 'voluptuous feeling' bestowed by recalling his time there as if in the present. His metaphor of Auschwitz as an 'undigested dumpling, its spices belching up', encapsulates the mixture of pleasure and difficulty he feels, as well as illustrating the comic edge of his self-representation. The old boy does not know whether 'memory itself is attended by that delight, irrespective of its subject', since a concentration camp is not 'exactly a bowl of fun' (*Fi*, 73). But whereas recollecting the experiences has greater reality for him than living them did, these memories are not the same as what he writes, for in the writing they become transformed so that his work is 'nothing else than a systematic atrophying of my experiences in the interest of an artificial — or if you prefer, artistic — formula' (*Fi*, 75).

Yet it is this very atrophying of the experiences that allows the novel to flourish as fiction. In *Dossier K.* Kertész insists on the distinction between fact and fiction, of autobiography and novel, by arguing that autobiography is a recollection whereas fiction is a creation of a world, however based on facts it is. Even if every detail is accurate, the 'world of fiction is a sovereign world that [...] follows the rules of art, of literature' and which is 'Remorseless in its laws' (*DK*, 10). Thus, he insists, 'In the novel [*Fateless*] I did have to invent Auschwitz' (*DK*, 9), and it is why he sees his 'proper place [...] not in the story but at the writing desk' (*DK*, 18). This same view is forcefully articulated by the old boy, whose experiences have been transformed into 'an irrevocable aesthetic standpoint' (*Fi*, 37): 'I was taken to Auschwitz not by the train in the novel but by a real one' (*Fi*, 75). So it is that words, over and above the concern with 'accurate portrayal' (*DK*, 129) take on their full significance from their place within the aesthetic whole. The shocking words 'happiness' and 'homesickness' change their ordinary meaning, just as bricks become part of a marvellous cathedral, because imagination is 'also a kind of reality' (*DK*, 130).

Kertész's work raises testing questions, both through its subject matter and exploration of themes, and in the way those themes are interwoven with the narrative fabric of the text. Through his eye for the joke and his comic sensibility, he interrogates representations of the 'greatest trauma of the twentieth century' (*DK*, 106) that seek to evoke horror through emotional identification, and confronts commonplaces of Auschwitz descriptions. This is at times both shocking and very funny, encapsulated in György's assertion that 'In any case, [...] I didn't notice any atrocities' (*F*, 256). The reader is unsettled by the possibility of a sick joke, one that she is drawn into enjoying, a voluptuous delight in reading divorced from the subject that perhaps hints, shockingly, that 'however sick a joke this may sound, Auschwitz proved a fruitful enterprise'.[7] Yet conversely, to deny 'aesthetic "pleasure"', to comply with the 'moral stink bomb' that censures Celan and Radnóti as barbaric, is also 'a sick joke' (*DK*, 105-6), for 'like it or not, art always regards life as a celebration' (*DK*, 104). Finally, his work asks us to think about the inevitable aesthetic mediation of experience, and, by resisting the conflation of the terms facts, accuracy, and reality, Kertész insists that the imagination must remain a plaything to create the reality in which certain issues can be addressed.

The constellation of issues that Kertész's work explores is at the heart of this study. It considers how 'voluptuous feeling' in the form of a comic aesthetic intersects with material that is not 'a bowl of fun' to interrogate the expectations and ethics of representing suffering and trauma. It examines the ways in which comedy functions to sustain or complicate the narrative perspective and modes of identification set up by the narrative. Thus comic devices may be used to sustain or challenge structures of empathy and identification that themselves depend upon a particular ethical or political position. Here the question of whose suffering is privileged, and how, becomes key, particularly with reference to the controversial issue of how German or Austrian suffering is depicted. Central to the book's enquiry will therefore be the question of what comedy contributes to debates around the ethics of representing trauma, victimhood, and suffering. It will also engage with the importance of comedy for interrogating and challenging our understanding of the notion of trauma and its prevalent use in cultural criticism: anxiety and moral disquiet around the pleasure we take in reading or watching suffering are especially acute in relation to suffering that has assumed significance as exemplary or as a cultural trauma. A final analytic thread will be a consideration of what comedy contributes to our understanding of melodrama and melancholy as two very differently evaluated articulations of suffering: melancholy as a privileged, masculine mode of perceiving and melodrama as a trivializing, feminine response.

'A Sense of a Certain Joke'

The relationship between the pleasures of art, others' suffering, and morality is a vexed one. Spectatorship of extreme events points to our 'degree of delight, and that no small one, in the real misfortunes and pains of others'.[8] This delight is, though, fraught, for it raises the question of what exactly it is we take pleasure in when we watch suffering from afar, whether this pleasure is the one of knowing oneself to be the survivor, of *Schadenfreude*, or the satisfaction of morbid curiosity. The transfiguration of the violent and traumatic event into an aesthetic object relieves the spectator of the accusation of being an actual bystander (for many spectators of atrocity are implicated in the event) and sanctions our pleasure in reading of or looking at another's suffering. As Susan Sontag observes in relation to Christian art, the depiction of violence has not provoked moral concern and the paintings offer both the 'satisfaction of being able to look at the image without flinching' and 'the pleasure of flinching'.[9] This is in contrast to the voyeurism of looking at a photograph of a real atrocity, unless the spectator is someone who can, like doctors, do something about the suffering.[10]

Sontag draws our attention to the transformation of reality by art, one that lessens the moral problems of voyeurism when it comes to fictionalized horror, however overwhelming it may be. But photography's indexical relationship to the reality it depicts means that it 'bears witness to the calamitous and the reprehensible' and as a result its inevitable aesthetic transformation of reality provokes moral judgement: 'Photographs that depict suffering shouldn't be beautiful'.[11] The anxiety caused by the pleasures elicited by representations of other people's pain is not, however, limited to photography, even if its indexical relation to reality is held to endow it with particular moral responsibility to its subjects. As is suggested by Sontag's juxtaposition of voyeurism with intervention or learning from, anxiety is commonly assuaged by the promise of moral improvement. Indeed, Martin Jay reminds us of Kant, for whom spectatorship is justified because 'by assuming the general viewpoint of the "world spectator" whose taste, imagination, and hope could transfigure events like shipwrecks or revolutions into ciphers of human improvement, one might transcend the despair aroused by a less elevated perspective'.[12] Thus the moral universe within which we may enjoy watching and reading of traumatic violence, or find ourselves fascinated by it, is normally carefully contained by a claim for a text's contribution to social, political, and ethical transformation one way or another.

The moral anxiety attending representations of violence and suffering, the fear that we are benefiting from the pain of others, is also contained by the boundaries of genre and the notion of appropriate form. The elevating catharsis of tragedy gives meaning to suffering, and the pleasure it gives rise to is part of a wider, ethically edifying experience. Yet if our pleasure in other people's suffering becomes too manifest as precisely that, pleasure, the response is anxiety, moral disquiet, and the devaluation of those modes of representation that clearly signal their association with pleasure, including comedy. It is precisely the unashamed association of comedy with pleasure that causes anxiety when representations of trauma and suffering include a comic dimension in their aesthetic. For comedy has, understandably, been commonly held to be incompatible with the tragic experience of another's death or suffering, or indeed the awareness of one's own finitude. This incompatibility has also been extended to aesthetic representation, where comedy is seen to be a by-product of more serious matters. This is typified in Cixous's attitude: 'I go to the theatre because I need to understand or at least to contemplate the act of death, or at least admit it, meditate on it; and also because I need to cry. And to laugh: but laughter is merely the sigh of relief that bursts forth at the scythe's passing: it missed us by a hair!'[13] Crying needs no excuse; laughter, however, is dismissed with a 'but' and a 'merely', typical of the generally lowlier status of comedy. Its association with the failings of the body, be this the reduction of the body to a mechanistic state or the ugly distortions of uncontrollable laughter, compares poorly with tragedy's emphasis on truth, and the usually male heroic gesture of reconciling individual will with necessity.[14]

However, the nature of the pleasure that we derive from comedy is more complex and ambivalent than the temporary relief of avoiding the scythe. The pleasures it offers include the affirmation of shared humour and its ability to confirm values, the hilarity of fooling around, the satisfaction derived from someone else's misfortune, the enjoyment of incongruity, the excitement of the macabre, and the thrill of provocation. However, these pleasures may be complicated by those aspects of comedy that are alienating, unsettling, and uncanny, which find expression in the German term 'das Komische' with its dual reference to both comedy and strangeness or peculiarity. Some types of comedy are more obviously associated with a feeling of unease or alienation, particularly irony and absurd humour, for they thrive on interpretative multiplicity and systematically question coherent meaning. Indeed, it is this unsettling dimension of comedy, particularly evident in cynical, bizarre, macabre, or naïve humour, which in its irritant effect may temper our pleasure, since it demands a critical response rather than one aimed solely at enjoyment.[15] Nevertheless, it is important to guard against any drift into schematization. Comedy's ability to cause pleasure, unease, reflection, or all of these — with unsettlement too so often offering a frisson of enjoyment — cannot be ascribed simply to type of comedy or content, but is inseparable from its function in a particular context.

The ethical implications of comedy reflect its complex nature and its ambivalent pleasures. Consequently, comedy neither entirely warrants the moral anxiety it provokes, nor totally abates it. Moral disquiet around comedy relates most obviously to the 'superiority' theory of comedy, which sees laughter being provoked in response to the inferiority of another, be that through ugliness of the body, character flaw, or behaviour. In this view, comedy is generated from the objectification or dehumanization of others, and the pleasure we take in our superiority depends upon exploiting their faults. As Hazlitt remarks, 'in general [...] we only laugh at those misfortunes in which we are spectators, not sharers'.[16] The superiority theory points to satire, to the comedy generated by ridicule and mockery, and it includes Freud's tendentious joke that constructs a butt to be laughed at. It is this aspect of comedy that is also linked to its negative evaluation as aggressive and debasing, and as a form of release of those emotions and drives that have been socially repressed. Yet any self-evident moral censure attaching to this understanding of comedy is destabilized by a consideration of context. For satire that ridicules the pretensions, weaknesses, and flaws of those in positions of power arguably has different moral effects from satire used in the service of sustaining a hegemonic ideology or particular social hierarchies. Kierkegaard recognizes the importance of different contexts in his consideration of the legitimate use of comedy, which varies even from individual to individual. Here, the polemical exposure of deficiency should not cause pain: 'It is absolutely necessary that the person concerned be himself happy in his ridiculous delusion; as soon as he is himself unhappy in his ludicrous delusion, he is not to be laughed at'.[17]

The variation in the appraisal of tendentious comedy is typical of a wider response to comedy, a moral ambivalence that is particularly evident around two of its key characteristics: distance and play. Distance from the object and the notion of 'laughing at' is inherent to the superiority theory, but it is also fundamental to more nuanced views of comedy based on incongruity. Here it is the coming together of different perspectives that produces humour, often through a sudden rupture of expectation. Thus, for example, Kant emphasizes the element of surprise and unexpectedness of comedy, and Schopenhauer suggests that the origin of laughter lies in suddenly recognizing the incongruity between concept and reality.[18] But incongruity may also involve the sustained holding together of mutually contradictory frames of reference or meaning. Hazlitt writes, for example, that the 'essence of the laughable is the incongruous, the disconnecting one idea from another, or the jostling of one feeling against another'.[19]

It is precisely these alternative possibilities and jostling feelings that demonstrate the limitations of any one particular perspective, evidence of a distance that makes comedy a threat to beliefs or acts that are held to be sacred, absolute, or all-consuming. Distance necessarily introduces an alternative point of view or exterior gaze that renders beliefs finite or relative, and that introduces the potential for critical detachment. The threat posed by comedy to the sacred, as well as the attempt to contain its pleasures, is reflected in the strong negative response in Christian thought to laughter, exemplified in Basil of Caesarea's assertion that 'it is clear that it is *never* the right time (*kairos*) for laughter for a faithful person'.[20] This tradition of thought is reiterated by Reinhold Niebuhr when he contends that 'laughter must be heard in the outer courts of religion; [...] but there is no laughter in the holy of holies. There laughter is swallowed up in prayer and humour is fulfilled by faith'.[21] In a very different holy of holies, that of sex in its 'ecstatic dimension', comedy renders ridiculous 'the moment of the utmost intimate engagement'.[22] Thus comedy can be understood as containing a corrosive influence, challenging both the seriousness of people's convictions and the notion that their outlook and values are either sacrosanct or universal, or both.

Yet the distance of comedy remains morally ambivalent. For while it is deemed a threat to values that are revered, be those religious, ethical, political, or social, the distance conferred by comedy is also held by some theorists to be a crucial virtue. This is largely because comedy facilitates a detachment from the immediacy of emotions and allows for the assumption of a sovereign position from which one can look down upon the human condition.[23] Schiller ascribes to such distance the greatest of value and describes comedy as the equivalent to the highest of man's goals: 'frey von Leidenschaft zu sein, immer klar, immer ruhig um sich und in sich zu schauen' [to be free of passion, always clearly, always calmly to look around himself and into himself].[24] Freud also draws on the notion of distance to valorize humour. He distinguishes between the comedy generated by the unconscious in pursuit of pleasure, and humour, which is based upon the mediation of the super-ego.[25] The pleasure of humour is more nuanced and more valuable, for in addition to causing pleasure it is also concerned to stave off suffering in a way that sustains spiritual health, unlike neurosis, ecstasy, or madness.[26] The ability to be humorous is highly prized by Freud, for it is a rare gift that equips an individual to joke about the perceived danger of the world and thereby lessen its threat.[27]

The ethical value of comedy is specifically addressed by Robert C. Roberts, who argues that a sense of humour reflects the ability to enjoy a range of incongruities and perspectives. Its virtue resides in the fact that it allows a person to transcend character and perceive her own moral failings. In contrast, an individual lacking in humour is 'in a spiritual straitjacket constituted by his own character'.[28] Crucially, Roberts argues, such a person is lacking in freedom and play. His emphasis on the notion of play is, in addition to the difficulties posed by distance, vital for understanding the moral ambivalence around comedy. If a key characteristic of comedy is its playfulness, then it raises the question of comedy's relationship to reality and how that inflects comedy's moral status. Thus, when discussing jokes, Roberts suggests that to 'get' a joke, the malicious element of the joke must be shared. To suspend one's disbelief and adopt the perspective of a racist in order to laugh at a racist joke is not tantamount to adopting racist beliefs. Rather, in William James's terms, this temporary sharing of perspective can be thought of as a 'moral holiday' and is testament to the plasticity of the human mind, which enables it to adopt and experiment with various and contradictory attitudes. Thus, 'there *is* something like malice in the enjoyment of malicious humour. However, it need not be malice itself, but only "something like" malice'.[29] It is precisely this playful quality of humour that is a source of its moral importance according to Roberts, because it means that the individual is not 'locked in' to a particular point of view. Nevertheless, as he admits, there is no guarantee that the 'something like' cannot end up becoming the thing itself.

Roberts's argument is lent further credibility by Christie Davies's study of 'national' or 'ethnic' jokes. Davies too emphasizes the importance of play in understanding jokes' non-correspondence with reality, arguing that there is a 'widespread tendency to confuse serious and humorous statements and to confuse playing with aggression in jokes with real aggression. [...] [J]oke telling differs fundamentally from other forms of communication, such as bona fide communication or lying'.[30] Jokes are, precisely, not serious, and it is possible for people to enjoy in a joke what, if said seriously, would shock: 'Humor is about mock shocks, mock frights and mock aggression'.[31] Like other creative forms, jokes 'are ambiguous, do not have clear meanings, break empirical and logical rules and have multiple uses. They are a form of play'.[32]

Comedy's role as a form of play, and its ability to maintain mutually contradictory frames of interpretation, are qualities that are inseparable from the complex perspectives and moral holidays that may be offered by fiction.[33] The intricate systems of identification and response involved when we know something to be real or fictitious, comic or serious, influence the moral response of the reader or spectator. Are there fundamental ethical differences in laughing at somebody being humiliated, laughing at someone being humiliated in fiction, whatever the form, and laughing at someone being humiliated within a clear comic structure? Most fiction signals itself as fiction even if the events it depicts bear a strong resemblance to reality, and such signposting of its artificiality offers precisely the freedom to transcend character that Roberts adduces as a moral virtue. Yet the question remains whether the freedom conferred by the distinction of fiction and the play of comedy is unconditional. For the imaginary is inseparable from the social, be that understood phenomenologically, where 'there is no division between social and psychic identification, [...] or indeed between the film experience and everyday life',[34] psychoanalytically, where 'so many of the images that come to us in fantasies, daydreams, and dreams are already symbolically determined or structured', or dialectically.[35]

As Laura Mulvey pithily remarks, 'history is, undoubtedly, constructed out of representations', and patterns and structures of representation construct and reinforce dominant discourses.[36] This is most succinctly illustrated in Franz Fanon's anecdote about the screening of a Tarzan film in the Antilles and in Europe: 'In the Antilles, the young Negro identifies himself *de facto* with Tarzan against the Negroes. This is much more difficult for him in a European theatre, for the rest of the audience, which is white, automatically identifies him with the savages on the screen'.³⁷ Fanon's example is not about comedy, and one of the claims for comedy is that its ability to hold together competing or contradictory perspectives strengthens its moral value. This suggests that the potential for comedy to resist being subsumed into a single purpose and to maintain a subversive quality is inherent in its distance and play. Yet it is also clear from Roberts's acknowledgement of humour's function as a bridge between virtue and vice and vice versa and from Freud's admission, with which Davies's study concurs, that the joke is always in service of an intention, that the effects of comedy as well as its ethical standing, relate to context.³⁸

'Moral Stinkbomb'

Despite the ethical complexity of comedy, the post-Holocaust context has undeniably intensified doubts about whether it is an appropriate form of response to suffering and death. The suspicion of comedy sits within the wider distrust of pleasure that has a long philosophical tradition and that was particularly sharpened by modernism. In her analysis of pleasure and modernism, Laura Frost sets out the hierarchy explicit in the difference between *hedone* (pleasure), which was associated with the body and the senses, and *eudaimonia* (happiness), which was more highly valued as being measured, metaphysical, and partaking of truth.³⁹ The distinction that Plato makes between the 'true' pleasures of reason and intellect and the 'false' pleasures of the body is typical of the pleasure hierarchy that persists into the modern period.⁴⁰ In modernity, this hierarchy manifests itself particularly in the 'Great Divide' between mass culture and high art.⁴¹ This divide sustained a polarity whereby mass culture was distrusted and disparaged in comparison to high art, with, for example, the commodified, feminized, and distracting pleasures of popular cinema being deemed inferior to the critical, reflective, and contemplative modes of viewing offered by art. Popular culture became quickly aligned with the easy, superficial, and fake pleasure of kitsch, a term that emerged with the ability to mass-produce cultural products. Seen as morally unsavoury, as an 'aesthetic form of lying', kitsch offers enjoyment without any effort.⁴² In contrast, modernism emphasized the hard cognitive work needed for true pleasure, which is achieved through the process of deciphering complex writing. Quick and easy sensory pleasures are disavowed as modernism teaches readers to strive hard for their pleasure: 'Difficulty becomes an inherent value and is a deliberate aesthetic ambition set against too pleasing, harmonious reading effects'.⁴³ Comedy is particularly suspect here, for it undermines the aspiration of high art as well as offending against topics considered serious or sublime: 'Wenn Komik ihre Funktion besonders gut erfüllt, meldet sich gleich das Mißtrauen des gebildeten Ästheten, der die hehre Kultur gefährdet sieht' [When comedy fulfils its function particularly well, the educated aesthete immediately becomes suspicious and fears that sublime culture will be threatened].⁴⁴

It is against this background of philosophical and aesthetic distaste for pleasure that the conviction that there is something inappropriate about it is radically intensified by debates around Holocaust representation. The impact of Adorno's 'moral stinkbomb', as Kertész puts it, that 'to write poetry after Auschwitz is barbaric', reflects a profound crisis concerning representation.[45] This crisis relates fundamentally to the problem of ethical representation, including the incongruity between the aesthetic pleasures of art and the extreme violence and suffering of the genocide. As Adorno went on to say, his assertion about poetry does not apply absolutely, 'but it is certain that after Auschwitz, because Auschwitz was possible and remains possible for the forseeable future, light-hearted art is no longer conceivable'.[46] The seriousness of art thus becomes further aligned with the seriousness of its ethical response to the events it depicts and the validity of its truth claim, a conflation that is compounded by the other key ethical worry: the extent to which the Holocaust can be represented at all, let alone with 'false' pleasures in mind. The result is 'Holocaust piety'.[47]

The unspeakability of the Holocaust has as a foundational reference point Primo Levi's statement that 'we, the survivors, are not the true witnesses. [...] those who saw the Gorgon, have not returned to tell about it or have returned mute'.[48] Yet while fundamentally problematizing the ability to witness, Levi links the attempt to do so with an ethical responsibility: 'My religious friend had told me that I survived so that I could bear witness. I have done so, as best I could'.[49] Memory and Holocaust studies have in various ways engaged with this double bind, the question of how a central traumatizing event can be articulated when the witnesses are dead or cannot speak, with the concurrent ethical insistence on witnessing. A prevailing tendency has developed which insists upon the impossibility of representing the Holocaust, evinced in George Steiner's claim that 'the world of Auschwitz lies outside speech as it lies outside reason'.[50] The Holocaust's unrepresentability is combined with an avowal of its absolute uniqueness and results in its elevation to the level of the sacred. Thus Elie Wiesel argues that to represent the Holocaust is to violate the absolute separate universe that it inhabits: 'A novel about Majdanek is about blasphemy. *Is* blasphemy', it is 'an act that strikes all that is sacred'.[51] Claude Lanzmann too assumes guardianship of the sacred flame when he speaks of the Holocaust as 'unique in that it created a circle of flames around itself, [...] a protected, safe zone that is not to be entered. Here, to transgress or to trivialize are alike'.[52]

Whether Kertész would consider Lanzmann's statement a 'moral stinkbomb' we do not know, but Dominick LaCapra certainly is critical of Lanzmann and generally wary of ways in which the Holocaust is constructed in an aesthetic of the sublime. He speculates that the sublime may be a secular manifestation of the sacred, assuming the form of 'a radically transcendent, inaccessible, unrepresentable other (including the alterity of radical evil)'.[53] To be a witness is, within this dominant tendency, itself to be confronted with the sublime. Thus Michael Bernard-Donals and Richard Glejzer, although pointing to the self-evident fact that the Holocaust has been represented, consider it unclear whether those representations actually offer knowledge or whether they rather provide 'something akin to a flash of horror that precedes and disturbs our ability to know'.[54] Such a flash of horror, by disrupting knowledge, may prevent replicating the rationality of the Shoah. Furthermore, this flash of something that exceeds comprehension offers a glimpse of the sublime that by rupturing harmony, be that the coherence of knowledge or of aesthetic pleasure, offers a type of redemption.[55] It is 'precisely the production of this sublime excess, which troubles testimony and narrative and forces the reader to confront the horror of the limit' that is redemptive: redemptive not 'as positive or transcendent' but in the glimpse of what is beyond the human.[56]

LaCapra expresses reservations about the invocation of the sublime, arguing that it resonates with a general trend away from accessible narratives to a celebration of aesthetic approaches that privilege rupture in various guises. The aporia has come to figure the purported ineffability of trauma and is part of a widespread tendency 'to transfigure trauma (including at times violence) into the sacred or the sublime'.[57] I would add, furthermore, that a crucial part of this transfiguring process is also the explicit bestowing of ethical value onto trauma per se, even if it is not explicitly figured as the sublime. The re-evaluation of trauma as an emotionally charged state that holds ethical value has arisen from developments in philosophy, psychoanalysis, and psychiatry.

The ethical privileging of trauma has been profoundly influenced by an increasing philosophical emphasis on the encounter with the other as ethical. A key figure in articulating this view is Emmanuel Levinas. For him the encounter with death is the confrontation with absolute alterity: death is ungraspable, for it cannot be experienced, and as such remains always utterly alien. It cannot therefore be assumed as in any way mine, but remains an obstacle, 'a menace that approaches me as a mystery'.[58] Far from being an 'event of freedom', from constituting the 'supreme lucidity and [...] supreme virility' of Heidegger's being-towards-death, for Levinas death is the cause of suffering which renders the subject passive.[59] The absolute alterity of death means that the relation to death is beyond the subject's possibilities, it is a relation that cannot be reduced to self-presence.[60] This is the crucial point that marks the subject as ethical, as constituted in relation to alterity: 'dying structures the self as Being-for-the-other'.[61] For Levinas, the encounter with alterity is figured as shattering, traumatic, and ethical. The traumatic, ethical encounter is, furthermore, located outside of reason, a realm in which the 'foreign being, instead of maintaining [...] its singularity, [...] becomes a theme and an object'.[62]

The universalizing of ethics as a shattering, or traumatic, encounter with the other, that exceeds reason and language, has strong parallels in psychoanalytic thought. In Freud's work on trauma, it is always conceived of as an interaction between an external event, a situation of danger that threatens the ego, and an individual's affective predisposition. Social and cultural context is also key, so as Clara Mucci summarizes:

> The impact of trauma even in quantitative terms is mediated by several factors: the quality of the attachment, the resilience and integrated level of the self, the cultural and personal meaning attached socially and individually to the event, the presence of support to the victims within society and in the family, the reiteration of the event and duration in time.[63]

Thus some people experience an event as traumatic when others do not, as Freud already observed in relation to shell shock, and as is indicated by the fact that on average only 20 percent of those who experience traumatic events develop posttraumatic stress disorder (PTSD).[64] The complex understanding of trauma as an interaction between an external event, psychic predisposition, and social context has, however, as Ruth Leys demonstrates, frequently been undermined by a polarization of external and internal. What she calls 'mimetic theory' emphasizes the traumatic experience as unavailable to normal memory, fating the victim to act out and identify with the original trauma unconsciously. In contrast, 'antimimetic theory' depicts violence as purely and simply an assault from without.[65]

Psychoanalysis has been crucial for universalizing trauma into an ethics through its focus on 'mimetic' theories on internal psychic trauma as common to everyone. Necessary developmental experiences such as birth, separation from the mother, loss of the primary love object, alienation from the primary wholeness, have all been figured as fundamentally traumatic events. As LaCapra points out, no differentiation is made here between absence and loss, as a result of which we are all victims of fundamental trauma. Yet there is an important difference between the two terms. He defines absence as a foundational absence of an absolute that was never there, but that is often perceived as a real loss, such as the *Volksgemeinschaft*, or harmonious pre-modern society. Loss, however, is the historical consequence of particular events.[66] Psychoanalysis commonly elides absence with loss to posit trauma as a structural universal, meaning that it can then become a foundational experience for identification with others. Such a move is evident in Cathy Caruth's suggestion that we all bear an ethical responsibility to speak and listen 'from the site of trauma' that relates not only to 'what we simply know of each other, but to what we do not yet know of our own traumatic pasts'. Hence 'trauma itself may provide the very link between cultures'.[67] By positing the radical link between ethics and trauma, psychoanalysis further severs the connection of ethics with reason. This rupture is particularly evident in Lacanian thought, where the ethics of psychoanalysis is not a question of what constitutes the Good, but of whether one is 'guilty [...] of having given ground relative to one's desire'.[68] This formulation links ethical action not with the ego and its subservience to the moral(istic) precepts of the super-ego, but with the subject's constitutive and traumatic relationship to her desire.

Thus influential strands of philosophy and psychoanalysis have contributed to trauma being understood structurally as a basis of our common humanity, and, furthermore, as being central to our status as ethical beings. American psychiatry, exemplifying Leys's 'antimimetic' approach to trauma, has in a very different way also been key in strengthening the status of trauma as ethically valuable. This is both surprising and paradoxical, because through its strong focus on defining the symptoms of PTSD, it divorces the event from its moral context. In 1980 the *Diagnostic and Statistical Manual for Mental Disorders-III* (DSM-III) adopted the term 'post-traumatic stress disorder' for the first time, and the term 'neurosis' to describe traumatic reactions was abandoned. This was significant because it marked a shift away from seeking the cause of trauma in the unconscious, to locating it solely with an unbearable event. The definition of trauma based only on adverse symptoms following an extreme event had another crucial consequence: the diagnosis of trauma became independent from perceived moral culpability. Perpetrators could suffer trauma as well as victims, suffering which showed that 'even if they expressed no remorse [...] they still shared in the humanity that their cruelty would seem to have destroyed'.[69] The DSM-III definition arose out of the specific US context of Vietnam war veterans showing symptoms of combat shock while also implicated in atrocities, but Fassin and Rechtman point to its global importance:

> It removed the moral dimension from clinical practice (since it refused to draw any distinction between the criminal and his victim) and articulated an ethical truth that lay beyond individual judgement (since it claimed to recognize the locus of the intolerable). From the moral to the ethical: this was clearly a profound change in the outlook on violence.[70]

Thus 'trauma' has become an ethically privileged category, yet it is one that through its increasingly generalized usage has worrying ethical consequences. There are three key areas where concepts are problematically blurred or where the term trauma is generalized. First, structural trauma, founded in absence, and historical trauma, based on particular loss, are blurred. This justifies claims that trauma is universal and conversely facilitates a movement whereby a historical event that caused trauma assumes foundational status akin to a myth.[71] Yet whereas structural trauma is significant for analyzing and understanding constructions of identity and national identity, historical trauma is specific to context and experience and cannot be claimed by all.[72] In his advocacy of the term 'cultural trauma' Jeffrey Alexander draws a similar distinction between events and their transformation into a collective narrative. He points out that an event can be hugely disruptive without being traumatic. For an event to become a cultural trauma it must first be actively constructed as one through its transformation into a narrative and disseminated through institutions and social hierarchies.[73] Alexander argues that cultural traumas are symbolic constructions and as such they are not descriptions of individual experience or events, but arguments conducted in the social realm about the interpretation and function of those events for a collective.[74]

The elision of structural and historical trauma may facilitate the translation of the term trauma to a social and cultural level in such a way that suggests that all individuals, often of one nation or society, inhabit the same position in relation to an event. Although Alexander insists on the constructed nature of cultural trauma, the employment of collective terms often reinforces and naturalizes the original event as a 'real' trauma for all, disguising the ways in which the event has been mediated or constructed as a trauma for social or ideological reasons, or for reasons of commodification.[75] The generalization of individual to collective trauma is further aided by the second conceptual blurring, that of the event and the traumatic response. A crucial consequence of DSM-III's emphasis on the external event in causing trauma has been a shift in terminology so that events themselves are described as traumatic, with those who experience it constructed as victims without reference to their affective response. The clinical and historical evidence that points to the importance of resilience is overlooked in favour of constructing victim status through tautological reference to a traumatic event. The specific analysis of how individual symptoms relate to a collective, why certain events do not result in 'collective trauma', and who exactly is traumatized become secondary.

The third blurring of categories is the conflation of the person who experiences trauma with victimhood. Fassin and Rechtman are tentatively optimistic that the increasingly broad application of trauma is a way of moving beyond the category of victim that was so central to the Holocaust model: 'By applying the same psychological classification to the person who suffers violence, the person who commits it, and the person who witnesses it, the concept of trauma profoundly transforms the moral framework of what constitutes humanity'.[76] Yet as their study goes on to demonstrate, the ever-expanding empire of trauma does not necessarily lead to the category of victim being productively questioned, but colludes in constructing more victims, including victims who are not the real victims.[77] The entrenched association of trauma with victimhood is why the term 'perpetrator trauma' is provocative. LaCapra refuses the alliance of trauma with victimhood, insisting that symptoms of trauma in those who commit atrocities, even if they can be understood as evidence of humanity, do not make someone a victim: '"Victim" is not a psychological category. It is, in variable ways, a social, political, and ethical category. [...] Not everyone traumatized by events is a victim'.[78] This is a vital point, for it insists on the importance of a specific context for the term to be meaningful.

'Similar Feelings'

The emergence of trauma and victimhood as ethically privileged states assumes a further twist in the context of Germany and Austria. By focusing on victims, questions of responsibility and culpability for the cause of suffering can too easily be marginalized. So how a text solicits empathy or identification and to what purpose becomes crucial to how victimhood is depicted. The politics of empathy with victims is particularly significant within a context where victimhood has been central to Austrian and German post-war narratives, both personal and national. The notion of victimhood was central to the construction of post-war Austrian national identity despite strong support by Austrians for the *Anschluss* in March 1938 and their far-reaching participation in the Third Reich and genocide. Indeed, Austrians were disproportionately involved in the Holocaust, providing half the concentration camp guards despite having only one-tenth of Germany's population before the war.[79] But in the Moscow Declaration of 30 October 1943 the foundation for the Austrian victim myth was laid when the allies declared that Austria was 'the first victim of Hitlerite aggression'. Austria's acknowledged status as victim was further confirmed as key to its self-definition when in the Austrian State Treaty of 1955 the allies omitted the clause referring to 'Austrian responsibility for her participation in World War II'. As Hella Pick remarks, the 'outside world was more interested in Austria's post-war achievements than in its Nazi record, its anti-Semitism or its reluctance to face up to its past; the four wartime allies still had no qualms about endorsing Austria's status as Nazi Germany's first victim'.[80]

The Austrian self-definition as victim rested on profound denial, as Jean Améry clearly states: 'Österreich jedoch, von seinen Politikern der Welt als ein Opfer Hitlers vorgestellt, steht vor der unerträglichen Nötigung, sich selbst ganz und gar zu verleugnen' [Yet Austria, presented to the world as a victim of Hitler by its politicians, suffers from the terrible compulsion to deny itself utterly].[81] This denial was not only an attempt at moral exculpation, but was also financially beneficial in that it led to the allies reducing Austria's reparation payments and also allowed Austria to divest itself of any responsibility for compensation to victims. Austria delayed payments to Israel and Jewish survivors, made the claim process very difficult and only recognized Roma and Sinti as victims from 1981. In contrast, injuries sustained from being active in the Nazi party or the *Wehrmacht* were fully compensated.[82] Austria's status as victim was publicly challenged when the Waldheim affair of the 1980s forced discussion and acknowledgment of Austrian support for the Nazi regime and anti-Semitism. In July 1991 the Social Democrat Chancellor, Franz Vranitzky, offered the first public revision of the 'victim' narrative, admitting that Austria could no longer avoid its moral responsibility for deeds perpetrated by its citizens.[83]

Although from the 1990s Austria's position as the first victim of National Socialism was no longer officially condoned, the case of Germany demonstrates that public and private discourses of victimhood do not necessarily match, and that widespread suffering can be cast as a type of victimhood. In Germany, a 'rhetorics of victimization'[84] has played a significant role in responses to the Second World War. The mass migration of up to fifteen million ethnic Germans at the end of the war, the mass rape of women and the bombing of German towns have been fundamental to narratives of victimhood in West Germany.[85] Discourses of victimhood were present in the domestic sphere from 1945 onwards, but also played a vital role in forging an identity for the united Germany.[86] If in the Federal Republic of Germany (FRG) narratives of suffering had offered collective legitimacy against East European communism and eased integration into the West, in the united Germany they offered a means for establishing cohesion.[87] Thus, for example, forced expulsion was viewed by the government as common to the history of East and West Germans and therefore as useful for a post-unification understanding of the past.[88]

To acknowledge German suffering does not necessarily mean avoiding issues of responsibility and guilt. As Rainer Schulze remarks, 'the moral obligation to remember the victims of National Socialism does not mean that it is not possible to remember the victims of the consequences of National Socialism'.[89] Yet his formulation is crucial, for German suffering is often decontextualized, becoming all too quickly equated with victimhood. Victimhood has been instrumental in diminishing or deflecting from questions of culpability for policies that led to war and genocide, a process that has occurred in three main ways. First, through uncritical or uncontextualized comparison which helps promote the 'indivisibility of *humanitas*'.[90] Thus, for example, the German experience of forced expulsion could be compared to other expulsions in order to highlight human suffering as such. This was the aim of the 'Erzwungene Wege' [Forced Paths] exhibition organized by the *Bund der Vertriebenen* [Association of Expellees] in Berlin in 2006, in which the Germans were featured alongside the Armenians, Greeks, Turks, Jews, the Finnish Karelians, and the populations of the former Yugoslavia. Underplaying differences and eschewing analysis, this exhibition was controversial and does not represent an accepted norm. Indeed, critics praised the exhibition 'Flucht — Vertreibung — Integration' [Flight — Expulsion — Integration] running concurrently in Bonn for its 'sober' approach.[91] But 'Erzwungene Wege' highlights the problem around implicit comparisons that establish equivalence or universality rather than using comparison critically to analyse and differentiate.[92] In this respect the exhibition was a further example of what was already explicit in the *Historikerstreit* of the late 1980s, when right-wing historians pointed to the suffering of ethnic Germans as on a par with that of holocaust victims. The exhibition was also a manifestation of what Bill Niven terms the 'implicit equation', which informs the belief that such comparisons are legitimate and which are articulated in the view that Czechs and Poles have not yet faced up to their past in the way that Germans have.[93]

The second way in which narratives of German suffering have distracted from questions of responsibility is through a process whereby history, be that historical events or the representation and reception of the past, has become increasingly subjective. As Daniel Fulda describes, this process encompasses human interest, self-reflection, historical reconstruction, and personal identification.[94] It is worth pointing out that such subjectification complements a further trend to emphasize vicarious experience rather than contemplation in approaching the past, a tendency that is also reflected in museum displays: 'Disinterested, contemplative spectatorship, drawing moral lessons from the disasters suffered by others, is less in fashion than a desire to experience the wreckage firsthand'.[95] The increased focus on the subject and subjectivity in history extends from the object of study through to questions of historical methodology, cultural representations, and public discourse. The academic interest in ego documents and memory studies has contributed to the shift from recounting experiences of suffering in private, which has always been a vital aspect of how the war is remembered, to narratives of personal experience moving into public discourse. The widespread focus on memory as a favoured term, one that has been generalized to incorporate all forms of accessing, recounting, and representing the past, has helped validate emotional responses to the past, most often through processes of identification. And complementing the role of the academy's interest in subjective accounts has been the huge impact of cultural representations of the German experience of the expulsions and bombings since 1989.[96]

The third reason for the uncoupling of German suffering from analysis of culpability is closely related to the subjectification of historical discourse and the accompanying emotional investment in the past: it is the wider concurrent shift towards the globalization of Holocaust memory and the universalization of trauma. As Niven argues, the globalization of the Holocaust and the duty to remember its victims has made Germany one of many nations involved in the process of remembrance, and no longer a pariah nation.[97] Furthermore, the critical emphasis on trauma has lent credibility to the German discourse of victimhood. This has occurred at the level of the event, since extreme events are accepted as de facto traumatic. But it has also occurred morally, for, as outlined in the discussion of trauma above, a traumatic event becomes a signifier of humanity regardless of the moral context in which it happened. It is particularly ironic in view of this shift to universalization of victimhood and the concern with the suffering of humanity in general that reference to German suffering and victimhood as a collective 'excludes once again the suffering of German Jews and other persecuted groups, such as Sinti and Roma' who are effectively posited as non-German.[98]

'An Artificial — or if You Prefer, Artistic — Formula'

Debates around Holocaust representation are weighed down by multiple ethical concerns, which have a far-reaching impact on how modes of representation and types of pleasure associated with them are evaluated. The cathartic pleasure of tragedy has always been affirmed and privileged because, as Simon Critchley suggests, the tragic paradigm provides a heroic response to the problem of finitude. Tragedy is the 'aesthetic form that would reconcile the freedom of the subject and the necessity of nature'.[99] It is through his struggle with suffering and death that the tragic hero finds redemption, or, as Karl Jaspers suggests, a burst of transcendence that brings with it a seed of hope.[100] Yet Kertész points to a fundamental problem with the tragic paradigm in relation to the Holocaust. If, following Jaspers, in tragedy man acts, and through his own actions enters tragic involvement in his fate, this cannot apply to the victims of Nazi atrocities whose fate had nothing to do with their actions but with genocidal policies of a state. Tragedy does not lend itself to the functioning of a bureaucratized state and to mass murder in which individual finitude plays no role. As the narrator of Kertész's *Kaddish for an Unborn Child* furiously argues, a 'dominating power' is 'simply a matter of decisions, decisions that are made or not made in individual lives, neither satanic nor unfathomably and spellbindingly intricate, [...] just vulgar, mean, murderous, stupid, hypocritical, and even at the moments of its greatest achievements at best merely well organized'.[101] This is also Friedrich Dürrenmatt's point when he writes that Hitler and Stalin cannot be made into Wallensteins, because their power has become too cruel and mechanical and often just pointless. The state itself has become 'unüberschaubar, anonym, bürokratisch' [immense, anonymous, bureaucratic] and thus without real representatives.[102]

The redemptive dimension of tragedy is also problematic in that it confers positive meaning on murders that have nothing ethical or transcendental about them. The emplotment of the Holocaust as tragedy explicitly or implicitly hints at ennoblement or grandeur. In relation to the victims it too easily figures the Holocaust as a 'necessity of nature' and casts them as heroically reconciled to their fate. The Holocaust thus ends by serving a higher ethical purpose and acquires a redemptive dimension. In relation to the perpetrators, tragedy affirms individual responsibility, but effectively invites moral consent for mass murders as well as conferring heroic stature onto the individual perpetrator. Nevertheless, as is evident from the discussions around the unrepresentability of the Holocaust and of trauma, critical reservations about tragedy have not obviated the desire for some type of redemption. The moral investment in victimhood and trauma, the tendency towards sacralization and the textual invocation of the sublime in order to achieve redemption, have resulted in a privileging of aesthetic modes that emphasize rupture, aporia, and loss.

Melancholy has assumed particular significance as the emotional and subjective state that seems to bear witness to the immeasurable loss and suffering of the Holocaust. At the individual level the subject, by internalizing the lost object, ensures that 'the existence of the lost object is psychically prolonged'.[103] Hence loss is not simply forgotten with time and the pain of suffering remains actual. Figuratively, melancholy can be understood as supporting the ethical injunction to remember and as ensuring that the lost other remains constitutive of how the past is approached and represented. Melancholy's affective intensity also serves as testament to the desolation of the human condition, serving, in its relationship to trauma, as a metonymy for being. Crucial to the privileging of melancholy as a representational mode that is adequate to human suffering is its association with the masculine genius and the melancholy man's 'keener eye for the truth'.[104] Thus historically melancholy has been seen as a particularly apt form of representation for male creativity as the artist uses his insight to transform suffering into a culturally valorized work of art.[105] As an 'exceptional individual', the melancholy man is a suitable heir to tragedy, for he embodies the suspicion that 'truth itself [might] be gloomy'.[106]

The 'true' and gloomy masculine pleasure of melancholy is in marked contrast to the 'false' feminine pleasures offered by melodrama. Despite being a mode of representation that places suffering and victimhood at its core, melodrama has traditionally been treated with suspicion as a debased form of tragedy. Its historical genesis in pantomime and music hall brings with it the taint of common entertainment, as does its tendency towards sensationalism. Its traditional emphasis on action and spectacle promotes an 'aesthetics of astonishment' that 'proposes the total enjoyment of excruciating situations in their unadulterated [...] state'.[107] Melodrama's fascination with overwrought feelings and pathos seem to confirm its superficiality, fuelling the view that its pleasures provide no more than a shallow emotional frisson which has no social or ethical worth.[108] Its promise of wish fulfilment makes it vulnerable to accusations that it trivializes suffering and relapses into kitsch.[109] Melodrama's low status is further compounded by its designation as 'woman's weepie'. The pleasures it offers are closely tied to the woman's body, both in terms of the suffering woman of the diegesis and the emoting reader or spectator. As Linda Williams argues, the woman's body functions as both the moved and moving. The bodily excess of melodrama, its lack of aesthetic distance and self-reflection, makes it, like pornography and horror, both inseparable from the feminine and highly manipulative. Together these genres employ the 'rhetoric of violence of the jerk': 'tear jerker', 'fear jerker', 'jerk off'.[110]

Comedy too can easily smack of the accessible but trivial amusements of mass culture. The effortless fun of much comedy makes it seem incompatible with the horror of atrocity and suffering, a view that is reinforced by comedy's unabashed relationship to joy or delight as ends in themselves. This opinion informs Gert Sautermeister's reading of Hilsenrath's *Der Nazi und der Friseur* as a voyeuristic product of the entertainment industry that displays a post-modern disregard for morality.[111] Comedy's association with the pleasures of the senses and of the debased body marks it as superficial and offensive, for comedy provokes the suspicion that someone is the object of amusement and that victims are being objectified for the laughter or smiles of others, even if it is through the medium of fiction. Instead of encouraging the empathy for another's suffering that is central to an ethical encounter, comedy can facilitate our pleasure in the other's reduced state.

Furthermore, the ethical value of comedy that derives from its characteristics of distance and play present a fundamental challenge to the orthodoxy of both Holocaust representation and the representation of trauma more generally. Distance from the passion of suffering can represent a betrayal of that suffering, a rejection of those who were murdered, or a rejection of those elements of one's identity that are inseparable from the experience of persecution and trauma.[112] As Jean Améry so forcefully articulates, even though the passing of time inevitably leads to the healing of wounds, such healing has something '*wider*moralisch' [*anti*moral] about it, a sentiment that can make any form of distancing highly ambivalent.[113] Thus comedy can be an affront to individual memory. It may also disrupt the attempt to keep trauma alive for moral and political legitimacy, and can challenge those who have an interest in representing trauma as collective and indelible.[114] The ability of comedy to generate and hold together incompatible perspectives, as well as its playful tenor, offends against the unspeakability of the Holocaust, and the tendency to ascribe to it a sacred or unique status. This is Rüdiger Steinlein's reservation: he worries that by detracting from the sacred Holocaust, comedy may undermine the scale of the Nazi crimes and the fundamental way in which they transgressed against humanity.[115] The intrinsic ambiguity and multi-dimensionality of comedy suggests that there are different views on suffering and on victimhood and this itself can be perceived as diluting the understanding of genocidal crimes as evil, or as undermining the moral integrity of the victim or traumatized individual.[116]

However, despite anxiety around comedy in Holocaust representations, it is both the case that comedy in post-Holocaust literature is as old as post-Holocaust literature and that such comedy has from the outset been recognized as significant and ethically valuable. Thus Tadeusz Borowski's *This Way for the Gas, Ladies and Gentlemen* (1947) has exerted a significant, and largely positive, influence on discussion of the comic in Holocaust narratives, as has Jurek Becker's *Jakob der Lügner* (1969). And canonical post-war writers such as Günter Grass, Thomas Bernhard, and Elfriede Jelinek are known for their use of biting comedy in their attempts to find an ethical response to atrocity. Not only has comedy been part of the canon of Holocaust representation, the reception of such comedy has frequently been positive, as the popular and critical success of Hilsenrath's *Der Nazi und der Friseur* demonstrates.

The embeddedness of different types of comedy in the canon of post-Holocaust literature has elicited surprisingly little scholarly interest. There are, however, notable and insightful exceptions. In 1982 Peter Stenberg suggested that the passing of time had led to enough distance and opened up a space for black comedy. Yet he remained concerned about the legitimacy of such comedy, arguing that only a member of the victimized culture, who has gained distance from the events, should break the taboo against comedy.[117] In contrast to Stenberg's qualifications, Terence des Pres argued forcefully in 1988 for comedy and laughter in Holocaust representation, which he judged to be restricted by expectations of what was appropriate. He was concerned by the limitations resulting from 'a seriousness admitting no response that might obscure [the Holocaust's] enormity or dishonor its dead'.[118] In his analysis of Borowski's *This Way for the Gas, Ladies and Gentlemen*, Leslie Epstein's *King of the Jews* (1979), and Art Spiegelman's *Maus* (1986), he presents the value of a comic approach as one which, by creating distance, permits 'a tougher, more active response' and which can 'foster resilience' and be 'life-reclaiming'.[119]

Des Pres does not address the question of authorship and legitimacy raised by Stenberg: his chosen authors anyway are survivors or belong to the victimized culture. But certainly any necessary relationship between the identity of an author or director and the ethics of comedy was increasingly questioned. In 2000, Sander Gilman historicized the relationship, maintaining in his analysis of Holocaust films that the need to justify comedy by evoking Jewish identity was characteristic of the 1970s. By the time of Roberto Benigni's *Life is Beautiful* in 1997, this was no longer the case, a shift that reflects the way in which the Shoah has become generalized as a human, rather than just Jewish, experience.[120] At the same time, Anne Fuchs problematized the relationship, commenting in response to Stenberg that being a survivor does not in itself 'justify employing the wrong register in portraying the Holocaust'. She also insisted on linking the ethical implications of comedy to a specific context and readership, arguing first, that the effect of comedy on a German readership should be considered. Secondly, she points out that the sense of guilt that is typical of the German post-war cultural climate, and that was reinforced by the 'negative but sacred boundary around Auschwitz', has contributed to 'collective repression'.[121] Her points reflect precisely the vacillation that characterizes the moral response to comedy generally: on the one hand fears about its tendentious impact, in this case the worry that it would reinforce anti-Semitic stereotypes and the attempt to normalize the Holocaust; on the other hand comedy's liberating challenge to norms, which here include stipulating the rules of Holocaust and trauma representation as well as condoning a culture of unselfcritical guilt.

It would be misleading to insist on a strict polarity between the two responses to comedy, for the sacralization of the Holocaust need not itself be devoid of tendentiousness. As Žižek remarks, the 'depoliticization of the holocaust, its elevation into the properly sublime Evil [...], can also be a political act of utter cynical manipulation, a political intervention aiming at legitimizing a certain kind of hierarchical political relation'.[122] Ofer Ashkenazi makes a similar point in relation to the specific German context in his discussion of contemporary comic representations of the Nazi past. Concentrating on visual representations, he distinguishes between pre-unification comedy that tends to depict Nazis returning into the post-war reality and post-unification images that emphasize the incongruity of Nazi ideology and appearance in contemporary mainstream society.[123] The humorous gap between the past and the present could be read as a form of escapism from responsibility, but, he insists, the humour is also a response to issues of representation: 'humor enables one to represent Nazism *beyond* the trauma and its mechanism of suppression. The humoristic references [...] are a reaction to, and a result of, the perceived obstructions of representation — not an escapist indifference to it'.[124]

Jill Twark situates the comic responses to the Nazi past within the general growth in humour culture in post-unification Germany, which is a result of greater openness among Germans, particularly younger Germans towards their history: 'Germans now possess enough self-confidence to be able to laugh at just about anything, including themselves and their turbulent history.'[125] Yet her assertion is perhaps rather too hasty. Although it is true that the question of whether Germans, and others, should or should not mock Hitler and the Nazis is no longer relevant because they do, comic depictions still cause controversy. Discussion around Mel Brooks's musical *The Producers*, Walter Moers's comic strip *Adolf, die Nazi-Sau* (1998–2006), and Dani Levy's film *Mein Führer — Die wirklich wahrste Wahrheit über Adolf Hilter* (2007) are testament to ongoing anxiety about Holocaust comedy, indeed around Holocaust 'impiety' more generally.[126] The heated responses to comic depictions indicate that German comedy and ridicule about the Nazi past can still be contentious, not least because some comic representations fuel concern that they are no more than '*Vergangenheitsbewältigung* "lite"' and a profitable commodity.[127]

It is significant that these examples focus on ridiculing or satirizing the Nazi perpetrators and their ideology and are therefore perhaps less likely to raise the complex ethical issues that comedy directed specifically at Holocaust victims does. Thus in his discussion of four comic films that are directly concerned with victims of the Holocaust, Žižek raises the question of the limits of comedy and its relation to the tragic. He suggests that the figure of the *Muselmann* is this limit: on the one hand his extreme destitution rules him out from being 'tragic', on the other this very destitution also prevents us from perceiving him as a comic character despite the fact that his relentless pursuit of food and automatic gestures are normally the stuff of comedy. Any attempt to treat the *Muselmann* as tragic results in him becoming a 'mocking parody of tragic dignity', yet treating him as comic will generate sympathy for his tragic predicament. 'The Muslim is thus the zero-point at which the very opposition between tragedy and comedy, sublime and ridiculous, dignity and derision, is suspended; the point at which one pole passes directly into its opposite'.[128]

Žižek's view of the *Muselmann* as potentially comic might seem extreme and even scandalous. But it brings us back to György's observations of the prisoners in Kertész's *Fateless* and with it to the question of how suffering is depicted. The aim of this book is not to analyze Holocaust comedies or indeed comic texts, but specifically to explore German language texts which are centrally concerned with the legacy of suffering caused by the Second World War and the Holocaust but which incorporate comedy into their aesthetic. The study thus addresses the dominant critical neglect of comedy over the last two decades and seeks to rebalance the approach to Holocaust representation that has focused intently and earnestly on themes of negative sacralization, trauma, and suffering.[129] It brings to the fore what has been an important, though marginalized, ethical tradition in Holocaust representation and scholarship, one which was already inherent to Adorno's understanding of post-Auschwitz poetics. For in his reading of Beckett's *Endgame*, Adorno insists upon the importance of the absurd, not because the absurd has no meaning, but because it requires a negotiation of meaning: 'The logical figure of the absurd [...] negates all the meaningfulness logic seems to provide in order to convict logic of its own absurdity'.[130]

As Stefan Krankenhagen points out, the importance for Adorno of the absurd is that it integrates self-reflexivity and the refusal to construct meaning (itself a secular *Bilderverbot*) into the formal fabric of representation. Through its formal refusal to affirm or confirm meaning, the artwork is made into a representation of Auschwitz and the society that allowed it to happen.[131] The absurd is only one dimension of comedy, one in which elements of weirdness and alienation are most distilled. But comedy's refusal of congruity is to various degrees one of its key characteristics, and it is the different ways in which comedy's interpretative duality contributes to and extends our understanding of suffering and trauma that is central to this analysis. With the exception of Hilsenrath's novel, the texts included in this study are not comedies, but combine a comic aesthetic with other representational strategies. They are texts that embody Benjamin's conjoining of comedy with mourning: 'Die Komik — richtiger: der reine Spaß — ist die obligate Innenseite der Trauer, die ab und zu wie das Futter eines Kleides im Saum oder Revers zur Geltung kommt' [Comedy — or more precisely: the pure joke — is the essential inner side of mourning which from time to time, like the lining of a dress at the hem or lapel, makes its presence felt].[132] The inclusion of comedy crystallizes the question of how we may enjoy portrayals of suffering, for by integrating comedy into texts that are predominantly concerned with the legacy of suffering, anxiety arising over the pleasure at others' pain is not contained by conventions of genre or form.

Furthermore, I consider the ways in which comic devices are deployed and with what aims: how they contribute to or challenge processes of empathy and identification that sustain particular identities and moral positions; and the extent to which they help perpetuate or question expectations of how suffering is both appropriately represented and responded to. I analyze what the incorporation of a comic aesthetic reveals about the values that attend particular artistic forms and representational modes, not least melancholy and melodrama. These values are of course neither rigid nor uncontested. Thus melancholy also brings with it a long history of criticism that it manifests a pathological 'complaisance towards sadness'.[133] The pathological dimension of melancholy, so important for privileging it as a form of negative sacralization, has been fuelled largely by psychoanalytic interpretations. However, as Mary Cosgrove demonstrates, melancholy also has a performative tradition, one that can offer space for comedy and for questioning the link between ethics and trauma.[134] Furthermore, melancholy, with its tendency towards emotional excess, especially in the tradition of sentimentality and *Empfindsamkeit*, can drift into melodrama. Melodrama too has garnered the interest of critics as being more than trivial women's weepies and for offering critical potential, not least in relation to feminist ethics. Thus the book aims to consider the obstructions and expectations that come with representation as well as the impact of comedy for interrogating the prevalent use and ethical privileging of trauma, traumatic subjectivity, and victimhood.

This study is not designed to be representative, but to be suggestive. I focus on authors and texts where the comic aesthetic has been marginalized in criticism or where it has been considered as a possible stylistic weakness or failure, as not sitting easily with the predominant tone of suffering. Thus I have not selected for analysis those authors where the comic aspects of their work have already been the focus of extensive study, as is the case, for example, with Jurek Becker, Elfriede Jelinek, and Thomas Bernhard.[135] By using comedy as a starting point the individual analyses will offer new interpretations of the authors' and directors' work. Each chapter offers a different context and raises different issues about the relationship of comedy to suffering. Chapter 1 explores how Ingeborg Bachmann combines comedy with melodrama as part of her focus on the suffering female victim. The interaction of melodrama and comedy continues to be key in Chapter 2, which analyzes the comic aspects of Rainer Werner Fassbinder's films in order to challenge the critical privileging of male masochism. The question of how suffering is gendered continues to be a theme in Chapter 3. Here I focus on the tension between two comic strategies in W. G. Sebald's work, one which constructs the figure of the masculine melancholy narrator as a privileged moral figure, and the other which points to the comedy of melancholy excess and sublimation as the ethical centre of the prose. In Chapter 4 I consider Reinhardt Jirgl's *Die Stille* in parallel with the post-reunification films of Volker Koepp in order to establish how their treatment of the former Eastern territories interacts with discourses around German suffering and culpability for atrocities. The study of Ruth Klüger's essays and memoirs in Chapter 5 raises questions about the role of comedy in relation to the boundary between fact and fiction and also considers how comedy might mediate between *ressentiment* and conciliation. Finally, in Chapter 6 I analyze two novels that draw upon comic devices in their representation of Nazi SS perpetrators, Edgar Hilsenrath's *Der Nazi und der Friseur* and Jonathan Littell's *The Kindly Ones*. Here the authors take the provocation of comedy to an extreme by using the device of fictionalized autobiography to engage with questions of self-exculpation, justice, and the limitations of tragedy.

Notes to the Introduction

1. Imre Kertész, *Fiasco*, trans. by Tim Wilkinson (New York: Melville House, 2011), p. 56. References will be given in parenthesis with the abbreviation *Fi*.
2. Imre Kertész, *Fateless*, trans. by Tim Wilkinson (London: Vintage, 2006), p. 111. References will be given in parenthesis with the abbreviation *F*.
3. Imre Kertész, *Dossier K.*, trans. by Tim Wilkinson (New York: Melville House, 2013), p. 183. References will be given in parenthesis with the abbreviation *DK*.
4. Michael Mulkay, *On Humor: Its Nature and Its Place in Modern Society* (Cambridge: Polity, 1988), p. 37.
5. Primo Levi, *If this is a Man and The Truce*, trans. by Stuart Woolf (London: Abacus, 1993), p. 28.
6. Ibid., p. 46.
7. Imre Kertész, *Kaddish for an Unborn Child*, trans. by Tim Wilkinson (London: Vintage, 2010), p. 41.
8. Edmund Burke, *A Philosophical Enquiry into the Origins of Our Ideas of the Sublime and Beautiful* (Basle: printed and sold by J. J. Tourneisen, 1792), p. 59.
9. Susan Sontag, *Regarding the Pain of Others* (London: Penguin, 2004), p. 37.
10. Ibid., p. 38
11. Ibid., p. 68
12. Martin Jay, *Refractions of Violence* (London: Routledge, 2003), p. 106.

13. Hélène Cixous, *The Hélène Cixous Reader*, ed. by Susan Sellers (London: Routledge, 1994), p.154.
14. Henri Bergson, *Le Rire: essai sur la signification du comique* (Paris: Quadrige, 1989).
15. See Wolfgang Preisendanz, 'Zum Vorrang des Komischen bei der Darstellung von Geschichtserfahrung in deutschen Romanen unserer Zeit', in *Das Komische*, ed. by Wolfgang Preisendanz and Rainer Warning (Munich: Fink, 1976), pp. 153–64 (pp. 160–61).
16. William Hazlitt, *Lectures on the English Comic Writers*, in *The Selected Writings of William Hazlitt*, ed. by Duncan Wu, 9 vols (London: Pickering and Chatto, 1998), v, 6.
17. Søren Kierkegaard, quoted in John Lippitt, *Humour and Irony in Kierkegaard's Thought* (London: Macmillan, 2000), p. 130.
18. See Immanuel Kant, *Kritik der Urteilskraft*, ed. by Wilhelm Weischedel (Frankfurt a.M.: Suhrkamp, 1996), p. 273; Arthur Schopenhauer, *Die Welt als Wille und Vorstellung II* (Zurich: Haffmans Verlag, 1991), p. 108.
19. Hazlitt, p. 5. Jean Paul (Johann Paul Friedrich Richter) offers a similar image when he describes how in humour the intellect dances back and forth with alternative possibilities. See Jean Paul, *Vorschule der Ästhetik*, in *Werke*, ed. by Norbert Miller, 10 vols (Munich: Hanser, 1980), v, 122.
20. Basil of Caesarea, *Regulae Fusius tractatae*, quoted in Catherine Conybeare, *The Laughter of Sarah: Biblical Exegesis, Feminist Theory, and the Concept of Delight* (New York: Palgrave Macmillan, 2013), p. 25 n. 9.
21. Reinhold Niebuhr, *The Essential Reinhold Niebuhr: Selected Essays and Addresses*, ed. by Robert McAfee Brown (New Haven, CT: Yale University Press, 1987), p. 49.
22. Slavoj Žižek, *The Plague of Fantasies* (London & New York: Verso, 1997), p. 176.
23. Comedy's dislocation from feeling is encapsulated in Nietzsche's aphorism that the joke is 'das Epigramm auf den Tod eines Gefühls' [the epigram on the death of a feeling], in Friedrich Nietzsche, *Menschliches Allzumenschliches II*, 202, in *Friedrich Nietzsche Menschliches, Allzumenschliches I und II. Kritische Studienausgabe*, ed. by Giorgio Colli and Mazzino Montinari (Munich and Berlin/New York: dtv/de Gruyter, 1988), p. 466. It finds equally witty expression in Horace Walpole's letter to Anne, Countess of Ossory, 16 August 1776, where he claims that 'the world is a comedy to those that think, a tragedy to those that feel'. See <http://archive.org/stream/lettersaddressedo2walpuoft/lettersaddressedo2walpuoft_djvu.txt> [accessed 1 September 2014].
24. Friedrich Schiller, *Über naïve und sentimentalische Dichtung*, *Werke*, Nationalausgabe, *Philosophische Schriften. Erster Teil*, ed. by Benno von Wiese (Weimar: Hermann Böhlaus Nachfolger, 1962), xx, 446; <http://www.schillerinstitute.org/transl/Schiller_essays/naive_sentimental-1.html> [accessed 3 September 2015].
25. Sigmund Freud, *Der Humor*, in *Sigmund Freud. Studienausgabe. Band IV: Psychologische Schriften* (Frankfurt a.M.: Fischer, 1989), p. 281.
26. Ibid., p. 279.
27. Ibid., p. 282.
28. Robert C. Roberts, 'Humor and the Virtues', in *Søren Kierkegaard: Critical Assessments of Leading Philosophers*, ed. by Daniel W. Conway, 4 vols (London: Routledge, 2002), IV, 293–315 (p. 307).
29. Ibid., p. 303.
30. Christie Davies, *The Mirth of Nations* (New Brunswick, NJ: Transaction Publishers, 2002), p. 202.
31. Ibid., p. 207.
32. Ibid., p. 227.
33. Mulkay, p. 28.
34. Jan Campbell, *Film and Cinema Spectatorship: Melodrama and Mimesis* (Cambridge: Polity, 2005), p. 17.
35. Bruce Fink, *The Lacanian Subject: Between Language and Jouissance* (Princeton, NJ: Princeton University Press, 1995), p. 189 n. 5.
36. Laura Mulvey, *Fetishism and Curiosity* (London: BFI, 1996), p. 39.
37. Franz Fanon, *Black Skin, White Masks*, trans. by Charles Lam Markmann (New York: Grove Press, 1967), pp. 152–53 n. 15.
38. Sigmund Freud, *Der Witz und seine Beziehung zum Unbewußten*, in *Psychologische Schriften*, p. 86. So when Mikhail Bakhtin points to the positive role comedy can play in liberating an individual

'from the great interior censor', there are contexts where the interior censor plays a valuable part in quashing people's intentions, as Ruth Klüger points out (see Chapter 5). Mikhail Bakhtin, *Rabelais and his World*, trans. by Hélène Iswolsky (Bloomington: Indiana University Press, 1984), p. 94.
39. Laura Frost, *The Problem with Pleasure: Modernism and its Discontents* (New York: Columbia University Press, 2013), p. 7.
40. Plato, *Philebus* (Harmondsworth: Penguin, 1982), p. 102.
41. Andreas Huyssen, *After the Great Divide: Modernism, Mass Culture, Postmodernism* (Bloomington & Indianapolis: Indiana University Press, 1986), p. viii.
42. Matei Calinescu, *Five Faces of Modernity* (Durham, NC: Duke University Press, 1987), p. 259.
43. Frost, p. 20.
44. Wendelin Schmidt-Dengler, Johann Sonleitner, and Klaus Zeyringer, eds, *Komik in der österreichischen Literatur* (Berlin: Erich Schmidt Verlag, 1996), p. 10.
45. Theodor Adorno, *Prisms*, trans. by Samuel and Shierry Weber (Cambridge, MA: MIT Press, 1983), p. 34.
46. Theodor Adorno, *Notes to Literature II*, trans. by Shierry Weber Nicholsen (New York: Columbia University Press, 1992), p. 251.
47. Gillian Rose, 'Beginnings of the Day: Fascism and Representation', in *Modernity, Culture and 'the Jew'*, ed. by Bryan Cheyette and Laura Marcus (Cambridge: Polity, 1998), pp. 242–56 (p. 243).
48. Primo Levi, *The Drowned and the Saved*, trans. by Raymond Rosenthal (London: Abacus, 1993), pp. 63–64.
49. Ibid., p. 63.
50. George Steiner, *Language and Silence* (New York: Atheneum, 1967), p. 123.
51. See Elie Wiesel, 'The Holocaust as Literary Inspiration', in Elie Wiesel, Lucy Dawidowicz, and others, *Dimensions of the Holocaust* (Evanston, IL: Northwestern University Press, 1977), pp. 4–19 (p. 7); Elie Wiesel, *From the Kingdon of Memory* (New York: Summit Books, 1990), p. 169.
52. Claude Lanzmann, 'From the Holocaust to "Holocaust"', in *Shoah: Key Essays*, ed. by Stuart Liebman (Oxford: Oxford University Press, 2007), pp. 27–36 (p. 30).
53. Dominick LaCapra, *Writing History, Writing Trauma* (Baltimore, MD: Johns Hopkins University Press, 2001), p. 93.
54. Michael Bernard-Donals and Richard Glejzer, 'Introduction: Representations of the Holocaust and the End of Memory', in *Witnessing the Disaster: Essays on Representation and the Holocaust*, ed. by Michael Bernard-Donals and Richard Glejzer (Madison: University of Wisconsin Press, 2003), pp. 3–22 (p. 3).
55. Michael Bernard-Donals and Richard Glejzer, *Between Witness and Testimony: The Holocaust and the Limits of Representation* (New York: State University Press of New York, 2001), p. 4.
56. Ibid., pp. 5 & 11.
57. Ibid., p. 67.
58. Emmanuel Levinas, *Totality and Infinity*, trans. by Alphonso Lingis (Pittsburgh, PA: Duquesne University Press, 1969), pp. 234–35.
59. Emmanuel Levinas, *Time and the Other*, trans. by Richard A. Cohen (Pittsburgh, PA: Duquesne University Press, 1987), pp. 70–71.
60. Ibid., p. 74.
61. Simon Critchley, *Very Little... Almost Nothing: Death, Philosophy, Literature* (London: Routledge, 1997), p. 75.
62. Emmanuel Levinas, 'Philosophy and the Idea of Infinity', in *Collected Philosophical Papers*, trans. by Alphonso Lingis (Pittsburgh, PA: Duquesne University Press, 1998), pp. 47–59 (p. 50).
63. Clara Mucci, *Beyond Individual and Collective Trauma: Intergenerational Transmission, Psychoanalytic Treatment, and the Dynamics of Forgiveness* (London: Karnac, 2013), p. 68.
64. Cécile Rousseau and Toby Measham, 'Postraumatic Suffering as a Source of Transformation: A Clinical Perspective', in *Understanding Trauma: Integrating Biological, Clinical, and Cultural Perspectives*, ed. by Laurence J. Kirmayer, Robert Lemelson, and Mark Barad (Cambridge: Cambridge University Press, 2007), pp. 275–93 (p. 278). See also Arieh Y. Shalev, 'PTSD: A Disorder of Recovery?', in Kirmayer, Lemelson, & Barad, eds, pp. 207–23.
65. Ruth Leys, *Trauma: A Genealogy* (Chicago: Chicago University Press, 2000), p. 299.

66. LaCapra, *Writing History, Writing Trauma*, pp. 43–64.
67. Cathy Caruth, 'Trauma and Experience: Introduction', in *Trauma: Explorations in Memory*, ed. by Cathy Caruth (Baltimore: Johns Hopkins UP, 1995), pp. 3–12 (p.11).
68. Jacques Lacan, *The Ethics of Psychoanalysis 1959–1960*, trans. by Dennis Porter (London: Routledge, 1992), p. 319.
69. Didier Fassin and Richard Rechtman, *The Empire of Trauma: An Inquiry into the Condition of Victimhood*, trans. by Rachel Gomme (Princeton, NJ: Princeton University Press, 2009), p. 94.
70. Ibid., p. 95.
71. LaCapra, *Writing History, Writing Trauma*, p. 82.
72. Ibid., p. 78.
73. Jeffrey C. Alexander, *Trauma: A Social Theory* (Cambridge: Polity, 2012), p. 15.
74. Ibid., p. 4.
75. See Roger Luckhurst, 'Traumaculture', *New Formations*, 50 (2003), 28–47.
76. Fassin & Rechtman, p. 21.
77. Ibid., p. 152.
78. LaCapra, *Writing History, Writing Trauma*, p. 79.
79. Tony Judt, *Postwar: A History of Europe since 1945* (London: Pimlico, 2007), p. 808.
80. Hella Pick, *Guilty Victims: Austria from the Holocaust to Haider* (London: IB Tauris, 2000), p. 3.
81. Jean Améry, *Geburt der Gegenwart: Gestalten und Gestaltungen der westlichen Zivilisation seit Kriegsende*, quoted in Gerhard Botz, *Gewalt in der Politik: Attentate, Zusammenstöße, Putschversuche, Unruhen in Österreich 1918–1938* (Munich: Wilhelm Fink Verlag, 1983), pp. 201–02.
82. Botz, *Gewalt in der Politik*, p. 207.
83. See Gerhard Botz, 'Historische Brüche und Kontinuitäten als Herausforderungen — Ingeborg Bachmann und post-katastrophische Geschichtsmentalitäten in Österriech', in *Ingeborg Bachmann: Neue Beiträge zu ihrem Werk*, ed. by Dirk Göttsche and Hubert Ohl (Würzburg: Königshausen & Neumann 1993), pp. 199–214 (p. 209n).
84. Robert G. Moeller, *War Stories: The Search for a Usable Past in the Federal Republic of Germany* (Berkeley, CA: University of Los Angeles Press, 2001), p. 48.
85. Pertti Ahonen, *After the Expulsion. West Germany and Eastern Europe 1945–1990* (Oxford: OUP, 2003), p. 1. Ahonen's figure of fifteen million is high and the figure remains contested, often cited as being between twelve or fourteen million. Differences stem in part from the different definitions used (distinguishing for example between *Vertriebene* and *Heimatvertriebene*) and because figures were used in post-war Germany to substantiate different sorts of political claims.
86. Helmut Schmitz and Annette Seidel-Arpaci, eds, *Narratives of Trauma: Discourses of German Wartime Suffering in National and International Perspective* (Amsterdam & New York: Rodopi, 2011), pp. 4–6.
87. Pertti Ahonen, *After the Expulsion: West German and Eastern Europe 1945–1990* (Oxford: Oxford University Press, 2003), p. 271.
88. Rainer Schulze, 'Forced Migration of German Populations During and After the Second World War: History and Memory', in *The Disentanglement of Populations: Migration, Expulsion and Displacement in Post-War Europe, 1944–9*, ed. by Jessica Reinisch and Elizabeth White (New York: Palgrave Macmillan, 2011), pp. 51–70 (p. 61).
89. Ibid., p. 64.
90. Bill Niven, 'Implicit Equations in Constructions of German Suffering', in *A Nation of Victims?: Representations of German Wartime Suffering from 1945 to the Present*, ed. by Helmut Schmitz (Amsterdam & New York: Rodopi, 2007), pp. 105–24 (p. 113).
91. Schulze, p. 62.
92. For a detailed analysis of the exhibition, see Niven, 'Implicit Equations'. Niven points to the way in which the exhibition failed to make clear that the expulsions were a '*reactive* policy (to a degree) as well as a *proactive* policy' on the part of the allies (p. 115). See also Ther's discussion of the strategically justifiable reasons for the population exchanges, which were designed to prevent renewed German expansion in East, achieve permanent peace in Europe and to stabilize the nation states of east and central Europe. How far these aims were realized is debateable (Philipp Ther, *Deutsche und polnische Vertriebene: Gesellschaft und Vertriebenenpolitik in der SBZ/*

DDR und in Polen 1945–1956 (Göttingen: Vandenhoeck & Ruprecht, 1998), p. 347).
93. Niven, 'Implicit Equations', p. 107.
94. Daniel Fulda, 'Abschied von der Zentralperspektive: Der nicht nur literarische Geschichtsdiskurs im Nachwende-Deutschland als Dispositiv für Jörg Friedrichs *Brand*', in *Bombs Away! Representing the Air War over Europe and Japan*, ed. by Wilfried Wilms and William Rasch (Amsterdam & New York: Rodopi, 2006), pp. 45- 64 (p. 58).
95. Jay, pp. 114–15. Aleida Assmann makes a similar point when she refers to the 'Wiederbelebung dieser Vergangenheit im Modus des emotionalen Nacherlebens' [bringing the past back to life by re-experiencing it emotionally] (*Der lange Schatten der Vergangenheit: Erinnerungskultur und Geschichtspolitik* (Munich: C. H. Beck, 2006), p. 194).
96. Key texts that fuelled debate include Sebald's *Luftkrieg und Literatur* (1999), Günter Grass's *Im Krebsgang* (2002), Jörg Friedrich's *Der Brand* (2002), Uwe Timm's *Am Beispiel meines Bruders* (2003) and Guido Knopp's *Die große Flucht* (2001). There is an extensive bibliography on the discourse of German suffering and victimhood, including accounts of the *Historikerstreit*, the Walser-Bubis debate on 'normalization', the impact of cultural representations on that debate, and the importance of memory culture. In addition to the works cited here, see: Laurel Cohen-Pfister, 'The Suffering of the Perpetrators: Unleashing Collective Memory in German Literature of the Twenty-First Century', *Forum of Modern Language Studies*, 41, 2 (2005), 123–35; the Bibliography in the special edition on German suffering, *German Life and Letters*, 57, 4 (2004), 354–56; also, the select bibliography in *Germans as Victims: Remembering the Past in Contemporary Germany*, ed. by Bill Niven (Basingstoke: Palgrave Macmillan, 2006), pp. 276–82.
97. Bill Niven, 'The Globalisation of Memory and the Rediscovery of German Suffering', in *German Literature in the Age of Globalisation*, ed. by Stuart Taberner (Birmingham: University of Birmingham Press, 2004), pp. 229–46 (p. 237).
98. Schmitz & Seidel-Arpaci, p. 7.
99. Simon Critchley, *Ethics-Politics-Subjectivity: Essays on Derrida, Levinas and Contemporary French Thought* (London: Verso, 1999), pp. 218–19.
100. Karl Jaspers, *Von der Wahrheit* (Munich: Piper, 1958), pp. 925–26.
101. Kertész, *Kaddish*, p. 40.
102. Friedrich Dürrenmatt, 'Theaterprobleme', in *Gesammelte Werke*, ed. by Franz Josef Görtz, 7 vols (Zurich: Diogenes, 1988), VII, 56–57.
103. Sigmund Freud, 'Mourning and Melancholia', in *The Standard Edition of the Complete Psychological Works of Sigmund Freud. Vol. XIV (1914–1916): On the History of the Psycho-Analytic Movement, Papers on Metapsychology and Other Works*, trans. by James Strachey (London: Hogarth Press, 1917), pp. 237–58 (p. 245).
104. Ibid., p. 200.
105. Juliana Schiesari, *The Gendering of Melancholia: Feminism, Psychoanalysis, and the Symbolics of Loss in Renaissance Literature* (Ithaca, NY: Cornell University Press, 1992), p. 8.
106. Paul Ricoeur, *Memory, History, Forgetting*, trans. by Kathleen Blamey and David Pellauer (Chicago: Chicago University Press, 2004), p. 76.
107. Peter Brooks, *The Melodramatic Imagination: Balzac, Henry James, Melodrama, and the Mode of Excess* (New Haven, CT: Yale University Press, 1976), p. 36. See also Ben Singer, *Melodrama and Modernity: Early Sensational Cinema and its Contexts* (New York: Columbia University Press, 2001), pp. 37–58.
108. Simon Shepherd, 'Pauses of Mutual Agitation', in *Melodrama: Stage, Picture, Screen*, ed. by Jacky Bratton, Jim Cook, and Christine Gledhill (London: BFI, 1994), pp. 25–37 (p. 25).
109. Steve Neale discusses the way in which the fantasy structure of melodrama sustains the hope for wish fulfilment even if the narrative of a particular melodramatic narrative does not fulfil the wish. See his article, 'Melodrama and Tears', *Screen*, 27, 6 (1986), 6–23.
110. Linda Williams, 'Film Bodies: Gender, Genre, and Excess', *Film Quarterly*, 44, 4 (1991), 2–13 (p. 5).
111. Gert Sautermeister, 'Aufgeklärte Modernität — Postmodernes Entertainment: Edgar Hilsenraths *Der Nazi und der Friseur*', in *'Wir tragen den Zettelkasten mit den Steckbriefen unserer Freunde': Ata-Band zum Symposion 'Beiträge jüdischer Autoren zur deutschen Literatur seit 1945'*, ed. by Jens Stüben and Winfried Woesler (Darmstadt: Häusser, 1994), pp. 227–42.
112. Ricoeur, p. 76; LaCapra, *History and its Limits*, p. 84.

113. Jean Améry, *Werke. Band 2: Jenseits von Schuld und Sühne. Unmeisterliche Wanderjahre. Örtlichkeiten*, ed. by Gerhard Scheit (Stuttgart: Klett-Cotta, 2002), p. 133; Jean Améry, *At the Mind's Limits: Contemplations by a Survivor on Auschwitz and its Realities*, trans. by Sidney Rosenfeld and Stella P. Rosenfeld (Bloomington: Indiana University Press, 1980), p. 72.
114. See Laurence J. Kirmayer, Robert Lemelson, and Mark Barad, 'Trauma in Context: Integrating Biological, Clinical, and Cultural Perspectives', in Kirmayer, Lemelson, Barad, eds, pp. 451–74 (pp. 471–72); Neil J. Smelser, 'Psychological Trauma and Cultural Trauma', in *Cultural Trauma and Collective Identity*, ed. by Jeffrey C. Alexander and others (Berkeley: University of California Press, 2004), pp. 31–59 (p. 42).
115. Rüdiger Steinlein, 'Das Furchtbarste lächerlich? Komik und Lachen in Texten der deutschen Holocaust-Literatur', in *Kunst und Literatur nach Auschwitz*, ed. by Manuel Köppen (Berlin: Erich Schmidt, 1993), pp. 97–106.
116. See Mulkay, pp. 22–38.
117. Peter Stenberg, 'Memories of the Holocaust: Edgar Hilsenrath and the Fiction of the Genocide', *Deutsche Vierteljahrsschrift für Literaturwissenschaft und Geistesgeschichte*, 56 (1982), 277–89 (p. 278).
118. Terence Des Pres, 'Holocaust *Laughter?*', in *Writing the Holocaust*, ed. by Berel Lang (New York & London: Holmes & Meier, 1988), pp. 216–33 (p. 217).
119. Ibid., p. 232.
120. Sander L. Gilman, 'Is Life Beautiful? Can the Shoah be Funny? Some Thoughts on Recent and Older Films', *Critical Inquiry*, 26, 2 (Winter, 2000), 279–308.
121. Anne Fuchs, 'Edgar Hilsenrath's Poetics of Insignificance and the Tradition of Humour in German-Jewish Ghetto Writing', in *Ghetto Writing: Traditional and Eastern Jewry in German-Jewish Literature from Heine to Hilsenrath*, ed. by Anne Fuchs and Florian Krobb (Columbia, SC: Camden House, 1999), pp. 180–94 (pp. 182–83).
122. Slavoj Žižek, *Did Somebody Say Totalitarianism?: Five Interventions in the (Mis)Use of a Notion* (London & New York: Verso, 2011), p. 67.
123. Ofer Ashkenazi, 'Ridiculous Trauma: Comic Representations of the Nazi Past in Contemporary German Visual Culture', *Cultural Critique*, 78, (2011), 88–118 (p. 98).
124. Ibid., p. 101. Ashkenazi is referring here to: Dani Levy's 2007 film *Mein Führer: Die wirklich wahrste Wahrheit über Adolf Hitler*, as well as Levy's response to *Der Untergang* as a film which made him laugh because of the absurdity of 'this amiable, old grandpa and his funny ideas in the bunker' (quoted on p. 96); the July 2002 cover of the satirical magazine *Titanic* which depicted an image of Hitler with the 'schrecklicher Verdacht' that he might be anti-Semitic; a film clip made by Florian Wittmann in 2008 which super-imposes a voiceover by the comedian Gerhard Polt on a clip of Hitler taken from Leni Riefenstahl's *Triumph des Willens* and shows Hitler getting very worked up about his encounter with a car leasing company (<http://www.youtube.com/watch?v=gSrTiIhMDn4> [accessed 30 August 2014]).
125. Jill E. Twark, 'Introduction: Recent Trends in Post-Unification German Humor', in *Strategies of Humor in Post-Unification German Literature, Film and Other Media*, ed. by Jill E. Twark (Newcastle upon Tyne: Cambridge Scholars Publishing, 2011), pp. 1–25 (p. 4).
126. Matthew Boswell discusses different types of Holocaust 'impiety' and argues that 'authorial biography and vague notions of sanctity' continue to be reasons for rejecting examples of Holocaust impiety. He cites the example of European critics' threat to boycott Uwe Boll's film *Auschwitz* before it had even been released in 2010. See: Matthew Boswell, *Holocaust Impiety in Literature, Popular Music and Film* (Basingstoke: Palgrave Macmillan, 2012), p. 6.
127. Annika Orich and Florentine Strzelczyk, ' "Steppende Nazis mit Bildungsauftrag": Marketing Hitler Humor in Post-Unification Germany', in *Strategies of Humor*, ed. by Twark, pp. 292–329 (pp. 294–95).
128. Žižek, *Did Somebody Say Totalitarianism?*, pp. 85–86. In his chapter 'Hitler as Ironist' he discusses Roberto Benigni's *Life is Beautiful* (1997), Peter Kassovitz's *Jakob the Liar* (1999), Radu Mihăileanu's *Train of Life* (1998), and Lina Wertmüller's *Seven Beauties* (1975).
129. Scholarly engagement with comedy and its potential for representing the Holocaust continues to be rare. Yosefa Loshitzy offers a brief analysis of *Life is Beautiful* and *Train de Vie*, which she sees as 'implicitly or explicitly [referring] to the taboo on imagining the Holocaust'. However, she does little to develop discussions around the ethics of comedy and representation. See

'Forbidden Laughter? The Politics and Ethics of the Holocaust Film Comedy', in *Re-Presenting the Shoah for the 21st Century*, ed. by Ronit Lentin (New York & Oxford: Berghahn, 2004), pp. 127–37 (p. 135). Discussion of comedy is typically absent from two other collected volumes dedicated to the representation of the Holocaust: *How the Holocaust Looks Now: International Perspectives*, ed. by Martin L. Davies and Claus-Christian W. Szejnmann (Basingstoke: Palgrave Macmillan, 2007); *Representing Auschwitz at the Margins of Testimony*, ed. by Nicholas Chare and Dominic Williams (Basingstoke: Palgrave Macmillan, 2013).

130. Theodor W. Adorno, *Notes to Literature I*, trans. by Shierry Weber Nicholsen (New York: Columbia University Press, 1991), p. 263.

131. Stefan Krankenhagen, *Auschwitz darstellen: Ästhetische Positionen zwischen Adorno, Spielberg und Walser* (Köln: Böhlau, 2001), p. 80.

132. Walter Benjamin, *Ursprung des deutschen Trauerspiels*, in *Gesammelte Schriften*, ed. by Rolf Tiedemann and Hermann Schweppenhäuser, 7 vols (Frankfurt a.M.: Suhrkamp, 1991), I.1, 304; *The Origin of German Tragic Drama*, trans. by John Osborne (London: Verso, 2009), pp. 125–26.

133. Ricoeur, p. 76.

134. Mary Cosgrove, *Born Under Auschwitz: Melancholy Traditions in Postwar German Literature* (Rochester, NY: Camden House, 2014), pp. 1–24. For further discussions of melancholy's comic potential see: Dieter Borchmeyer, ed., *Melancholie und Heiterkeit* (Heidelberg: Universitätsverlag, 2006); Bettina Baur, *Melancholie und Karneval: Zur Dramatik Cecilie Løveids* (Tübingen & Basel: Francke, 2002); Peter Sillem, ' "der du gedeihen läßt und zerstörst": Melancholie, Karneval und die zwei Gesichter des Saturn', *Zeitsprünge: Forschungen zur Frühen Neuzeit* 5, no. 1/2 (2001).

135. Wendelin Schmidt-Dengler asserts that Thomas Bernhard's 'chief concern, to exaggerate somewhat, is a poetics of comedy', a view echoed by Stephen Dowden who writes that he is a 'satirist of Swiftian sensibilities': he offers 'a "comic" insight into the basic human plight' and in his work the 'unredeemed absurdity of the cosmos simply offers itself as the setting for his austere comedy of catastrophe, despair, and mockery'. Martin Huber too does not limit the comedy in Bernhard's work to satire but sees it serving many different functions, and Caroline Markolin understands his concern with Austria as 'a comic and grotesque metaphor for the wretchedness of human existence'. Elfriede Jelinek's work too has long been understood in the tradition of Austrian satirists. Margarete Lamb-Faffelberger describes her as 'one of Austria's foremost political satirists', in the tradition of Nestroy, Kraus, and Horváth. And Sigrid Löffler comments of *Die Klavierspielerin* that Jelinek treats her subject with 'a coolness equally humorous and scornful', a description which is applied to much of her prose. See: Wendelin Schmidt-Dengler, 'Thomas Bernhard's Poetics of Comedy', in *A Companion to the Works of Thomas Bernhard*, ed. by Matthias Konzett (Rochester, NY: Camden House, 2002), pp. 105–15 (p. 110); Stephen D. Dowden, *Understanding Thomas Bernhard* (Columbia, SC: University of South Carolina Press, 1991), pp. xii, 4–5; Martin Huber, 'Rettich und Klavier: Zur Komik im Werk Thomas Bernhards', in *Komik in der österreichischen Literatur*, ed. by Schmidt-Dengler, Sonleitner, & Zeyringer, pp. 275–84 (p. 284); Caroline Markolin, 'Too Late to Seek, too Early to Find?: Philosophical and Aesthetic Aspects of Contemporary Austrian Fiction', in *Shadows of the Past: Austrian Literature of the Twentieth Century*, ed. by Hans H. Schulte and Gerard Schapple (Oxford: Peter Lang, 2009), pp. 125–38 (p. 127); Margarete Lamb-Faffelberger, 'In the Eyes of the Press: Provocation — Production — Prominence: A Critical Documentation of Elfriede Jelinek's Reception', in *Elfriede Jelinek: Framed by Language*, ed. by Jorun B. Johns and Katherine Arens (Riverside, CA: Ariadne Press, 1994), pp. 287–302 (p. 287). Sigrid Löffler, quoted in Lamb-Faffelberger, p. 291.

CHAPTER 1

Ingeborg Bachmann: Comedy and the Women's Weepie

In his essay on Beckett's *Endgame*, Adorno recounts a joke about a threesome: 'stupid August, who catches his wife with his friend on the sofa, cannot decide whether to throw out his wife or his friend, because he cares too much about both of them, and hits on the solution of selling the sofa'.[1] Ingeborg Bachmann's version of the threesome drama, *Malina*, is no joke: brevity and distanced observation have been replaced by length and personal suffering; the startling lateral thinking of the perhaps not so stupid August has been replaced with the depressingly realistic punishment of the woman and the cutting punch-line 'it was murder'; humour and the pleasure it arouses have apparently been replaced with despair.[2] Yet with regard to this last point, one further fundamental shift in emphasis has occurred. Adorno uses fiction as part of an argument that sees humour as a debased aesthetic medium under late capitalism, 'without a place of reconciliation from which one could laugh, and without anything harmless on the face of the earth that would allow itself to be laughed at'.[3] He seems to want to take back the force of the story's humour and the laughter it provokes. *Malina*, however, is fiction; like much of Bachmann's prose work it tells of trauma, of the harmfulness of the earth, and of despair.

In interviews Bachmann repeatedly confirmed the view that the primary focus of her late prose was suffering and trauma, referring in interview to a permanent state of war in which people kill each other slowly.[4] Bachmann's narrative exploration of suffering and victimhood, her concern with the question of how trauma and the memory of trauma can be represented, and what the ethical implications of such representations are, are central to her fiction. It is no surprise, therefore, that she has increasingly been cited as an example of female melancholy.[5] Melancholy is particularly evident at those points in Bachmann's work where the protagonists are yearning for a lost, pre-genocide, and multi-ethnic Austria-Hungary, often embodied in one figure. Evident examples are 'Drei Wege zum See' [Three Paths to the Lake], the *Prinzessin von Kagran* sections of *Malina*, and Franza's 'Heimkehr nach Galizien' [Return to Galicia]. However, such melancholy is held in check, is indeed overshadowed, by the combination of melodrama and comedy in her work. Bachmann characterized her attitude to her protagonists as 'bösartig liebevoll' [maliciously loving], and was aware of the absurd dimension of their suffering. Nevertheless, 'Das Lächerliche an den Menschen ist für mich etwas, das nur zur

Fassade gehört. Und solange nur die Fassade beschrieben wird, sind die meisten Menschen, auch das Ich, oft lächerlich. Nur hinter der Fassade ist kein Mensch lächerlich' [For me, people's ridiculous side only belongs to the façade. And as long as only the façade is described, most people, including the *Ich*, are often ridiculous. But behind the façade no one is ridiculous]. Behind the façade everyone has their own tragedy.[6] The author's juxtaposition of ridiculousness, what makes someone laughable, with tragedy is significant, for it points to a pervasive tension in her writing. Yet whereas Bachmann seems here to restrict that tension to a dichotomy of surface relief giving way to cathartic depth, I wish to suggest that a slightly different relationship is at play: one between comedy and melodrama. The interaction of these representational modes both crystallizes and complicates Bachmann's narrative concerns. It signifies a playing out of the tension between emotion and distance at an aesthetic level. Furthermore, both melodrama and comedy have an unabashed association with pleasure, so their presence extends Bachmann's exploration of narrative ethics. They signal Bachmann's concern around the relationship of pleasure and ethics while at the same time ensuring that pleasure remains a central component even of narratives of suffering. And finally, the nature of that pleasure is interrogated not least because both comedy and melodrama are modes that put the moral elevation of tragedy into question.

Melodrama

The linking of melodrama and comedy in Bachmann's work has been perceptively analyzed by Hans Höller in his article focusing on comedy in *Malina*. In it he identifies a comically melodramatic dimension in *Der gute Gott von Manhattan*, and points to similar violent episodes in certain poems and in particular manifestations of the murderous father in *Malina*.[7] Höller relates these grotesque scenes to the tradition of the 'Hanswurst' character of the *Volkstheater*, thereby establishing a direct link between aspects of Bachmann's work and the extreme thrills of traditional stage melodrama.[8] He then goes on to point out that Bachmann laid aside the tragic victimhood of *Das Buch Franza* in order to write the more complex *Malina*. Early editions of *Malina* had a blurb dripping with the tone of cloak and dagger melodrama, leading the reader to anticipate a page-turning whodunit based on a failed love triangle: 'Mord oder Selbstmord? Es gibt keine Zeugen. Eine Frau zwischen zwei Männern. Ihre letzte große Leidenschaft. [...] Ein Leichnam, der nicht gefunden wird. Das verschwundene Testament. [...] Zerwischte Spuren. Schritte. Jemand also, der noch auf und abgeht in dieser Wohnung — stundenlang: MALINA' [Murder or suicide? There are no witnesses. A woman between two men. Her last great passion. [...] An undiscovered corpse. The vanished will. [...] Traces removed. Footsteps. Someone still pacing up and down in the flat — for hours on end: MALINA]. Höller suggests that Bachmann was ironic in proposing a melodramatic mode of reading and that the blurb text encouraged initial misinterpretations of the novel as superficial and, precisely, as a melodramatic love story.[9] He thereby implies that melodrama is a superficial mode and thus not to be taken seriously.

Yet this unabashed signalling of melodrama need not be understood as ironic since the novel is indeed permeated with characteristic traits of melodrama. These include the space of innocence from which virtue is expelled (the 'Ungargassenland'), the figure of the victim (the *Ich*) pursued by the villain (the father, the murderer, men in general), gestures of muteness (the *Ich* is silenced) and an emphasis on the body for communicating meaning (shaking, trembling, collapsing), a fascination with nightmare (central section), betrayal (Malina), the incorporation of music (Schönberg), and unlikely resolutions (disappearing into a crack in the wall). Thus the melodramatic dimensions of the novel were rightly identified, but wrongly criticized upon the novel's publication. As Peter Brooks argues in his fundamental re-appraisal of melodrama as a literary form, it is not a debased form of tragedy, but a response to the loss of the sacred and the moral certainties it guaranteed. A tragic vision of humanity is no longer available in modernity, for such a vision is dependent upon sacred truths. One reaction to this loss of absolute truth has been an ironic and anti-metaphorical mode of writing exemplified by Flaubert, Beckett, and possibly Joyce, who privilege an aesthetic of suspicion. In contrast, melodramatic writers such as Henry James or Joseph Conrad form part of a 'metaphorical quest' to reintroduce the notion of the sacred and of ethical striving. In modernity this is only possible, however, 'in personal terms'.[10] So melodrama refuses to accept that transcendence is absent from the world and seeks moral meaning in the world. Consequently, 'things and gestures of the real world, of social life, act as kinds of metaphors that refer us to the realm of spiritual reality and latent moral meanings'.[11]

Brooks points to the battles between good and evil played out at a personal level and how in consequence ethics is associated with emotional states. Thus the experience of suffering assumes a moral agency, for in the polarized scheme of good versus evil, suffering is the result of virtue overpowered by the very real presence of evil in the world. Tragedy, of course, is also concerned with suffering, but melodrama expresses suffering without restraint and, furthermore, commonly shows passivity in the face of suffering rather than assertion or decisive action. And fundamental to melodrama is the fact that all of its themes are suffused with an extreme intensity of emotion, particularly of love and suffering, that offends social norms. This rather ignoble lack of emotional restraint is one of the reasons for melodrama's poor reputation, yet importantly, Brooks insists that overwrought emotion and the schematization of good and evil need not be equated with a lack of subtlety. He points to the example of Henry James, in whose novels evil lurks below the good manners of the upper classes and where evil may mean 'denying to someone the means to free realization of his or her full potential as a moral being'. Conversely, the good may be an individually held ethical imperative to which the individual aspires, rather than a recognized social norm. Overall, then, Brook concludes that 'melodrama becomes the principal mode for uncovering, demonstrating, and making operative the essential moral universe in a post-sacred era'.[12]

Bachmann's late prose both belongs to and engages with traditions of melodramatic writing. The melodramatic aspects of her work are immediately apparent in the suffering of the female protagonists, suffering which acquires far-reaching moral significance. This is most marked in the figure of Franza, who in her pursuit of ideals is a stark example of re-sacralization. The moral dimension of her suffering is evident: the innocent girl who has brought up her younger brother (even saving him from drowning) is caught up in the villainous machinations of the psychiatrist Jordan, who systematically sets out to destroy her. Beyond this personal conflict of good and evil, Jordan is the emblematic white man, more generally responsible for the destruction of aboriginal peoples and the Jews, and the oppression of women. And just as Franza sees in Jordan the embodiment of a greater meaning, so too is her excessive horror at the sight of the dead camel and the cretin an immediate response of perceiving them to be more than they are.[13] The *Ich* too elevates Ivan to the level of the sacred by referring to him as her Mecca and her Jerusalem (*M*, 320) and her suffering is a moral response to the murderousness of a society in which terrible crimes are committed that remain unknown and untried (*M*, 617). The villains are cast as men; their individual crimes are fuelled by their pathological attitude to women, and through the archetype of the father and the dreams of torture, destruction, and the Holocaust, her suffering is a symptom of a wider, social evil. Also, in the *Goldmann/Rottwitz* fragment, Eka strives to think of her relationship to Jung as 'vollkommen' [complete], and after being raped thinks in absolute terms, believing she has finally become a woman: 'es war die Vollendung' [it was the completion].[14]

Melodramatic suffering is associated with female figures who are virtuous victims of villainous men. Fanny Goldmann is exploited and manipulated by the ambitious Marek, becoming depressed, alcoholic, and suicidal. Eka Kottwitz, the highly acclaimed political journalist, is intellectually sophisticated, knows no nastiness, and is clearly presented as emotionally innocent (*GR*, 416). In a manner reminiscent of Jordan's objectification of Franza, Jung uses Eka's extensive knowledge of literature and her social connections to further his own career as a novelist. As a result of his systematic belittling of her and his exploitation of their relationship as material for his work, Eka despairs and throws herself from a window, remaining permanently paralyzed. This dramatic gesture is in itself an important component of melodramatic expression, for in melodrama the body and its gestures become the means for articulating emotion when language fails. In the confrontation with evil, the victim is frequently rendered mute and physically devastated. Thus Eka withdraws almost entirely from society, silent and paralyzed. Franza, unable to voice her unhappiness and fear stops eating, shakes uncontrollably, makes gestures of wiping something off her clothes (*DBF*, 167), weeps, has convulsions (*DBF*, 155), vomits in response to those she sees as desecrating the corpses in Egypt (*DBF*, 290), and finally dies. For the *Ich*, intensity of feeling can only be articulated through gesture and the body. As a child she became ill rather than take an oath (*M*, 574), she feels that even her skin and hair are involved when she speaks to Ivan (*M*, 306), and she becomes still in his presence, displacing her feelings onto polishing his shoes (*M*, 314). Her elevation of her love for Ivan to an absolute would only be matched by the absolute gestures of throwing herself in to the Danube for him, or flinging herself in front of a car (*M*, 586). Conversely, her response to trauma is physical collapse, panic attacks, headaches, and pain.

Passivity, the 'space of innocence', and thwarted escape are characteristic tropes of melodrama and of Bachmann's late prose. Franza is not only unable to resist Jordan's cruelty, but in a grotesque masochistic attempt to conform to the figure of virtuous victim she lies on the bathroom floor praying that she may love him even more (*DBF*, 211). Fanny and Eka likewise do not take action against their abusers, and the *Ich* feels at the mercy of others' demands. The action they do take is to try and flee, be this Franza's escape to Galicien or the desert, the *Ich*'s retreat into the safe enclave of the Ungargasse, away from the intrusive evils outside, or Eka's withdrawal to the isolation of the Kottwitz flat. But escape proves futile, and the space, and state, of innocence cannot be regained.

The Failure of Melodrama

It is quite evident from the progression of her work that Bachmann saw melodrama as inadequate in its 'pure' form. The pathos of melodrama and its focus on the victim's perspective is fundamentally problematic. Bachmann was acutely aware of the destructive danger of emotional entrapment in a position of victimhood, as we know from her devastatingly honest, and unsent, letter to Celan: 'Das ist Dein Unglück, das ich für stärker halte als das Unglück, das Dir widerfährt. Du willst das Opfer sein, [...] Du sanktionierst es' [That is your misfortune, that I consider worse than the misfortune that befalls you. You want to be the victim, [...] you sanction it].[15] Her work would seem to suggest that melodrama is not adequate for representation, an unhappiness that is reflected in her dissatisfaction with the *Franza* text and in the complexity of the narrative strategies in *Malina*, which expose the limitations of unmediated melodramatic expression. The treatment of melodrama in *Malina* is important, for the novel was designed as the overture to a planned trilogy of novels, the *Todesarten*.[16] Bachmann's project was unfinished at the time of her death in 1973, but the fragments tell the stories of women who are figuratively or literally murdered by men, husbands, and lovers, and of the murderous society that condones their actions through silence. As an overture, *Malina* is Bachmann's most complex engagement with the literary, philosophical, and ethical foundations of narrative. The novel explores and establishes key themes, particularly the question of how trauma and suffering, and the victim's voice, can be adequately articulated and ethically represented. It engages with ways in which intense emotion, be that passion or suffering, can be translated into story or narrative form when narrative presupposes structures of past, present, and future. And it asks how justice can be done to the authenticity of emotion without objectifying it through language.

The excesses of melodrama are exemplified in the figure of the *Ich*. She is presented as victim of three different men and of a pre-history of trauma that has caused her current terror. This dark story is also linked to a man, associated as it is with Vodka and orange, the memory of someone trying to fling her from a window (*M*, 477), with a plate from Vietri (*M*, 481), and with throwing a ring into the Danube (*M*, 499; 550). Her relationships to men and masculinity can all be understood as having a destructive effect. In her affair with Ivan, the *Ich* experiences the euphoria and despair of passionate love, and he becomes everything for her. Only he gives her life meaning and she yearns to please him with gestures of absolute love. Here we see the *Ich* as masquerade, the image of desirous womanliness constructed by and for men. In relation to Malina the feminine *Ich* is cast as other to the male title figure.[17] In Malina, the emotional, sensual *Ich* is faced with a reasoning, incisive, and questioning mind, and feels constantly challenged and undermined by his distance. His refusal to listen to her intensifies to the point where he simply ignores her altogether, a denial of voice that is tantamount to murder. The woman is silenced, for there is no place for her stories, her language within male discourse. The dream sequences offer the most extreme forms of violence perpetrated against the *Ich*, here by the father. She is incarcerated, beaten, humiliated, gassed, electrocuted, blinded, frozen, silenced, raped, her valuable books are destroyed, and more. The details of the torture inflicted by a man against a woman are graphic and realistic. But the process of condensation and metaphorization of dreams also confers upon the father a symbolic position: he becomes the personification of the abusive authority of patriarchy under which women are the victims of arbitrary power, their agency limited to becoming complicit with that violence.

The *Ich*'s victim position is suffused with extreme emotion and suffering. It is in the nature of the *Ich* that she can only exist in the present: hers is the immediate emotional response to what is experienced and felt in the moment. The present for the *Ich* is the permanent 'today' of the novel from which all awareness of the past and of the change implied by the future must be banished: 'Nie wollte ich denken, wie es im Anfang war [...] Ehe gestern und morgen auftauchen, muß ich sie zum Schweigen bringen in mir. Es ist heute. Ich bin hier und heute' [I never wanted to think about how it was in the beginning [...] I have to silence yesterday and tomorrow within me before they surface. It is today. I am here and today] (*M*, 469). Existence in the present precludes a reflexive stance, for this presupposes a distance from which analysis and historical contextualization become possible, both of which inevitably kill off pure emotion. The *Ich* lives in the emotional simultaneity of the now, admitting to Malina that she wants everything to make an impression on her at the same time (*M*, 638). But the excessive excitation of emotion is pathological and destructive, which the *Ich* knows but cannot resist, and she admits: 'ich fürchte, es ist "heute", das für mich zu erregend ist, zu maßlos, zu ergreifend' [I fear that it is 'today' that is too exciting for me, too excessive, too moving]. Her pathological existence means that even the life-giving passion of ecstatic love becomes a cause of suffering, for it cannot be reconciled with the mundane reality of Ivan. Her suffering is pervasive and undifferentiated, be it caused by Ivan's absence, the screaming child, the knowledge of disease, or the horror of the 'Todesarten' [modes of death], and is manifested through her body. Like other heroines of melodrama, she comes to life in and yet is incapacitated by her emotional response.

The figure of the *Ich* exemplifies traits associated with melodrama, and it is therefore significant that her perspective of excessive suffering and victimhood is associated with the failure of storytelling and the ability to represent her all-consuming perspective. The *Ich* is a well-known author, who, like her creator, is working on a project entitled *Todesarten*. Ivan is irritated and asks her to write a book with a title like 'Esultate jubilate' to reflect those moments in which she feels intense joy' (*M*, 334). The result is the legend of the Princess of Kagran, a utopian myth set by the Danube in a time before states and borders, in which the princess is rescued and falls in love with a stranger. The love is so strong that she knows they will meet and recognize one another again in centuries to come. Here the *Ich* draws upon conventions of fairy tale and myth to articulate her yearning for a better world, but the book fails in a number of ways: it neither expresses nor elicits happiness; by displacing emotions onto the distant past and impossible future it does not translate the *Ich*'s experience of immediacy into narrative form and slips into melancholy; its vision of a better world remains indebted to clichés of conventional idealized femininity in the image of the princess with golden hair; and it does not satisfy Ivan's desire for a pleasurable read.

Letters too are testament to the impossibility of writing the moment. A selection of the *Ich*'s abandoned draft letters is included in the text, in which she addresses various people with surprising, and very funny, directness. Thus, for example, she informs the President of her alienation on receiving his birthday greetings since her birth is a matter of intimacy between her parents. This example exhibits two failures: the President's letter does not have its desired effect on the addressee, and the *Ich*'s is not sent. The failures are evidence of the fundamental *Briefgeheimnis* [privacy of the post] that the loyal postman Kranewitzer has comprehended. He suddenly stops delivering the post and begins to hoard it, unopened, at home until his crime is discovered. For the *Ich,* he has attained a philosopher status for he has understood the paradox that a letter cannot truly convey the authenticity of the moment; the present becomes the past once the letter is received. This is why all real letters should be torn up: 'weil sie von heute sind und weil sie in keinem Heute mehr ankommen werden' [because they are from today and because they will no longer arrive on any Today] (*M*, 277). The *Briefgeheimnis* is, furthermore, of ethical significance. The *Ich*'s letters are written in the passion of the moment, but with a hand that is burned by her 'flammenden Aufrufe' [flaming appeals] and 'flammenden Begehren' [flaming desire] (*M*, 576). Letters that are opened betray the moment of that passion, expose it to the other's objectifying gaze. Letters that burn with passion also destroy themselves; passion transforms into charred pieces of paper (*M*, 576).

The *Ich*'s third failure to transform her immediate suffering into narrative is in the recounting of the dream sequences. How to articulate suffering is a question which is particularly acute in relation to the representation of trauma, since trauma is by definition that which has not been symbolized in language, but around which the subject circles. Clearly the dreams do articulate the experience of trauma and suffering, and in their refusal of conventional time, they are always 'last night's dreams', remaining ever present. But the dreams are the psychic equivalent of the burning letter that destroys itself and its message. They remain in themselves moments of the primary trauma that are experienced as such in the dreaming, and indeed in the re-telling. For in the form that the *Ich* recalls the dreams to Malina, she finds no distance to the suffering, cannot make sense of it by integrating it into a structuring narrative. It is Malina who asks the questions that might lead to such a narrative of understanding, a narrative which would certainly kill the immediate emotion of the traumatic moment, that is, kill the *Ich*, but which would incorporate the knowledge of the trauma into the subsequent narrative. The alternative is the destruction of the *Ich* by the very trauma whose truth she wishes to convey.

The *Ich* cannot, therefore, tell of her own trauma or seek to comprehend its significance, she can only live all emotion at once. Malina tells her: 'wenn man überlebt hat, ist Überleben dem Erkennen im Wege, du weißt nicht einmal, welche deine Leben früher waren und was dein Leben heute ist' [if one has survived, then survival inhibits understanding, you don't even know which were your previous lives and what your life is today] (*M*, 552). The *Ich* gradually begins to recognize that it is impossible for her to tell the story and admits: 'ich kann nicht erzählen' [I can't narrate] (*M*, 597) and 'ich zerbreche an jeder Erinnerung' [I shatter with every memory] (*M*, 598). However reluctantly, she recognizes that it is Malina who should tell what she feels: 'Übernimm du die Geschichten [...]. Nimm sie alle von mir' [You take over the stories [...]. Take them all from me] (*M*, 688–89). Malina's assumption of the task of narrating the *Ich*'s stories can therefore be understood as a necessary act of transformation. A persona emerges to tell the story, but he is a different self from the *Ich*. He is not a self that disregards or discards the *Ich* and Malina reminds her that he exists alongside her (*M*, 640). Rather, he is a self that comprehends and is empowered to tell of suffering, who can comply with the *Ich*'s paradoxical wishes: 'Ich möchte das Briefgeheimnis wahren. Aber ich möchte auch etwas hinterlassen' [I want to protect the privacy of the post. But I also want to bequeath something] (*M*, 682). So, although the *Ich* seems distraught that Malina throws away her legacy, arguably he is safeguarding her secret, guaranteeing discretion. And although the *Ich* has hidden and locked her precious letters in a drawer, she has also put the key in the pocket of Malina's dressing gown that she is wearing, entrusting him with what she describes as 'das ganze Feuer' [all the fire] (*M*, 576). As Bachmann said of her protagonist, 'Malina wird uns erzählen können, was ihm der andere Teil seiner Person, das Ich, hinterlassen hat' [Malina will be able to tell us what the other part of his self, the I, has bequeathed him].[18]

In a fine example of close reading of the novel, Joachim Eberhardt sustains this reading of Malina as a positive figure. He analyzes the episode when Malina and the *Ich* spend the evening at the Gebauers. The *Ich* wants Malina to play an extract from Schönberg's 'Pierrot lunaire', and she starts playing it on the piano. She does so clumsily, and without accompanying the music with the relevant text, 'O alter Duft aus Märchenzeit' ('O ancient scent from fabled times').[19] Then Malina pushes her away (*M*, 672), and takes over, but he 'spielt wirklich und spricht halb und singt halb und nur hörbar für mich' [really plays and half speaks and half sings and so only I can hear it] (*M*, 673). The fact that Malina pushes the *Ich* away need not be read as an example of the suppression of the feminine voice. He does what she wants him to do; he plays for her, and, as she herself says, he plays 'really'. He adds to, indeed completes what she plays, for not only does he include the text that she omitted, he begins with the lines that precede: 'All meinen Unmut geb ich preis' ('All of my gloom I've set aside').[20] This episode thus pre-empts the end of the novel, but at a point in the story where the *Ich* is still in control of the narrative and therefore aware of Malina's ability to sing, or speak, for her. It is she who uses the adjective 'wirklich' [really] to characterize his playing. As Eberhardt writes, this 'Wirklichkeit besteht [...] darin, daß es das Spiel des Ichs *enthält* und übertrifft' [reality consists of the fact that it *includes* the I's playing and exceeds it].[21] Malina sings 'I' at a point where the *Ich* is unable to use it. Eberhardt thus rejects the view of those critics who see Malina's rationality as silencing the *Ich*'s perspective, and invokes Schönberg's view that reason broadens rather than diminishes the scope for expressing emotion. He points out that for both Schönberg and Bachmann, rationality was not a dirty word.[22]

Sigrid Weigel situates the final death of the *Ich* in a broad philosophical context within which writing itself is related to death. She refers to Roland Barthes's assertion that the novel is a type of death: 'The Novel is a Death; it transforms life into destiny, a memory into a useful act, duration into an orientated and meaningful time'.[23] By making death central to the very act of representation itself, Barthes is expressing a view prevalent in much twentieth-century philosophy and poetics, of which Maurice Blanchot's is also typical. In his writing death and literature are intimately related, and conveyed through the figures of Orpheus the writer, driven by his desire to bring beauty, Eurydice, out of nothingness into the light as a work of art. On the one hand Orpheus can only bring Eurydice into the light by not gazing upon her, by representing her and not seeing her; on the other he is driven by his desire to see her as herself, in the darkness, as fully other. 'Orpheus does not want to make the invisible visible, but rather (and impossibly) to see the invisible as invisible'.[24] Bringing Eurydice into the world is that aspect of writing inseparable from the possibility of death: the writer seeks to represent alterity in aesthetic form, in meaningful language, yet the process of aesthetic transformation depends on the negation of the reality it seeks to represent. Indeed for Blanchot the very articulation of subjectivity is dependent on death: 'when I speak: death speaks in me. My speech is a warning that at this very moment death is loose in the world'.[25]

Malina can undoubtedly be understood as a fictional affirmation of such a poetics. The absolute alterity represented by the *Ich*, the utter immediacy of her traumatic experience, must die in the process of representation. It is a poetics that has particular resonance in critical interest in Bachmann as a post-Holocaust writer, for the recognition that death is central to representation overlaps with the problem of how to represent a traumatic event of such magnitude. The theoretical and narratological issues identified by the poetics are intensified by the double death at the core of a novel that thematizes Holocaust representation, an event that is emblematic of unrepresentable horror: representation, already a form of death, is here seeking to represent the unrepresentable, for the millions of witnesses of death are dead.[26] Bachmann is acutely aware of the self-referential or negating dimension of representation, of the way in which what can be said is determined by language's relationship to what cannot be said; as Caitríona Leahy so convincingly argues: 'in struggling to tell a story, [she] was struggling to rethink the way in which language might refer to something other than itself, might *point to* a real, historical *Grund*, even when it could not say it'.[27]

Melodrama's Pleasures

Yet ironically the centrality of death to representation is undermined at the very point where it is apparently most definitively stated: 'Es war Mord' [It was murder]. For who is speaking here? If, like the rest of the novel, it is from the *Ich*'s perspective that the accusation is made, then she is not dead. If the perspective has shifted to Malina or an impersonal third-person narrator, the assertion nevertheless confirms what has preceeded; it validates the *Ich*'s perspective and contradicts Malina's outright denial that she existed. The very assertion that murder has taken place functions as an affirmation of that other voice. Thus Bachmann offers a profound exploration of what constitutes the I and of the irreconcilable tension between the here and now of the feeling self and the historical time of narrative; what the *Ich* wittily describes as the 'Raum- und Zeitproblem' [space-time problem] (*M*, 656) that she has never been able to resolve. Bachman neither undermines the importance of the I, nor does she deny its agency. Indeed, she intensifies the absolute link between the I and the notion of emotional authenticity. But she refuses to accept this as adequate: the I is vital but limited, and the truth of emotional authenticity is powerful but destructive and circumscribed. Bachmann privileges the I as the 'Platzhalter der menschlichen Stimme' [placeholder of the human voice] and irreducible, therefore, in its importance. Nevertheless, it must be transformed or incorporated into a wider perspective: the third person.[28] The status of the I as necessarily preceding narration is why Sigrid Weigel argues for understanding the *Ich* as Malina's other, rather than the common response of viewing Malina as the *Ich*'s alter ego. As she says, the *Ich* 'geht [...] dem Erzähler voraus; es wird gewesen sein, wenn er erzählen wird' [preceedes the narrator; it will have been, when he narrates].[29]

Malina thus ends with an ambiguous interplay of presence and absence, an interplay that aptly comments on the complexity of representation itself: for all that representation might involve the death of that which it represents, for all that it might be a self-referential fiction that masks the death of being at its core, it is never only this. For in its depiction of its object, narrative, including the most disturbing attempts to engage with death, trauma, or suffering, is necessarily productive in its creation of real effects and of real affects in the present. As we see from the figure of the *Ich*, language is inseparable from emotion, and for Bachmann it is precisely language's emotional impact that affirms life. When asked in interview about the 'Stellenwert' [place value] of a Rimbaud quotation, Bachmann replies:

> Es gibt für mich keine Zitate, sondern die wenigen Stellen in der Literatur, die mich immer aufgeregt haben, die sind für mich das Leben. Und es sind keine Sätze, die ich zitiere, [...] weil sie schön sind oder weil sie bedeutend sind, sondern weil sie mich wirklich erregt haben. Eben wie Leben.[30]

> [For me there are no quotations, just the few places in literature that have always excited me, which for me are life. And I don't quote sentences because they're beautiful or because they're meaningful, but because they have really excited me. Precisely like life.]

In the spirit of Bachmann's refusal to evaluate the 'place value' of a phrase, 'Es war Mord' is more important than providing a starting point for a discussion of poetics. For it is a powerful, angry accusation. But why does the novel end with such force given that the *Ich* recognizes the need for Malina to take on the task of narrating her stories, and asks him to do so? Why, when in interview Bachmann sees Malina as someone who helps the *Ich* find death, does she conclude with such drama, melodrama even?[31] The shift from 'finding death' to murder, is vital, for it insists on and validates the power of emotion that is so markedly absent from Blanchot's account of death in literature. The 'Es war Mord' articulates Eurydice's fury at Blanchot's sovereign misogyny. The novel cares about emotion, and the last line adamantly reminds us of the importance of those aspects of the text that respond passionately to cruelty, suffering, and also to love. Specifically, however, 'Es war Mord' returns the reader to the importance of melodramatic conventions of representing suffering and victimhood and suggests that Bachmann's blurb, which directs us towards melodrama, is not simply ironic.

The melodramatic ending of *Malina*, and with it the final chords of the overture that heralds further murderous tales, affirms the relevance of that mode of representation to narratives of suffering and traumatic events. It is telling in this respect that the *Ich*'s failed attempts to narrativize her perspective do not draw upon melodramatic conventions, but that the *Fanny Goldmann* and the *Rottwitz/Kottwitz* drafts narrated by Malina do. Of course, the complexity of narrative strategies in *Malina* exposes the limitations of unmediated melodramatic expression, and the pathological solipsism of its perspective is set as a limit. Furthermore, imposing a limit continues to be a function of Malina's subsequent role as narrator. But a limit is not a negation, and melodrama continues to be an important mode in these texts, not least in the constellation of morally evaluated victimhood and the suffering women endure at the hands of villainous men. Thus far from trivializing suffering by association with the 'women's weepie', the incorporation of melodramatic tropes reinforces the centrality of emotion to meaning. This is made explicit in *Malina*, for without the intensity of emotion Malina is unable to evaluate what he observes. Without moral evaluation, change is impossible: 'Ich glaube, daß Malina Änderung und Veränderung in jeder Hinsicht kalt lassen, weil er ja auch nirgends etwas Gutes oder Schlechtes sieht [...] Für ihn ist offenbar die Welt, wie sie eben ist' [I think that change and alteration leave Malina cold in every respect because he simply doesn't see anything good or bad anywhere [...] For him the world is evidently just as it is] (*M*, 582). Crucially, however, melodrama, like the *Ich*, points to a particular relationship between emotion and meaning. It insists on the value of extreme emotion, on pathological suffering as a commensurate response to real evil. The I in *Malina* is not a generic I of emotional authenticity *tout court*, but is constructed as a melodramatic I: one that emphasizes the suffering of life, investing pain and its cause with absolute moral values even while demonstrating that individual desire cannot be reconciled with an absolute, and that values are, anyway, contingent. In the face of such contingency the melodramatic self is nevertheless determined by the quest for meaning in the present. The quest for moral truths is acted out in personal terms and plenitude is only ever provisional, but the contingent truths and facts of the historical and emotional moment are no less real and have no less impact. So even while Bachmann recognizes that the melodramatic victim position is not one that can be productively inhabited, it nevertheless conveys suffering that cannot be redeemed by tragedy's conflation of self with higher necessity.

The *Ich*'s ignominious retreat into a crack in the wall is not a tragic death even if it is murder. The final accusation, with its narratively ironic affirmation of the *Ich*'s voice, marks a significant development in Bachmann's treatment of yearning. In one of her most striking images from the closing lines of *Die Zikaden*, she presents the terrible transformation and cost of yearning:

> Die Zikaden waren einmal Menschen. Sie hörten auf zu essen, zu trinken und zu lieben, um immerfort singen zu können. Auf der Flucht in den Gesang wurden sie dürrer und kleiner, und nun singen sie, an ihre Sehnsucht verloren — verzaubert, aber auch verdammt, weil ihre Stimmen unmenschlich geworden sind.[32]

> [The cicadas were once people. They stopped eating, drinking and loving in order to be able to sing the whole time. During their escape into song they became thinner and smaller, and now they sing, lost to their yearning — enchanted but also damned, because their voices have become inhuman.]

Throughout her work, Bachmann's characters are shown in various ways to be striving for the fulfilment of their ideals, absolute values, and completeness, the pursuit of which leads to both positive transformation and the intensification of perception, *and* to their destruction. There are repeated examples of this double transformation, including the characters in *Die Zikaden* whose very existence on the island is the attempt to live their fantasies while sinking deeper into loneliness and the protagonists of the stories in *Das dreißigste Jahr* who in various ways negate the value of the present through their yearning for a better world and a rupture with the present. It is in Bachmann's later work that the theme of yearning becomes more melodramatic and extensively intertwined with the abusive dynamics of relationships and of traumatic suffering. Franza strives constantly for the absolute, be that the British officer, Sire, the desire to die as a martyr, or the desert. Here too the pursuit of ideals is double-edged; her desire to submit to a higher moral authority enables her to recognize the atrocities perpetrated against her and other victims, while her need to sustain an ideal leads to self-deception and blindness. In *Malina*, the *Ich*'s elevation of emotion and the concomitant lack of reflexivity fuels a potent moral anger directed against the complacency, injustice, hypocrisy, and cynicism of contemporary society, and yet causes a debilitating inability to live in real time and normal society. This shift to the melodramatic mode ensures that the yearning voice does not become detached from the immediate experience of relationships and the social, but remains resolutely mundane and human.

Perhaps surprising given melodrama's focus on suffering, is its importance in contributing and drawing attention to narrative pleasure. Melodrama, in its emotional excess and its strategies of eliciting emotional identification with its protagonists, is peculiarly honest about the troubling relationship between representations of suffering and enjoyment: finitude is terrible and we will jolly well suffer and have a good cry. The pejorative association of melodrama as the 'women's weepie' is fuelled by melodrama's excess, an indulgence in suffering that encourages the pleasures of self-pity. This pleasure is neither ennobling nor redemptive and therefore draws attention to the fact that storytelling is also about pleasure, whatever the content of that fiction. The victim's uncontained emotion is acted out in personal terms, the enjoyment of which serves no higher moral or cathartic purpose. The pleasure of melodrama also differs from tragedy in that in its emphasis on emotional excess it can acquire traits of comic hyperbole. Normally, given melodrama's emphasis on female suffering, it is tears rather than laughter that figure in discussions of the genre. Yet film studies scholars have long pointed to that side of melodrama that leans towards the parodic aspects of comedy. Many have insisted that film melodramas are, at their best, complex parodies of social norms, and that they achieve their parodic critique precisely through their techniques of emotional and stylistic excess. Those critics who support this view frequently point to Douglas Sirk as a director who used these excesses as a form of Brechtian alienation to reveal the ideological contradictions of bourgeois ideology.[33] Thomas Elsaesser too highlights the comic potential of the discrepancy that can arise out of melodrama when he writes of George Cukor's *The Chapman Report* that 'it underlines the ambiguous discrepancy between displaying intense feelings and the circumstances to which they are inadequate — usually a comic motif but tragic in its emotional implications'.[34]

In Bachmann's work the comic potential of melodrama is not incidental, but is part of her incorporation of comedy into her narratives of trauma and suffering. Indeed, as Daniela Strigl points out, although Bachmann's comedy arises from the clash of irony and pathos, it is the pathos that critics have focused on.[35] Like melodrama, comedy triggers anxiety around the pleasurable and entertaining dimension of fiction that is concerned with trauma and its effects.

Comedy and Laughter

There is an interesting parallel between the relationship of weepy melodrama to ennobling tragedy and the relationship of two types of comedy. On the one hand, comedy's association with the failings of the body, be this the reduction of the body to a mechanistic state, the ugly distortions of uncontrollable laughter, or aggression, have been seen as demeaning. On the other hand comedy is taken very seriously when it can be divorced from the physical, when it fulfils its Schillerian goal of being free from passion, calmly looking on. Comedy is also taken seriously when it assumes tragic dimensions, conforming to the poetics of negation, when in writers like Beckett and Kafka it is held to produce the 'laughter of despair' in the face of nihilism.[36] This is precisely how Höller evaluates the comedy in *Malina*. In his view the comedy is deeply unfunny, and is, through the motif of laughter, thematically linked with the idea of suffocation. At the Institut Français the *Ich* leaves the room before she starts to laugh and refers to her 'ersticktes Lachen' [smothered laughter] (*M*, 369). And as she perceives her relationship with Ivan changing, the *Ich* remarks: 'In meinem Hals steckt ein wahnsinniges Lachen, aber weil ich fürchte, daß ich dann nie mehr aufhören könnte zu lachen, sage ich nichts' [Wild laughter sticks in my throat, but because I'm afraid that I would never be able to stop laughing, I say nothing] (*M*, 667). Echoing Schiller, Höller argues that rather than pointing to a free and sovereign self, such comic moments are evidence of the self's pre-rational responses. As such they are central to a comedy of despair, functioning in Adorno's words as 'die ästhetischen Statthalter von Negation' [the aesthetic governor of negation].[37]

All uncontrollable laughter can be understood as a form of negation of reason, as a disruption of ordered value systems, including ethical systems. Christine Kanz reinforces Höller's emphasis on laughter as a sign of the self under threat, arguing that along with its potential to cause disorder, laughter can also upset the stability of the ego. This is exemplified when Franza's laughter becomes a symptom of her decomposition (*DBF*, 287), so that laughter assumes an association with madness.[38] Gürtler too makes this link, commenting that laughter is liberating for the women, symbolizing their madness.[39] It is laughter's challenge to reason and the ego, and its association with an uncontrolled body, that have led to those aspects of comedy associated with the body, and consequently with the emasculating loss of reason, being so devalued. As part of a general re-evaluation of laughter, Simon Critchley is right to praise it as something that 'returns us to the limited condition of our finitude, the shabby and degenerating state of our [...] bodily strata'.[40] He is wrong, however, to reduce finitude only to shabbiness and degeneration. For as the *Ich* asserts of her pre-history of happiness: 'damals hatte ich nie Angst, aber oft Glücksgefühle [...], ich konnte vor lauter Glück stundenlang lachen' [I was never scared then, but often happy [...], I could laugh for joy for hours] (*M*, 655). The *Ich* values Ivan's gift, that he can make her laugh again (*M*, 309), frequently laughing with him (*M*, 342; 367) and banishing unhappiness through laughter: 'ich [muß] lachen und ich lasse das Unglück anderswo geschehen' [I [have to] laugh and I let the unhappiness happen somewhere else] (*M*, 334). Franza and Martin too laugh together when they meet (*DBF*, 220), and Franza's time with Ödön, a period when she is always strong and joyful, is also the time when she laughed most (*DBF*, 237). Kanz argues convincingly that laughter thus functions as a weapon against fear and as an assertion of the protagonists' own desires. Franza realizes briefly that she can undermine Jordan with laughter (*DBF*, 190); and the *Ich* uses laughter subversively in the face of the father's order in her dream: 'ich lache, tanze' [I laugh, dance] (*M*, 554).[41]

Franza's and the Ich's coupling of happiness with laughter insists upon the dimensions of laughter and of finitude that Höller omits to mention: that its pleasures and joys are real and immediate, and indeed, that laughter, in and of itself, is part of that immediate experience of joy. In these examples laughter is a manifestation of positive emotion and wellbeing, even if that wellbeing cannot be the same as that of the pre-traumatic existence. Elisabeth Matrei too affirms the connection between wellbeing and laughter when she describes her marriage to the homosexual Hugh as one based on sharing friendship and a joyful home.[42] Later she tells her father that the marriage was very funny: 'fast das einzig Komische in meinem Leben' [almost the only funny thing in my life] (*S*, 417). The importance of laughter and pleasure is not limited to the protagonists' experience, however, but is explicitly stated as being fundamental to narration. As Malina says to the *Ich* before she starts telling him her opinion of men: 'Bitte aber keine Geschichten oder nur einige Stellen aus ihnen, wenn sie komisch genug sind' [But please no stories or only some parts if they're funny enough] (*M*, 606). Malina's demand for amusing entertainment is duly met, and the *Ich* combines a scathing analysis of men's pathological treatment of women with an extremely witty account of how this manifests itself in practice: a man who likes kissing feet will go on to kiss the feet of fifty women and assume they like it; the woman whose feet gets kissed has to reconcile herself to the fact that it is now the turn of her feet. But there is more:

> Sie muß sich unglaubliche Gefühle erfinden und den ganzen Tag ihre wirklichen Gefühle in den erfundenen unterbringen, einmal damit sie das mit den Füßen aushält, dann vor allem, damit sie den größeren fehlenden Rest aushält, denn jemand, der so an Füßen hängt, vernachlässigt sehr viel anderes. (*M*, 609)
>
> [She has to invent unbelievable emotions and spend the whole day reconciling her real emotions with the invented ones, first so that she endures the thing with the feet, but mainly so that she endures the even bigger, missing Rest, because someone who is so keen on feet, neglects so much else]

The *Ich*'s ability to combine a story about the basic asymmetry in the relationship between men and women with the need to amuse her listener signals much of what Bachmann achieves in her narratives. Missing from this quotation is the suffering that results for the woman by being reduced to an interchangeable body part, but that suffering is a more evident feature of her writing. Here we see evidence of the comic aesthetic that is present in her late prose in various ways. Most obvious, and most commented upon, is Bachmann's satirical eye. The shadowy journalist Mühlbauer is undoubtedly a figure of fun, caricatured as the cliché-pedalling hack who is utterly non-plussed by the *Ich*'s unconventional answers. The Altenwyls are a marvellous example of comic characters, their comedy enhanced by the fact that they keep popping up in the different *Todesarten* texts as sincere guardians of Viennese upper-class decorum. At the same time, they epitomize that society's indiscretion and superficiality. So when Jordan contravenes the rules of good conversation by giving a lecture on the technicalities of shark attacks, a few days later his chunk of information has been transformed into a palatable conversational ragout. It is a ragout that Awi Altenwyl is particularly good at serving: 'Awi [sah] so kokett um sich, als wollte sie den nächsten Haifisch ersuchen, es bloß mit ihr aufzunehmen' [Awi looked around so coquettishly, as though she wanted to dare the nearest shark to take her on] (*GR*, 383). Other guardians of Austrian decorum are Fanny Goldmann's aunts, who are unanimous in considering the period after the *Anschluss* as dreadful. It takes the Jewish Goldmann a while to understand that their 'dreadful' refers to the ensuing bad manners and is not an expression of horror (*GR*, 355).

In contrast to the well-behaved Austrians for whom the offence against manners is worse than the offence against humanity, foreigners are satirized for their vulgarity. In *Franza* the American woman is caricatured with little sympathy as a witch (*DBF*, 295), as are the sunburned Dutch, who are likened to figures from Breughel (*DBF*, 289). In 'Besichtigung einer alten Stadt' satiric comedy is at its most sustained and is aimed at both the Austrians and their history, and at Americans. Malina and the *Ich* gain a whole new insight into Vienna by going on a tour aimed at foreign tourists, learning about the:

> most famous water, [...] the most famous Austrian chocolates, [...] the most famous composer of all the times, [...] the most famous and dreadful illness, [...] the greatest singing successes and singing accidents in the world, [...] the oldest and most famous dramas and murderings in Europa.[43]

Here the hyperbolic pretentions of the Austrian tourist industry are exposed, as are its idealization and trivialization of history.[44] Conversely, the simplistic enthusiasm of the American group is humorously derided, their desire for superficial gratification reflected in their consumption of imitation *Mozartkugeln*.

'Besichtigung einer alten Stadt' was removed from *Malina* before publication on the suggestion of Martin Walser and the publisher.[45] Looking at other removed sections further confirms the comic potential of the lesser figures in *Malina*. In 'Lina' the *Ich* describes her 'cat and mouse' relationship with the housekeeper Lina, who, from the *Ich*'s point of view is undoubtedly the cat. Through rigorous policing of the division of labour and of class, enforced through careful deployment of her moods, Lina seeks to protect herself, the *Ich*, and Malina from the demeaning encroachments of change and the Germans. As Karen Achberger points out, and as is clear from the tour guide's English, the comedy is further enhanced by the way in which characters' modes of speech are reproduced.[46] Lina's adept manipulation of the *Ich* as well as her dislike of Germans is precisely conveyed when with a raised duster she reports on a phone call: 'wenn Sie mich fragen, gnädige Frau, aber mich fragen gnädige Frau ja nicht, gesprochen hat er ohne Manieren' [if you ask me, madam, but of course madam isn't asking me, he spoke without manners] (*BS*, 708).

As well as being typical of Bachmann's satire, the *Ich*'s interaction with Lina gives rise to humour based on the apparent incongruity of an event and the *Ich*'s response to it. What for Malina remains an uncomplicated relationship has a quite different impact on the *Ich*, resulting in what Achberger sees as a tension between appearance and inner emotions.[47] The mismatch between what a character feels and the events they are responding to are a pervasive source of comedy in the texts. An early example exists in the judge Wildermuth's scream in court in immediate response to the question of whether two buttons can be identical. Beatrix finds everything 'grauenvoll' [horrendous], including the problem of finding matching underwear and the burden of ill-fitting bras. Her extreme reaction to being badly made-up has comic elements, as does Miranda's wilful refusal to see anything. This spares her the sight of women with hair on their upper lips and legs, leads her to believe that she is brushing her leg against a man rather than a chair leg, and culminates in her slapstick collision with a glass door (*S*, 256, 255, & 274). For Eka the gap between her complex understanding of psychopathology, sexology, perversion and fetishes, and her ignorance of what orgasm is, is an unbridgeable gulf (*GR*, 419).

Examples of comic excess and incongruity arise from some of the protagonists' most desperate moments. When Franza mistakes a sea cucumber for a vision of God, the comic potential is intensified by the narrator's previous ironic comment about her inability to differentiate (*DBF*, 180). In response to the horror of seeing a slaughtered camel lying in a pool of blood, Franza's self-identification as a victim leaves her oblivious to the grotesque comedy of her assertion: 'Ich weiß, wie ich aussehe. Ich sehe aus wie das Kamel, das mich ansieht' [I know how I look. I look like the camel that's looking at me] (*DBF*, 280). The *Ich* is in utter turmoil during her encounter with the man from Bulgaria, a country about which she knows nothing except that its people are meant to live long because of the yoghurt. Sadly, with his Morbus Buerger, the man fails to conform to this healthy image. The *Ich* is internally on the verge of collapse through the horror that she feels by being confronted with disease and mortality, while externally remaining polite and empathetic. Similarly, she is tortured by the din of the child in the nearby flat, her agony suitably relativized by the fact that Malina barely notices the noise. Fanny Goldmann ends up fumbling around on the floor picking up the contents of her handbag just as her lover tells her the devastating news that he is now with a new woman (*S*, 311). And in a moment of intense emotional drama when Eka first tries to kill herself by driving at speed into a wall, the rather more mundane fear of the police intervenes with almost slapstick results: the police lights give her such a shock that she nearly crashes into the police car instead (*GR*, 405). Far from slapstick, and in what is perhaps the most extreme example of grotesque comic incongruity, is the end of the rape scene. Eka's drawn out ordeal of pain and objectification concludes with the Somali student apologizing that he has only managed two hours, declaring his love for her, calling her 'Liebchen' [darling] and cutting off a lock of her hair. The narrator comments ironically that the Countess Kottwitz was no Lady Chatterley (*GR*, 426), thereby viciously satirizing the relationship between romantic gesture and the violent imposition of male fantasy onto women that it masks.

Bachmann's protagonists do not themselves recognize the comedy that their responses generate. Martin explicitly remarks that his sister has no sense of humour (*DBF*, 195), a description that fits with her 'Schwerfälligkeit' [ponderousness] (*DBF*, 236), even during the time she was with Ödön. Indeed, Franza's ponderousness recalls the earnest and humourless tone of the *Kagran* legend, and the *Ich* too is consumed by the immediacy of her suffering. Thus the comedy does not arise from the women's perspectives, but from their perspective being represented in an incongruous relation to events or to another point of view. The narrative of *Malina* is built around the juxtaposition of perspectives, and this more readily facilitates a comic response to the *Ich*'s hyperbolic responses to her passions. The operatic constructedness of the dialogues with Malina, the condensation of the telephone exchanges with Ivan and the many unsent letters ensure that an ironic structure permeates the novel. In Bachmann's more conventionally realistic works, it is through the complex interplay of different narrative perspectives that comic incongruity is generated. For this reason the comedy in *Franza* has been neglected, because the narrative complexity of this unfinished draft is often undervalued.[48] Although those sections of the story narrated by Franza or articulating her point of view display little humour, it is the incorporation of the perspectives of Martin and the third person narrator that introduce a comic dimension.

Martin never quite comprehends the degree of his sister's mental desolation, does the best he can, but is frequently placed in unexpected and unwanted situations. He hates anything happening (*DBF*, 173) but has events thrust upon him that he would never have thought possible, starting with the three-side long telegram full of 'stop und stop und stop' [stop and stop and stop] (*DBF*, 135). His methodical approach to life is fundamentally challenged and his defensive retreat into rationalizations becomes comically exaggerated as he desperately casts around for solutions to the Franza problem. Just as he is swigging Steinhäger gin in the kitchen, comforting himself that Alda will sort it all out, Franza appears at the door and ruins his fantasy. When in desperation Franza jumps into the river and is rescued by a passing motorcyclist, Martin has to deal with the social consequences: not only does the motorcyclist finish Martin's Steinhäger, but Martin has to give him his nearly new winter suit so that he can finally ride off after midnight, a slightly wobbling cowboy (*DBF*, 202). Martin's fury at Franza's inexplicable behaviour culminates in a typical example of the comic relief afforded by surprising juxtapositions, and he has to laugh when he realizes that she has been deeply engrossed in the financial pages of the newspaper (*DBF*, 203). His anger at Franza's odd behaviour and anxiety about her false passport is offset by her consummate performance of unruffled confidence as she looks at the border officials with brazen friendliness (*DBF*, 205). The comedy is further heightened by the clash of Martin's furious fantasy of flinging her off the train with her repeated decorous requests that he do something for her: 'macht es dir etwas aus, mein Lieber, und bitte' [do you mind, love, and please] (*DBF*, 205).

Much of the general ironic tone of the first section of *Franza* is closely identifiable with Martin's general outlook and his sceptical turns of phrase. He is appalled when he sees that Jordan has two warts on his face like their father did, shocked at what he thinks of as 'Warzen als Heiratsgrund' [warts as grounds for marriage] (*DBF*, 154). He is also somewhat incredulous at the discrepancy between Franza's ideals and her lack of pragmatism when preparing the first aid kit:

> Es stellte sich heraus, daß sie auch davon nichts verstand, weil von Magen und Darm und von Gelbfieber bis Malaria in ihrer Welt nichts vorgekommen war, nur die Psyche der Weißen, die offenbar bedrohter war, als er es sich vorstellen konnte. (*DBF*, 199)
>
> [It became clear that she didn't understand anything about that either, because nothing to do with the stomach or intestines or with yellow fever or malaria had entered her world, just the psyche of the Whites, who were obviously more threatened than he could imagine]

But the ironic tone cannot solely be ascribed to Martin's voice. His perspective, as well as much of Franza's, is mediated through the voice of a third person narrator. The narrator's presence is felt predominantly, though not exclusively, through the use of *erlebte Rede*, when the narrative voice and the voice of a character converge in what Pasolini describes as 'an exchange of linguistic ardors'.[49] An invaluable narrative strategy for giving access to the inner life of a character while at the same time maintaining an external perspective, this exchange allows the subjectivity of the character to be articulated while ensuring a certain distance necessary for reflection and criticism. The external gaze is maintained even at profoundly subjective moments, so the reader must hold these different perspectives together concurrently. Although not in itself comic, such distance is conducive to irony and to a heightened awareness of comic incongruity. The *erlebte Rede* also means that an ironic tone cannot be attributed specifically to either Martin or the narrator, but remains ambiguously both.

So far from being dissociated from an ironic perspective, the narrator in *Franza* validates the incorporation of a comic aesthetic, even if overall Bachmann was not content with the text's representation of trauma. Indeed, the narrator's enjoyment of comedy is confirmed at the end of the story, when a drunk Martin leaves the Altenwyls after an evening watching a film about Egypt. On this occasion Martin comes closest to comprehending Franza's devastation, her critique of the white man, and her uncompromising expectation of love, to the point where her phrases enter his head: 'Die Liebe aber ist unwiderstehlich' [But love cannot be withstood] (*DBF*, 332). This is a potentially pathos-laden occasion, but although Martin feels a terrible gloom, comic devices ensure that the pathos, without being denied, is heavily mediated. We are again presented with situation comedy: Martin ignores the rules of polite society in which manners and appearance are all, and where gloom is not only an emotional state, but an opportunity for Antoinette to hide her glasses and Atti to suppress his yawn. But more importantly in terms of the narrator's affirmation of comedy, the narrator enjoys a pun with 'unwiderstehlich' [withstand]. Barely able to withstand the effects of alcohol, Martin is forced to take a taxi home: 'Er zahlte nicht ganz dreißig Schilling für die Unwiderstehlichkeit und kam nachhause' [he paid just short of thirty shillings for not being able to withstand and went home] (*DBF*, 332).

The narrative strategies that contribute to comic elements in *Franza* become more pronounced in the *Todesarten* fragments and in *Simultan*. Here the movement between perspectives is fluid, with frequent shifts between subjective and objective, internal and external voice, between direct speech and third-person narrative comment. Bachmann's comedy is at its most evident and sustained in *Simultan*, particularly in 'Ihr glücklichen Augen' and 'Probleme, Probleme'. But even when faced with the apparently ludicrous figures of Beatrix, for whom every exertion except her regular makeover is 'grauenvoll' [horrendous], and Miranda, who tries only to see the good in life by refusing to wear her glasses, the women are never made figures of ridicule. As Bachmann says, 'Die Lächerlichkeit ist eine Kategorie, die ein Schriftsteller wirklich nicht kennt' [ridiculousness is a category that a writer really doesn't know] (*S*, 20), an assertion that points to her concern about the ethical implications of comedy.

Comedy and Ethics

When Malina tells the *Ich* to tell him her stories about men if they are funny enough, he adds: 'Sag, was sich ohne Indiskretion sagen läßt' [say what can be said without indiscretion] (*M*, 606). In his insistence on discretion, a point on which he is in full agreement with the *Ich*, Malina articulates a fundamental narrative tenet of Bachmann in her search for ways of representing suffering ethically and without objectifying the sufferer. The demand for the stories to be funny, or, in a broader sense, to be entertaining, must be combined with an ethical limit. The link between comedy and discretion that Malina makes, signalling that comedy, like any other representative mode, has ethical implications, is rather more crassly reinforced at an earlier point in the novel when the *Ich* recounts how she and Ivan make each other laugh without laughing at someone's expense (*M*, 307). The specific intention to belittle or humiliate someone through comedy and ridicule is portrayed as murderous in the *Todesarten*-texts, but any laughter may be problematic: 'Allein, was ein Freund mit einem besorgten Gelächter einem Freund antun kann, dem er zu helfen meint damit, das ergibt eine unabsehbare Geschichte' [Even the harm someone can do by giving a concerned laugh when he thinks he's helping a friend can result in a quite unpredictable story] (*GR*, 358). And as the *Ich* acknowledges, the question of who can laugh at whom can be a complicated one. She recalls the occasion when on a ship to America a man began to burn holes in his hand with a lit cigarette: 'Nur er hat darüber gelacht, wir wußten nicht, ob wir auch lachen durften' [He was the only one who laughed about it, we didn't know if we were allowed to laugh] (*M*, 623). Although the onlookers are clearly discomforted by the ambiguity of the situation, the *Ich*'s use of 'dürfen' [to be allowed] here exemplifies the way in which laughter, and more generally comedy, relates both to the question of perspective and, crucially, is subject to moral evaluation.

The importance of the relationship between what or who is comic and the person who finds it amusing is explicitly thematized in the *Goldmann/Rottwitz-Roman*. Jordan finds the circumstances of Maria Malina's death by shark attack so unbelievable that anyone would laugh when hearing about it. Antoinette's indignant observation that no one is laughing seems to be informed by her suspicions about what goes on in private for those people who die in such a macabre way. After all, she insists that she knows what she is saying when justifying her scepticism about a hanged man's purported suicide (*GR*, 382). Antoinette's reprimand to Jordan chimes with a likely reader response that the strange circumstances of Maria Malina's death are anything but funny when seen in connection with this murderous psychiatrist. Thus the wider context of the comic perspective is key, whether it forms part of a process of objectification and belittlement of another or not. So Jung becomes, like Jordan, murderous because he seeks to destroy Eka through a calculated process of 'Lächerlichmachen' [ridiculing] (*GR*, 417). Crucially, however, Jung is not necessarily wrong in seeing the laughable side of someone, but he is wrong to forget that he too is laughable: 'Er war durchaus scharfsinnig, das wirklich, er hatte sehr bald herausgefunden, daß diese verdammten Rottwitzens [...] lächerlich waren, aber er sah nicht, daß er sie lächerlich sah, weil er es selber war' [He was definitely astute, he really was. He found out very quickly that these damned Rottwitzes were ridiculous, but he didn't realize that he saw them as ridiculous because he himself was] (*GR*, 438). Jung is far too restricted in his vision to situate himself within a wider comic framework and it is this that effectively empowers him to assume a superior view. This is in stark contrast to Malina's comic gaze, which is perspicacious but not destructive. So the young author Maleta feels that Malina sees right through him with his undefinable smile, but with no ill intent (*GR*, 341). If Malina does harbour negative views than he keeps them to himself, as he does when young Austrian authors ludicrously pretend not to have read anything written by a German: 'er lachte für sich' [he laughed to himself] (*GR*, 375).

Malina's role as a key narrating voice in the later *Todesarten* drafts points to the importance of an empathetic framework if the incorporation of comedy as an important part of representing suffering is to remain ethical. He is a crucial figure in the framework narrative of the *Goldmann/Rottwitz-Roman*, which is narratively more complex than the earlier *Requiem für Fanny Goldmann*, and also funnier. Malina explicitly describes himself as someone else's double (*GR*, 399), whom we know to be the *Ich*. He incorporates her experience of and perspective on suffering within his narrative strategies and knows of the many ways in which women are murdered. It is his constant emotional and moral empathy for the women which permits an often comic awareness of their plight and their faults. Similarly it is Martin's fundamental sympathy for his sister, however incomprehensible she is to him, that ensures comedy does not tip into ridicule. The importance of empathy is further reinforced by the use of *erlebte Rede*, for the emotional reality of the women's suffering, including their own responsibility for that suffering, is powerfully presented alongside comedy. Unlike Jordan's experimentation with Franza, Jung's treatment of Eka as literary material, or Elizabeth's photos of the Algerian war, *erlebte Rede* facilitates the representation of suffering women without objectifying or instrumentalizing them. A necessary distance to the solipsism of suffering is maintained without ascribing to the comic perspective a position of emotional or textual superiority. So in contrast to Jordan's 'höhnisches Gelächter' [scornful laughter] (*DBF*, 224) when he learns of Franza's affair, Martin, Malina, and the narrator are not simply positioned above the protagonists and the comic devices do not serve the purpose of belittlement and humiliation. Indeed, however privileged Malina's evaluation of Marek or Jung may be in the *Goldmann/Rottwitz-Roman*, the fact that he is distinct from the authorial narrator means that his perspective remains subject to ironic qualification, the more so because he, and we, are cognisant of a previous murder. Thus the intermingling of voices, the shifting between and holding together of incongruous perspectives means that the position of superiority often associated with comedy is unsustainable.

The insistent link in Bachmann's work between comedy and a sympathetic narrative perspective seems to exemplify the *Ich*'s refusal to laugh at someone's expense (*M*, 307). However, this rather self-righteous interjection cannot naively be regarded as a final statement of Bachmann's narrative intent when it comes to comedy, for comedy cannot so easily be tamed by good intentions. Antoinette may not find the story of the shark attack funny, but that does not prevent the reader finding the incongruity of sharks and Viennese high society amusing. Indeed, many of the examples offered here of comic incongruity, from Franza thinking she looks like a camel to Eka nearly colliding with the police car, to Miranda's actual collision with a glass door, may or may not be amusing for different readers, may or may not be amusing for the same reader on different occasions. Nadja aptly conveys this unpredictable, arbitrary dimension of comedy, which necessarily exceeds narrative control, in *Simultan*. In response to the story Ludwig Frankel tells her about the woman who was followed by a dolphin, but thought she was being chased by a shark, and never went swimming again, Nadja says: 'oh das ist eine komische — sie unterbrach sich — es ist eine traurige Geschichte' [oh, that's a funny — she interrupted herself — it's a sad story] (*S*, 125). Narrative ethics could be understood as being undermined by those elements of comedy that exceed the intention to impose ethical parameters. However, in Bachmann's work, unpredictability and an unwillingness to define others are themselves of great ethical importance, so far from being in opposition, it is the often arbitrary nature of comedy that becomes part of its value.

Malina asks the *Ich* to combine comedy and discretion in her stories, a discretion that demands the avoidance of ridicule. But discretion can also be understood more broadly as the refusal to assume one can know everything there is to know about another. It is the villains in Bachmann's work who proceed with this assumption and make a weapon of knowledge: Jordan as a psychiatrist who analytically dissects people (*DBF*, 219), and Jung who as a writer observes them to the point of objectification (*GR*, 416), rendering them caricatures. In the *Goldmann/Rottwitz-Roman* the totalizing, defining narratives of the psychiatrist and writers are contrasted with unfinished stories, those in which ambivalence lingers. Indeed, narratives are portrayed as necessarily unfinished, not only because the causes of actions often lie in unnoticed, transitory moments that cannot therefore be systematically explained, but because knowledge of a person is always incomplete: 'Nichts ist [...] verwerflicher als die Freundschaft, die meint, den andren zu erkennen' [Nothing is more reprehensible than the friendship that thinks it comprehends the other] (*GR*, 359). This is what leads Malina to say of his own stories: 'meine Geschichten sind wahr. Sie haben den Vorzug dieser Unvollkommenheit' [my stories are true. They have the advantage of this incompleteness] (*GR*, 365). Going yet further, he suggests that a story's incompleteness does not derive just from the narrator's ignorance of his characters, but from the obscurity and incompleteness within the narrator himself: 'in uns selber ist es taghell bis dunkel mit allen Schattierungen' [we have all shades within us, from daylight to darkness] (*GR*, 432).

Such ambiguity, the impossibility of knowing all, is vital thematically, and becomes a governing aesthetic and ethical mode in Bachmann's work. Ambiguity is placed at the centre of Bachmann's narrative precisely because in *erlebte Rede* the fusion of voices blurs the boundary between character and narrative voice and with it the ability to attribute the origin of an utterance with any certainty. And by placing it at the heart of her language Bachmann points too to language's incompleteness, demonstrated so graphically by the death of the *Ich* and the failures internal to narration. The impenetrability of the subject, an impenetrability that is inseparable from 'the impossibility of saying everything in language', is what guarantees her sovereignty.[50] The subject's incalculability ensures that she remains unknowable and therefore not wholly determined by discourse and its laws. Eka is very aware of the relationship of arbitrariness and humanity: 'Meinst du nicht, daß die Menschen viel größer, viel ungeheuerlicher, viel zarter und unberechenbarer sind, fragte Eka erregt' [Don't you think that people are more magnificent, more monstrous, much gentler and more unpredictable, Eka asked excitedly] (*GR*, 416). Eka's 'Erregung' [excitement] is telling, for it recalls Bachmann's own use of the word to explain why she does not quote sentences for their meaning but because they have truly excited her.[51] Bachmann explicitly separates excitation from meaning; its cause is not explicable through reference to its importance to others and it is felt uniquely. Arbitrariness and emotional profundity are emphasized by the image of the lightning strike in describing Maria Malina's impact on the young Maleta: she 'hatte dort eingeschlagen, wo manchmal eine Buchseite, eine Katastrophe, eine Stimme, eine Musik [...], wovon andre nie begreifen werden, daß es ein Blitz für Menschen sein kann und für immer' [she had struck him where sometimes a page in a book, a catastrophe, a voice, music does [...] in a way that others will never understand how it can be a lightning strike for a person and for ever] (GR, 343). The reasons for this impact cannot be known by others, or even by the individual themselves; the causes of excitation are famously elusive, inexplicable and unpredictable.

The unknowability and arbitrariness of 'Erregung' are presented in Bachmann's work as safeguards of individuality against dehumanizing definition. That part of comedy that is unpredictable, the laughter that is not fully constrained by moral considerations, belongs to the many forms of excitement to which she refers. If the sovereign freedom of a self is associated with rationality, as it is by Höller, then the laughter of the pre-rational, or the non-rational, can only be understood as a threat to sovereignty and even its negation. Höller's view echoes Schiller's privileging of comedy's cerebral quality, whereby comedy is ennobling precisely through the negation of emotion and the body. Yet the comedy that Bachmann offers us is a radical rejection of this tradition. Her narrative strategies and the predominance of *erlebte Rede* mean that the ever-present suffering body is not left behind in a movement to some higher freedom, but remains central to and part of the narrative voice. Freedom is situated not in the cerebrality of comedy but in its unpredictability, which is inseparable from the unpredictability of the emoting individual. As Critchley writes in his critical study of the philosophical privileging of the tragic paradigm, laughter acts as 'a site of resistance to the alleged total administration of society'.[52] As Bachmann too demonstrates, comedy as a mode of non-identity has an ethical function returning us to the ordinary while being at the same time a refusal of everyday speech.

'Second-hand pain'

In David Grossman's *Falling Out of Time*, the Centaur, a figure who like the others in the book is overwhelmed by the anguish and despair at the death of a child, is struggling to write of his pain. In contrast to the Town Chronicler's 'regurgitating' what people have told him, the Centaur '*must recreate it in the form of a story!* [...] And it must have plots! And imagination!'[53] But he also speaks of the inevitable difference between the experience of losing a child and the response of others to its representation: 'What could be more titillating than someone else's hell? And besides, I'm sure you'll agree that second-hand pain is far better than first-hand. Healthier for the user and also more "artistic" in the sublime — I mean, the castrated — sense of the word'.[54]

The Centaur echoes key tenets of Bachmann's narrative poetics. Her work explores passion, cruelty, the suffering they cause, and the possibility of articulating them. But it does not replicate the despair it depicts not least because suffering is consistently coupled with the transformative potential of yearning. The intense emotional desire for the absolute in the face of a murderous society, coupled as it is with the inevitable limitations of the 'schlechte Sprache' [bad language], sustains both an intense ethical critique of the status quo and an affirmation of narrative pleasure. By insisting on the centrality of emotion to language and to representation, Bachmann confirms the productive effect of language, and with it the pleasures of fiction. The importance of pleasure is clear from the way in which Bachmann's work draws on comedy and melodrama, both of which have an unabashed association with pleasure. So the *Ich* may not have much cause to laugh, but her suffering must and can only be mediated and this mediation incorporates enjoyment. After all, it is not Bachmann's intent that we should become like one of her worst villains, Jordan the psychiatrist, who is described by his victim wife Franza as having eyes which can neither laugh nor cry (*DBF*, 223). Thus our enjoyment is condoned, but it is also complex: we are invited neither just to cry and to identify ourselves with the victim position, nor just to laugh and retain a distance that facilitates pity or distain. The immediacy of suffering is set a limit by the distance of comedy so that empathy neither becomes uncritical identification nor premised on maintaining a position of superiority. The self-reflexivity of Bachmann's writing requires us to reflect on our pleasure as part of the necessary process of mediation rather than itself becoming a site of emotional immediacy and indulgence.

Melodrama and comedy are also important in Bachmann's work for the anti-heroic paradigm they adhere to. Following Critchley's argument, the tragic paradigm is a response to finitude, but one that '*disfigures* finitude by making the human being heroic'.[55] This heroism is achieved through the triumph of freedom, attained by reconciling individual freedom with the necessity of fate or nature. In contrast, Bachmann's deployment of melodrama and comedy to achieve a complementary affirmation of emotion and the body roots us in the physical emotions of finitude. This affirmation both affirms and complicates the gendered representation of emotion and suffering. Melodrama is firmly linked with the woman's victimhood and the unbounded, unreflected nature of immediate emotion: it is the woman's body that becomes the symptom of men's and society's murderousness. The ability to reflect and analyze, to achieve distance from incapacitating emotion and open up the space for comedy is figured as masculine. Yet together, these two modes function to affirm the body and emotion and thereby implicitly question the heroic aspiration of tragedy.

In Rainer Werner Fassbinder's work these modes of representation are also inseparable from questions of sexual difference. Here too melodrama and its limitlessness play a central role, as do moments of excessive, hyperbolic comedy. His work frequently pushes the enjoyment of excess and suffering to ludicrous levels, excesses that also seem to challenge ethical constraint and its relationship to gender.

Notes to Chapter 1

1. Adorno, *Notes to Literature I*, p. 258.
2. Ingeborg Bachmann, *Malina*, in *'Todesarten'-Projekt*, ed. by Monika Albrecht and Dirk Göttsche, 4 vols (Munich: Piper, 1995), III.1. All further references will be to this edition and will be given in parenthesis with the abbreviation *M*.
3. Adorno, *Notes to Literature I*, p. 257.
4. Ingeborg Bachmann, *Wir müssen wahre Sätze finden: Gespräche und Interviews*, ed. by Christine Koschel and Inge von Weidenbaum (Munich & Zurich: Piper, 1991), p. 111. See also p. 69.
5. See, for example, Katya Krylova, *Walking Through History: Topography and Identity in the Works of Ingeborg Bachmann and Thomas Bernhard* (Oxford: Peter Lang, 2013), pp. 16, 37–59. Mary Cosgrove also sees Bachmann as a melancholy writer in *Born Under Auschwitz*, p. 29 n. 50.
6. Bachmann, *Wir müssen wahre Sätze finden*, p. 98.
7. Hans Höller, ' "Das Komische, mehr als das Tragische, hat seine Noten, seine nationalen": Ingeborg Bachmanns *Malina*', in *Komik in der österreichischen Literatur*, ed. by Wendelin Schmidt-Dengler, Johann Sonnleitner and Klaus Zeyringer (Berlin: Erich Schmidt, 1996), pp. 263–74 (p. 264).
8. Ibid, p. 264.
9. Ibid, p. 267.
10. Brooks, p. 16.
11. Ibid., pp. 4–11.
12. Ibid., p. 15.
13. Ingeborg Bachmann, *Das Buch Franza*, in *'Todesarten'-Projekt*, ed. by Albrecht and Göttsche, II. All further references will be to this edition with the abbreviation *F*.
14. Ingeborg Bachmann, *Goldmann/Rottwitz-Roman*, in *'Todesarten'-Projekt*, ed. by Albrecht and Göttsche, II, 420 & 429. Henceforth all references will be given in parenthesis with the abbreviation *GR*.
15. Unsent letter from Ingeborg Bachmann to Paul Celan, Zurich, after 27 September 1961. See *Herzzeit: Ingeborg Bachmann — Paul Celan: Der Briefwechsel*, ed. by Bertrand Badiou and others (Frankfurt a.M.: Suhrkamp, 2008), p. 155.
16. Bachmann, *Wir müssen wahre Sätze finden*, p. 95.
17. Sigrid Weigel, *Ingeborg Bachmann: Hinterlassenschaften unter Wahrung des Briefgeheimnisses* (Vienna: Paul Zsolnay Verlag, 1999), p. 530.
18. Bachmann, *Wir müssen wahre Sätze finden*, p. 96.
19. Arnold Schönberg, *Pierrot lunaire*, trans. by Andrew Porter, 1984, <http://www.da-capo.org/html/PierrotEnglish.html> [accessed 29 July 2015].
20. Ibid.
21. Joachim Eberhardt, *'Es Gibt für mich keine Zitate': Intertexutalität im dichterischen Werk Ingeborg Bachmanns* (Tübingen: Niemeyer, 2002), p. 317.
22. Ibid., p. 319.
23. Roland Barthes, *Writing Degree Zero*, trans. by Annette Lavers and Colin Smith (New York: Hill and Wang, 1999), p. 39. Quoted in Weigel, p. 529.
24. Critchley, *Very Little... Almost Nothing*, p. 43.
25. Maurice Blanchot, *The Gaze of Orpheus and other Literary Essays*, trans. by Lydia Davis, ed. by P. Adams Sitney (Barrytown, NY: Station Hill, 1981), p. 43.
26. There has been a marked critical focus on Bachmann's work as predominantly a response to the Holocaust and its unrepresentability. On occasion this focus has led to generalization about Bachmann's whole work, and some unconvincing analyses. Examples include arguing that the absence of references to the Holocaust is nevertheless an absence that points to a positive 'Leerstelle' [empty place] or to a 'Latenz der Erinnerung' [latent memory] (see Eberhardt, p. 260; for a full critical discussion of approaching Bachmann as a post-Auschwitz writer, see pp. 251–62); or that Bachmann's work as a whole is a response to the 'Chiffre Auschwitz', a term which has ominous echoes of 'der Marke Ivan' (see Bettina von Jagow, *Ästhetik des Mythischen: Poetologien des Erinnerns im Werk von Ingeborg Bachmann* (Cologne: Böhlau, 2003)). More

sophisticated analyses situate the references to the Holocaust within a wider consideration of themes of memory and forgetting in response to trauma. Thus the figure of Fanny Goldmann can be seen as a personification of forgetting, as she discards her uniform, that of a 'deutschen Flakhelferin' [German anti-aircraft auxiliary], and dons her purple dress (*GR*, p. 289). The *Ich*'s insistent living in the present can be understood as a multifaceted exploration of how memories, indeed, memory, can be avoided: 'Das Traumkapitel eröffnet eine Möglichkeit, die Vergangenheit zu repräsentieren, ohne sich zu erinnern' [The dream chapter creates the possibility of representing the past without having to remember it] (Eberhardt, p. 260). And in her *Walking Through History*, Krylova demonstrates through her analysis of the topography of Vienna and Austria how the Nazi past and Jewish genocide are part of Bachmann's intricate concern with space and history.

27. Caitríona Leahy, *'Der wahre Historiker': Ingeborg Bachmann and the Problem of Witnessing History* (Würzburg: Königshausen und Neumann, 2007), p. 225.
28. Ingeborg Bachmann, *Frankfurter Vorlesungen* (Munich: Piper, 1989), p. 61.
29. Weigel, p. 530.
30. Bachmann, *Wir müssen wahre Sätze finden*, p. 69.
31. Ibid, p. 102.
32. Ingeborg Bachmann, *Die Hörspiele* (Munich: Piper, 1992), p. 96.
33. Christine Gledhill, ed., *Home is Where the Heart Is: Studies in Melodrama and the Woman's Film* (London: BFI, 1987), pp. 6–7.
34. Thomas Elsaesser, 'Tales of Sound and Fury: Observations on the Family Melodrama', in *Imitations of Life: A Reader on Film and Television Melodrama*, ed. by Marcia Landy (Detroit, MI: Wayne State University Press, 1991), pp. 68–91 (p. 87).
35. Christa Gürtler, '"Malina sieht mich so listig an, dann lacht er, ich lache auch": Ingeborg Bachmanns komische Geschichten', in *Frauen verstehen keinen Spaß*, ed. by Daniela Strigl (Vienna: Paul Zsolnay Verlag, 2002), pp. 97–105 (p. 100).
36. Höller, p. 270.
37. Ibid.
38. Christine Kanz, *Angst und Geschlechterdifferenzen: Ingeborg Bachmanns "Todesarten"- Projekt in Kontexten der Geenwartsliteratur* (Stuttgart: Metzler, 1999), p. 184.
39. Christa Gürtler, 'Ironie und Komik in Ingeborg Bachmanns Erzählband Simultan', in *Klangfarben: Stimmen zu Ingeborg Bachmann*, ed. by Pierre Béhar (St. Ingbert: Röhrig Universitätsverlag, 2000), pp. 12–145 (p. 130).
40. Critchley, *Ethics-Politics-Subjectivity*, p. 235.
41. Kanz, pp. 183–86.
42. Ingeborg Bachmann, *Simultan*, in *'Todesarten'-Projekt*, ed. Albrecht and Göttsche, IV, 403. Henceforth all references will be given in parenthesis with the abbreviation S.
43. Ingeborg Bachmann, 'Besichtigung einer alten Stadt', in *'Todesarten'-Projekt*, ed. by Albrecht and Göttsche, III.2, 698–99. Henceforth all references will be given in parenthesis with the abbreviation BS.
44. For a detailed discussion of the significance of the sites and spaces for understanding the representation of the Austrian and Habsburg past, see Krylova, pp. 154–60.
45. Bachmann, *Todesarten-Projekt*, III.2, 801.
46. Karen Achberger, "Bösartig liebevoll" den Menschen zugetan: Humor in Ingeborg Bachmanns Todesarten — Projekt', in *"Über die Zeit schreiben": Literatur- und Kulturwissenschaftliche Essays zu Ingeborg Bachmanns "Todesarten" — Projekt*, ed. by Monika Albrecht and Dirk Göttsche (Würzburg: Königshausen & Neumann, 1998), pp. 227–43 (pp. 233 & 236).
47. Ibid, p. 234.
48. Even Achberger asserts that *Franza* shows 'keinerlei spuren von Humor' [no sign of humour]. Achberger, p. 233, f26.
49. Pier Paolo Pasolini, quoted in Joan Copjec, *Imagine There's No Woman: Ethics and Sublimation* (Cambridge, MA: MIT Press, 2002), p. 214.
50. Joan Copjec, *Read my Desire* (Cambridge, MA: MIT Press, 1994), p. 211.
51. Bachmann, *Wir müssen wahre Sätze finden*, p. 69.
52. Critchley, *Ethics-Politics-Subjectivity*, p. 235.

53. David Grossman, *Falling Out of Time*, trans. by Jessica Cohen (London: Jonathan Cape, 2014), p. 78.
54. Ibid., p. 64.
55. Critchley, *Ethics-Politics-Subjectivity*, p. 220.

CHAPTER 2

Rainer Werner Fassbinder: Ludicrous Melodrama and Comic Double Vision

Franz Walsch listens unmoved to a recording of Karl Valentin's 'Maskenball der Tiere' [The Animals' Masked Ball] in *Götter der Pest*. He lies impassive, apparently indifferent to the comedy of the piece, which is no more than nonsense.[1] Although Walsch himself does not seem to derive any obvious pleasure from the humour, the viewer does: the song is played in full, barely interrupted by dialogue. Walsch's lack of response suggests that the simple pleasure of responding to nonsense rhymes is a thing of the past, no longer available to a man so passively trapped in melancholy criminality. Yet this homage to Valentin also serves to emphasize the dreariness and narrowness of Walsch's humourless perspective, one that largely dominates the whole film. This perspective, I wish to argue, is not that of Fassbinder. The homage points to an important aspect of this director's *oeuvre*, the way in which the depiction of entrapment, melancholy, and suffering is combined with comedy in various ways. This comedy can be seen to be in the tradition of Valentin's wide-ranging satire in as far as ordinary people's weaknesses and foibles are exposed. However, in a radical departure from Valentin's work, the comic effects are rarely light-hearted or nonsensical, and, with the exception of the three self-evident comedies, *Rio das Mortes*, *Satansbraten* and *Die dritte Generation*, are rarely signalled as 'comedy'. Indeed, Peter Jansen and Wolfram Schütte argue that despite the occasional attempts at comedy, Fassbinder's films are fundamentally humourless and what laughter they may provoke is tortured rather than liberating.[2]

Not all critics concur with this view. Wallace Steadman Watson, for example, is adamant that 'even [Fassbinder's] bleakest films contain moments of comic irony (often ignored in the predominantly somber commentary on his work)'.[3] He also points to specific instances of humour, such as the job interviews in *Der Händler der vier Jahreszeiten*, Franz sneaking past the doorman at the nightclub and the American tourist searching for money while he escapes from the hotel in *Götter der Pest*. Both he and John Sandford acknowledge the self-conscious humour of *Warnung vor einer heiligen Nutte*, and Stephen Holden wrote in his review of *Martha* that 'you don't have to agree with its premise — that middle-class marriage equals sadomasochism — to respond to the bravura comic glee with which the director lays it out'.[4] The

New York Times hailed *Mutter Küsters Fahrt zum Himmel*, released in the United States with the screenplay's original comic ending, and that preferred by Fassbinder, as a humorous political comedy.[5] In his study of Fassbinder's theatre, David Barnett sees *Satansbraten* as being in the tradition of Joe Orton's farces, a fact that may have made its comedy more easily accessible to an English-speaking audience: 'its bitter irony and quirky misanthropy tapped into a comic tradition that was eminently recognizable'.[6] Nevertheless, despite the intermittent references to comedy in Fassbinder's work, the prevailing critical response is to emphasize his cinema as one of entrapment, suffering, and despair.

Suffering in Fassbinder is played out in the domestic sphere and is inextricably linked with the emotional and financial demands of relationships. Relationships are where the ideals of love and personal fulfilment are sought but inevitably fail, for any relationship is a complex system of exchange. Love, as well as the articulation of desire, is caught up in power structures that result in exploitation and abuse. Emotions are the tools of power play, but are themselves formed by, and also inform, wider historical, social, and economic interactions. Thus the intensely personal space of Fassbinder's films is also social and economic, and relationships are a symptom of wider systems of social and economic exploitation, typically of bourgeois capitalism. Furthermore, these are German spaces, and the systems of emotional, political, and economic exchange and exploitation are situated in relation to Nazism and its legacy, even if, as in *Effi Briest*, it is set in a time before. Fassbinder's films are concerned with the destructive effects of bourgeois capitalism and its values, and the failure of its ideals that both fed and refused to learn from Nazism. His work traces the 'sellout of bourgeois morality, the free market of humanistic values, and the meritocracy turned black market of the emotions'.[7] This destructive effect is figured in terms of victimhood and suffering, for relationships cannot flourish in a system where value is governed by commodification and competition. Melodrama emerges as Fassbinder's key representational mode, for the ideological fissures that run between ideals of fulfilment (personal and social) and actual antagonism manifest themselves in the suffering body of the individual and in the excesses of *mise en scène* and emotion. As a symptom of this inescapable rift, the suffering victim is ascribed moral value, for her suffering becomes a sign of a potential that has been betrayed.

Fassbinder's interest in the suffering German body functions as a vehicle for criticism of unjust power relations. But it is also problematic: it raises questions about the purpose of identifying with and inhabiting a victim position in a context where Germans perpetrated atrocities upon others. Elsaesser is sympathetic to Fassbinder's fascination with victimhood, arguing that the 'self-abandonment' occasioned by becoming victim is a means of 'experiencing for oneself the Otherness of the Other', thereby assuming a form of responsibility.[8] Yet identification with suffering is commonly a form of usurpation and self-indulgence that denies otherness and which concurrently obfuscates the question around the perpetration of abuse. This particular German context is though inseparable from the issues arising from a wider general trend in theory and criticism that increasingly ascribes ethical value to victims, a trend that underpins melodrama as a mode of representation that enjoys and valorizes suffering. It is through an exploration of the films' comedy that Fassbinder's concern with suffering will be considered. The chapter follows Watson's lead in insisting that comic structures and humorous effects in the films are more pervasive than generally acknowledged: the first section thus suggests various modes and examples of comedy that span Fassbinder's *oeuvre*, and serves to contextualize what follows. The focus is therefore on those of his films that are not presented as 'comedies'. Rather than comedy being noteworthy only in as far as it can be immediately dismissed as simply tortured, comic devices ranging from irony through to hilarity and the ludicrous, both facilitate a playful response on the part of the spectator and play a crucial role in imposing a limit to the melancholy and melodrama of his work. The presence of comedy supports a shift from understanding Fassbinder's cinema as one of vicious circles to one of double vision, and undermines the recent privileging of the negative utopia, including that of male masochism, in his work. Although all Fassbinder's films are not of a type, and not all evidently utilize comic devices, his style is nevertheless characterized by a comic edge, intended and unintended, that crucially mitigates against the moral valorization of the suffering, shattered self that has become prevalent in trauma and shame theory.

'Convulsions of the diaphragm'

Fassbinder's films are interlaced with comic moments and humorous social interactions, including examples of strong visual humour. In *Liebe ist kälter als der Tod*, the gangster Bruno has terrible difficulties removing the punter's corpse, worried that he will be spotted trying to steal a car, yet dangling the corpse off another car while he does so. In a neat touch, placing one of the gangsters in a Fiat 500 highlights the ineptitude of Bruno's gangster organization. In *Warnung vor einer heiligen Nutte*, the moody tension between Jeff and Ricky as they look across the room at one another is undermined by the body of the Spanish receptionist, who is collapsed over the desk like a corpse and who has been visually placed near the middle of the screen. Two other figures who are well placed for comic effect are the very statuesque naked men in the sauna scene in *Faustrecht der Freiheit*, one reclining on the reception desk, the second standing directly behind and to the side of Max's head. So while Max is suggesting to Fox the very investment that will later ruin him, it is difficult for the viewer not to be distracted by the prominent penis and tan-line, just as, one might argue, Fox is disastrously distracted by Eugen('s). A comic high point is achieved in *Martha* when the camera cuts directly from the moment Martha falls asleep in the sun, unprotected by sun cream at the request of her sadistic husband, to her lying stretched out, naked and bright red on the hotel bed, the redness of the burns intensified by the white stripes left by her bikini. A more muted effect is achieved when cutting from Martha with an elegant hairstyle, to a new head of doll-like curls she has had done to please her husband.

Much of the comedy in the films is generated by incongruity, whether within the diegesis or through formal means. A vital constituent of comedy is precisely those moments or situations that allow for incongruous perspectives and responses to be held together without one necessarily diminishing the other, the 'disposition to enjoy a certain range of incongruities as such'.[9] However, there is no clear explanation for why some incongruities are funny and others are not, and as Roberts points out, not all incongruity is comic even if it is enjoyed. It is not possible to determine the precise shift from enjoyment to amusement in the response to incongruity. However, it is important to emphasize first that the context provides a frame for which incongruities are found funny: Anglo-American critics have been more receptive to Fassbinder's comedy than German critics.[10] Secondly, the ambiguity and volatility of laughter points to an indeterminacy of response that also applies to incongruity: not all viewers will find the many incongruities in Fassbinder's work comic as I do, or as I frequently or sometimes do: that variation belongs to the indeterminacy of response. But Fassbinder's particular insistence on incongruities necessarily opens a space for comedy. In the section that follows I suggest moments and episodes that manifest this comic potential in order to suggest a further frame for responding to his films.

In the muted but sensitive *Angst vor der Angst*, a comic perspective is introduced through the repeated shots down onto the road from a window, replicating the gaze of someone watching Margot below. The shot highlights the sense of oppression and apparently unaccountable anxiety felt by Margot, who can never escape others' appraising gaze, yet the repeated shots with variations, which punctuate the film, also function as brief comic intermezzi. We see variations on a theme of Margot leaving the building, meeting with Herr Bauer, and repeatedly running to the chemist. And in a moment of marvellous incongruity, Margot is juxtaposed with an armoured car that happens to be passing through the leafy suburb. The symbolic importance of the armoured car, which Sandford sees as 'the political equivalent of Margot's valium: an attempt to quell the symptoms by those who are too shortsighted to cure the illness', does nothing to lessen the comic moment.[11] As Margot's crisis worsens, so does the incomprehension of her mother- and sister-in-law, who relish the opportunity it gives them for self-righteous interference. The tension culminates in a darkly funny scene: Margot is reclining on the floor in alcohol-fuelled ecstasy, listening to the Rolling Stones 'We love you' through headphones. Oblivious to the fact that her distraught daughter Bibi has been brought home by her teacher, she does not open the door. When Margot's in-laws then enter the flat with Bibi and the teacher, they stand stunned at the sight of her, while she is, momentarily, blissfully unaware of their seething indignation.

The enjoyment of social incongruity also resonates in other works, even when certain scenes are excruciating to watch. In *Warum läuft Herr R amok?*, Kurt seems consistently out of place and his ineptness culminates in the episode when at the firm's Christmas dinner he proposes drinking *Bruderschaft* with his boss, persisting while the boss and his wife flee. *Martha* opens with the confrontation between the repressed, valium-swallowing, emphatically bourgeois Martha and a strange Arab man who starts undressing with the intention of having sex, emphasized by the close-up of him slowly undoing his fly. When the receptionist tells her that he sent the man up after seeing Martha wink at him, Martha, with quivering, but unconvincing indignation retorts: 'Es ist nicht meine Art zu zwinkern' [It is not my style to wink] (03:23). In *Faustrecht der Freiheit*, Eugen's snobbery is set against Franz's haplessness for laughs, a dynamic that is repeated in the Italian restaurant in *Angst essen Seele auf*, and Emmi's horror at the prospect of rare steak. In *Lola* von Bohm's naivety is related to moral purity, and the fact that he is an outsider from East Prussia, rather than class, but perceived social blunders are still the result: overdressing in plus-fours for his walk with Lola, and inviting his housekeeper to eat at the dinner at which he was planning to introduce his fiancée to the so-called elite. His naivety also facilitates a version of mistaken identity, where he does not know that Lola is a nightclub singer and prostitute, and that his housekeeper is Lola's mother, who similarly does not know that his fiancée is her daughter. So when von Bohm compliments his housekeeper on the table, only the spectator sees the irony of his words: 'Für ihre eigene Tochter hätten Sie es nicht schöner machen können' [You couldn't have made it nicer if it was for your own daughter] (59:12).

Comic effect in Fassbinder's films is often closely related to two seemingly opposite traits: a deadpan, distanced response to events on the one hand, and a heightened, often seemingly exaggerated, emotional response on the other. The deadpan response is most in evidence in the early films of 1969 and 1970, and dominates in *Katzelmacher*. Here, the swearing, bitching, and outbreaks of violence are conducted in a mood of indifference and boredom. When Helga and Paul are sitting in the pub, he tells her to shut her mouth when she asks about his mysterious friend and then, unprovoked, smacks his hand on her head. The long silences, the blandness of tone and expression, and the incongruity between the words, the action, and the bored passivity, are typical of how a comic dimension is added to the depiction of small-minded bigotry. Sex and love are similarly passionless, and Franz's attempt to get some affection from Rosi when he pays her for sex results in a painfully funny scene: he embraces her in silence as her bored face looks over his shoulder, until she finally says 'das langt' [that's enough] (27:33). Formally, the deadpan tone is intensified by the static camera and the repeated use of the same setting, particularly the rails in the yard. Such repetition draws attention to the small differences in composition that reflect the change in relationships, and also magnifies the effect of the movements that do take place. So when in one of the early scenes six of the characters are lined up along the railing, preening themselves, smoking, looking around, all in silence, the exaggerated significance of each self-important gesture becomes funny, as does the emerging juxtaposition of their dependence on one another and their relentless bickering rivalry.

Following *Katzelmacher*, it is largely at the level of formal techniques that a 'deadpan' effect is achieved, rather than being produced by the characters themselves. There are obvious exceptions where the peculiar non-responsiveness of the characters does offer potential for comic effect, largely through the incongruity that results. In *Der amerikanische Soldat*, the chambermaid morosely recounts the tragic story of Emmi and Ali while sitting on the bed in which Ricky and Rosa are starting to have sex. They, and the camera, are unperturbed by the incongruity of the scene. In *Herr R* the reserved and quiet Herr R simply gets up and bludgeons a neighbour, his wife, and his son to death without any display of emotion. On the whole, however, the deadpan effect is achieved formally. Even as Fassbinder's camera became more mobile with his growing success, his frequent emphasis on framing and non-naturalistic *mise en scène* guarantees a distance between diegesis and spectator that facilitates comedy. In *Die Niklashauser Fart* Fassbinder makes use of the tableau-effect again, and of a surprising and incongruous *mise en scène*. While this works to emphasize the allegorical side of the film and its concern with why revolutions fail, as well as the role art and performance play in revolutions, it undoubtedly has comic effect. Thus, for example, Penthesilea's speech calling on Ares to help in her final duel with Achilles is declaimed by a woman whose stylized speech is matched by the stylized dripping blood. The effect slips into comedy when we see Penthesilea flanked by two women, one of them naked and rather gormless, standing on a smoking landfill site.

In tandem with the deadpan effect and vital to moments of comic incongruity, is the other common characteristic of Fassbinder's work, the tendency to heightened, unrestrained emotions. The chambermaid in *Der amerikanische Soldat* stands in raptures after being kissed by Ricky, and when Ricky briefly returns home, his brother crushes a glass in his hand in repressed passion for Ricky then collapses in tears on the piano. In *Die Niklashauser Fart* the rich woman is in raptures over the prophet while feeding her bedridden and hated husband. The 'fire in her belly' (51:48) as she terms her passion, promptly leads her to set fire to the hangings and curtains in her husband's room amid orgasmic moans of pleasure. She finally murders her husband by stabbing him twenty-one times on the steps of their house in an orgiastic frenzy, while members of the sect simply sit as though nothing were happening. Like them, the camera remains static throughout this excessive display. Also in this film, the Bishop is a childish, emotional figure, excited by the fact that a commoner stinks, bursting into tears when he hears of the murder plot, begging his 'Mutti' to put him in a cloister where he cannot be harmed, and crying again when the American GIs are killed.

More realistically, the opening scene of *Warnung vor einer heiligen Nutte* is nevertheless an outstanding sequence of controlled exaggeration. A spectrum of human interaction is on show, with emotions that are in part justified by the diegesis, the characters' self-indulgent and self-obsessed concerns intensified by having to wait around. However, the emotions and moods within the scene are further exaggerated by being put on stark display by a camera that moves from one group to another, not linked to any one perspective, and not interested in exploring the interiority of the characters. The bitching, complacency, tedium, aggression, bored lust, and unrequited love are thrown into comic relief by a camera that in this sequence is interested in dissection rather than identification. The comedy is at its most pronounced in the figure of Fred, whose unrequited love for the Spanish hotelier, Candy, leads to idiosyncratic outbursts of passion: he bursts into tears in front of the uncomprehending Spanish receptionist, then again in front of the barman, and clutches at Candy on his knees. His passion culminates in him shouting in all seriousness at Sacha: 'Ich hasse dich Satyr!' [I hate you Satyr!] making the sign of the cross, and then turning and shouting at the woman who has been dancing oblivious to all throughout the whole sequence: 'Und dich auch, du Hexe!' [And you too, you witch!] (08:43).

A film in which the extremes of 'Liebe und Leiden' [love and suffering] (45:33) are combined with extensive distancing techniques is *Die bitteren Tränen der Petra von Kant*. The stark contrast between the emotional intensity of Petra's desire, her manipulation, and her final suffering on the one hand, and the highly stylized camerawork and *mise en scène* on the other, is not merely thought-provoking, as alienating effects are so frequently held to be, it is funny. The unrestrained excess of feeling is both reflected in Petra's intense articulation of feeling, the costumes, the excessive décor, and the mannequins, and also rendered comic by the extreme stylization of that excess. The costumes are parodies from the cat-walk, but are worn with the utmost earnestness: the moment when Karin, in a pseudo-Greek dress with a pointed metallic, almost armour-plated, bust meets Petra in her harem-style-cum-bondage dress is extremely humorous, as are the copulating mannequins. Also humorous are the manner and tone of many of Petra's comments, uttered either in anachronistic, formal German ('mich dürstet' [I feel thirst]) or beautifully pronounced German that seems inadequate to the emotion being expressed: 'wie schrecklich!' [how awful!] she says with a solemnity fuelled by desire when Karin tells her that her father killed her mother and then hanged himself.

The comedy of *Die bitteren Tränen der Petra von Kant* is finely judged. In an excellent analysis of the film, Timothy Corrigan emphasizes the role of the camera in deconstructing the way in which the image of the woman is fundamental to supporting patriarchy and the structures of classical cinema. By eschewing the reverse angle cut in favour of 'lavish tracks and zooms', Fassbinder keeps the spectator 'outside the action' and can thereby show how classical cinema naturalizes the process of 'maintaining the status of woman's body as an erotically controlled image'.[12] He too sees the comic potential of this outsider perspective, arguing that the camerawork '[undercuts] the sympathetic identification of tragedy with the distance of an uneasy laughter'.[13] However, I would like to expand on Corrigan's conclusion, for it remains dependent on emphasizing the incompatibility of tragedy and laughter. Yet if moments of comedy are precisely those in which incongruous perspectives are held together without one necessarily diminishing the other, then the strength of *Die bitteren Tränen der Petra von Kant* is not that it offers the spectator a distanced position of criticism, but that it insists upon the concurrence of both melodramatic identification with Petra's suffering and critical distance: it is this that opens the space for comedy.

This jostling together of appraising distance with intense emotion is a feature of many of Fassbinder's melodramas. There are even moments in the emotionally gruelling but less emphatically stylistic *Angst Essen Seele Auf* which allow the spectator to hold together competing perspective in a way that can tip into comedy. The shots that are held for so long that the spectator is disquieted by her own complicity with the judgemental and disapproving social gaze, are also at one level darkly humorous. The very calculatedness of these discomforting, even embarrassing, shots is also that which offers scope for the spectator to savour the comic side of excruciating social intercourse. There are certain scenes in particular where the balance between powerful emotion and critical distance facilitates such a response: the opening scene where Emmi does not stop talking in response to the silent staring; the occasion when Emmi proudly introduces her new husband to her uncomprehending children; and the scene when the delighted Emmi encourages her friends to feel the belittled and stony-faced Ali's muscles.

'Opportunities for thought'

The unsettling nature of certain of Fassbinder's shots, and the sense of complicity with the social look that they provoke, raises the question of how implicated the spectator becomes if she finds herself amused or laughing at scenes that are also concerned with suffering. Does she not then align herself with the sadistic laughter of Martha's husband laughing at his wife's hair, or with the belittling scorn of the waiter forced to serve two unwelcome customers? Indeed, the concern articulated in this question about the aggressive, humiliating potential of comedy can be extended to the way in which comic exaggeration in the films is often inseparable from caricature, however mild, and the depiction of types. This trait is reinforced by the director's persistent typecasting, so Margit Carstensen is usually cast in the role of the emotionally intense, bourgeois woman, Irm Hermann as the calculating bitch, Kurt Raab often as the over-emotional and rather foolish Queen, and Hark Bohm as an establishment figure, frequently a corrupt one. However, the anxiety surrounding the aggressive potential of comedy and the ethical implications of spectator amusement too easily ignores the nature of play, with its attendant associations of pleasure, role-play, and flexible perspectives, and, by extension, the play of perspectives within fiction.

Comedy depends upon being able temporarily to adopt alternative perspectives. So, as Roberts points out, to identify someone enjoying a sexist joke as being themselves sexist is to 'underestimate the plasticity of the human mind for adopting attitudes in experimental mode'.[14] The interdependence of play with flexibility of perspective is fundamental to fiction in general, with its facility for exploring and sustaining multiple perspectives and incongruities. These traits are crystallized in comedy, which thrives on and takes pleasure in incongruity and indeed which demands plasticity of mind. For comedy to be used tendentiously, then, the less its playfulness or fictionality is signalled the better. Yet it is the very foregrounding of artifice in Fassbinder's work that makes it surprising that the comic side of his films has not been more emphasized, for there are very few films that neither signal their artificiality nor contain comedy. It is this insistence on artifice too that opens the space for a playful response on the part of the spectator. Indeed, it is the pervasiveness of artifice that has led certain critics to describe his cinema as camp, which, as Sontag argues, is itself 'a comic vision of the world': 'The whole point of Camp is to dethrone the serious. Camp is playful, anti-serious'.[15] Studies of the role of camp in Fassbinder's work have been crucial for understanding his films. Elsaesser describes the films as registering feeling 'on the razor's edge [...] between risibility and tragedy, camp and kitsch', where 'pathos becomes less a call to righteous anger [...] than a sophisticated aesthetic effect that confirms inevitability'.[16] And Alice A. Kuzniar, by relating camp to allegory, a representational mode which '[admits] its ultimate failure to unveil that to which it would refer', sees camp as always including 'the awareness of the *failure* of the imitation'.[17]

Elsaesser and Kuzniar focus less the comedy of camp than on camp's all-encompassing and apolitical aestheticism and its denial of ontological wholeness. And it is perhaps not surprising that the comic vision offered by camp is forgotten in the face of Fassbinder's treatment of entrapment, exploitation, and the failure of utopias at all levels, personal and social, especially as this treatment depends so heavily on melodramatic conventions. The melodramatic insistence on the value of the suffering victim and the suffering body as an articulation of the evils of society does not sit easily with camp's refusal of 'both the harmonies of traditional seriousness and the risks of fully identifying with extreme states of feeling'.[18] Yet even the most conventionally melodramatic of Fassbinder's films drift towards the comic. They fail to evince the degree of identification that would make them effective weepies precisely because of Fassbinder's tendency to exaggeration. Here, melodramatic excess is itself excessive: Fox and Mutter Küsters become near-parodies of naivety, Hans's passivity borders on the inert, and Martha quite quivers with emotional repression. The melodramatic elements of these films are, additionally, comically framed or disrupted: the first half of *Faustrecht der Freiheit* is in large part a comedy of manners, from which the subsequent decline of Fox cannot be separated; Fassbinder's preferred ending of *Mutter Küsters Fahrt zum Himmel* was the comic one, which at the very least retroactively opens a different perspective; and Watson points to comedy as one of the things that interrupts the 'stylistic tact' of *Der Händler der vier Jahreszeiten*. I would argue, however, that not only is such an interruption not limited to that film, it is an integral part of Fassbinder's tactless signature.

It is through the films' tactless drift towards comedy that it is possible to identify some interesting points of convergence between melodrama and camp as well as between melodrama and comedy more generally. It is in the nature of melodrama that it tends towards exaggeration, and it is this quality of excess that brings it close to what are also qualities of comedy: hyperbole, amplification of recognizable situations and types, unbelievable plot twists, shock, overwrought emotions, and tension. The slippage from melodrama into comedy, from responding with pathos and tears to responding with amusement or laughter, is often seen as a failure of melodrama, but it may also be understood in relation to the nature of melodrama. Melodrama:

> not only exposes us to the fraudulence, the inauthenticity of the world, but also presents a particular kind of response to it. It attempts to redress the particular failure it perceives by making up for what appears to cause it. In brief, it responds to the absence of any limit by imposing imaginary limits on it.[19]

This 'violent imposition of imaginary boundaries on a world' leads to the creation of 'flimsy structures, [...] and they are marked as such'.[20] The slippage into comedy can, then, be understood as a moment of awareness and enjoyment of that artificiality, illustrated in Jacky Bratton's insistence that nineteenth-century melodramas 'easily accommodated the comic response, without embarrassment'.[21] Here, too, the proximity of melodrama and camp can be seen, for camp too depends on seeing the world 'in terms of the degree of artifice', 'a victory of "style" over "content"'.[22] Both melodrama and camp recognize the ungroundedness of the world; both are decisively modern forms of response to the post-sacral world: Copjec as well as Sontag thus identify the eighteenth century as the 'dividing line' after which these sensibilities develop.

I have pointed to the centrality of artifice, of 'imitation of life' to both melodrama and camp in order to suggest that there is a certain compatibility of vision that prevents the drift of melodrama into the comedy of camp being dismissed as a necessary aesthetic lapse: the ungroundedness and inauthenticity of the world remains, even if the mode of response, and with it the mode of enjoyment, shifts. Having said this, each mode interestingly functions to impose a critical limit on the other. The comedy of camp, and comic structures more generally, in their recognition of the flimsy structures of melodrama, expose the restricting and solipsistic nature of the melodramatic vision, which is, in Copjec's view, that of the hysteric: it entails 'active manipulation designed to sustain the illusion that there can be an existence that evades inclusion in social space'. Melodrama, like the beautiful soul that is the hysteric, 'stages a theatre of satisfaction while keeping herself unsatisfied, disgusted with the whole mess'. Comedy, and the comic dimension of camp, acts as a safeguard against the spectator's absorption into the hysteric's world by revealing it as imaginary imposition. Comedy therefore also exposes the suffering position as the manipulation of the beautiful soul, who becomes 'superego to the world'.[23]

This exposure goes some way to address critical reservations concerning Fassbinder's love of Hollywood and melodrama. Elsaesser argues that Fassbinder's notion of realism admits 'of the habitual functions of escapist entertainment: encouraging daydreams, private fantasies, wish fulfilment ... except that he talks about liberation and utopia rather than escape'.[24] I would argue, however, that it is often the comic elements of the films that draw attention to the excesses of the melodramatic vision and which help signal its hyperbolic artifice. It is worth drawing on an extreme example in order to clarify this point. In Fassbinder's only western, *Whity*, the exploration of social conflict within the domestic sphere is taken to an extreme, with race and sexuality played out in a family drama set in exotic antebellum America. In one central scene, Frank discovers his step-mother's sexual interest in the black slave Whity, who is also his father's illegitimate son, a revelation that is staged as a horror film. Frank's shadow looms behind the door before he confronts his mother; he himself is reminiscent of both Nosferatu and his victims, with his unnatural white make-up and scrawny frame, and his hysterical fleeing from the scene, so hysterical, indeed, that the film either has, or looks momentarily as though it has, been speeded up for effect (also, of course, reminiscent of Murnau's *Nosferatu*). The sheer funniness of this scene, and it is typical of the whole film, actively discourages the spectator's capacity for fantasy fulfilment and entry into an exotic and highly eroticized world. Rather, that world is signalled, not least by the comic elements, and the moments when melodramatic excess tips into comedy, as the singularly constructed daydream of the hysteric.

If comedy is important for revealing the solipsism of melodrama, conversely, melodrama's concern for the victim, its insistence that good and evil persist in the post-sacral world, ensures that the underlying structures of identification and sympathy with the victim are not sacrificed to comic distance. It addresses spectator anxiety about laughing 'at', for example, the woefully sunburned Martha, by clearly identifying the villain, and thus refuses a simple replication of the structures of humiliation or exploitation of the diegesis. In many ways melodrama can be seen as intensifying a quality that Sontag sees as anyway belonging to camp, its 'love for human nature', 'a tender feeling' that is not 'laughing at' but enjoying.[25] Yet it is precisely these moments of proximity and overlap between melodrama and camp that also raise the question of the nature of camp's perspective. If so many qualities of melodrama are also those of camp, including excess, extravagance, the vision of the world as artifice, then the rather pressing question arises whether camp can itself be understood as the disavowal of hysteria through comedy. On this view, the limit set on the melodramatic perspective by camp humour, and comedy more generally, is, crucially, mirrored back onto camp itself: it too stages a retreat from the world, fuelled not by moral distain but by boredom. If camp distinguishes itself from melodrama by disavowing its own hysterical positioning through comedy, when it is set alongside melodrama that disavowal is revealed. Thus the comic sensibility of camp is crucial to its attempt to universalize the image of the world as artifice, but in Fassbinder's distinct intertwining of melodrama and camp, comedy is a vehicle for setting a critical limit to melodrama, and it in turn reveals camp's perspective as flimsy. In Fassbinder's work, therefore, comedy is both part of camp's artifice and also betrays its vision as limited.

I have argued here not that the slippage between melodrama and certain forms of comedy, including camp as a comic sensibility, leads to their conflation, but to a relationship in which each form exposes the limited perspective of the other. Although both depend upon and revel in the representation of the world as artifice and imitation, the mutual limit prevents the total subsumation of the spectator into the world of image and role-play, since this world is so evidently framed as imaginary imposition. So although Fassbinder's cinema, in its representation of the world as artifice, is justifiably viewed as one of 'vicious circles', I would suggest that it actually opens up the space for a double vision, or in Peter Ruppert's phrase, a 'dialectical structuring': we are always looking in on artifice, on the circle, however much we are absorbed by it.[26] Comedy both belongs to the vicious circle of the artifice in the form of the camp sensibility, but also exceeds it, critically contributing to maintaining the outside view, the looking in on those restricting imaginary impositions. This double role of both being part of the artifice yet also exceeding it, facilitating the double vision of absorption and 'looking in', is one that extends to the inclusion of Fassbinder himself in his films.

The director appears in many of his early films, among others as the Greek *Gastarbeiter* in *Katzelmacher*, a gangster in *Liebe ist kälter als der Tod* and as Fox. Fassbinder's appearance in the films and his tendency not to change his appearance or acting style from one role to another (Fox being an obvious exception), at once makes him a player in his own fantasy world, but also includes him within the critical, and often comic framework. This is very evident in *Die Niklashauser Fart*, a film that explores the contribution of a vanguard to bringing about revolution through performance and role-play. Fassbinder is of course one of the vanguard, directing his comrades, slouching around, and perpetually smoking: acting himself. The comic effect of Fassbinder's repeated appearances, as of those of his leather jacket, has received no comment. His involvement in his own films has been criticized as egotistical indulgence, the unmediated playing out of his own problems or fantasies, or as a positive mode of identifying with his protagonists. Thus Kaja Silverman analyzes Fassbinder's involvement in *In einem Jahr mit 13 Monden* and *Berlin Alexanderplatz* in relation to male masochism and the exploration of non-phallic masculinity. Yet the comedy forms part of another crucial effect of his presence within his films: the self-contained fantasy of the film is ruptured by his entry into it. This gesture of rupture, and its relation to watching and identifying with suffering, becomes particularly explicit in *In einem Jahr mit 13 Monden* and *Berlin Alexanderplatz* and it is to these that I shall now turn.

Rupture and Identification

Although Fassbinder does not appear in *In einem Jahr mit 13 Monden*, he is credited as director and with all the production roles, and Silverman therefore justifiably sees the film as a uniquely personal reflection on his ex-lover Arnim Maier's suicide. Most critics emphasize the film's stark portrayal of the suffering wreaked by a society that insists upon polarized gender: Silverman argues that it depicts a society whose 'system of sexual differentiation' is unable 'to accommodate a figure who can be assimilated neither to masculinity nor to femininity'; and Kuzniar that it shows how the 'attempt at conformity meets with ridicule and isolates one further from others'.[27] Similarly, Robert Burgoyne sees Elvira as 'the excess which must be repressed in patriarchal society'.[28] Here, Elvira's suffering functions as a critique of the society around her, her masochism, in true melodramatic mode, acquires moral leverage. Indeed, in Silverman's suggestive reading, while recognizing that masochism is inseparable from the structures of the symbolic, she nevertheless posits male masochism as a mechanism of reaction against the dominant fictions of the symbolic: the 'male masochist deploys the diversionary tactics of demonstration, suspense, and impersonation against the phallic "truth" or "right", substituting perversion for the *père-version* of exemplary male subjectivity'.[29] Although she does not argue for the male masochist as 'a model for a radically reconstituted male subjectivity', the critical potential of that figure resides in its contribution, certainly in Fassbinder's work, to the 'ruination' of conventional masculinity. Masochism is thus privileged as a utopian moment of bliss in as far as it involves the ecstatic 'divestiture of "self"' rather than a new masculine subjectivity.[30]

However, as Burgoyne concedes, there are identifiably comic elements to the film, not least the abattoir scene and its juxtaposition of the slaughtering and dismemberment of cattle with Elvira, walking around in heels, quoting Goethe's *Tasso*.[31] For Silverman Elvira's identification with the cattle is a further example of divestiture of self, an intensification of her masochistic bliss. Yet to equate masochism with the divestiture of self is problematic, for masochism is itself strategic. As Gilles Deleuze says of male masochism, 'What insolence and humour, what irrepressible defiance and ultimate triumph lie hidden behind an ego that claims to be so weak'.³² In *In einem Jahr mit 13 Monden* it is the moments of insolent dark comedy that point to precisely this triumph, and which by doing so rupture the possibility of replicating the unmediated identification as well as the attempt to privilege it. These moments include the abattoir scene, the excessive excess of Elvira herself whose suffering tips at times into parody, Bergen-Belsen as a password, the persona of Saitz as a man who re-enacts scenes from gangster films and musicals, the ridiculousness of the (masochistic) man who looks up at Saitz's building day after day, and Elvira's appearance-as-man in front of her wife and daughter where her cut-off trousers are reminiscent of a clown. And perhaps funniest of all, the scene in which Elvira encounters the man about to commit suicide, who quotes Schopenhauer to her before hanging himself in a perfectly matter-of-fact way.

Comedy exposes the limit of Elvira's masochistic hysteria, and of that dimension of the film that suggests Fassbinder's identification with the suffering protagonist or which encourages the identification of the viewer. Silverman rightly comments that Elvira, lacking the 'ironic distance between "appearance" and "actuality"' cannot be camp, but this lack is not the lack of the film.³³ Comedy serves this important limiting purpose in *Berlin Alexanderplatz* too, another film in which male masochism and suffering are extensively explored. In relation to *Berlin Alexanderplatz* Silverman is quite clear that the exploration of male masochism does not lead to the discovery of a new masculine subjectivity, for the film, despite exposing the extremes of violence against and exchange of women upon which conventional masculinity depends, remains pessimistic about an alternative. Nevertheless, the eroticization of the suffering male body, tipping into ecstasy, can be understood as utopian, for it undermines masculine norms. It does so both through the insistent gaze on the men's brutalization of women as a prop to their masculinity, epitomized in the repeated flashbacks of Franz beating Ida to death, and through displaying the suffering body in un-valorized ways: urinating, vomiting, belching, having sex, sweating profusely, and disfigured. The eroticization of suffering is emphatically not situated in the woman's suffering body, for cruelty against women in *Berlin Alexanderplatz* is shown to be precisely that: relentlessly un-ecstatic. Rather, it is the suffering male body that is central to any utopian moment through the 'sudden overcoming of limits [...]; from pleasure seized against all odds because of a desire which will not cease making its always exorbitant demands'.³⁴

Elsaesser too sees in Biberkopf the attempt to find a non-phallic masculine identity, though he is reluctant to see a utopian dimension in masochistic bliss. Rather, he suggests that this dimension lies 'in the insistence [...] that the couple as a love relationship can only exist when it recognizes its place in other circuits of exchange'.³⁵ Franz strives to break out of exchange systems based on binary opposites, such as homosexual/heterosexual, employed/unemployed, and seeks to establish relationships that are 'polymorph, non-exclusive'.³⁶ Biberkopf's tragedy is that other characters prevent this. Although Elsaesser and Silverman both insist that *Berlin Alexanderplatz* displays the brutality of the violence inflicted on women, and thus offers a critique of phallic masculinity, their emphasis on Biberkopf's moments of masochistic bliss or rejection of phallic power as utopian moments remains problematic in view of what Elsaesser himself admits remains a 'male-centred utopia'.³⁷ It is difficult to see how male-centeredness does not replicate a phallic structure. Indeed, the basic sustaining structure of a patriarchal man whose self-exploration and development is achieved at a cost borne by women remains unaltered. The women remain fundamentally interchangeable in their eagerness to please, comply, forgive, affirm, and, in the perfect enactment of male fantasy, to gratify Biberkopf sexually. Throughout the film, his attitude to women does not change, illustrated in his repeated biting of his lover's neck, a gesture that recalls the *Ich*'s scathing attack on men who like women's feet in Bachmann's *Malina*. This context of unconditional love, unlimited sex, and no commitment, of relationships in which Biberkopf lays down the terms, is the context within which the interesting question of male-male subjectivity can be explored. Women can be discarded or exchanged; one neck is, after all, much like another. And there is little evidence of 'divestiture of the self' in Biberkopf's laughter when he learns that Mieze has been murdered, his laughter of relief at finding out that she has been murdered and has not left him: murder as affirmation of his masculine ego.

Biberkopf's laughter, as well as his forgiving smile to Reinhold at the murder trial, recalls the defiance and triumph that Deleuze reveals behind masochism, and it is the insolence and humour particularly of the epilogue that complicates the spectator's understanding of identification with suffering and notions of the self. The epilogue is a surreal condensation of and commentary on the themes of the preceding episodes and it emphasizes the suffering body and the violence inflicted upon it, as well as exploring the psychic damage caused by violence and suffering. It is also ambiguous and multifaceted in its function and, very importantly, opens a sometimes scathing critical perspective on Biberkopf's behaviour by showing him finally confronted with the consequences of his actions. While hallucinating, he is accused by Reinhold, dressed as Death, of judging people without trying to understand them and by Eva of being responsible for Mieze's death by using her in his joust with Reinhold. He is also confronted by Ida, who cannot walk properly because he beat her to death and even Meck condemns Biberkopf's attitude, characterizing it sarcastically as 'ich und ich und was für Unrecht ich erleide' [I and I and what injustice I suffer] (XIV, 01:03:16). After thirteen episodes of being exposed largely to Biberkopf's perspective, it is gratifying to see his self-pity no longer indulged. Nevertheless, critical focus on the themes of suffering, masochism, and sacrifice has eclipsed the critical dimension of the epilogue that warns us against indulging Biberkopf, however much narrative sympathy lies with him as the protagonist: 'wir wissen, was wir wissen, wir haben's teuer bezahlen müssen' [we know what we know, we had to pay dearly for it]. Elsaesser relates the epitaph to the experience of understanding what it is to be, and become once again, German through the figure of an Everyman. Yet the epilogue suggests that it is precisely Biberkopf's approach, (that of a man) which prevents the confrontation with a history of violence leading to greater self-knowledge or insight. Suffering and keeping one's eyes shut are what Biberkopf excels at, and the price is indeed a heavy one: his courtroom smile at Reinhold shows the persistence of temptation over critical reflection, and the film ends with the prescient strains of the Horst-Wessel Lied.

The critical interest in suffering and masochism has also obscured the strategic use of comic devices in the epilogue. Right at the outset, we are presented with two angels who will decide whether it is worth taking Biberkopf away from purgatory and giving him a new existence. Both angels are dressed in suspenders, with golden tunics and golden, glittering hair, and with a few black costume feathers at their shoulders. The camp appearance of these judging angels visually ironizes their serious task and earnest tone, and sets the pattern for much of what follows: a camp dimension of the *mise en scène* in many of the most ostensibly serious scenes. When Reinhold is whipping Biberkopf in the presence of the rest of the Pums gang, all of whom are criticizing Biberkopf's stupidity, a disco-ball revolves above him, a fitting match for Reinhold's long false eyelashes. Death appears in the figure of Baumann, wearing a shimmering gold cape, and the piled-up, writhing bodies in the slaughterhouse have glinting nipples and pubes. The high camp of many scenes finds comic resonance too in the juxtaposition of ridiculous images presented with an air of deadpan. Not only do Pums and his gang, dressed in eveningwear, sit in mud while Reinhold whips Biberkopf in their midst, but suddenly an athletic naked man appears, dragging himself prone but energetically through the mud, pursued by another man in a top hat and fur coat who is whipping him. In a later scene, Biberkopf is having his heart cut out, screaming in pain, while Bruno, dressed in women's underwear, is suggestively licking his shoes and Pums's wife is sitting knitting.

The ironic and ridiculous juxtapositions, camp representations, and visual humour of the epilogue culminate in the two nativity tableau scenes. These scenes have received particular critical attention for their relevance to themes of suffering, masochism, and sacrifice. In the background is a massive reproduction of the central panel of Hieronymus Bosch's triptych, *The Garden of Earthly Delights*. In the foreground is recognizably a nativity scene, but with odd variations: reproducing the earthly delights are a naked couple who make love throughout; the Virgin Mary, standing next to Joseph, holds a baby Nazi doll which bears a strong resemblance to Biberkopf; a classical male nude stands in the foreground, with first a table in front of him, then with crates of beer at his feet; in the first tableau there is an incinerator, in the second there is a crane, used to hoist up the cross upon which Biberkopf is crucified. The climax of the scene in the crucifixion of Biberkopf is seen by many critics as pivotal to Fassbinder's treatment of masculinity and death and his rejection of redemption. For Elsaesser it suggests 'an eternity without transcendence'; Wolfram Schutte draws the distinction between Döblin's cry of 'saved, judged, redeemed' and Fassbinder's whisper, 'definitely lost, finished'; and for Silverman it is a disassociation from Christian utopianism in which death can be redemptive.[38] Hers is the most complex reading, one in which she points to the condensed imagery of the whole, where the simultaneity of Eden, the Nativity, and Calvary, of Nazism and the nuclear bomb collapse 'diachrony into synchrony, and effectively foreclos[e] upon the possibility of transformation'.[39]

What these critical responses fail to convey and certainly do not consider, is the funny side of what is on show. The whole tableau is a triumph of artifice, an overt pastiche of Christianity and history, and, in addition, a lampooning of how they have been represented. The nativity scene is a caricature of all those amateur and school nativity plays, cut-out crowns and all, the characters stiff and well-meaning in their determination to play such world-important parts. Most of the images are hilariously juxtaposed with others: Christian iconography with classical buttocks; live sheep with what looks like a stuffed cow's head; high art with folk theatre; Nazi jodhpurs with a tea towel middle-eastern look. There is a fundamental mismatch in the exaggeratedly earnest devotion of the spectators as they watch the cross being raised, and the figure that they are adoring: the overweight Biberkopf. The two critical moments of death and resurrection are treated with visual comedy: Biberkopf's 'death' is accompanied by cartoon flames that leap up and then vanish, leaving a new backdrop of an overcast sky (XIV, 2:33:47). His resurrection too is marked by a cartoon image: the nuclear explosion is shown as the animated caricature of a flash, liberating the attendant associations of Tom-and-Jerry-like explosions, that then expands into real footage of an unfolding mushroom cloud to the accompaniment of Glenn Miller's joyous 'In the Mood' (XIV, 2:34:26).

The observation that the tableau scenes excel in the art of pastiche fits well with the critical emphasis on Fassbinder's cinema as a vicious circle, endlessly repeating the very normative discourses that it seeks to criticize. However, it is comedy that secures us another mode of viewing that prevents absorption into this circle. Far from being an abstract assertion, the insistence on comedy and double vision is explicitly thematized in the second vital scene, that of the slaughterhouse. Here we see a pile of bodies being processed as though they are animals in an abattoir. It is undoubtedly shocking: the bodies are treated as though they are animal cadavers, but they are not yet dead. The iconography of the piled up bodies is also powerfully reminiscent of the bodies in the death camps, establishing a direct and problematic link between Biberkopf's suffering and that of the murdered Jews. In the foreground a body is hanging upside-down from a butcher's hook, Biberkopf's body is immersed in hot water and then scraped with a butcher's knife, blood is everywhere, and a woman's screaming combined with an operatic aria is the constant refrain. Watching the scene are the two angels who will decide whether it is worth taking Biberkopf away from purgatory and giving him a new existence, and next to them, in the shadow, is the figure of Fassbinder himself, who remains silent.

Silverman reads the scene through the lens of Fassbinder's essay 'Man's Cities and His Soul', in which he discusses his fascination with Döblin's novel and his intense identification with Franz Biberkopf. Silverman argues that by standing next to the angels and being an onlooker, Fassbinder neither assumes a divine nor conventionally omniscient authorial position, but rather invites the viewer to realize that he, Fassbinder, is himself part of Biberkopf's suffering body. This is, crucially, a moment of heteropathic identification, in which the 'I' is 'so overwhelmed and [...] fettered' by the other self that its 'formal status as a subject is usurped by the other person's personality'.[40] In contrast to idiopathic identification, a process by which the other self is absorbed into one's own thereby denying its otherness in an act of despotism, heteropathic identification is founded in the 'acknowledgment of the "otherness" of all identity', thus denying 'the imperialism of the "self"'.[41] As in her discussion of *In einem Jahr mit 13 Monden*, Silverman privileges the extreme of heteropathic identification, the ecstasy of masochist abandon, as an 'assault on male subjectivity, and even [...] a way out of the vicious circle of masculinity'.[42] Silverman's is a thought-provoking reading. However, the notion of heteropathic identification and self-abandon seems to reinforce the visual link of Biberkopf's, and by extension Fassbinder's, suffering with that of murdered Holocaust victims.

Yet the scene is more complex than Silverman's reading suggests, for she does not take account of the fact that the figure of the watching Fassbinder is part of wider dynamic that includes a comic dimension. The scene is characterized by a degree of exaggeration that tips into hyperbole. This element of exaggeration is generated from all sides. The intrusive operatic aria expresses heightened emotional states not normally associated with the butchery of a slaughterhouse. Visually, the physicality of the bodies is always to the fore, yet these very bodies also display glimmering nipples and pubes, the cause of which is revealed to be glitter and nipple-tassels. The acting of the butchers is too stylized to be realistic and contrasts sharply with the unabashedly anaesthetic display of the butchered bodies. These examples are typical of the way in which everything is just too much, too emphasized, too excessive, to allow for either a response based on, or based only on, identification or horror. The 'too much' tips easily into caricature, the grotesque, and even hilarity. Adding further to this sense of excess is the contribution of the three observers. The two angels are dressed in suspenders, with golden tunics and golden, glittering hair, with a few black costume feathers at their shoulders. Their camp appearance visually ironizes their serious task of deciding Biberkopf's fate, and the commentary they offer on the scene is comic in its sing-song tone and nursery-rhyme simplicity: Sarug's expression is one of amused delight as he speaks: 'schwing, hack, hack; schwing, schwing, hack'. Terah happily responds: 'schwing, hack' [swing, hack] (XIV, 57:00). Next to them, the gloomy presence of Fassbinder also has a comic dimension. Like a caricature of all his previous roles, he slouches to the left of the screen, the ubiquitous cigarette raised to his lips, looking like a gangster in his shades and hat.

At the most basic level, the comic aspect of this scene means that the response demanded is not only an earnest one. It suggests that heteropathic identification and masochism may be on display, but they are not the only things on display. Furthermore, heteropathic identification is denied to the spectator of the scene. She may well identify with Biberkopf, either as the fictional character of the film, or as emblematic of suffering humanity, but the accumulation of comic and ironic effects mitigate against any sort of abandon. Indeed, the inclusion of Fassbinder in the scene further contributes to the process of ironizing any such abandon. By placing him and the angels next to each other, two contrasting perspectives on the scene are concurrently held in the same frame, one of identification, the other of (amused) observation. Neither excludes the other, nor is either reducible to the other. Furthermore, the appearance of Fassbinder within the diegesis, although possibly demonstrating the importance of heteropathic identification as a mode of response to suffering, is not the equivalent of privileging that response. The entry of Fassbinder into the fictional space explicitly draws the spectator's attention to the ambiguity of the relationship between Fassbinder the director, the character of Fassbinder the director, and shifting perspectives of the camera. This explicit ambiguity certainly ruptures a conventionally authorial position, as Silverman suggests, but by no means supplants that perspective with that of the character Fassbinder. Should one wish to argue that the camera is here showing Fassbinder's perspective, then that perspective cannot be reduced or equated to the perspective of the character Fassbinder, framed alongside that of the angels. Thus the absorbed gaze, here associated with identification with the position of the suffering hysteric, is doubly ironized: first by the concurrence of the look of the Fassbinder figure, emblematic of heteropathic identification, with that of the amused angels, and secondly by the moment of filmic ambiguity. Crucially, this process of ironization also has as its object the iconographic alignment of Biberkopf's suffering with that of murdered Jews, as well as modes of identificatory spectatorship that draw the viewer into elevating the status of her own suffering through such visual equivalence.

An interesting contrast exists between the model of spectatorship presented in the slaughterhouse scene and a scene in which Biberkopf and Max, the publican, disagree about the appropriate response to a family tragedy. Biberkopf reads in the newspaper about a father who has drowned his three children after first drowning his wife, and finds the story funny. Max is appalled by Biberkopf's laughter and seeks to persuade him of the tragedy by referring to film: 'Das ist ein trauriger Fall. Wenn du sowas im Kino siehst, dann heulst Du' [That's a sad case. If you saw something like that in the cinema, you'd cry] (III, 01:01:48). Here we are presented with opposite poles: a scandalous response where laughter rests on the absence of identification with others' suffering; and a scandalized response that finds justification in the intense emotional identifications of the melodramatic weepie. These irreconcilable positions are emphasized through the shot-countershot face-off of the two men during their exchange, unlike the slaughterhouse scene in which Fassbinder and the angels watch Biberkopf's suffering together. Here, comedy and heteropathic identification ambiguously coexist in a microcosm of the film overall. The comedy offers a critical interrogation of both heteropathic identification and masochistic ecstasy, yet at the same time the sole perspective of the amused onlooker is not privileged as utopian either: the angelic way in which Sarug and Terah dump bodies into a pile while describing the march of death through history, in itself darkly humorous, exposes the objectification or callousness that accompanies an absence of identification.

The significance of combining modes of identification with a comic aesthetic is most explicitly explored in the epilogue, but also established at the outset of *Berlin Alexanderplatz* in Biberkopf's decisive encounter with the two Jewish men, Nachum and Eliser. It is from this meeting that he draws the resolve to face the perceived threat of the metropolis after four years in gaol. Nachum seeks to help the overwhelmed Biberkopf by telling him the story of the successful conman Zannowich, only to have his version 'corrected' by his brother-in-law Eliser, who insists on recounting Zannowich's unhappy end as a corpse on the knacker's cart. Foiling Nachum's hopes, it is from Eliser's part of the story that Biberkopf takes heart, identifying angrily with the story of a man who, like him, once made a mistake while onlookers stood and did nothing. It is, however, from Nachum's part of the tale that he draws the method for re-entry into Berlin: 'Sie haben mir doch erzählt von der Aujen und der Beene. Ick hab' sie noch' [You told me about the eyes and the legs. I still have 'em] (1, 24:30). Importantly, Nachum is played for comic effect, an unusual, quirky figure, particularly in juxtaposition with the stolid Biberkopf. Biberkopf is quick to call him various names, including monkey, and accuses him of being quite crazy. Nachum happily admits: 'Das eine Mal bin ich 'n Affe, das andere Mal meschugge' [Sometimes I'm a monkey and sometimes meschugge] (1, 14:48) and is quick to point out that he is not the one choosing to sit on the floor when a sofa is on offer. He thus does not hesitate to resort to comedy in his interaction, laughing at Biberkopf's taunt that he lives 'auf dem Mond' [behind the times]: 'Das ist gut! Jetzt werden wir sprechen vom Mond' [That's good! Now we'll talk about time] (1, 16:26).[43]

The meeting with the Jewish men is no mere exotic interlude, but a reflection on fictional representation, identification and engagement with the world. In Nachum we have a figure who is comic, who accepts the comic effect he creates as positive, who takes suffering seriously, and who combines these in his pleasurable storytelling. Juxtaposed to him, in the figure of Biberkopf, we have the self-absorbed suffering of a man who 'sees' the relevance only of that bit of the story with which he can utterly identify: the disregard shown to Zannowich's corpse. The difference between these two figures marks the difference between a response based on identification alone and the blindness it assumes, and one which combines acknowledgment of suffering with the comic. At the character-level we are offered a version of the difference between a mode of response to storytelling that identifies with suffering and privileges it, and one in which suffering is not divorced from the pleasure, including comic pleasure, of narration. And crucially, it is Nachum, the figure who can laugh at himself, who takes a risk and acts spontaneously when he sees Biberkopf, a rare event in Fassbinder's films, where characters are normally embroiled in relationships of exchange.

Style and the Trouble with Shame

Fassbinder's presence in his films is evident not just from his appearances but also from his distinct style. Comedy is a vital component of his style, and it both contributes to and is itself fuelled by other alienation effects. These effects include the alienation caused by the sheer ludicrousness running through the director's work, a sense of the ridiculous that frequently stems from poor acting or from shoddy *mise en scène*, with the unintended comedy that results (*Whity* being one of the more obvious examples). As Paul Coates points out, scholarship seems:

> often oblivious of the flaws caused by an indifference to acting quality, marshalling camp and Brechtianism as alibis, and of the effects of Fassbinder's preferred one-take aesthetic [...]: flaws swept under the carpet of the works' political utility, or an auteur status ensured by stylistic and thematic continuities stewing monotonously.[44]

The blatant flaws of Fassbinder's aesthetic go beyond what John David Rhodes characterizes as the 'obviousness of its belabored appearance', and should not be divorced from a style that is marked by his repeated appearances.[45] Yet in keeping with the wider theoretical tendency to invest extreme victimhood and traumatic abjection with ethical value, Rhodes too interprets style in relation to the divestiture of the self. By quoting D. A. Miller's comment that shame is 'style's encrypted alter ego', where style serves 'as the stylist's best defense against shame', Rhodes forges a link between Fassbinder and shame.[46]

Shame, like trauma, has undergone a theoretical shift into being valorized as ethical. In sociological and historical definitions of shame, shame is understood as historically contingent and as fundamental to the social regulation of the individual. Shame performs 'a social function moulded according to the social structure', and is a means to police and reinforce moral codes and values through shaming practices.[47] The inseparability of shame and moral values means that taken one step further, the admission of shame is interpreted as a sign of a morally better person. Thus when Primo Levi describes the Germans as having no shame, we understand that they had no morality. In psychoanalytic discourse the link between shame and socially enforced morality is complicated through notions of interjection and subject formation and it becomes fundamentally coupled with an ethics of the subject. The privileging of shame as an emotion linked with ethical standards stems from shame being understood as an emotion of the self. It results from a fundamental undermining of the self, a shattering of the ego and is felt as the extreme pain of worthlessness. For Copjec, shame assumes ethical value because it reveals the truth of the subject as split: 'To experience shame is to experience oneself not as a despised or degraded object, but to experience oneself as a subject. I am not ashamed of myself, I am the shame I feel'.[48] Eve Sedgwick summarizes the value of shame as the emotion that 'monitors our sense of self': 'one *is something* in experiencing shame'.[49] For Agamben, shame is 'the fundamental sentiment of being a subject'.[50] And in keeping with his views on the value of the traumatic challenge presented to the self by the other, Levinas praises shame for putting into question 'the I for its naïve spontaneity, for its sovereign coincidence with itself in the identification of the Same. This shame is a movement in a direction opposed to that of consciousness, which returns triumphantly to itself and rests upon itself'.[51]

There are strong parallels between shame and trauma in terms of their effect on the self and how that effect is interpreted as offering evidence of our wider humanity.[52] Both have become inseparable from conceptualizations of the self; both lead to a shattering of the ego, the pain of worthlessness, and a rupture of integrated narratives of self, resulting in a breakdown of symbolic and affective functioning; both act as an attack on the self's attachments to both interior and exterior objects and consequently as an attack on the ability to relate to others. It is precisely this abjection that Elsaesser, like Silverman, posits as the ethical centre of Fassbinder's films, arguing that the victims 'have completely fallen out of the symbolic order' with nothing left to exchange or sell, even their bodies. They thereby reveal a 'new truth of the subject [...]. The purpose of this ethics of becoming a victim is to strip the self of all its physical, psychic, and symbolic means of exchange, and in this way to achieve a radical openness towards life'.[53] However, it is not incidental that the protagonists particularly singled out by Elsaesser, Elvira and Veronika Voss, die.

This rather dilutes any claim for their openness towards life; death seems, rather, an inevitable outcome if a subject is stripped of the possibility of physical, psychic, and symbolic interaction.

Ruth Leys is highly critical of the privileging of shame, for the focus on shame as a marker of the subject undermines the potential for analysis: 'how can there be an argument about the meaning of an emotional situation if the issue for us is simply how we feel?'.[54] Indeed, critical and theoretical trends that consider the ruptured self to be ethical because it reveals the truth of the subject as incoherent, shift ethics into the idealized realm of abstract potentiality removed from the murky reality of action and interaction. Without the movement out of traumatic or shamed abjection the ethical encounter with another remains foreclosed, for it is precisely interrelational attachment that has been ruptured by shame and trauma. Of course there is no guarantee that the re-assertion of the self will result in new forms of ethical encounter with the other, hence the theoretical attraction of the 'shattered self' as an embodiment of abstract potentialities that are by definition not put to the test. Indeed, the ethical reality of the victim is often far from ideal. As Zygmunt Bauman remarks, 'Victimization hardly ever humanizes its victims. Being a victim does not guarantee a seat on the moral high ground', and he continues by quoting Antonina Zhelazkova: 'How to escape from the pain and humiliation — the natural thing is by killing or humiliating your executioner or benefactor. Or, by finding another, weaker person in order to triumph over him'.[55] In his discussion of ethics Bauman emphasizes the morality of the spontaneous act that must not serve a purpose but be 'nothing but an innately prompted manifestation of humanity'.[56] Uncertainty itself is not idealized as a moral state. Rather, the spontaneous act, whose outcome is unknown, is a response to the proximity of the other human being: 'we are challenged to act — to help, to defend, to bring solace, to cure or save'.[57]

The spontaneous act returns us to Nachum, who is challenged to act while not identifying with Biberkopf's masochistic suffering. More generally, Fassbinder's comedy, flawed style and all, interrupts the process of identification with victimhood, or with masochistic abjection, that the films undoubtedly invite. Indeed, it requires considerable effort to get sucked into the vicious circles that the characters inhabit because of the stylistic excess. So far from Fassbinder's style evoking shame through the effacement of the director, it flaunts his presence.[58] His appearances in the films, normally as an outsider who challenges bourgeois norms, do not serve to stigmatize but if anything to affirm Deleuze's suspicion of 'irrepressible defiance and ultimate triumph'. The director's style is shameless, ranging from its disregard of flaws, its unmasking of normative moral hierarchies, through to offence. If an ethical impetus is to be sought anywhere in Fassbinder's work, it is as a result of the ambivalent and unsettling confrontation of, on the one hand, the invitation to identify with those entrapped in structures of melodramatic suffering and on the other the excessive, often comic or ludicrous, disregard that characterizes his style, be that in his treatment of theme or mode of representation. It is at the level of this ambivalence, and not in the stewing monotony of suffering, that the uncertainty is generated out of which an ethical choice is made. The fact that this choice is in response to fictional representation means that the challenge to act may consist of no more than the spectator questioning her own values and expectations, with no guarantee of an 'ethically proper and laudable' outcome.[59] But as Bauman remarks, 'blunders *and* right choices arise from the same condition'.

Blunders and Right Choices

It is precisely the question of blunders and right choices that assumes a particular charge when thinking of Fassbinder's representations of Jews. As Rosalind Galt sets out, critics disagree fundamentally on how significant the theme of German anti-Semitism is in his work. There are very few important Jewish characters in his films, which otherwise engage extensively with Nazism, the legacy of the Second World War, and capitalism. For some critics this neglect typifies a wider German failure to address the central role of anti-Semitism, whereas Justin Vicari views all the films as being in some way about the camps.[60] Furthermore, critics disagree fundamentally on whether Fassbinder's treatment of Jews is anti-Semitic, with discussion centering on his play *Der Müll, die Stadt und der Tod*. Fassbinder argued in defence of the play that it explores the way in which anti-Semitism interacts with capitalism to construct the very figure of the rich Jew that in turn reinforces anti-Semitism. Furthermore the play exposes how those in power exploit the rich Jew, using him to do their dirty work knowing that post-war philo-Semitism will protect him, and them, from criticism.[61] Critics who concur with Fassbinder point to the difference between the words of the characters and of the author, the necessary break with philo-Semitic representations of Jewish characters, the anti-redemptive trajectory of his *oeuvre* in general in which victims are themselves brutalized, and the positive alignment of the rich Jew with the queer underworld. Others are not persuaded. They point to the absence of voices that relativize the hate speech of the anti-Semitic characters, the language of infestation and pollution, and the association of the rich Jew both with capitalist exploitation and sexual lasciviousness. Many critics remain torn.[62]

I would argue that it is Fassbinder's shameless style that is the condition out of which, understood broadly, blunders and right responses arise. What is a blunder and what is right is both debatable and contextual. I would contest, however, that it was a blunder to prevent performances of the play in Germany in 1975, 1978, 1984, 1985, and 1998 for its apparent anti-Semitism, as well as in the Netherlands in 1987. These cancellations seem particularly regressive given the near total indifference shown to performances held in Bochum in 1979, and in the USA, Scandinavia, Italy, and Israel amongst others since then, as well as to the film adaptation, *Schatten der Engel*, on general release in 1976.[63] It was right, though, for protesters to demonstrate and occupy the Frankfurt theatre in 1985 for precisely the same apparent anti-Semitism. As Daniel Cohn-Bendit commented, this marked the Jewish community's 'first decisively public stand in any political controversy in the postwar period', part of their protest against wider attempts at 'normalization' encapsulated in Helmut Kohl's 'Gnade der späten Geburt' [Grace of late birth] speech to the Knesset in January 1984 and his visit to Bitburg with Ronald Reagan in May 1985.[64] Thus in terms of presenting a challenge to act, the uncertainty and controversy around whether the play is anti-Semitic or not was productive at a particular historical juncture and in a particular form, that of a theatre performance in state-subsidized theatre.

It is significant in this respect that *Schatten der Engel* elicited no such response. This film is largely faithful to the play, and is a Fassbinder vehicle in as far as he wrote the screenplay, he and his standard actors populate the roles, and its visual style displays all the characteristics of Fassbinder's *oeuvre*. His style, then, is very much in evidence, flaws and all: stilted acting, portentous language, abusive relationships weighed down by a sense of fateful importance, all made to fit a vague city-thriller plot in which the queer pimp (Fassbinder of course) becomes victim. Seen within the context of Fassbinder's films, it is both ludicrous and tedious, with little comic edge to offset the suffering of the entrapped characters. It is worth noting, however, that the figure of the rich Jew is played by Klaus Löwitsch, an actor who in Fassbinder's type-casting schema, plays positive roles. Furthermore, in *Schatten der Engel* the anti-Semitic stereotype of lascivious Jew is explicitly one that is projected onto him by others. He pays the prostitute Lily Brest to listen to him, but she recounts tales of his physical and sexual prowess to her pimp Raoul to satisfy his emerging homosexual desire. It is also significant that *In einem Jahr mit 13 Monden* elicited no controversy, the film in which the figure of a rich Jewish speculator appears, who, like the rich Jew, has been used to do the dirty work for the conspiring gentile capitalists. Anton Saitz, learning from his experience in Bergen Belsen, has risen through the ranks of capitalist exploitation, learning his trade in prostitution and butchery. A victim turned exploiter, he is juxtaposed to the suffering body of Elvira, a shift of suffering from Jewish to queer German body that Gertrud Koch sees as potentially anti-Semitic. Potentially she is right, but this view is fuelled by an uncritical response to Elvira's suffering that ignores how the film's comic edges problematize the lachrymose indulgence of identifying with her position.

'Opportunities for Thought'

Fassbinder was interested in what happens in the head of the spectators, hoping that his films would bring them closer to a utopia. Most critics are in agreement that the utopian moment in Fassbinder is, at best, a negative one since the films replicate the patterns of entrapment they seek to criticize. Yet Fassbinder's comic streak ruptures or interrupts this negative recession in ways that might, perhaps, be understood as utopian, but which are certainly productive. The comic double vision guarantees the spectator the space from which to see the operations of the vicious circle and resist absorption into the perspective that sustains it. Furthermore, comic moments generate an affective response, of amusement, laughter, astonishment, that escapes the negative circuitry. Not only does this affective response retain a degree of volatility and unpredictability that eludes patterns of entrapment, but it is the comic incongruities in the films that positively generate such a response. The comedy is one manifestation of the shamelessness of Fassbinder's style, a style characterized by the willingness to play with the comic impact of ludicrous melodrama, with its hyperbolic, hysterical suffering and inauthentic *mise en scène* and acting to match. This play exposes the limits of melodramatic indulgence as it also counters the ethical privileging of abjection, of the shattered self, be that through shame or trauma, that has gained widespread currency.

This is why the comic effects are not merely one more example of taking the 'stylization of the given syntax to its limits', one more concession to entertainment.[65] Tony Pipolo might wish to remind us of the limits imposed on Fassbinder's critical agenda by his love of Hollywood, quoting Benjamin's warning that 'the bourgeois apparatus of production and publication can assimilate astonishing quantities of revolutionary themes, indeed, can propagate them without calling its own existence, and the existence of the class that owns it seriously into question'.[66] But Benjamin also offers another perspective:

> It may be noted that there is no better trigger for thinking (the kind of thinking that would alienate the public from the conditions in which it lives, i.e., revolutionary thinking) than laughter. In particular, convulsion of the diaphragm usually provides better opportunities for thought than convulsion of the soul.[67]

Notes to Chapter 2

1. Michael Schulte, ed., *Alles von Karl Valentin* (Munich: Piper, 1978), p. 181.
2. Peter W. Jansen and Wolfram Schütte, eds, *Rainer Werner Fassbinder* (Frankfurt a.M.: Fischer, 1992), pp. 122–23.
3. Wallace Steadman Watson, *Understanding Rainer Werner Fassbinder* (Columbia: South Carolina University Press, 1996), p. 3.
4. Stephen Holden, 'A Grim Fassbinder on the Marriage Bond', *New York Times*, 24 Sept 1994. Quoted in Watson, p. 145.
5. Vincent Canby, 'Mother Kusters Goes to Heaven', *New York Times*, 7 March 1977, quoted in Beate Uhrmeister, '"It was indeed a German Hollywood Film": Fassbinder-Rezeption in den USA: Notizen zu einem produktiven Mißverständnis', *Text + Kritik*, 103 (1989), 80–85 (p. 82).
6. David Barnett, *Rainer Werner Fassbinder and the German Theatre* (Cambridge: Cambridge University Press, 2005), p. 220.
7. Thomas Elsaesser, 'R. W. Fassbinder: Prodigal Son, Not Reconciled?', in *A Companion to Rainer Werner Fassbinder*, ed. by Brigitte Peucker (Oxford: Wiley-Blackwell, 2012), pp. 45–52 (p. 50).
8. Ibid., p. 52.
9. Roberts, 'Humor and the Virtues', p. 294.
10. This difference between the American and German reception of comedy concurs with Beate Uhrmeister's study of the differences in early Fassbinder reception more generally. Uhrmeister argues that American critics have been more interested in the formal and stylistic aspects of his films than their political dimension. Although this leads to some fundamental limitations in interpretation, it in other ways frees up critics' appreciation of Fassbinder's work. See Uhrmeister, pp. 80–85.
11. John Sandford, *The New German Cinema* (London: Eyre Methuen, 1981), p. 89.
12. Timothy Corrigan, *New German Film: The Displaced Image* (Bloomington: Indiana University Press, 1994), p. 49.
13. Ibid., p. 51.
14. Roberts, p. 302. See too the discussion of Roberts and of the importance of play in the Introduction above.
15. Susan Sontag, 'Notes on Camp', in *A Susan Sontag Reader* (Harmondsworth: Penguin, 1982), pp. 105–19 (p. 116).
16. Thomas Elsaesser, 'A Cinema of Vicious Circles', in *Fassbinder*, ed. by Tony Rayns (London: BFI, 1979), pp. 24–36 (pp. 31, 32).

17. Alice A. Kuzniar, *The Queer German Cinema* (Stanford, CA: Stanford University Press, 2000), pp. 10, 74.
18. Sontag, 'Notes on Camp', p. 115.
19. Copjec, *Imagine There's No Woman*, p. 123.
20. Ibid., p. 124.
21. Jacky Bratton, 'The Contending Discourses of Melodrama', in *Melodrama: Stage, Picture, Screen*, ed. by Jacky Bratton, Jim Cook, & Christine Gledhill (London: BFI, 1994), p. 38.
22. Sontag, 'Notes on Camp', pp. 106, 115.
23. Copjec, *Imagine There's No Woman*, p. 127.
24. Elsaesser, 'A Cinema of Vicious Circles', p. 33.
25. Sontag, 'Notes on Camp', p. 119.
26. Peter Ruppert, 'Fassbinder, Spectatorship, and Utopian Desire', *Cinema Journal*, 28, 2 (1989), 28–47 (p. 31).
27. Kaja Silverman, *Male Subjectivity at the Margins* (London: Routledge, 1992), p. 216; Kuzniar, p. 80.
28. Robert Burgoyne, 'Narrative and Sexual Excess', *October*, 21, Rainer Werner Fassbinder (1982), 51–61 (p. 61).
29. Silverman, p. 213.
30. Ibid., p. 265.
31. Burgoyne, p. 59.
32. Gilles Deleuze, 'Coldness and Cruelty', in *Masochism*, trans. by Jean McNeil (New York: Zone Books, 1991), p. 124.
33. Silverman, p. 222.
34. Ibid., p. 247.
35. Thomas Elsaesser, *Fassbinder's Germany: History, Identity, Subject* (Amsterdam: Amsterdam University Press, 1996), p. 253.
36. Ibid., p. 228.
37. Ibid., p. 225.
38. See Elsaesser, *Fassbinder's Germany*, p. 236; Wolfram Schutte, 'Franz, Mieze, Reinhold, Death and the Devil: Rainer Werner Fassbinder's Berlin Alexanderplatz', in *Fassbinder*, ed. by Ruth McCormick (New York: Tanam Press, 1981), p. 109; Silverman, p. 283.
39. Silverman, p. 279.
40. Ibid., p. 264.
41. Ibid., p. 265.
42. Ibid., p. 265.
43. Literally: 'on the moon' and 'That's good! Now we'll talk about the moon'.
44. Paul Coates, 'Swearing and Forswearing Fidelity in Fassbinder's Berlin Alexanderplatz', in *A Companion to Rainer Werner Fassbinder*, ed. by Peucker, pp. 398–419 (p. 410).
45. John David Rhodes, 'Fassbinder's Work: Style, Sirk, and Queer Labor', in *A Companion to Rainer Werner Fassbinder*, ed. by Peucker, pp. 181–203 (p. 197).
46. D. A. Miller, *Jane Austen, or The Secret of Style* (Princeton, NJ: Princeton University Press, 2003), p. 48. Quoted in Rhodes, p. 195.
47. Norbert Elias, *The Civilizing Process* (Oxford: Blackwell, 2000), p. 117.
48. Joan Copjec, 'The Object-Gaze: Shame, *Hejab*, Cinema', *Filozofski vestnik*, 27, 2 (2006) 11–29 (p. 15).
49. See Donald Nathanson, 'Understanding What is Hidden: Shame in Sexual Abuse', *The Psychiatric Clinics of North America*, 12, 2 (1989), 381–88 (p. 381); Eve Kosofsky Sedgwick, *Touching Feeling: Affect, Pedagogy, Performativity* (Durham, NC: Duke University Press, 2003), p. 37.
50. Giorgio Agamben, *Remnants of Auschwitz: The Witness and the Archive*, trans. by Daniel Heller-Roazen (New York: Zone Book, 2008), p. 107.
51. Emmanuel Levinas, 'Transcendence and Height', in *Basic Philosophical Writings*, ed. by Adriaan T. Peperzak and others (Bloomington: Indiana University Press, 1996), p. 17.
52. See the discussion of trauma in the Introduction, and also Fassin & Rechtman, pp. 58–97.
53. Elsaesser, 'R. W. Fassbinder', p. 51.
54. Ruth Leys, *From Guilt to Shame* (Princeton, NJ: Princeton University Press, 2007), p. 186.

55. Zygmunt Bauman, *Liquid Love* (Cambridge: Polity, 2003), p. 86.
56. Ibid., p. 92.
57. Ibid., p. 94.
58. In his analysis of Jane Austen's style, Miller is not suggesting that style *tout court* is the alter ego of shame, but that Austen's style, based as it is on the split between narration and character, assumes this function. Her style, with its stringent 'refusal to realize its author personally', ensures that she remains outside of the representation within which, having failed to attain the state of 'perfect happiness' through marriage, she could only appear as stigmatized (Miller, p. 56). This is very different from Fassbinder's repeated attempt to realize himself personally in his films.
59. Bauman, p. 93.
60. Rosalind Galt, 'Jolie Laide: Fassbinder, Anti-Semitism, and the Jewish Image', in *A Companion to Rainer Werner Fassbinder*, ed. by Peucker, pp. 485–501; Elsaesser, *Fassbinder's Germany*, p. 175; Justin Vicari, 'Fragments of Utopia: A Meditation on Fassbinder's Treatment of Anti-Semitism and the Third Reich', *Postmodern Culture*, 16, 2 (2006), 1–30 (p. 19).
61. Rainer Werner Fassbinder, 'My Position on *Garbage, the City, and Death*: A Statement', in *The Anarchy of the Imagination: Interviews, Essays, Notes*, ed. by Michael Töteberg and Leo A. Lensing, trans. by Krishna Winston (Baltimore, MD: Johns Hopkins University Press, 1992), pp. 119–20. Also reproduced in *A Companion to Rainer Werner Fassbinder*, ed. by Peucker, pp. 37–38, n. 22.
62. See Galt, pp. 488–95.
63. Wanja Hargens, *Der Müll, die Stadt und der Tod: Rainer Werner Fassbinder und ein Stück deutscher Zeitgeschichte* (Berlin: Metropol, 2010), pp. 204–07. For a full account of the performance history of the play and its reception, including the performance in Mülheim an der Ruhr in 2009, see Hargens, pp. 74–153.
64. Daniel Cohen-Bendit, quoted by Anrei S. Markovits, Seyla Benhabib, and Moishe Postone, 'Rainer Werner Fassbinder's Garbage, the City and Death: Renewed Antagonisms in the Complex Relationship between Jews and Germans in the Federal Republic of Germany', *New German Critique*, 38 (1986), 3–27 (p. 10).
65. Tony Pipolo, 'Bewitched by the Holy Whore', in *October*, 21, Rainer Werner Fassbinder (1982), 82–114 (p. 89).
66. Walter Benjamin, 'The Author as Producer', in *Reflections* (New York: Schocken, 1986), 229. Quoted in Pipolo, pp. 88–89.
67. Walter Benjamin, *Selected Writings*, ed. by Michael W. Jennings and others, trans. by Howard Eiland and others, 4 vols (Cambridge, MA: Belknap/Harvard University Press, 1996–2003), II, 779.

CHAPTER 3

❖

W. G. Sebald: Melancholy's Seduction and the Pleasures of Comedy

One of the funniest episodes in *Die Ringe des Saturn* depicts the narrator arriving in a desolate, run-down Lowestoft, the spectre of the once *'most salubrious'* coastal resort, where the ruined facades of the terraced houses, their grotesque front gardens, the dubious Bed & Breakfasts and the stinking games arcades reflect years of decline.[1] The narrator finds it hard to reconcile the Victoria with its description in his guidebook as a hotel *'of a superior description'* (RS, 57; *Rings*, 42), but he goes in and finds himself apparently the sole resident. When the receptionist finally appears, she is a terrified young woman who either keeps her eyes on the ground or stares through the narrator. Later she also takes on the role of waitress in the empty hotel restaurant, and then of chef, serving very English fish and chips: the fish, exhumed from years of burial in the deep freeze, is singed in patches and its breaded armour-plating causes the fork prongs to bend. The struggle to penetrate this hard exterior, which is all the so-called fish consists of, leaves the narrator's plate looking like a battlefield: 'Die Sauce Tartare, die ich aus einem Plastiktütchen hatte herausquetschen müssen, war von den rußigen Semmelbröseln gräulich verfärbt, und der Fisch [...] lag zur Hälfte zerstört unter den grasgrünen englischen Erbsen und den Überresten der fettig glänzenden Chips' ('The tartare sauce that I had had to squeeze out of a plastic sachet was turned grey by the sooty breadcrumbs, and the fish itself [...] lay a sorry wreck among the grass-green peas and the remains of soggy chips that gleamed with fat') (RS, 58; *Rings*, 43).

The description of the narrator's evening in Lowestoft brings together different types of humour evident in Sebald's work: good-humoured social satire, often with a particular eye for English mores; satirical descriptions in which hostility to the modern world is uppermost, and its inhabitants are tainted by or become a symptom of their damaged environment; grotesque exaggerations of the observed or experienced environment into which the narrator has entered as an outsider with a privileged sensitivity to signs of decline; and comically disproportionate responses by the narrator to his environment. But at the same time, a pervasive and fundamental tone of melancholy often suffuses Sebald's writing, distracting the reader from or disguising the comic moments in the texts. Thus the Lowestoft scene finishes with the narrator looking out onto the coast: 'es bewegte sich nichts, weder in der Luft noch am Land, noch auf dem Wasser' ('nothing was moving, neither in the air nor on the land nor on the water') (*RS*, 59; *Rings*, 43). This melancholy is also inseparable from another marked feature of the scene, the absence of contact between the narrator and the woman running the hotel. Such lack of interaction is central to Sebald's work and is connected with his view of human beings as windowless monads — albeit ones whose fate makes them suffer.[2]

It is well-known that Sebald's concern with suffering, with the devastating effects of a traumatic past upon a devalued present, and with the catastrophic impact of history, particularly of modernity as a history of destruction, are among his dominant interests.[3] He is also fundamentally concerned with how that suffering can be represented. His writing explores the ways in which the history of catastrophe can be witnessed, and how the perspective of the spectator or narrator constructs the survivors or victims and our affective response to them. He describes in 1997 how the author/narrator stands at the edge of catastrophe in order to tell of it, a position of distance from events that Sebald considered central to his ethical project.[4] In several of his interviews from the late 1990s, he stressed the ethical importance of his 'detached narrative style', describing it as an alienation device that should enable the reader to feel that the narrator is not taking advantage of what he describes.[5] At the same time, however, his writing is characterized by a profound empathy with those who have suffered as a result of violence and destruction, exemplified by the Holocaust, leading to a dynamic tension in his prose fiction between empathy and distance.

This tension is to a large degree played out through his aesthetics of melancholy. As Mary Cosgrove argues, writing about melancholy and writing about the Holocaust are structurally affiliated, for in both, 'the effort to find words that capture the object without distorting it raises the issues of knowing and representation and determines that these are the central concerns of the signifying process'.[6] Yet this structural similarity notwithstanding, the moral implications of representing suffering through a melancholy lens remain complex and controversial. Freud's description of melancholia as the internalization of the lost object in order to preserve it, results in symptoms that may be pathological since the lost object is unconscious and remains obscure. In contrast, in mourning the lost object is identifiable and the loss can be worked through. This difference has led to a highly critical evaluation of melancholy as an emotional mode through which to respond to and represent limit events, since it inhibits the healthy work of mourning. Paul Ricoeur argues for this view in his alignment of mourning with working through and melancholy with acting out, as does Dominick LaCapra, who sees in melancholy 'a compulsive preoccupation with aporia' which functions as a 'secularized displacement [...] of the sacred'.[7] Melancholy facilitates the elision of a generalized, timeless absence with a historically and socially specific loss, which in turn leads to easier (self-)identification as victim by those who are not victims.

In contrast to this negative evaluation of melancholy, the melancholic's profound sense of loss has also been seen as fertile ground for creativity and imagination in post-War discourse.[8] This understanding of melancholy, which develops the long-standing association of melancholy with genius, is one that Cosgrove defends in pointing to the performative dimension of melancholy. Here melancholy is not understood as an individual or social pathology, but as a shifting literary discourse that plays with cultural icons of sadness to explore the post-war moral universe. Sebald uses melancholy performatively to great effect, so that 'against the postwar German characteristic of the inability to mourn, Sebald's special brand of sadness emerges as insightful, mnemonic, and ethically driven mourning work cross-dressed in traditional melancholy apparel'.[9] Yet Maya Barzilai is sceptical of the ethical scope of Sebald's melancholy, pointing towards precisely the danger of identification that concerns LaCapra. She wonders whether 'the particular melancholic lens of [Sebald's] narrator secures him against the accusation of deriving pleasure from the misery of others'.[10] This vicarious pleasure might be manifested in his narrators' identification with the protagonists to so great a degree that they often wish to share their victims' fate, 'to join their travails, even in retrospect'.[11]

But the narrator of *Die Ringe des Saturn* shows little interest in sharing this Lowestoft woman's fate, categorizing her as disturbed and physically rather repulsive, with mention of red patches that creep up her neck (*RS*, 58; *Rings*, 43). As Barzilai has also noted, the melancholy lens of the narrators is gendered: 'the main protagonists of Sebald's works are consistently male, whereas women appear either as conduits of male memory or as dead mothers/lovers', and she concludes that 'Sebald privileges a viewpoint that filters all incomprehensible or horrific events through male anxiety'.[12] However, when this viewpoint is further complicated by different types of comedy, and when that viewpoint is itself subject to comic treatment, the vexed questions around the ethics of representing suffering are intensified. In what follows I explore the constellation of suffering, the question of whose suffering is privileged and how it is represented, by considering the function and status of the comic in Sebald's four works of prose fiction. First I look at the way in which satirical and derisive comedy is directed against women and the masses in order to sustain patterns of melancholic identification. I then show how, at critical points, a further comic dimension is at play, whereby the melancholy of the narrators tips into amusing hyperbole, thus ironizing and complicating the pervasive sorrowful tone. I argue that melancholy excess can be understood as a form of potentially ethical comedy, not only by demonstrating the indulgent masculine solipsism that melancholy can entail, but crucially, by celebrating the pleasure of aesthetic transformation. Through the comedy generated by melancholy hyperbole a limiting moral universe sustained by idealization of lost wholeness is relativized and surpassed by one that, whilst narrating loss, takes pleasure in language and image. Finally, the comedy of melancholy excess places the bond between suffering and pleasure at the heart of the text, compelling us to consider not only the nature of the narrators' enjoyment of others' woes, but also our own.

Satire and the Debased World

Sebald's melancholic tone, delicately constructed with language that evokes the rhythms and prose of an earlier time, is periodically inflected by moments of humour, satire, and even grotesque comedy. At its most fundamental level the humour of the texts resides in what is funny in the world that the narrators observe, read about, and clearly find worthy of note. They draw attention to the idiosyncrasies of names, the optician who is called Susi Ahoi,[13] Selwyn's horses Herschel, Humphrey, and Hippolytus, and the string of towns along State Highway 17: 'Monroe, Monticello, Middletown, Wurtsboro, Wawarsing, Colchester und Cadosia, Deposit, Delhi, Neversink and Niniveh'.[14] The two American aircraft that collided over Somerleyton after an apparently playful dogfight, were, as though enacting the impossibility of the sexual encounter, called 'Big Dick' and 'Lady Loreley' (*RS*, 55; *Rings* 40). Moreover, the comic impact of Big Dick failing to get his Lady Loreley is further enhanced by the fact that the aircraft was, it seems, 'Big Dick II', thus conjuring up a sequence of Big Dicks prematurely cut off.[15] The narrators' observations form the basis of effective social satire, which is particularly amusing when it touches on English mores. Aurach cannot sleep in the English beds because they hold him down by having the blankets tucked under the mattress. His school uniform with its black shorts, bright blue knee socks and blazer, orange shirt, striped tie and tiny cap, is an apt reflection of his carnivalesque boarding school, combining eccentricity with institutionalization (*DA*, 282–83; *TE*, 189). The narrator wryly refers to the combination of serving trolley and hotplate used to serve dinner at Selwyn's as '[eine] Art Patentkonstruktion aus den dreißiger Jahren' ('some kind of patented design dating from the Thirties') (*DA*, 22; *TE*, 13), a response reminiscent of his fascination with the functional but weird 'teasmade' (*DA*, 228; *TE*, 154).

The teasmade, with its pragmatic aspiration to a touch of class, is elevated to the status of an '*electric miracle*' by Gracie Irlam, just as the colourful ladies who come and go in the evenings are transformed by her, without irony, into '*the gentlemen's travelling companions*' (*DA*, 229; *TE*, 155). The gulf between reality and aspiration is also evident in the mismatch between the hotel's very English combination of flowery carpet, violet print wallpaper, and candlewick eiderdown with its evocative alpine name, *Arosa* (*DA*, 225; *TE*, 153). In *Die Ringe des Saturn* the Swan Hotel's unassuming name (referred to as the Saracen's Head in the English translation) belies the ambition of the bedroom, in which the head of the pink bed consists of a huge altar-like construction of black-marbled formica which is not to be outdone by the dressing table, embellished with gold flourishes (*RS*, 295; *Rings*, 249). If the pursuit of something classier is satirized in these examples, so too is the opposite movement. The narrator captures the decline of the landed aristocracy and the eagerness with which the masses pay for an infantilizing experience of the aristocratic dream in one parodying image: tourists visiting Somerleyton sit on the miniature railway carriages like dressed up circus dogs or seals, driven by their very own animal trainer, the current Lord Somerleyton, Her Majesty The Queen's Master of the Horse (*RS*, 44; *Rings*, 32).

Whilst the humour in the preceding examples is often based on the narrators' affection for the England they observe, there are many instances in Sebald's work where the satire assumes an aggressive tone, at times tipping into ridicule and stereotyping, elements of which are already present in the image of tourists as circus animals. It is, of course, in the nature of satire to be tendentious and to present its object from a particular viewpoint. But what links Sebald's narrators is their tendency to satirize or ridicule either women or members of the common masses. Women, certainly, are vulnerable to becoming objects of derision to varying degrees, as is clear when the narrator refers to the 'Weiberschaft von W., die ausnahmslos fast aus kleinen, dunklen, dünnzopfigen und bösen Bäuerinnen und Mägden bestand' ('womenfolk of W., who were almost without exception small, dark, thin-haired and mean farmers' wives and wenches') (*SG*, 257; *V*, 235, adapted). Women in particular can become the grotesque physical symptom of an underlying malaise. In Ivrea, the soprano who unleashes such feeling of joy in the young Beyle has a missing tooth and a left eye that squints whenever she sings a difficult coloratura, as though presaging the emotional and syphilitic love pains that Beyle himself will soon start to endure (*SG*, 13; *V*, 10). The black woman in the tube station embodies the threat of the empty, unsettling station, her sole characteristic being that she is a 'dunkle[] Frau' [dark woman] (*SG*, 283–84).[16] In *Die Ausgewanderten*, Hedi Selwyn is negatively portrayed as an extremely efficient industrialist's daughter, who is estranged from her husband, frequently leaves home on business trips, and manages to remark on the narrator's newly whitewashed bathroom in such a way that he perceives it as a devastating judgement on his whole life (*DA*, 16; *TE*, 9). But her warped and truncated emotions take on hysterical form in Aileen, the real female presence in the house who acts like the return of Hedi Selwyn's repressed. She looks like an inmate of a (mental) institution, her room is full of carefully dressed-up dolls, and she breaks out into strange, neighing laughter without evident cause (*DA*, 16–18; *TE*, 9–10).

Similarly, Deauville's sad decline is exemplified by the state of its women. The narrator has the feeling that the whole place consists of invisible women condemned to an eternity of dusting, who lie in wait to give passers-by a signal with their dusters (*DA*, 172; *TE*, 117). Within the economy of Sebald's work, where dust offers potential for a positive mediation with the past, the characterization of these women takes on a negative hue, reinforced by the resonance of the German 'düster' [sinister]. The visiting ladies too mimic the decline of the resort and the architectural monstrosity of the Grand Hotel. They remain oblivious to its and their decay, going for walks along the promenade with their ulcerated poodles and pekingeses (*DA*, 175; *TE*, 119). And in a final, ludicrous Deauville image, the narrator describes the Baroness Dembowski, who takes her angora rabbit out on a lead. She is '[a]uf das geschmackloseste zusammengerichtet und auf das entsetzlichste geschminkt' ('dressed in the most tasteless of styles and appallingly made up') (*DA*, 186; *TE*, 126).

The narrator thus repeatedly draws attention to women's bodies and links them with decline and the threat of death. The most grotesque female body belongs to the dying Gwendolyn, Austerlitz's adoptive mother, who, like Aileen, acts out the perverse effects of an absence of love and the stunting effect of an all-pervasive emotional coldness in her repulsive death. Compulsively applying talcum powder to herself, she covers the house in a mucus-like layer of slime.[17] In much less extreme form, Mary Frances FitzGerald is presented as woman with a terrifying bosom next to whom her husband appears utterly insignificant (*RS*, 234; *Rings*, 197).

Crucially, satire and the comic marginalization of women point us clearly towards the wider marginalization of women by the narrators, whether this is done through satire or not. As Barzilai demonstrates, the narrator of *Die Ausgewanderten* uses women to gain access to the male protagonists, such as Lucy Landau who tells him about Paul Bereyter, or Aunt Fini whom he visits in order to hear about Ambros Adelwarth. Although in *Die Ringe des Saturn* the narrator speaks positively of Janine Rosalind Dakyns, likening her to the figure of the angel in Dürer's *Melancholia*, most of what we know about her is what she tells the narrator about Flaubert, a writer whose uncompromising approach to his writing clearly fascinates the narrator. Dakyns also puts him in touch with the surgeon Anthony Batty Shaw, the key to his research into Thomas Browne. When not mediating between men, women appear as lost mothers or lovers, such as Aurach's mother Luisa Lanzberg or the spectral German-speaking woman who appears to the artist from his Berlin past. Similarly, in *Austerlitz*, Agáta and Adela function as erotic mothers, Vera helps Austerlitz remember his childhood years in Prague, and Marie de Verneuil is the lost beloved about whom we learn little. Women in Sebald's prose fiction tend to be of significance only in the various ways they act as props for the lives and the fulfilment of men. Penelope Peacefull is important for the role she inadvertently plays in triggering Austerlitz's memory by listening to the radio broadcast about the *Kindertransport* (*A*, 203; *AusE*, 199), Florence Barnes is vital as Le Strange's housekeeper (*RS*, 80; *Rings*, 62), and Menuchah is named only as the wife of the Rabbi Heschel or the mother of Dan Jacobson. She, a woman who emigrated to South Africa with nine children after the death of her husband, is of little interest to a narrator for whom Jacobson's search for his grandfather's kingdom provides parallels with, and therefore a sanction for, his own exploration of Austerlitz's past (*A*, 415; *AusE*, 413).

In Sebald's works, women are also crucial for the literary achievements of men. Caroline, Métilde, and Mme Gherardi become notches on Beyle's tally of lovers and vital ingredients in his musings upon love. As the narrator points out, Mme Gherardi herself is probably no more than a fantasy figure who functions as a cipher for Beyle's other, unindividuated women (*SG*, 26; *V*, 21). Sebald's narrators also turn women into ciphers for their symbolic universes. It is not surprising that when he is under the influence of morphine, his nurses Katy and Lizzie should become hovering beings who, with voices that combine angels' music and the song of the sirens, represent both salvation and seductive threat (*RS*, 28; *Rings*, 18). But even without the help of opiates, women are interesting as bearers of mythological meaning, rather than being of interest in themselves: the three Jewish women in the ghetto become Nona, Decuma, and Morta, and the narrator concurs with Austerlitz's transformation of the barwoman in Antwerp station into the goddess of past time (*A*, 12; *AusE*, 8).

The interest that the narrator shows in Luciana Michelotti, the Italian hotel proprietor, is unusual in Sebald's work because the narrator seems initially to relate to her as an equal. She is the same age as him and on the day he arrives she appears somewhat melancholy. Yet the fascination she exerts is quickly transformed into that of a muse for a writer, for she stands at the terrace bar and he derives particular satisfaction from being able to look over to her frequently (*SG*, 109; *V*, 95). On this occasion he is inspired to write as on no other: 'das Schreiben ging mir mit einer mich selbst erstaunenden Leichtigkeit von der Hand' ('I wrote with an ease that astonished me') (*SG*, 107; *V*, 94). When she touches him, he admits that being touched by a strange woman has always had something 'Gewichtloses, Geisterhaftes' [weightless and ghostly] (*SG*, 111) about it, thereby drawing attention to another key device by means of which women can be hastily overlooked as subjects in their own right: they are made insubstantial, associated with phantoms, floating, or with realms of abstraction. Agáta and Adela too are linked to floating or hovering, Agáta through the silk scarf that floats across her face, thereby disguising its form (*A*, 233; *AusE*, 229), and Adela who is said to hover in the air longer than gravity allows (*A*, 161; *AusE*, 158). Even the cashiers in the Ferrovia buffet, who are seated enthroned above the crowd of customers, seem to be floating (*SG*, 77; *V*, 67). It is therefore in keeping that as Luciana drives off, she should seem to be following a curve that leads away to another world (*SG*, 118; *V*, 103). From the perspective of the melancholic narrator, women seem to be either too much of this world in their scandalous physicality, or else they are insubstantial and not of this world.

One woman stands out as an individual who escapes satirical treatment, and who is presented neither in relation to hysterical physicality nor as ethereal or mythological unreality nor as mediator between the narrators and another man. Mathild, one of three unmarried sisters, a keen reader of key socialist thinkers and advocates of women's rights, was in Munich at the time of the *Räterepublik*, and continued an independent, proud life back in the village, despising the villagers around her. Her status is confirmed in the narrator's eyes by the fact that his grandfather paid her weekly visits involving card games and lengthy discussions. Perhaps the gesture of the handshake between them offers a clue to her unusual representation: she is seen as an authority by her sisters (*SG*, 239; *V*, 219) and becomes an honorary man both for the grandfather and for the narrator. Nevertheless, the tantalizing glimpse of an unusual and challenging life, one that is interlinked with world-historical importance, is not pursued any further: Mathild is not fascinating as a subject for further research. For this, too, there is a clue. Despite considerable suffering, for she returns from Munich in disarray and almost speechless, far from being melancholy she has a cheerful disposition (*SG*, 247; *V*, 226). Her response to loss, here the collapse of hope for radical change in the immediate aftermath of the First World War, as well as the devastation of the war itself, is not a model with which the narrator identifies.

But Sebald's narrators do not limit their caustic observations to women, for other individuals or groups are cast as complicit actors in or bystanders to his unfolding narrative of catastrophic decline and destruction. Like the circus animals, the Japanese in Deauville allow themselves to be herded around the globe and into the casino, where they stoically spend all day on the gaming machines, delighting if they ever win (*DA*, 176–77; *TE*, 120). After reading Luisa Lanzberg's account of her childhood, the narrator travels to Kissingen and Stenach to pursue his research. During the last stage of his journey the moral and social deformity of the Nazi years seems to take on human form when a monstrous man sits opposite him. This man has a blotchy face, squints, and pushes food remains around his mouth with an unshapely tongue. The narrator offers a repulsive but amusing description: 'Die Beine gespreizt, saß er da, Bauch und Unterleib auf eine grauenerregende Weise eingezwängt in eine kurze Sommerhose' ('There he sat, legs apart, his stomach and gut stuffed horribly into summer shorts') (*DA*, 328; *TE*, 219). For the narrator, this man is a monster, regardless of whether his appearance is caused by psychiatric problems, congenital disability, or too much beer. In contrast to Kissingen's pre-Nazi harmony, its modern ghastliness is further manifested in the mean-spiritedness of the woman in the same train who takes an hour to eat an apple, and an old couple in the hotel who stare at the narrator with barely concealed hostility, and smuggle food up to their room in claw-like hands (*DA*, 329; *TE*, 219).

In *Die Ringe des Saturn*, those who appear grotesque are complicit in the cruelty of colonial exploitation. The narrator is hilariously uninhibited in his characterization of Belgians:

> Tatsächlich gibt es in Belgien [...] eine besondere, von der Zeit der ungehemmten Ausbeutung der Kongokolonie geprägte, in der makabren Atmosphäre gewisser Salons und einer auffallenden Verkrüppelung der Bevölkerung sich manifestierende Häßlichkeit, wie man sie anderwärts nur selten antrifft. (*RS*, 149)

> [And indeed, [...] one sees in Belgium a distinctive ugliness, dating from the time when the Congo colony was exploited without restraint and manifested in the macabre atmosphere of certain salons and the strikingly stunted growth of the population, such as one rarely comes across elsewhere.] (*Rings*, 122)

As though to prove his point, the narrator notices the hunchbacked old woman whom he links by her age to the completion of the Congo railway (*RS*, 153–54; *Rings*, 126–27). Less harsh, but prescient in view of bankers' increasingly demonstrable greed, is the narrator's characterization of the City workers in *Austerlitz* as an animal species, who in a system that extols the virtues of individual freedom, nevertheless all look and behave the same as part of their increasingly drunken horde (*A*, 57; *AusE*, 53–54). If the capitalist banker remains an as yet uncategorized beast, the workers of the state-run hotel in Marienbad are as sloths in a stultifying system that enforces a different type of cruel habitat. The skinny receptionist, the lines of whose brow descend to the bridge of his nose, moves with comic slowness, as does the porter, who, struck by a debilitating tiredness, climbs the stairs as though straining to reach the highest alpine peak (*A*, 296–97; *AusE*, 293).

In the preceding examples, where satire tips into ridicule and the absurd, it is clear that the objects of the narrators' comic derision are individuals or groups that they identify with a debased world, people who collude knowingly with homogenizing systems of modernization, cruelty, and exploitation. Or else, through their willed or lazy obliviousness to anguish, they become metonyms of those forces of destruction. Conversely, those that are left untouched by mocking humour are those figures to whom the narrators are attracted by their suffering and melancholy, normally men. Indeed, the melancholic perspective of the narrators privileges those who manifest a particular sensitivity to loss and decline and whose suffering is linked to or caused by the history of destruction: the French Revolution, the Napoleonic Wars, colonialism, forced exile, the Holocaust, the Irish civil war. Furthermore, the suffering figures are exemplary in various ways: they are landed gentry who move in elite circles, writers or artists, teachers who resist the encroachments of a pedagogy that is driven by ideological and market-forces and who strive for education and knowledge that is not subject to instrumental reason. The lure of the elite and the hierarchy of values that follows from it is clear from the narrator's fascinated and admiring description of Cosmo's luck at roulette that is set against his denigration of the spinning slot machines. His observation, that he has never seen a Japanese person playing roulette (*DA*, 177; *TE*, 120), assumes a moral weight that is unsustainable in view of the similarly utterly arbitrary nature of both types of gambling.

Other men whose suffering is privileged have either suffered profound loss, like Aurach or Austerlitz, or are acutely aware of the processes of destruction that continue unabated and disavowed into the present. The suffering caused by failed relationships, unfulfilled love, fraught family ties, or dashed desires are not of interest in themselves, but only if they have a link with a grander history of destruction. So where Korzeniowski's (Conrad's) love-entanglements and subsequent duel or suicide attempt are humorously dismissed as suitable material for an Offenbach operetta (*RS*, 137; *Rings*, 112–13), Austerlitz's failed relationship with Marie de Verneuil is treated seriously because it is viewed as a consequence of his traumatic past and loss of his parents. That is not to say that these suffering but exceptional men are not shown to have a funny side, for they are often bizarre or eccentric in their behaviour. Selwyn is counting blades of grass when the narrator first sees him. The entirely fictional Le Strange lives up to his name by eating dinner in silence with his housekeeper every day, and by apparently dressing up in an antique, canary-yellow frock coat because he does not wish to buy new clothes (*RS*, 82; *Rings*, 64). Swinburne incongruously combines an underdeveloped body and pathological avoidance of any stimulation with a rapacious appetite and consumes immense portions of beef in a way that is reminiscent of the voracious silkworm *Bombyx mori* (*RS*, 198; *Rings*, 165). And Mr. Squirrel the coffin bearer, whose ambition it is to be an actor but who can only remember the names of the dead, spends a year learning his lines when he is finally given a role in *King Lear*. After the performance he continues to recite them, but on the most unlikely occasions such as when he returns Anne Hamburger's good morning greeting with '*They say his banished son is with the Earl of Kent in Germany*' (*RS*, 226; *Rings*, 189).

Crucially, however, the comic effect of these examples is inseparable from the suffering that lies behind or causes the behaviour. So although Selwyn's grass-counting 'pastime' (*DA*, 11; *TE*, 5) remains funny, he himself does not become a comic figure or the butt of a joke. Rather, he is linked both to a glamorous past of a twenties and thirties highlife, and to the sorrows of East European Jewry: he emigrated from Lithuania with his family in 1899 and with age increasingly feels the burden of exile and homesickness for his lost home. The theme of loss is further emphasized through the sorrow that is caused him by the death of the mountain guide Nagele, who, like the memories of his Lithuanian childhood, returns from oblivion when his corpse is disgorged by the glacier. Similarly, Le Strange has apparently witnessed the liberation of Bergen Belsen; Swinburne had an extreme nervous breakdown and Mr. Squirrel has always worn mourning, hinting at a profound loss. These are men for whom the catastrophes and sorrows of the past and the ongoing destruction of the present have nurtured a sensibility and experience of pain that makes living a burden.

The discernible division in Sebald's texts between those treated with mockery or comic derision and those whose suffering sensibility is explored, is articulated by the narrator of *Schwindel. Gefühle* when he admits how implausible the past seems to be: 'denn nichts an ihr sei normal zu nennen, sondern es sei das allermeiste lächerlich, und wenn es nicht lächerlich sei, dann sei es zum Entsetzen' ('for nothing about it could be called normal; most of it was absurd, and if not absurd, then appalling') (*SG*, 231–32; *V*, 212). Yet, as Bachmann reminds us, no-one is absurd behind the facade.[18] In Sebald's texts the people who remain risible are those whose facades are not penetrated, for the narrators are uninterested in suffering that is not linked with a particular melancholy sensibility, or indeed their own aesthetic constructions of it. Thus, where Selwyn's emotional burden of exile is explored with sympathy and ascribed considerable importance, the pain of exile felt by Aunt Theres is described with great humour so that she becomes a figure of fun, even though her description is not without affection. When visiting Germany from her country of exile, the United States, she cries almost without pause, for the first three weeks, out of joy at being home, and for the second three weeks in the anticipation of renewed separation. Consequently, visits of less than six weeks cause consternation, for it is impossible to tell whether she is crying from joy or dread (*DA*, 100; *TE*, 69), and within the economy of the text, it is no surprise that this excess of female physicality results in death.

A final good example of the comic depiction of women whose suffering is only mentioned in passing, is the very funny description of Babett and Bina — B&B –, the two spinster sisters who ran the Café Alpenrose. The narrator admits with some sympathy that the two women had lived a life of disappointment, dashed hopes, and mutual dependency, all of which had diminished them as women. He then offers a lengthy humorous account of their failed café: how they both waited in vain, Bina rushing around, Babett endlessly refolding tea-towels, for a customer who never came; how the weekly baking of a cake took on the dimensions of a 'Staatsaktion'; and how they had to eat the cake themselves at the end of each week, Babett with a cake-fork and irritated by Bina dunking it in her coffee (*SG*, 237; *V*, 218). In this case, their suffering, which is related only to their personal hopes and desires, and so is full of melodramatic potential, is subordinated to the construction of their life as a comic double act. In contrast, the comic potential of Selwyn's predicament is marginalized in favour of what lies behind the facade.

Entering the Comic Frame

Sebald's comedy is not limited to good-humoured observation of strange mores or more or less tendentious satire, but the stories of others' despair and suffering are also composed in such a way as to show a funny side. A central feature of many humorous episodes or observations in Sebald's prose fiction is the incongruity of the perspectives they involve. By juxtaposing differing perceptions of events and then adding their own, Sebald's narrators transform the events from being merely tragic, devastating, disappointing, or otherwise sad examples of pain and suffering, and make them, in addition, amusing. Thus in *Die Ausgewanderten* the emigrants stand on deck watching out in vain for the Statue of Liberty after a miserable week's passage to 'Amerikum'. Only after disembarking do they realize that they are in London and many continue to believe that London is New York (*DA*, 32; *TE*, 19). The means by which events that were not at all amusing for the participants are transmuted into something humorous is in certain cases quite transparent. The narrator relates how Beyle is unable to survive even a few days 'ohne Métilde SEHEN zu können', and so disguises himself, perhaps hoping to be mistaken for Goethe's Werther. He dons a yellow jacket, dark-blue leggings, an extra-high velour hat, and a pair of green glasses (*SG*, 24; *V*, 20) and then follows her from a distance, happily humming his own tune '*Je suis le compagnon secret et familier*', unaware of the deep offence he is causing and the imminent rejection that will follow. The capitalized 'sehen', followed by the colourful list of conspicuous clothes *à la* Werther, directs the reader to laugh at Beyle.

In the case of Dr K.'s spa treatment in Riva, the careful composition of text and image draws attention to a narrative perspective that fashions a space for humour. We are told of the suffering that descends upon Dr K., and are concurrently shown four thumbnail sketches that apparently depict the cold-water therapy he is receiving (*SG*, 171). But these cartoonish sketches are at odds with the debilitating depression he is suffering. The first three show a man having water poured over his head through a watering can, then having his legs hosed with cold water and finally having his upper thigh watered. In fact one needs to look carefully at this third sketch to ascertain whether the therapy on offer is not in fact rather more pleasurable than enduring cold water, since it looks at first glance as though a more amorous exchange of fluids is the recommended treatment. The final sketch illustrates the very verb into which it is, literally and wittily, inserted, 'hineinsenken': a man relaxing in a tub with his feet up.[19] The pictures here are in evident tension with the simultaneous textual insistence on suffering and this double optic actively forges an amused distance from the narrated events.

What emerges from these examples is the extent to which Sebald's narrators enjoy the narrative transformation of events. Not only do they display a satiric eye, they also construct and narrate scenes in such a way that they can be read comically. Their pleasure in comedy is also discernible in the jokes they play upon the reader, in particular the way in which they interweave fact and fiction with no indication of when one finishes and the other starts: the textual equivalent of a 'completely straight face'.[20] Thus the narrator of *Die Ringe des Saturn* observes drily that the scientists who are researching the fate of the North Sea herrings are appropriately called Herrington and Lightbown, without indicating that any scholar would struggle to find them (*RS*, 76; *Rings*, 59). Similarly there is no evidence that the carriages of the narrow-gauge train running between Halesworth and Southwold were originally designed for the Emperor of China (*RS*, 166; *Rings*, 138), and we will never know whether the little Manchester rat-catcher Renfield is good at this job because, like his namesake R. M. Renfield, he is under the influence of Dracula (*DA*, 226; *TE*, 153).[21]

Crucially, however, the play with perspective in Sebald's prose fiction extends to the figures of the narrators, whose extreme self-absorbed melancholy itself generates comedy. In a grotesquely funny episode during the narrator's walk along the Suffolk coast in *Die Ringe des Saturn*, the narrator catches sight of a couple having sex just as he is trying to recover from a vertigo attack on the edge of a cliff. Seen from above and with the man lying on top, only the woman's spread legs are visible, and together they appear like 'ein von weit draußen hereingetriebenes, vielgliedriges, doppelköpfiges Seeungeheuer' ('a many-limbed, two-headed monster that had drifted in from far out at sea') (*RS*, 88; *Rings*, 68). The sight induces panic in the narrator rather than voyeuristic pleasure, and he rapidly retreats. Here again, comedy is linked to the grotesque body of a debased world, which is no surprise, for comedy has long been associated with materiality and the limitations imposed upon us by our deficient physicality. What is interesting about this comic episode, however, is that although the body is central, it is the narrator's reaction to the unexpected physicality that is comic, not his own body's failure, as would be the case in slapstick, or if he had fallen off the cliff and betrayed his presence. The shock induced by the primal scene interrupts his lofty musings on the way in which humans project their diseased understanding of the world onto inferior beings and causes him to do precisely that: to project his consternation onto the image of a lesser being, the mollusc. Here then, the narrator himself, along with his response to the world, enters into the frame of comedy.

There are a number of such occasions when the narrator's perspective enters the comic frame, not least in certain photographs. Blackler convincingly points to the photograph of the window in *Die Ringe des Saturn* as one such example, which is apparently the window from which he can see the sky from his hospital room. 'The absurdity lies in the reader's imagining the paralysed narrator somehow managing to photograph (hence the odd angle) his own view of the sky through the hospital window'.[22] Over and above the comedy of this particular image, the photograph raises the question of what is being documented, and poses that question as a joke. If the narrator is recording his own absurd position both physically and metaphysically in his search for meaning, then 'is this a moment when we glimpse the author's wry smile at the intensity of the narrator's self-preoccupation [...]?'[23] The narrator's perspective, as well as that of Sebald, is also subject to visual comedy through the photograph of the reissued passport, for here the lugubrious expression on Sebald's face, who here merges with the figure of the narrator, is cut through by a black line, which thus cancels the validity of the very document that confers identity and puts a question-mark over the confident assertion that his identity is now secured (*SG*, 129; *V*, 113). Not only is the reader being asked the question of whose perspective is being presented, but a joke about the lines between fact and fiction is being made this time with a genuinely deadpan expression.

The narrators' melancholy sensibilities and reactions are frequently central to the comic scene. The battle with the armoured fish in Lowestoft is one such event, as are episodes in which the narrative persona takes on certain characteristics of the innocent abroad, wide-eyed and horrified by what he encounters. For the narrator of *Schwindel. Gefühle* the act of buying a coffee in the Venice Ferrovia is akin to an emasculating final judgement. The place is monstrous, the noise is hellish, the passage to the counter a fight, and the general mood one of panic (*SG*, 76–77; *V*, 67). Enthroned above the desirous throng, impassive women dispense receipts arbitrarily, and, alongside the waiters, appear like higher beings passing judgement on 'ein von endemischer Gier korrumpiertes Geschlecht' [on the endemic greed of a corrupted species] (*SG*, 78). Similarly, the surroundings of the pizzeria in Verona are such that the narrator is reduced to leaving the town in terror: its blue walls and fishing nets induce the feeling of being hopelessly lost at sea, a sentiment that is confirmed by a framed picture of a boat about to plunge into the yawning deep. Terrified by this vision of imminent catastrophe, the narrator clings to the table like a seasick traveller clinging to the railing (*SG*, 89; *V*, 77). His fear is exacerbated by reading about a string of unsolved murders, and by the waiter's name, Cadavero, which apparently leads him to imagine that he may be the next in line to end up a corpse, especially as the waiter stares at him, the sole customer, with contempt. So the narrator rushes, panicking, from the pizzeria and from Verona, in a response that is comically incommensurate with the banality of the vulgar little eatery. Although not as extreme, his reaction to Innsbruck is also marked by a heightened sensibility for awfulness. It is a place with horrendous weather, where the station is full of down-and-outs with a penchant for alcohol-fuelled philosophizing (*SG*, 187–89; *V*, 170–73). Here, in the most miserable of all station restaurants he knows, matters deteriorate even further when the waitress is extremely rude to him. (*SG*, 190; *V*, 174).

The narrator's sometimes almost wilfully naïve absorption in his own perspective is central to the comic effect. The reader sees nothing unusual in the plastic-covered chairs of the pizzeria or in Cadavero's telephone conversation. We notice that what for the narrator is a 'not unfriendly' remark to the Innsbruck waitress about Tyrolean chicory coffee is probably a criticism of its poor quality. We can also see the embarrassingly funny side of the incident when the narrator accosts a German tourist and almost compels him to take a photograph of the now closed Pizzeria Verona. But the narrator fails to persuade the tourist to take another photograph of the pizzeria covered in pigeons, choosing to blame a clingy fiancée rather than notice his own gauche imposition (*SG*, 142–43; *V*, 126–27). In one extreme example, the narrator does realise how odd his behaviour appears, but persists in it regardless. On the bus to Riva he espies twins, fifteen-year-old Kafka look-alikes. First he looks at them over his shoulder, then he tries to converse with them, then he tries to convince the parents that his interest in the boys has to do with a '*scrittore ebreo*', and finally, in order to remove all suspicion, he informs them that he would be satisfied if they just sent him a photograph of the boys to his home in England (*SG*, 102–03; *V*, 89–90). In fact, he has satisfied them that he is an English paedophile, and he leaves the bus covered in shame.

Another example of a melancholy narrator being comically overwhelmed by his alienating surroundings is the scene in *Die Ringe des Saturn* where the narrator is wandering through a deprived area of The Hague, characterized particularly by 'oriental' men, shops, and a mosque. Suddenly he is confronted by an extraordinary sight: 'Eine mit Lichtern bestückte, chromglänzende amerikanische Limousine mit offenem Verdeck, in der ein Zuhälter in einem weißen Anzug saß, mit einer goldumrandeten Sonnenbrille und einem lachhaften Tirolerhut auf dem Kopf' ('An open-top American limousine studded with lights and gleaming with chrome [...], and in it sat a pimp in a white suit, wearing gold-framed sunglasses and on his head a ludicrous Tyrolean hat') (*RS*, 101; *Rings*, 82). Distracted by this remarkable sight, the narrator finds himself dramatically caught up as a shield between two 'dark-skinned' men, one of whom, dressed in a chef's apron, is wielding a huge, flashing knife that narrowly misses his ribs. What makes this incident comic is the conflation of surprise, stereotype, and incongruity, as though the narrator has suddenly and unwittingly found himself in the middle of an over-acted and clichéd crime shoot. Particularly evident in this scene is the extent to which the jolt of comic absurdity is clearly a product of the narrator's own perceptions. For even before the eruption onto the scene of the limousine and the knife-wielding cook, the narrator has already commented on the unfamiliarity of the area and built up suspense by referring to the man who slips past him, and the groups of men doing business on the streets. This is for him an almost 'extraterritorial' area, in which he feels like a criminal on the run even in the very familiar McDonald's. What we see clearly here is how the narrator fashions his surroundings in a certain way, arising out of a distinct sentiment or mood: he has arrived in The Hague after a bad night. Furthermore, he reconstructs the scene from memory one year later, which is significant because he has been musing on the transformation of memory in dreams, and asking the question: 'Was ist das für ein Theater, in dem wir Dichter, Schauspieler, Maschinist, Bühnenmaler und Publikum in einem sind?' ('What manner of theatre is it, in which we are at once playwright, actor, stage manager, scene painter and audience?') (*RS*, 99; *Rings*, 80) The performative transformation that he describes here in dreams is also at play in the theatre of his own memory: The Hague has become The Corner.

These scenes tacitly offer a comic perspective on the narrators from which their melancholy projections and excessive 'self-stylization' are not condoned but ironized.[24] Thus, in the scene in The Hague, the narrator's perspective on his environment, which slips all too easily into the criminalization of dark-skinned men, suddenly appears as incongruous and laughable as the pimp with the Tyrolian hat, who perhaps is not a pimp at all. Perhaps his transformation by the narrator into something almost supernatural (*RS*, 101; *Rings*, 82) is a variation on a comparably comic elevation of a limousine driver that the narrator of *Schwindel. Gefühle* made when he was a boy. He remembers how he saw the extraordinary sight of a black man driving a pink and green limousine through his remote village, and recognized him as King Melchior because his crib figure of the black sage wore the same colours (*SG*, 267; *V*, 244). This is an early example of the process whereby the narrator projects his own understanding of his world onto the events around him. Yet by entering into the comic frame himself, a wedge is driven, even if momentarily, between the emoting narrator, object of narrative, and the enunciating narrator. This splitting, however temporary, is crucial for understanding the scope of the comedy since the narrator's superiority is deflated by showing him to be human and fallible like all those around him. He worries about the declining herring population but eats his mass-produced breaded fish; he despairs about the homogeneity of modernity but buys his chips in McDonald's rather than venture into a local eatery; he suffers agonies of national association at the rowdy sound of the south German dialect being spoken without inhibition in the Italian hotel, but shows little respect for local convention in his intrusive behaviour towards the Kafka look-alikes.

Despite the hurdles, Sebald's narrators keep on walking and in the end always continue on their way. In their tenacious progress, they bear a resemblance to Alenka Zupancic's archetypal comic figure, the toffee-nosed baron who 'slips on a banana peel (thus demonstrating that even he is subject to the laws of gravity), yet the next instant he is up again and walking around arrogantly, no less sure of the highness of His Highness'.[25] Taking this figure as a starting point, Zupancic distinguishes between two different ways in which comedy grounds us as 'human'. The first lays emphasis on the fact that the baron is 'also' a man, thereby encouraging us to accept our material and physical limitations. However, this comedy leaves the position and concept of the baronage itself untouched for it is the individuals who bear the title who are limited by being only human. She argues that this is a conservative paradigm, for 'we identify with heroes' weaknesses, yet their higher calling (or universal symbolic function) remains all the more the object of respect and fascination'.[26] In relation to the narrators, we see that they are fallible, but remain sympathetic to their intensely felt melancholy and motives. The second, subversive, paradigm is that which points to the baron's very belief in his own importance as the real human weakness: what is comic here is the fact that he gets up and continues in his belief regardless, not that he slips. Subversive comedy reminds us that the belief itself, 'the ego-ideal directly *is* a human weakness'.[27] In Sebald's work the narrators do not solely reveal their own fallibility, they also transform their suffering into a form of hyperbolic melancholy, the comedy of which creates a critical space with which to probe their own melancholy perspective and the ideals that are posited by that perspective. Through comic excess they place the ethically troubling relationship of pleasure and suffering at the heart of the texts, and it is to this relationship that I now turn.

Comedy and Ethical Discontent

Although the narrators' eye for the comic leads them to construct scenes in such a way that the reader can see the funny side, however absurd or grotesque, the comic effect of certain scenes is not clearly signalled and may, for many readers, not be comic at all. Whether an episode is perceived as comic relies frequently on the arbitrary response of the reader who is surprised, shocked, or jolted by what she reads. In *Austerlitz* the episode of the bombed cinema offers one such example. One Sunday afternoon a bomb falls on the cinema of a small valley town in Wales. The accidental bomb arbitrarily hitting the target as though it were a bullseye in the middle of rural Wales, and in broad daylight, combined with the simple certainty with which the preacher Elias sees the event as God's punishment on the sinners who dared watch a film on the Sabbath, has always struck me as funny (*A*, 74; *AusE*, 70). So too has the scene when Elias is unable to preach to his horror-struck congregation and stands silently in the pulpit (*A*, 96; *AusE*, 92), the moment when upon being told that he is not Dafydd Elias but Jacques Austerlitz the boy politely says 'Thank you, Sir' (*A*, 98; *AusE*, 94), and when the adult Austerlitz wonders whether lettuces dream (*A*, 138; *AusE*, 134). While it is unlikely that all readers will consider these, and other examples, to be comic anecdotes, Sebald, the metanarrator of *Austerlitz*, acknowledges this arbitrariness of response, which can cause a narrated event to be funnier for some than for others. Furthermore, he connects this arbitrariness with the question of ethics and appropriateness of response. Thus he has his narrator tell Austerlitz of the carpenter who after the death of his wife carefully builds a guillotine, which, after careful research, he has concluded is the most reliable way of killing himself. This he then does successfully, and is found with the pliers with which he cut through the wire still in his rigid hand. Austerlitz does not respond to this story for a long time, leading the narrator to worry that he was tasteless to dwell on the story's absurd side (*A*, 143; *AusE*, 139). Similarly, in *Die Ausgewanderten*, Aurach tells the narrator of a newspaper report he read about the photo-lab technician who has absorbed so much silver over the years that he became a type of living photographic plate whose face and hands turned blue in strong light as they 'developed'. The narrator remarks that Aurach recounts this tale of poisoning totally seriously, thereby betraying that his own response had included seeing a funny side (*DA*, 244; *TE*, 165).

Following Cosgrove's persuasive argument that the narrators are 'overdetermined through the doe-like narrative gaze of unconditional contrition' they bestow upon the Jewish other, it is easy to see here how the narrators concede the moral high ground and doubt the moral probity of their own sense of humour.[28] Yet it would be a mistake to accept the narrator's anxiety about the 'tastelessness' of humour as an overall negative judgement upon comedy in the face of suffering. Austerlitz's identification with the carpenter rests upon his unsupported assumption that the man has led an unhappy life and it takes no account of the man's profoundly caring relationship with his wife. Consequently, it is Austerlitz's flawed projection that makes him unable to acknowledge the absurd aspect of the guillotine suicide, and this inability is a symptom of Austerlitz's trauma that prevents him from having exactly the kind of loving relationship that the carpenter enjoyed. And as though to emphasize this point, Austerlitz himself relates positively how Marie de Verneuil, the woman whose love he was unable finally to accept, had a very unique sense for comic excess (*A*, 299; *AusE*, 295).[29] Thus, Austerlitz's traumatic experience of suffering impoverishes his range of responses to others' suffering and invites the reader to resist viewing Austerlitz as a 'model of ethical behavior' as the narrator does.[30] In contrast, the positive figure of Marie demonstrates the possibility and attractiveness of such a range of reactions, for her sensitivity to suffering does not preclude a sense of humour.

Indeed, the reactions of Austerlitz and Marie de Verneuil evoke in microcosm two aspects of Sebald's prose fiction, with their attendant modes of reading and different ethical implications. The first is an unbounded melancholy through which the world is understood in terms of loss and decline, and which sustains a moral hierarchy in which the experience of melancholy suffering is privileged and perpetuated. The second, as Marie demonstrates, takes pleasure in the comedy of excess, which in Sebald's texts becomes melancholy excess. So when the narrator recounts Austerlitz's description of an ice cream, it is possible to see it as one more example of pervasive decline, much like the armoured cod: 'Wir hatten [...] ein Eis bestellt, beziehungsweise, wie es sich zeigte, ein eisähnliches Konfekt, eine gipserne, nach Kartoffelstärke schmeckende Masse, deren hervorstechendste Eigenschaft es war, daß sie sogar nach Ablauf von mehr als einer Stunde nicht zerging' ('we ordered an ice cream, or rather, as it turned out, a confection resembling an ice cream, a plaster-like substance tasting of potato starch and notable chiefly for the fact that even after more than an hour it did not melt') (*A*, 303; *AusE*, 299). Yet the description is also a very amusing metaphor of Austerlitz's own stiff melancholy, unable to soften even in the empathetic company of Marie. So as with melodrama's slippage into comedy, the slippage of melancholy into comic hyperbole exposes the solipsistic danger of an unconstrained melancholy perspective; one which harnesses satire to its particular moral sensibility, while being suspicious of comedy more generally out of moral concern. Such concern also dominates the reception of Sebald's work.

The narrators' anxiety about the appropriateness of humour in the representation of suffering signals the ethical complexity involved in the texts' interplay of melancholy and comedy. The melancholy of the prose fiction has been positively understood as being central to Sebald's ethical project. The narrators display profound sensitivity to people's lives marked by dehumanizing destruction and trauma, and derive from this the ability to tell the stories and memories of exile and suffering with tact. It is this tact to which the narrator of *Die Ausgewanderten* explicitly lays claim when he condemns his own attempts to visualize Paul Bereyter's death: 'Solche Versuche der Vergegenwärtigung brachten mich jedoch [...] dem Paul nicht näher, höchstens augenblicksweise, in gewissen Ausuferungen des Gefühls, wie sie mir unzulässig erscheinen und zu deren Vermeidung ich jetzt aufgeschrieben habe, was ich von Paul Bereyter weiß' ('Such endeavours to imagine his life and death did not [...] bring me any closer to Paul, except momentarily, in certain gushes of emotion of the kind that seem inadmissable to me and to avoid which I have written down what I know of Paul Bereyter') (*DA*, 45; *TE*, 29, adapted). To avoid such tactless emotionalism, the narrators remain discreetly in the background and use the mediating layer of reported speech to recount the disastrous effects of trauma and repression without trivialization or sensationalizing.[31] Following Thomas Bernhard, Sebald called this mode of narration 'periscopic' and maintained that this telling of events 'through layers of hearsay' involves a narrator with a strong presence and a clear 'moral makeup'.[32] The narrators thus display an urgent concern for how suffering and disaster are represented, reflecting Sebald's own clear moral responsibility to people in old photographs who ask him to 'please take care of us for a while'.[33]

The tactful narration, conducted by narrators whose clear 'moral makeup' mirrors the that of the author, has underpinned the view that Sebald's prose fiction stands as an example of 'empathic unsettlement', LaCapra's term for an affective response to another's suffering that recognizes 'the difference or alterity of the other' through its 'special stress on modes of address'.[34] While recognizing that Sebald's style at points suggests an ahistorical melancholy, LaCapra himself cites Sebald as an example of 'subdued empathic unsettlement'.[35] Anne Fuchs and Michael Niehaus condone his view by arguing in different ways that Sebald's mode of narration resists appropriating the victim position of the other through identification.[36] Yet readings that acclaim the narrative ethics do not take account of the highly restricted nature of the narrators' identification and the moral values it favours. The melancholy narrators use and direct their satiric comedy to sustain their own elevated perspective on their environment, setting themselves apart from the banal world that is also strongly associated with materiality and the feminine. This melancholy stance is figured in microcosm in the narrator's attraction to Le Strange's eccentric isolation from the world and his strange request for total silence from his housekeeper (RS, 80; Rings, 62). The bizarrely comic request — and the woman is duly rewarded for keeping her mouth shut, so apparently all's well that ends well — actually displays a refusal to engage with another. And the fact that this other is female is crucial for understanding the ethical failure of an unbounded and unchallenged melancholy vision.

Sebald's narrators seek out others with a melancholy perspective who respond to the world as they do, or who, like them, also creatively transform their reality. Their identification with these others is intense, and 'facilitates an exchange of roles and situations which obliterates distinctions between experience and imagination, subject and object'.[37] For the narrator of *Die Ringe des Saturn* such obliteration is so powerful that when he visits Michael Hamburger for the first time, he feels as though he had lived and worked in his house, and he draws attention to the points of similarity between the lives of the two men (RS, 218; Rings, 182–83). In *Die Ausgewanderten*, the narrator visits a Jewish cemetery and identifies with the losses of survivors like Max Aurach as though they are his loss (DA, 337; TE, 224). The narrators repeatedly put themselves into situations that conform to and confirm their perspective, and through a sustained use of targeted satire and ridicule they construct a privileged group of sufferers, whose exceptional, never mundane, stories relate them to the sweep of world history and its sensitive cultural and social elite. The 'clear moral makeup' of the narrators is considerably less clear when its hierarchy of value is exposed: by identifying themselves with the privileged group of melancholy sufferers, the narrators bestow upon themselves the positive aura of Freud's 'keener eye for the truth', which depends fundamentally on disregarding women and the masses.[38] They assume and affirm the heightened sensitivity associated with melancholy, thereby signalling that they are equal to the narration of the history of destruction that is modernity and lending 'a sense of moral greatness to the task of working through the past'.[39]

Furthermore, the 'layers of hearsay' that are central to the narrators' tact, facilitate a movement by which they can assume the voices of those with whom they identify, for there is 'not a great deal of difference between all of these voices'.[40] The mirroring of the narrators' melancholy in the melancholy narratives of others extends to the mirroring of the author with his narrator and the protagonist, and is visually re-enforced by the ghostly reflection of Sebald in the window of the antique shop in Terezín, even though Austerlitz is said to be the photographer (*A*, 280; *AusE*, 276). Here, in a powerful image in which mirroring is demonstrated literally, both the authorial self and the narrator are conflated with Austerlitz. The image serves as a microcosm of how the narrators' melancholy becomes parasitic upon the melancholy of others: their actual loss becomes his fantasy of loss. As Niehaus points out in relation to Austerlitz, he 'can, by standing in for the first person narrator, achieve what the narrator is denied'.[41] This confluence of male bodies, voices, and emotion undermines notions that the 'brotherly homoerotics [...] allow for the possibility of encounters with the other'.[42] Far from recognizing alterity, the narrators' assertion of their melancholy worldview relies upon their systematic construction of the female, material world as other and beyond empathy.

Crucially too, the feminized material world is held up as lacking in the face of the fascinated gaze upon the lost past. Through a melancholy lens the lost past is constructed as a time against which the present is measured. As Sebald remarked, 'the past, horrendous though it is, with all its calamitous episodes, nevertheless seems to be some kind of refuge'.[43] Melancholy is intertwined, therefore, with a process of idealization, of 'believing in a world that is elsewhere, in a place to which one can withdraw in solitude to safeguard the precious core of one's being'.[44] Through idealization, the melancholy narrators becomes moral arbiters who present the past as a seductive, though indeterminate, escape, implying that there was once a time when authentic individuality was possible. Measured against this time, both the present and the future can only be found wanting, and the narrators are then themselves also implicated in the inadequacy of the present, never able to live up to the moral demands the past makes upon them. Thus the narrator of *Die Ausgewanderten* describes his writing as a labour: 'ein äußerst mühevolles, oft stunden- und tagelang nicht vom Fleck kommendes [...] Unternehmen' ('It was an arduous task. Often I could not get on for hours or days at a time') (*DA*, 344; *TE*, 230). Yet the harder he works, the more his scruples grow that his writing does not do justice to the past. He is as though 'enslave[d] [...] to a force or measure to which [he] can never quite measure up and to which [he] is compelled to sacrifice [his] efforts and pleasure in an attempt to do so'.[45]

In this respect, the fact that the narrators, and Sebald, feel indebted to the unattainable measure of an indeterminate yet idealized past, the narrators differ from the hysteric, who also sets herself apart from the world, but who does so by herself assuming the position of superego. The comparison with the position of the hysteric is not incidental, however, since the narrators' debasement of a present that falls short of the fantasy of a more authentic past has parallels to that of the hysteric: both are outside observers of a world which is insufficient and from which they withdraw. The narrators, like the hysteric, frequently manifest physical symptoms of the debased world: in *Schwindel. Gefühle*, for example, the narrator lies immobile in bed for two days, and suffers vertigo attacks and nausea, as does the narrator in *Die Ringe des Saturns*. Indeed, this text begins with his reference to 'das lähmende Grauen' ('the paralysing horror') that he felt when faced with the long history of destruction that he frequently witnessed on his walk (*RS*, 11; *Rings*, 3). The proximity of the narrators' position to that of the hysteric presents the danger of slippage from a melancholic sensibility, associated as it is with a masculine sensitivity that finds cultural sanction through its association with genius, into the socially despised figure of the feminine hysteric.[46] Thus from the outset the narrator of *Die Ringe des Saturn* is careful to link certain physical and spiritual illnesses with the sign of Saturn and hence with melancholia. This is typical of the narrators' general anxiety to guard against any such slippage, and they hold at bay any hints at or incursions of the hysterical and the feminine body, not least through their deployment of satire. The moral claim underpinning the notion of tact is inseparable from this motivation, for the worry about 'gushes of emotion' also functions as a defence against the drift into melodrama.

The melancholy disposition of the narrators sustains a moral universe in which the past becomes the measure against which to berate the present, and in which the process of idealization and its fantasy of coherence depends upon constructing the feminized, material world of modernity as abject. However, the very fear of slippage from tactful melancholy into emotional melodrama is itself suggestive of a tendency towards excess that runs through the prose works. For all that the narrators experience the anguish of loss and responsibility towards victims, in their aesthetic transformation of that experience their melancholy assumes a hyperbolic intensity that betrays their pleasure in comedy. It becomes evident that the narrators craft their narratives in such a way that the funny side of a dreadful event may emerge in its representation, including their own suffering. The comedy of melancholy excess, becoming almost melodramatic at times, ironizes the narrators' own melancholy identifications, and points to a very different way in which the ethical thrust of the texts may be understood: the pleasure in narration itself.

Pleasure and Sublimation

The evident pleasure the narrators take in comic representation makes explicit the more general pleasure they derive from aesthetic transformation, humorous or not. The comic moments magnify a tension that is discernible in the books more generally. On the one hand is the persona of the narrator, whose melancholy knows no bounds, who is burdened by a world of suffering and decline, and for whom writing is a task of mourning a lost past. On the other is the narrator who in his melancholy aesthetic incorporates and reveals the comic excess of the experience of melancholy solipsism and thereby imposes a limit upon it. In the process of transforming experience into representation, the world is cast into mesmerizing and often humorous prose, and writing becomes more than a process of mourning loss. At this level of the texts we see the love of constructing complex representations through text and image, the delight in language, and the play of perspectives. And it is this level that produces the powerful pleasurable effect of the prose, a pleasure that is not sought from melancholy identifications but from writing itself, the here and now from which past events are remembered, structured, enjoyed, and from which coincidences are constructed, evidence is deployed, and slippages played with. If in

Sebald's prose an unironized melancholy sensibility nourishes, and is nourished by, a moral universe whose values are constructed and maintained through processes of idealization, the pleasure attaching to narration itself points to a very different ethical realm: that of sublimation. As Joan Copjec argues, sublimation is the satisfaction that the drive takes in the object: it 'does not finish [...] easily with its object, but keeps turning around it'; it does not idealize by aiming 'beyond the ordinary object at the satisfaction to be attained on the other or thither side of it'. So whereas idealization involves 'the representation [...] of a noumenal beyond' against which the object can only be found wanting, sublimation results in a *'changing of the object itself'*.[47]

The fascination of the drive with its object, the element of compulsion entailed in circling it, is reflected in the quality of impersonal compulsion that is characteristic of Sebald's work. The author commented of his own writing that 'I never thought it would take over, but you write one thing, and then you feel compelled to write another. It's a kind of compulsive disorder. Writing is quite painful'.[48] He also referred to writing as 'devotional work. Obsessive'.[49] This trait of being driven to write is also discernible in the narrators' references to their own practice. In *Austerlitz* the narrator briefly fantasizes about the salvation that would come with premature blindness, for he would be freed from the compulsion to read and write (*A*, 52; *AusE*, 48). It is a compulsion that is evident in the attempts to take photographs, themselves an integral part of the creative drive, and taken to extremes in *Schwindel. Gefühle*. It manifests itself too in what Jan Ceuppens sees as Sebald's furious will to describe, which is clearly illustrated in the prose works' fascinating and irritating love of, or obsession with, detail.[50] Ceuppens cites numerous examples: in *Die Ausgewanderten* the vegetables in Selwyn's garden, the items for sale in the Bereyter family's emporium, the holy and philanthropic buildings in Jerusalem; in *Austerlitz* the list of animal and street names; and in *Die Ringe des Saturn* the place names. The narrators' compulsion, their devotional work a reflection of Sebald's own, is testament to their love for language itself, the satisfaction it offers in all its immediacy, ranging from its potential for complex play through to the lists that exert huge fascination for the narrators but may induce boredom for the reader.[51]

The satisfaction taken in the object is just as much in evidence in the photographs and images included in the texts. Alongside the function of photographs to act as a form of testimony to the past and to help in the moral task of mourning, they are also testament to the narrators' devotion to the play of representation. Alongside the complex functions and meanings of the images, they also very powerfully evoke the concrete and physical properties of what they depict.[52] The haptic quality of many of the photographs draws attention to the centrality of the depicted object over and above the generation of particular meaning. The texture, density, and consistency of the objects become almost tangible, so in the very first sequence of photographs in *Austerlitz*, our attention is not limited to the gaze of the animal and human eyes. The four faces out of which they stare are just as noticeable, and our eyes are drawn to the lustre of the animal hair and the lined surface of the men's ageing skin. Many of the photographs in Sebald's texts are not of people but of things or places, and here, too, the surface qualities of objects, their grain and mass, are emphasized.

Indeed, a vivid sense of space is conveyed precisely because the texture of what is depicted elicits the feeling that the viewer can touch it and so enter into that space, such as the files and papers in Austerlitz's room, the sodden London mud with its uncovered skeletons (*A*, 47 & 189; *AusE*, 43 & 185), the oily Manchester canal (*DA*, 235; *TE*, 159), the bird in its cage (*RS*, 50; *Rings*, 37), or the derelict house (*SG*, 51; *V*, 44).

Many of the photographs represent the 'thingness' of the object they depict or the tangibility of a space, transforming the objects into things of value. So where Silke Horstkotte rightly criticizes certain critics for their 'mistaken understanding of the photograph as reference to the real',[53] understood as empirical reality, it is nevertheless possible to see in the photographs the effect of a very different real whereby the objects are 'elevated to the dignity of the Thing' by the very action of the drive itself.[54] Crucially, however, Horstkotte also points to the fact that 'Sebald's photos may be understood as pictures *of* photographs that *quote* the original photograph. Hence, we are never dealing with actual photographs [...] but always with representations *of* photographs'.[55] This adds a further layer of transformation: not only do we see in the photographs the narrators' fascination with the objects they depict, we see that photographs too are such objects of fascination. It is a fascination that is not limited to type: we are presented with photographs of paintings, of objects, including different types of text, of people, and of spaces. And, as has been widely observed, the photographs are not exceptional in style or quality, for most are ordinary snapshots. Finally, the provenance of the photographs is insignificant: we do not necessarily know who took them, whether or not they relate to what is described in the text, or how the narrators found them. Yet it is precisely their normality, even in some cases banality, that signals the narrators' compulsive enjoyment.

The narrators' love of photographs as such, and the subsequent inclusion of very varied images, opens up an ethical space that, like moments of comedy, eludes the constructions of the solipsistic melancholy narrator. Undoubtedly the photographs can be subsumed within his unbounded melancholy sensibility, but they also bespeak a dynamic world that does not necessarily conform to his patterns of identification and judgement. We see Aunt Theres smiling, sitting with others around a table enjoying an event (*DA*, 104; *TE*, 71); we see a humdrum receipt for a pizza meal rather than a record of a terrifying encounter (*SG*, 90; *V*, 79); rather than a Jewish victim, we see a driver in the Wehrmacht who successfully contributed to the German war effort for six years and survived (*DA*, 82; *TE*, 55); we see homes of various shapes and sizes, including the terraced houses of Lowestoft, that may evoke familiarity and homeliness rather than alienation (*RS*, 55; *Rings*, 41). The dilapidated carpet shop in The Hague might, for many inner-city urban dwellers, conjure an association of cultural vibrancy rather than serve as an image of decline (*RS*, 100; *Rings*, 81). The dam across the Danube appears an impressive piece of engineering (*SG*, 49; *V*, 42), whereas the pictures (as well as the description) of the encroaching piles of papers point to defensive battlements erected against the world by intellectuals rather than any academic engagement with and intervention in the world (*RS*, 18 & 219; *Rings*, 8 & 184; *A*, 47; *AusE*, 43).

The satisfaction that the narrators derive from language and photography emancipates them from an ethics in the service of 'fear and pity'. These, as Copjec argues, are 'those emotions that facilitate our subservience to the superego and the imaginary ideals it sets up in order to berate us with our shortcomings'.[56] It is the purging of fear and pity through sublimation that gives the narrators the freedom, in Sebald's words, to 'arrange coincidences retrospectively', through 'sleight of hand',[57] and which, put provocatively, offers each narrator the freedom to be 'an accomplished liar'.[58] This is no longer the moral universe of narrators constrained by unlimited melancholy, evoking an unattainable beyond, but of those whose love of representation through language and image offers satisfaction in the present. That love also offers them the freedom to transform the experience of unlimited melancholy into aesthetic hyperbole, which, through its comic excess, imposes a critical limit. It is at this level of the texts that the narrators evade, even if only temporarily, the 'rigorous program of critical self-observation at all times, a constant splitting of the self into ever more policed parts'.[59] The tension between the two ethical paradigms is not resolved, and Sebald was himself unable to reconcile the two, seeing pleasure and moral obligation as contradictory. Thus he insisted that people in old photographs have an 'appellative presence'[60] and repeatedly acknowledged his sense of moral debt to the past, a stance that entailed deep suspicion of his own satisfaction: 'even when you do produce a passage which you feel is quite good, you feel like a swindler at that moment, because you get a sense of gratification, of having pulled something off'.[61] But the swindle being perpetuated here, and one which Sebald falls victim to, is the one in which the moral duty of care becomes the evaluating lens through which the love of writing and the satisfaction it provides is cast as a guilty pleasure and its ethical significance is denied.

The tension between the moral outlook sustained by an unbounded and unironized melancholy sensibility and idealization, and the ethical importance of 'gratification', to use Sebald's term, is not resolved in the texts. However, the comic dimensions of Sebald's works that are not limited to the tendentiousness of the melancholy narrators, but which, broadly speaking, can be described as relating to the pleasures of play, language and narration, serve a vital function in exposing that tension and the moral expectations implicit to it. The non-tendentious comedy reveals the moral limitations attached to the 'appellative presence' of the past. It also points to the ethical importance of the freedom the narrators take from their love of and delight in language, narration itself, and image, which enables them to intervene, through writing, in the present. Comedy, as part of the amorous relation to language, is key to the narrators' ability to transform lived experience into mediated experience, or, to use Walter Benjamin's terms, to move from *Erlebnis* into *Erfahrung*, 'the sense of a wisdom drawn and communicated from experience'.[62] The enunciating narrators, on those occasions where they aestheticize their melancholy experience into melancholy excess, demonstrate the potential of ethical comedy: while maintaining the acknowledgment of suffering, their comic excess opens the possibility of a range of emotional responses to that suffering, not its replication. This transformation counters the restrictions of the super-ego. For this reason the enunciating narrators are not subject to the same self-censorship as the emoting narrators, for their prose is driven by more than idealization and the moral duty of care. So far from conforming to the view that comedy entails rising above emotion and passion, Sebald's comedy suggests that the freedom to invest and intervene in the present is in fact derived from passion, the transformative passion of sublimation. Nevertheless, the fact that there is no consistency to the presence of comedy in the four prose fiction texts, that in *Die Ausgewanderten* and *Austerlitz* there is noticeably less comedy, means that in these two texts the seduction of an unrestrained and narcissistic melancholy and its apparent moral superiority, becomes all the stronger.

Notes to Chapter 3

1. W. G. Sebald, *Die Ringe des Saturn* (Frankfurt a.M.: Fischer, 2007), p. 61. All further references will be given in parenthesis with the abbreviation *RS*. *The Rings of Saturn*, trans. by Michael Hulse (London: Harvill, 1998), p. 45. All further references will be given with the abbreviation *Rings*.
2. Ruth Klüger, 'Wanderer zwischen falschen Leben: Über W. G. Sebald', in *Text + Kritik*, 158 (2003), 95–102 (p. 96).
3. See J. J. Long, *W. G. Sebald: Image, Archive, Modernity* (Edinburgh: Edinburgh University Press, 2007), pp. 15–16.
4. W. G. Sebald, interview with Andrea Köhler, 'Katastrophe mit Zuschauer', *Neue Zürcher Zeitung*, 22 November 1997, p. 52.
5. See, for instance, Sebald's interview with Sigrid Löffler, '"Wildes Denken": Gespräch mit W. G. Sebald', in Franz Loquai, *W. G. Sebald* (Eggingen: Edition Isele, 1997), pp. 135–37.
6. Cosgrove, *Born Under Auschwitz*, p. 7.
7. Ricoeur, pp. 68–80; LaCapra, *Writing History, Writing Trauma*, p. 23. See also LaCapra's *History and its Limits*, p. 63. Here LaCapra confirms the view that melancholy is like 'the affect or "feel" of aporia and absolute paradox', but while he argues that it may 'block any significant [...] working through traumatic symptoms, however hesitant, limited, or self-critical', he also sees the positive benefits of melancholy in that it 'prevents closure or turning the page of the past'.
8. Cosgrove, *Born Under Auschwitz*, p. 22.
9. Ibid., p. 151.
10. Maya Barzilai, 'Melancholia as World History: W. G. Sebald's Rewriting of Hegel in *Die Ringe des Saturn*', in *W. G. Sebald and the Writing of History*, ed. by Anne Fuchs and J. J. Long (Würzburg: Königshausen & Neumann, 2007), pp. 73–89 (p. 87).
11. Ibid., p. 88.
12. Maya Barzilai, 'Facing the Past and the Female Spectre in W. G. Sebald's *The Emigrants*', in *W. G. Sebald — A Critical Companion*, ed. by J. J. Long and Anne Whitehead (Edinburgh: Edinburgh University Press, 2004), pp. 203–16 (p. 215).
13. W. G. Sebald, *Schwindel. Gefühle* (Frankfurt, a.M.: Fischer, 2009), p. 111. All further references will be given in parenthesis with the abbreviation *SG*. *Vertigo*, trans. by Michael Hulse (London: Vintage, 2002), p. 97. All references will be given with the abbreviation *V*.
14. W. G. Sebald, *Die Ausgewanderten* (Frankfurt, a.M.: Fischer, 2008), pp. 11 & 153. All further references will be given in parenthesis with the abbreviation *DA*. *The Emigrants*, trans. by Michael Hulse (London: Harvill, 1997), pp. 6 & 105. All references will be given with the abbreviation *TE*.
15. For a list of bomber serial numbers and their fates see <http://www.joebaugher.com/usaf_serials/1942_4.html> [accessed 17 October 2014]. 'Big Dick II' and 'Lady Lorelei' are listed under 42–76119/76364 and 42–74615/74964 respectively.
16. The translation offers 'black inspector', but the point of her being 'dark' is that the same adjective is used to describe the ominous 'dunkle Vorhalle' [dark ticket hall] of which she seems to be a guardian.

17. W. G. Sebald, *Austerlitz* (Munich: Süddeutsche Zeitung/Bibliothek, 2008), p. 90. All references will be given in parenthesis with the abbreviation *A*. *Austerlitz*, trans. by Anthea Bell (London: Hamish Hamilton, 2001), p. 86. All references will be given with the abbreviation *AusE*. For a full discussion of this scene and its implications for understanding touch in *Austerlitz*, see my article, '"Er gab mir, was äußerst ungewöhnlich war, zum Abschied die Hand": Touch and Tact in W. G. Sebald's *Die Ausgewanderten* and *Austerlitz*', *Journal of European Studies*, 41, 3–4 (2011), 359–75.
18. Bachmann, *Wir müssen wahre Sätze finden*, p. 98.
19. This visual joke is not reproduced in the translation.
20. Richard Sheppard, 'Dexter — Sinister: Some Observations on Decrypting the Morse Code in the work of W. G. Sebald', *Journal of European Studies*, 35 (2005), 419–63 (p. 428).
21. Bram Stoker, *Dracula* (London: Penguin, 2003), p. 69.
22. Deane Blackler, *Reading W. G. Sebald: Adventure and Disobedience* (Rochester, NY: Camden House, 2007), p. 148.
23. Ibid.
24. Cosgrove, *Born Under Auschwitz*, p. 151. Greg Bond fails to recognize the humour that attaches to the melancholic narrator, content to understand the comedy arising out of the melancholic tone as 'involuntary', a 'stylistic faux pas' resulting from the narrative insistence on sustaining the melancholic gaze 'at all costs'. See his article 'On the Misery of Nature and the Nature of Misery: W. G. Sebald's Landscapes', in *W. G. Sebald — A Critical Companion*, ed. by Long & Whitehead, pp. 31–44 (p. 40).
25. Alenka Zupancic, *The Odd One In: On Comedy* (Cambridge, MA: MIT Press, 2008), p. 29.
26. Ibid., p. 31.
27. Ibid., p. 32.
28. Mary Cosgrove, 'The Anxiety of German Influence: Affiliation, Rejection, and Jewish Identity in W. G. Sebald's Work', in *German Memory Contests: The Quest for Identity in Literature, Film, and Discourse Since 1990*, ed. by Anne Fuchs and others (Rochester, NY: Camden House, 2006), pp. 229–52 (p. 243).
29. The German specifically invokes the notion of excess by referring to Marie's 'Sinn für alles ins Komische überzogene' [sense for comic exaggeration]. This is missing from the English translation, which refers to 'her strong sense of the comical'.
30. Cosgrove, 'The Anxiety of German Influence', p. 243.
31. Sometimes the defensive layer is threefold: 'sagte Věra zu mir, sagte Austerlitz' ('Vera told me, said Austerlitz') (*A*, 246; *AusE*, 242).
32. W. G. Sebald, interview with Kenneth Baker, 'Up Against Historical Amnesia', *San Francisco Chronicle* 235, 7 October 2001, R2.
33. W. G. Sebald, interview with Toby Green (1999), <http://www.amazon.co.uk/gp/feature.html?ie=UTF8&docId=21586> [accessed 13 May 2013].
34. LaCapra, *History and its Limits*, p. 65.
35. Ibid., pp. 64 & 65.
36. See Michael Niehaus, 'Sebald's Scourges', in *W. G. Sebald and the Writing of History*, ed. by Fuchs & Long, pp. 45–57 (p. 57), where he argues that the narrator 'does not place himself on the same level as the victims' even if he is 'infected' by catastrophe. See also Anne Fuchs, *Die Schmerzenspuren der Geschichte: Zur Poetik der Erinnerung in W. G. Sebalds Prosa* (Cologne: Böhlau, 2004), p. 32. Here she describes Sebald's project as one which does not solely tell the repressed stories of his protagonists but which also articulates the difficulty of mediating their experiences. 'Der mittels solcher Techniken produzierte selbstreflexive Diskurs lotet den Abstand zwischen Selbst und Anderem genauestens aus, um so die zuvor thematisierte Identifikation des Ich-Erzählers mit den Protagonisten von vornherein zu unterlaufen'.
37. Peter Morgan, 'The Sign of Saturn: Melancholy, Homelessness and Apocalypse in W. G. Sebald's Prose Narrative', *German Life and Letters*, 58, 1 (2005), 75–92 (p. 80).
38. Freud, 'Mourning and Melancholia', p. 200.
39. Cosgrove, *Born Under Auschwitz*, p. 11.
40. John Cook, 'Lost in Translation? A Conversation with John Cook', in *Saturn's Moons: W. G. Sebald — A Handbook*, ed. by Jo Catlin and Richard Hibbitt (Oxford: Legenda, 2011), pp. 357–64 (p. 363).

41. Michael Niehaus, 'W. G. Sebalds sentimentalische Dichtung', in *W. G. Sebald: Politische Archäologie und melancholische Bastelei*, ed. by Michael Niehaus and Claudia Öhlschläger (Berlin: Erich Schmidt, 2006), pp. 173–87 (p. 186).
42. Helen Finch, *Sebald's Bachelors: Queer Resistance and the Unconforming Life* (London: Legenda, 2013), p. 130.
43. W. G. Sebald, interview with Michaël Zeeman, in *W. G. Sebald: History, Memory, Trauma*, ed. by Scott Denham and Mark McCulloh (Berlin: de Gruyter, 2006), pp. 21–29 (p. 23).
44. Copjec, *Imagine There's No Woman*, p. 77.
45. Ibid., p. 126.
46. See Schiesari, *The Gendering of Melancholia*.
47. Copjec, *Imagine There's No Woman*, pp. 38, 39.
48. W. G. Sebald, interview with Susan Salter Reynolds, 24 October 2001, *Los Angeles Times*, <http://articles.latimes.com/2001/oct/24/news/cl-60893/4> [accessed 28 April 2011].
49. W. G. Sebald, interview with Arthur Lubow, August 2001, quoted in Blackler, p. 91.
50. Jan Ceuppens, 'Realia. Konstellationen bei Benjamin, Barthes, Lacan — und Sebald', in *W. G. Sebald: Politische Archäologie und melancholische Bastelei*, ed. by Niehaus & Öhlschläger, pp. 241–58 (pp. 242, 241).
51. See Iris Denneler, *Von Namen und Dingen: Erkundungen zur Rolle des Ich in der Literatur am Beispiel von Ingeborg Bachmann, Peter Bichsel, Max Frisch, Gottfried Keller, Heinrich von Kleist, Arthur Schnitzler, Frank Wedekind, Vladimir Nabokov und W. G. Sebald* (Würzburg: Königshausen & Neumann, 2001), p. 151.
52. For the function of images in Sebald's prose texts, their relationship to the narrative and to the work of mourning and their ambivalent relationship to reality, see particularly: Carolin Duttlinger, 'Traumatic Photographs: Remembrance and the Technical Media', in *W. G. Sebald and the Writing of History*, ed. by Fuchs & Long, pp. 155–71; Silke Horstkotte, 'Photo-Text Topographies: Photography and the Representation of Space in W. G. Sebald and Monika Maron', *Poetics Today*, (Spring 2008), 49–78; and Jonathan J. Long, 'History, Narrative, and Photography in W. G. Sebald's *Die Ausgewanderten*', *Modern Language Review*, 98, 1 (2003), 118–37.
53. Horstkotte, p. 53.
54. Lacan, *The Ethics of Psychoanalysis*, p. 112.
55. Horstkotte, p. 54–55.
56. Copjec, *Imagine There's No Woman*, p. 8–9.
57. W. G. Sebald, interview with Zeeman, p. 26.
58. W. G. Sebald, interview with Maya Jaggi, in 'Recovered Memories', *The Guardian*, 22 September 2001, at <http://www.theguardian.com/books/2001/sep/22/artsandhumanities.highereducation> [accessed 16 October 2014].
59. Cosgrove, 'The Anxiety of German Influence', p. 239.
60. Steve Wasserman, 'In this distant place: A conversation with Steve Wasserman', in Catling and Hibbitt, pp. 365–76 (p. 367).
61. W. G. Sebald, interview with Toby Green.
62. David S. Ferris, *The Cambridge Introduction to Walter Benjamin* (Cambridge: Cambridge University Press, 2008), p. 111.

CHAPTER 4

Volker Koepp and Reinhard Jirgl: Comedy and Monologic Histories

The works of the author Reinhard Jirgl and the documentary filmmaker Volker Koepp display a strong interest in the *Ostgebiete* and the longer span of history within which events and movements of peoples have taken place. The Eastern Territories, those areas that before 1945 were part of Greater Germany, including West and East Prussia and Pomerania, are areas that experienced the extreme violence of war, persecution, and genocide. The artists explicitly present these areas both as having a long history of conflicts as well as being places where different ethnic groups lived alongside each other over centuries. Albeit in very different ways, their work constantly alludes to the deep legacy of suffering left by the violence of the Second World War and the Cold War. Their concern with the *Ostgebiete*, as well as with Eastern Germany, straddles their personal histories and wider discussions around migration, German suffering, and national identity. Jirgl was born in Salzwedel in 1953, the grandson of German expellees from the Sudetenland. Koepp was born in Stettin, now Szczecin, in 1944, and fled westward with his mother, settling and growing up in East Berlin. Both concur that the *Wende* of 1989 led to new opportunities for exploring the history of the areas. Jirgl refers to the opening of archives post-1989 as crucial for enabling literature to populate the narrative gaps of history without perpetuating *ressentiment* and accusations of guilt.[1] Koepp describes his greater psychological openness to the East following the fall of the Berlin Wall, as well as the freedom to travel to areas that had been inaccessible even from the German Democratic Republic (GDR).[2]

Yet the reunification of Germany in 1990 has provoked questions about the nature of German national identity and Germany's place in relation to its past as well as its position within the expanding European Union. As Helmut Schmitz writes, 'any new German identity would have to confront anew the legacy of National Socialism and the question as to what place the period of the Third Reich and the Holocaust should occupy in the self-image of the new Germany'.[3] Jirgl's hope that patterns of mutual suspicion and recrimination might be broken seems optimistic in view of the vexed legacy of the Third Reich. This legacy is particularly fraught in relation to the *Ostgebiete* because these areas particularly are associated with German suffering and victimhood. The mass migration of up to fifteen million ethnic Germans at the end of the war, including those who were expelled from land East of the Oder and

Neisse rivers, have made these territories central to German narratives of violence, trauma and loss.[4] Before 1989 these narratives were particularly prevalent in West Germany, where the *Bund der Vertriebenen* used the violent losses as justification for restitution claims. Although the influence of expellee groups in the FRG declined from the 1960s, not least because of increased affluence and generational changes, they continued to exert pressure on the Christian Democratic Union (CDU) and the Christian Social Union of Bavaria (CSU) for territorial revisions.[5] In the GDR the 'Umsiedler' problem was declared solved by the early 1950s[6] and there was strict repression of discussion of the Oder-Neisse line.[7] Here, as in the FRG, narratives of suffering were moulded by Cold War allegiances, and the focus for German suffering was on the allied bombings, perpetrated largely by the USA and Britain, rather than on the flight and expulsions in the East in which the Soviet Union was a key agent.[8]

Following reunification and the formal confirmation of the Polish-German border in 1990–91, the potential for land revisions was nullified. Nevertheless, expellee lobbying continued to have an effect on relations with Germany's neighbours: the *Sudetendeutscher Heimatbund* intervened to delay the final Declaration on Reconciliation in 1997 between Germans and Czechs, and Polish fears about land acquisition in former German territories persisted even as Poland entered the EU.[9] Yet arguably more significant than any political concessions achieved by the *BdV* was their emphasis on suffering, for this was key to the expellees' identity and consolidated their status as victims. They were thus vital in contributing to the more widespread 'rhetorics of victimisation' that informed West German national identity.[10] And in the reunified Germany too, the experience of expulsion provided a common German narrative of suffering which could easily slip into narratives of victimhood that avoided issues of responsibility.[11] Representations of German war suffering, including the experience of traumatic violence, therefore raise acute questions: how far do they invite critical consideration of the relationship between suffering and victimhood? How far is suffering emotionally and morally privileged at the cost of analysis? And how far can the acknowledgment of suffering facilitate a notion of German-ness that, by being freed from the right-wing instrumentalization of victim discourses, can become less rigid in its definitions of German identity?

Jirgl's *Die Stille* and Koepp's documentaries offer an interesting contribution to debates around suffering and responsibility. Their approaches to the past are fundamentally different: the one is a novel writer, drawing self-consciously on avant-garde techniques and misanthropic in tone; the other a documentary filmmaker, using oral history techniques and humanist in his outlook. In both men's work, unlike the works explored in previous chapters, comic devices do not form part of a self-reflexive or critical tension. Rather, they are deployed to consolidate the wider textual strategy in each case. In Jirgl's novel, they confirm the view that war and abusive power relationships are the norm, for *Schadenfreude* is the prevalent comic mode. In contrast, in Koepp's work the comic aspects of his presentation are gentle, kindly even. They help construct a moral universe within which the victims of traumatic experiences, whatever the context, become virtuous by embodying the possibility of reconciliation. Koepp's benevolent humour, when seen in contrast with the ruthlessness of Jirgl's *Schadenfreude*, points to the significance of genre when considering the ethical impact of comedy: can documentary film that explores the real impact of suffering and loss afford to ridicule its subjects or take pleasure in their suffering?

Reinhard Jirgl

In *Die Stille*, Henry Schneidereit's face contorts with bitterness over the perceived neglect by his son Wilhelm, contortions which provoke a particular type of comedy: 'grause Komik [...], wie der Anblick von Krieg's & anderen Krüppeln mit zerschlagenem Leib, wenn sie humpelnd & wackelnd & schlenkernd durch die Straßen sich entlangraupen' [cruel comedy, like the sight of war & other cripples with shattered bodies when they caterpillar their way along the streets, hobbling & wobbling & swinging].[12] The comedy generated here is firmly on the side of the observer, who sees the grotesque physical results of suffering and violence. The combination of horror and the grotesque contortions of pain, with comedy, concentrates disquiet about our enjoyment at the pain of others. Although we are told that the observer would not want to laugh at Henry and by implication at the 'cripples', the very choice of word points to a fundamental lack of empathy between the observer and those suffering. The enjoyment of the comedy thus becomes an undiluted form of *Schadenfreude*, which is not surprising given Jirgl's stated aim: 'das in den sozialen und mentalen Wirklichkeiten bestehende Unrecht zu benennen, zuzuspitzen, um es zu verneinen!' [to name and intensify the very real social and mental injustice that exists in order to negate it!]. He defends himself against accusations that his works are gloomy and pessimistic by laying claim to the politics of negation as an aesthetic strategy to effect change in the mind of his readers.[13] Following Jirgl's logic of negation, it is clear that his comedy can be understood as one more vehicle for intensifying both the awareness of injustice and our response to it. Yet when comedy is intertwined with a persistent lack of empathy and *Schadenfreude*, the question arises whether the professed critical aims of negation collapse instead into further disparagement of the object. In this particular example, the cruel comedy triggered by the sight of the disabled might be read positively as drawing our attention to the devastation of war and at the same time making us cognizant of how we ourselves respond to that sight. Within the misanthropic economy of Jirgl's text, however, it might do no more than confirm the narrative perspective that casts 'cripples', along with most other people, as objects of disdain. It is by looking at *Die Stille*, a novel that can be understood as condensing Jirgl's themes and approach hitherto, that this tension will be explored.[14]

Permanent War

Die Stille tells the story of two families, the Baeskes and the Schneidereits, from the late nineteenth century until the present of 2008. The families become linked through the marriage of Friedrich Baeske and Johanna Schneidereit in 1922. The Baeske family stems from the *Niederlausitz*, an area that from 1815 belonged to Brandenburg, and which after 1945 was part of the GDR, with the areas east of the Neisse becoming part of Poland. The Schneidereit family originates from Gumbinnen in East Prussia, which in 1945 was renamed Gusev and became part of the Kaliningrad Exclave. The family histories are intertwined with a broader, largely twentieth-century history of Germany: the two world wars, the division of Germany and unification, but with a particular focus after 1945 on life in the GDR as both the home of the Baeskes and a new home for the refugees from East Prussia. The perspective from which wider and devastating historical events are represented is insistently personal and familial: as Helmut Böttiger remarks, 'den monströsen gesellschaftspolitischen Entwicklungen im Deutschland des 20. Jahrhunderts entspricht das Monströse in den Familien' [the monstrous socio-political developments in twentieth-century Germany correspond to the monstrousness within the families].[15] Events assume significance through their impact on the members of the two families, on their emotional development and material wellbeing. In *Die Stille*, the personal and the familial are inseparable: individuals are always caught up in the power-play of family relations, so wider historical events are mediated through the dynamics of family, and past events continue to have an impact in the present through complex inter-generational relationships.

The importance of the family network for exploring the reverberations of war upon individuals is emphasized through the novel's structure and narrative devices. The book consists of one hundred sections, each of which represents one of the one hundred photographs in a family album. Each section is preceded by a cursory, italicized description of the people in the photographs, place and date, from which we know that the photographs depict individuals and family groupings from both sides of the family dating back to 1914 and continuing to 1980.[16] Although there is a loose association between the dates of the photographs and general time period being treated in the main text, there is no evident connection between a particular photograph and the narrative of the section. Rather, the album is the symbol of a past that cannot be escaped and which looms over and links family members now, even if they wish to escape their inheritance. As it is passed from Felicitas Adam to her brother Georg, from Georg to his son Henry, to his wife Dorothea, and then to the journalist who is investigating Dorothea's life, so too the narrative voice shifts. Each character assumes a key point of view in narrating the family history and their own position in it. However, the point of view of each character is not presented in isolation, for as the album passes between them, it is in conversation with each other that they reconstruct the past. Yet they do so from a position of tension, guilt, and hostility, for the relationships between Felicitas and Georg, Georg and Henry, Henry and Dorothea, are themselves products of a damaging history. And even when not directly in dialogue with each other, their different narrative voices are engaged in internal struggle with each other and with other voices from the past. Here, seeking to understand the past and one's relationship to it offers little hope for change in the present, for the past can only continue to be understood through the prism of relationships determined by it.

In *Die Stille*, as in Jirgl's work generally, relationships, and the individual family members, are burdened by wave upon wave of ghastly incidents and horrendous human behaviour: 'Es geht um Leben und Tod, um beschädigte Identität, um Spielsucht und Inzucht, um Kriege als Vergangenheits-, Gegenwarts- und Zukunftstraumata, um Hassliebe, Mord und Selbsttötung' [It is about life and death, damaged identity, compulsive gambling and inbreeding, war as past, present and future trauma, love-hate, murder and suicide].[17] To give the example of just the central family strand, August Adam, Felicitas and Georg's father, is murdered by his father-in-law and left to die by his brother for inheritance purposes. His widow Theresa kills herself, whereupon Georg and Felicitas are sent to a hellish orphanage, a place where systemic abuse is a pedagogical tool. As adults, Felicitas and Georg have a one-off incestuous encounter that leads to the birth of Henry. Georg, able only to see his son Henry as the embodiment of '*Blutschande u Schmach*' [incest and shame] (*St*, 186), relentlessly torments his son, who becomes a loner and is severely bullied at school. Burdened by his incestuous origins, Henry does not want children and is therefore relieved when his child with Dorothea, conceived in the same bed as he was, is stillborn. Before leaving for the USA in an attempt to escape his family origins, Henry admits to his father that he gave Henriette, his adoptive mother and Georg's wife, the tablets with which she then killed herself. She did this to avoid a painful, inevitable death from heart failure, not knowing that Georg was, the very evening of her suicide, arranging specialist treatment for her. The hatred between the men culminates in Henry hitting his father in a fight, nearly killing him, and he only evades prosecution because Georg refuses to speak to the police. Once in the USA, Henry abandons his job to travel to Alaska, where, in a moment of paranoia, he shoots his companions, believing they wish to kill him. He returns to Dorothea, asks her to shoot him, but dies quickly but painfully of throat cancer anyway. Dorothea, who had been unable to kill her husband, moves to the family house in Thalow with Georg, and in answer to the compulsory purchase of Thalow and its demolition by EL, an international energy corporation, she murders its director.

These are only the terrible experiences of the key contemporary characters. Other members of the family also suffer a litany of awful events, including the lifelong battle against those who make claims on the family house in Thalow, and the attempt to maintain a business in the face of inflation, the crash, the war, the black market, and state ownership. Unrelenting awfulness dominates the lives of all the characters, who even in the domestic realm are embroiled in damaging psycho-sexual relationships and derive no joy from their children. Within the world of *Die Stille*, it makes perfect sense that Dorothea interprets one miscarriage and one stillbirth as an inevitable response to a world of 'Vielschmerz Vieltrauer Demütigungen Heimtücke Verrat Pein Schande & Schmach' [much pain much sorrow humiliations maliciousness betrayal agony disgrace & shame] (*St*, 444). There is very little room in the novel for a more positive response to life, and as one of the key narrators of the families' past, Georg undoubtedly sets the tone here. His misanthropic outlook constructs the world as irredeemably negative, where no period is free from degeneracy and decay (*St*, 47) and where emotions, because of their persistence, are people's cruellest burden (*St*, 86). In his view there is no difference between love and hate (*St*, 285), and Werner Baeske's brave rescue of his wounded friend Wilhelm Schneidereit from no-man's-land is the start of a new type of unbearable illness, for Werner becomes responsible for the rest of Wilhelm's life (*St*, 154). It is no wonder that Henry has similarly corrosive views. For him man is no more than an animal: '& bestenfalls wird er so behandelt, von Seinesgleichen wie von Seinesungleichen' [& at best he's treated like one, by his equals as well as his non-equals] (*St*, 287).

The tone of cynical misanthropy is not limited to the focalization of the characters and thereby relativized. The fiction that the story is being told by key figures is diluted by the similarity of tone and voice, and is frequently undermined by passages that are more akin to conventional third person omniscient narration, hence Katrin Hillgruber's reference to an omniscient narrator.[18] The conventions of omniscient narration are particularly drawn upon in those parts of the novel predating the memories of Georg and Felicitas, where family and national history are described in detail, including characters' emotions and motives. Maintaining the fiction, one might ascribe this level of dense narration to the figure of the journalist who interviews Dorothea in prison and to whom she finally gives the family album. Yet his voice remains marginal, and as a figure who only emerges late in the novel his perspective too is subsumed into the overarching narrative voice that has access to historical detail and to the characters' interiority. The aggressive, misanthropic suffering of the key protagonists of *Die Stille* is thus condoned by being indistinguishable from a narrative voice that embeds the ubiquity of familial abuse within a wider context of all-encompassing historical and political ghastliness.

Thus, although there is undoubtedly a montage of voices in the novel, it is a montage that produces one coherent meaning and which is monologic in tone. The confluence of voices is reinforced by Jirgl's orthographic system, which he uses to produce highly specific meanings. Thus, where and why abbreviation, punctuation, and numbers are employed in his 'alphanumerical code' is clearly set out and included at the end of some of his novels as explanation.[19] For Jirgl, this code is not a rigid system or dogma,[20] but a mutual liberation of numbers and letters from the threat of the other: 'zum einen versucht er, die Vergewaltigung der Zahlen durch die Buchstaben [...] aufzuheben; zum anderen widersetzt er sich (der Hypothese) einer (restlosen) Ablösung der Buchstaben durch den digitalen Code' [on the one hand he is attempting to annul the rape of numbers by letters; on the other hand he is resisting (the hypothesis that) letters (are) being (totally) replaced by digital code].[21] The code is a form of resistance. The play with words and letters causes a shift from the two-dimensionality of the written word to three-dimensional 'Körper-Welten' [body-worlds], which, like the human body, disrupt the totalizing biopolitics of modernity.[22] Nevertheless, it is precisely this emancipatory intention of the code that contributes to and exemplifies the monologic nature of Jirgl's writing. The code is harnessed for Jirgl's express purpose of naming and negating injustice, and far from being associated with a particular perspective, the meta-meaning of the code permeates all textual utterances. This fundamentally limits how far Jirgl's novels can be understood as 'polyphone Stimmen-Montagen' [polyphonic voice-montages].[23] Indeed, the code forms part of a different type of totalizing trajectory in which all individuals' experiences are in the service of and subsumed into a wider critique of modernity. As Erk Grimm points out, the critique is a generalized one, for Jirgl conjures up injustice as something that exists independently of specific identities.[24]

Central to the accusation of pervasive injustice is war. Protagonists and narrator overlap in their monochrome representation of the Moloch of war, which is indiscriminate in whose flesh it consumes: '*Schuldigen Nichtschuldigen Beteiligten Unbeteiligten*' [the guilty, the innocent, those involved, those not involved] (*St*, 34). War is ever-present (*St*, 119), the Second World War is no more than the perpetuation of the First (*St*, 109), the post-war period is a war carried on with different means (*St*, 155), and the need of the defeated to re-assert themselves against the victors means that there will be no end to war (*St*, 195). When states win wars, the masses are always the losers (*St*, 206) and it is the perpetual state of '*Immerkrieg*' [perpetual war] (*St*, 183) that diminishes and humiliates people, and that results in people's indifference to each other: '*weil es nicht der Schmerzen lohnt, an anderen Menschen Seele die eigene Seele zu binden*' [because it is not worth the pain to bind your own soul to the soul of other people] (*St*, 184). Justifications given for war are no more than lies or hypocrisy, and there is little difference between those who support war or peace. Thus those who legitimized the Iraq War are scathingly described as: 'Frieden's Engel in Nobelhotels, [die] Denhunger Daselendderwelt bei Kaviar & Schampanjer "beklagen"' [Angels of Peace in Nobelhotels who 'lament' hunger and themiseryoftheworld with caviar & shampayn] (*St*, 216).

In a world in which war is abstracted as being everywhere, where all wars are similar and there is little to distinguish perpetrators and peacemakers, it is also logical that there should be no difference between states, leaders, and functionaries. In international terms, 'Hitler&stalin' (*St*, 66) are as one in person and their countries are as one in deed: the Polish town of Przemysl is divided between them, the Russians round up and deports citizens on the east side, the Germans do so on the west (*St*, 280). In national terms, the equivalence of the Nazi, the GDR, and the post-*Wende* German States is summarized in the table setting out side-by-side three different correspondence templates for writing to the respective bureaucracy. The templates differ only marginally, for example in the address ('Werter Volksgenosse/Sehr geehrter Genosse/Sehr geehrte(r) Frau (Herr) [Valued National Comrade/Dear Comrade/Dear Sir or Madam]), the valediction ('Heil Hitler!/Mit sozialistischem Gruß!/Mit freundlichen Grüßen' [Heil Hitler!/Best socialist wishes/With kind regards]), and in the significance of the petitioner's request: 'für die Deutsche Volksgemeinschaft und den Endsieg/die sozialistische Volkswirtschaft/die Entwicklung des Wirtschaftandorts Deutschland' [for the German National Community and ultimate victory/for the Socialist Peoples' Economy/for the development of Germany's economic standing] (*St*, 342–44). The equivalence between German States is mirrored in the seamless transition of vindictive village youths into Hitler youths (*St*, 27), and of loan sharks into brown-shirts for whom Nazi membership is another means to exact property (*St*, 33).

Humans Stink: Victims and Empathy

The description of Przemysl is typical of *Die Stille*'s emphasis on how war produces a mass of victims and how these victims are alike, whether these are the hordes in the east of the town, the rows of refugees from the East, or the Poles and Jews in the western area (*St*, 280). Thus Henry Schneidereit's fate of having to flee his home is one he shares with roughly sixty million others (*St*, 13). The fact, to give just one example, that Schneidereit has a family and house he can flee to and Isolde Przemysl, who is Jewish, does not, or that he can exchange one grave for another but that she has no grave in Theresienstadt, is irrelevant. It is precisely this undifferentiated grouping of victims that has led to some critics charging Jirgl with diminishing the responsibility of the Nazis by drawing attention to the suffering of expellees. A particularly clear example of this is the way in which the expulsion of Sudeten Germans from Czechoslovakia is described in *Die Unvollendeten* using language associated with the deportation and genocide of the Jews.[25] These concerns are also relevant to *Die Stille*. Yet the extent to which the portrayal of non-Jewish German suffering is privileged over the suffering of the victims of National Socialism is inseparable from the question of empathy and of who inflicts suffering upon whom.

The dominating negative and cynical tone of the text overall, which reinforces the misanthropic outlook of Georg and Henry, does little to invite empathy with individuals' suffering. Just as in the personal realm abuse and suffering are part of a self-perpetuating cycle of cruelty over generations, so too the violence engendered by suffering is manifested socially. This is particularly evident in the stark portrayal of the destitute expellees. Described as a 'Lumpenkreuzug' [lumpencrusade], the stream of ethnic Germans fleeing westwards is thoroughly depersonalized: 'Ausgelaugt, böse, lauernd, kalkbitter, Todesangst stinkt Wut stinkt Hunger stinkt Krankheiten stinken = Menschen stinken' [exhausted, angry, furtive, chalkbitter, fear of death stinks anger stinks hunger stinks illnesses stink = humans stink] (*St*, 370). Their extreme suffering does not lessen their cruelty to others: the profoundly traumatized woman whose family was shot by soldiers of the Red Army and who was raped many times, quickly becomes a burden. Soon it is the refugees who are beating her and driving her away, and the mothers in particular are concerned about the moral degradation of their children when she compulsively lifts her skirts to put balls of snow between her legs as though to wash herself clean (*St*, 333). Although it is difficult not to feel a degree of pity for this traumatized woman, crucially this is pity for someone who has been reduced to the status of the creaturely: she is finally adopted by a vagrant horse with which she disappears. She has been forced out of the civilized human world of nastiness and self-interest.

The fate of the German refugees from the eastern territories is central to the book and is shown to be extreme. But the hardship and the atrocities suffered by the ethnic Germans are not presented as inflicted or caused only by the allied bombardments or the Red Army. When Henry Schneidereit wishes to flee East Prussia, it is not the Russians who are the problem, but the '*eSeS*' (*St*, 209). Any German trying to leave would be executed by the SS as a traitor or deserter. As the

Germans try to reach the Oder, the SS use violence to prevent them: 'Längst ist das-eigene-Volk=Derfeind' [for a long time now one's-own-people=theenemy] (*St*, 331). Yet it is then the SS who secretly flee at night, leaving the population to panic at the rumours of terrible Russian atrocities. Even though such atrocities are referred to, and their effects shown to be devastating, as we know from the traumatized woman, the focus of the narrative is on what the Germans do to themselves and each other: children are murdered by their mothers, and the women commit suicide or kill each other to escape the Russian threat. The descriptions of mass suicides do little to invite empathy with the women who drown their children, force them to their knees to prepare for hanging, or for the old woman who chases her daughter down the road and axes her to death (*St*, 373).

More generally in *Die Stille* it is Germans who cause the suffering of other Germans. This is evident in abusive familial relations and in the functioning of the state, which systematically exploits its citizens in the exercise of power. The political make-up of the state is irrelevant. Werner Baeske's discharge papers exemplify the humiliation and degradation of the front-soldier by his state by belittling his conduct in the face of extreme experiences as the norm (*St*, 113). Again he is humiliated by the ingratiating functionary of the GDR who attempts to mollify Werner in the process of expropriating his business by claiming that as a refugee from the East he too had everything taken from him (*St*, 348). And after 1989, the EL corporation works with full support of the local and federal government to claim the land and forcibly resettle the local population. Just as the ideological constitution of the state makes no difference to its abuse of its citizens, so too ideology does not play a part in how suffering is experienced. Thus the repeated attempts to expropriate the family house are more central to the characters, and therefore to the book, than the systematic confiscation of Jewish property. Hedwig's defensive war to keep her house is not affected by regime change, and to that extent she is neither for nor against the Nazis. Her resistance to their demands is not ideological or political but visceral (*St*, 199).

Suffering is rigorously, if not rigidly, un-sentimentalized and has no redemptive qualities. Combined with the almost exclusive focus on non-Jewish Germans, this is significant in a number of ways. The depiction of the extreme events and suffering do not serve to fuel an emotionally charged discussion around German victimhood. Suffering is shown without ascribing to those who suffer any moral status, let alone that of innocent victim. Indeed, the experience of extreme events and suffering results in further cruelty towards others. To this extent the text departs fundamentally from the process that Fassin and Rechtman describe, whereby traumatic events and trauma more generally have acquired a 'current status more as a moral than as a psychological category'.[26] Suffering is represented almost callously, and Jirgl thus resists any moral equation of German suffering with the victims of Nazi racial policy. The novel simply does not entertain a view that suffering transforms Germans into innocent victims and thus he resists eliding suffering with victimhood as an ethical position. He thereby also denies the reader any comfort that suffering is redemptive. On the contrary, the cycle of Germans and the German states inflicting suffering on other Germans undermines the notion of collective German suffering on which discourses of German victimhood have thrived.[27] In this reading, the fact that references to the genocide and systematic murder of homosexuals are limited to passing references and near silence leaves open the possibility that innocent victims is precisely what they are.

However, although *Die Stille* discredits the idea of a German collective, it constructs a different, and differently problematic generalization, that of a universal, human collective. In the world of the novel, war and abuse are ubiquitous and, in an irrefutable tautology, all violence is attributable to war and abuse. Dorothea voices Henry's reason for refusing to assume blame for attempting to murder Georg: 'Niemand ist tatsächlich der-Schuldige gewesen außer Der-Ewigen-Feindschaft *Fremder gegen Fremde, doch* Feindschaft *kann niemand anklagen*' [no-one was actually guilty except for *the-eternal-enmity* of strangers against strangers, but no-one can charge enmity] (*St*, 492). Her statement applies equally to the tautology, for the inescapable cycle of war and abuse at once elevates suffering to an existential condition and absolves individuals of their responsibility for perpetuating the abuse. Only the state, as an institution of war, can be blamed, but since all states are the same, blaming the state becomes little more than an exercise in apolitical *ressentiment*. The remorseless totalizing conception of war as a human condition that breeds further abuse and indifference introduces a relativizing lens through which judgement or the analysis of responsibility become impossible. The only clear blame is placed on 'the state', a further abstraction that prevents concrete political analysis and evaluation. Collective guilt has been replaced by collective ghastliness. After all, humans stink.

Just Vengeance

On rare occasions other perspectives challenge the pervasive vicious circle of negativity. Felicitas berates Georg for failing to counter the 'Stachel-des-Bösen' [thorn-of-evil] triggered by their father (*St*, 22), thereby suggesting that there is an alternative to his destructiveness, just as her love for Henry acts as a foil to Georg's hatred of him. Similarly, through Dorothea's eyes we see that Georg's abusive response to Henry is far from inevitable, since incest is common and hardly worth mentioning (*St*, 421). It is also Dorothea who looks after the seriously injured Georg although she does not have a strong relationship to him, who accepts her husband back after his disappearance in the USA, and who finally moves with Georg to the house in Thalow. But these glimpses of how cycles of violence may be interrupted are swamped by the relentless onslaught of terrible behaviour and are rendered futile. Felicitas's attempts to counter Georg's cruelty to Henry cannot prevent his self-loathing, and her hope for reconciliation between them is shattered by Henry's violent assault on his father. In Dorothea's case, it is not her love for Henry, but the simple fact of his death that stops his ongoing hatred: '*Ich hasse euch bloß*' [I just hate you all] (*St*, 489).

Dorothea herself, the character who as 'die Stille' of the title privileges silent acts of love and generosity over talking of the past, and thus seems to offer some hope of redemption, ends by committing murder. She shoots the director of the

EL corporation in protest against the systematic disempowerment and bullying of individuals by corporate and state interests and the compulsory purchase of their land for economic gain. State and industry compound this iniquity by insisting the policy is in those individuals' best interests. Within the context of the systematic abuses of power by the state, Dorothea's act is presented as just. It emerges as a necessary reaction to over a century of family suffering and largely futile struggle against the encroachment of various, indistinguishable authorities. It also follows from the story of the old couple from Rogow who resist money and threats in order to stay in their house. Fighting the case in the courts despite intimidation, and scared even to leave the house after finding their dog dead in their yard, they lose all appeals and are forcibly removed. In view of this story, Dorothea's act of murder becomes an emotionally comprehensible gesture and an example of righteous anger in the face of the cynical steamroller of power. Although she admits that the murder is pointless and childish, she nevertheless justifies it as an act that finally overrides the fear, patience, and compliance that people show to those in power. Since justice does not exist in this world, each individual should themselves pursue '!Sein=Recht' [!His=Right] (*St*, 522).

Yet although we are invited to empathize with Dorothea's act, it remains one of violent revenge. By suggesting that the murder is a gesture of 'die-Rächzflege' [cultivating-rightribution] (*St*, 522), she conflates justice with revenge, and thereby reinforces the inevitability of violent cycles where a violent intervention cannot force change. Interestingly, her view at the end of the book echoes Georg's attitude at the start, when he asserts that every death is a violent death that must be avenged. Death is murder that leads inexorably to the next murder (*St*, 16). Thus Dorothea, by fusing justice not only with revenge but also with the individual's right to impose justice, seems to affirm Georg's understanding of the world. She lends credibility to his misanthropy by adopting a comparable attitude of aggressive contempt: she murders the official 'Weil das einen GOTZVERDAMMTEN SPASS macht, nem Drecksack das Licht auszublasen [...]. Immer=hin: 1 Schweinekerl weniger Aufderwelt' [because it's GODDAMNED FUN to get rid of a dirty bastard. Any=way: 1 filthyswine fewer intheworld] (*St*, 521).[28] Dorothea's pleasure in killing a 'swine' that is deemed by her to be representative of society's ills is once again a moment when history repeats itself in microcosm.

The fact that Dorothea's act fits within the dominant economy of a text in which violence can only breed violence invalidates its claim to be just and therefore ethical. Her act is not an intervention that changes existing structures or ways of understanding, for it reinforces the symbiotic antagonism of state and individual that is already fundamental to how the main protagonists view the world, as well as being a structuring feature of the novel itself. Dorothea's is a gesture through which she eschews politics in favour of violence, which is no more effective than politics is shown to be. It is undoubtedly a gesture that confirms her view of the world as debased, full of 'swines' and the gullible masses, and it also effects her retreat from that world through incarceration. She views justice as something that can only exist in another world (*St*, 522), which makes her claim to be promoting justice disingenuous, and exposes her violence as a rejection of an unchangeable present. And so she joins the ranks of other family members who seek escape from humanity: Henry by fleeing to Alaska and then asking Dorothea to shoot him, Felicitas who withdraws into a convent, and Georg who devotes his time to taking photographs that are devoid of people.

Dorothea's act is also unconvincing as either just or ethical because it cannot even be taken at face value as a reaction to corporate greed. For, conforming to the logic of the text, where violence is a necessary response to previous abusive relationships, she murders as a result of the fundamental antagonism in her marriage to Henry, and, more specifically, her failure to kill him when he asks. The official, as well as being a corporate representative, becomes, in the moment of being shot, a projection of the emotional reality of Dorothea's marriage. In murdering him, Dorothea symbolically kills Henry as he requested, and rids herself of a weak and broken husband who showed her no love. She enacts a fantasy of revenge, imagining a jealous Henry crying out in despair: '*?Was hat 1 popeliger Angestellter, was !ich ?nicht habe*' [?What's 1 pathetic little employee got that !I ?haven't] (*St*, 520).

If Dorothea's fantasy of revenge places her firmly within webs of despair and loathing, the question remains whether the reader's desire for justice is whetted by this imaginary act, thereby achieving Jirgl's aim of eliciting a critical response to injustice in the mind of the reader.[29] Dorothea's refusal to compromise and subsequent exclusion from society might function as a model for ethics in the way that Antigone does, who also asserts her individual and family ethics against the interest of the state. Yet as Frances Restuccia argues, the importance of *Antigone* for understanding ethics does not lie in holding up Antigone's willingness to die as a model of ethics.[30] Restuccia refutes the notion that Antigone exemplifies Lacan's insistence that ethics means not ceding on one's desire. Rather, Antigone manifests pathological *jouissance* and with it 'precisely the acceptance of death', a site where desire cannot thrive but is necessarily extinguished.[31] However, the fact that Antigone regrets the life that she will lose from a position of imminent death reflects desire's relation to death. It is a relationship that must be mediated through the signifier for otherwise it collapses into the *jouissance* of annihilation. The subject must enter the zone of 'those who go crazy through a trance' but she must return, pull out, having gained a sense of what she is not. Otherwise she risks wreaking the destructiveness of martyrs: 'the day when the martyrs are victorious will be the day of universal conflagration. The play is calculated to demonstrate that fact'.[32] Lacan's reference to the play is key, for it is through figures like Antigone that the subject can enter the zone of those who go crazy and retreat. As Restuccia argues, Antigone is not paired by Lacan with the desiring subject, but with the analyst, while the spectator of the play takes up the position of the analysand: 'In the course of the play, her morbid beauty draws out our fascination, as the analyst attracts the analysand; but she vanishes, just as the analyst is eventually exposed as a false love object'. But 'the seeds of desire have been planted'.[33]

Thus, even if Dorothea's violent act is not ethical, the text itself might offer an aesthetically mediated relationship to death. Yet I would argue that it does not. Whereas Antigone values life from the position of imminent death, Dorothea is not herself engaging with death but killing someone else. More broadly the novel, although full of death, depicts characters who exact their anger and despair on others, and who function in the service of the overall textual premise, that life is no more than war. Of course, following the logic of negation, reading a novel that depicts life as systematically horrendous might be akin to entering the zone of those who go mad, from which the reader then retreats with an enriched critical view on life. But Jirgl's writing is so relentlessly monologic, content and form are so systematically in the service of his politics of negation, that the space for the reader to develop a response that is not simply subsumed into that logic, is quashed. If the text, like the analyst, attracts our fascination by '[holding] the place of what cannot be said', then Jirgls's unrelenting aim to change what goes on in the reader's mind effectively fills that place on our behalf.[34]

Schadenfreude

'Ein wesentlicher Grund zum Schreiben von Stücken ist Schadenfreude. Sie ist die Quelle allen Humors, die Freude daran, daß etwas schiefgeht und daß man in der Lage ist, das zu beschreiben' [One of the main reasons for writing plays is *Schadenfreude*. It is the source of all humour, the joy when something goes wrong and one is in the position to describe it].[35] Even if Jirgl does not explicitly share Heiner Müller's motivation for writing, Müller's harsh and somewhat limited view of humour has strong resonances with Jirgl's work. In *Die Stille*, the link between *Schadenfreude* and comedy is glaring. The story of Henry Schneidereit's grave is an early and recurring example. When his wife dies in 1926, he is only sixty-one, but assumes he will die soon and so has his grave dug next to that of his wife. Eighteen years later he abandons the grave to flee west. But in those eighteen years he visits his grave nearly daily, maintains it by jumping in and securing the walls, and by removing the corpses of animals who have drowned in it after heavy rain. He not surprisingly becomes the butt of a children's prank: they remove the ladder from the grave when he is in it, and he is unable to get out. When it starts to rain, the grave slowly starts filling with mud and water, and he fears drowning in his own grave. Suddenly a large clod of earth falls in, and he finds himself staring in horror at the contents of the neighbouring grave: 'So hat er im letzten Dämmerlicht Nachjahren seine "Frau" wiedergesehn' [So after manyyears he saw his 'wife' again in the dusk] (*St*, 208).

This grotesquely funny anecdote is typical of the way humour is generated from death, misfortune, or desperation. Another example is Kommandant Oberst von Sowieso's suicide attempt. Hearing of the wave of German suicides as the Red Army advances, he decides to kill himself too. His first shot to the temple merely grazes the skull. The second shot follows exactly the same trajectory with the same result. Desperate, he throws himself from the top of the building, only to land on the canvas roof of a lorry parked below. The canvas tears, and the force of his falling body kills two soldiers. The Kommandant survives, only to be later arrested by Red Army soldiers in a case of mistaken identity and executed for another person's war crimes (*St*, 374). The hearse with Paul Karge's body is incongruously embroiled in the May Day celebrations, a 'blecherne(s) Mementomori auf Rädern' [a tin mementomori on wheels] (*St*, 112), and the sight of Georg chasing Henry along the path beside the River Main, both men gasping for breath and with an old dog jumping between them, is a comic sight for the group of drug dealers. It is additionally comic for the reader watching the dealers watching the men and knowing that the drug enforcement police are also observing the whole fiasco (*St*, 308). Few people or situations are immune to the scathingly negative observations that function like amusing fairground distorting mirrors. Thus children of ageing parents have something unbecoming about them, as though they are the result either of a '*Verkehr-Unphalls*' [traffic-accident][36] or of a gymnastics routine: '*die Frau nach dem Erguß Unterleib & Beine hoch damit drinbliebe & anschlage was der Herr gesäet*' [the woman with raised lower body & legs after ejaculation in order that what the man soweth should stay within and take effect] (*St*, 242). When Henriette goes to a men's toilet to buy a condom, the obese attendant personifies the misshapen sexual double standards in the GDR: she looks at Henriette with disgust from a face that looks like a Königsberger dumpling swimming in sauce with eyes like capers (*St*, 405).

Such grotesque descriptions give rise to a hostile humour that ruthlessly reduces people to being the butt. The frequent wordplay has the same effect, reinforcing the view that human interaction and motives are self-interested, exploitative, and actually de-humanizing. Thus *finanzieren* [to finance] is the behaviour of animals and becomes 'viehnan-zieren' (*St*, 33), and it is Werner's financial success that allows him entry to the businessmen of Mathildenburg's 'Mülljöh', with *Milieu* transformed into 'Müll' [rubbish] (*St*, 239). With a pun on *Narzisse* [narcissus], Hedwig is described as being '*keine Nazisse*' (*St*, 212), which concisely conveys the self-aggrandizement and self-interest of those in the Nazi party. This is reinforced by the description of people acquiring Nazi membership for economic reasons as acquiring brown life-jackets (*St*, 260). The constant punning throughout the text can be an amusing way of crystalizing criticism, which is why Jirgl sees the *Kalauer* [corny joke] as the common man's Molotov cocktail that disrupts the culturally sanctioned meanings of words.[37] Thus *Ehrgeiz* [ambition] becomes 'ehr-Geiz' (*St*, 11), emphasizing that meaness (*Geiz*) is the main constituent of ambition; and *Fantasien* [fantasies] is transformed into 'Fant-Asien' [fant-asia] (*St*, 24), which exposes a view of fantasy as an immature process of escapism and exoticizing of distant lands. With the aural association of *Fand* with *Pfand* [deposit], fantasy is also brought within the realm of transactions, where the present is paid as a deposit for a future that will not actually materialize.

The *Schadenfreude* and the *Kalauer* are an integral part of Jirgl's strategy of intensifying injustice in order to negate it. Both align the reader with the dissecting and un-empathetic narrative perspective and the extra-diegetic purpose it serves. In Fassbinder's and Sebald's work there are crucial points where the narrator or director is brought into a comic frame. These moments form part of a wider tension within their work that challenges their representational modes and the forms of identification attaching to them. In *Die Stille*, the comic strategies are part of the systematized 'Text-Machart' [text-design] and thus reinforce the dominant, monologic voice.[38] However, having said that, there are strong elements of unintended comedy in the novel, many of which arise out of his orthographic system and use of fonts.

The use of different fonts is part of Jirgl's critical strategy, and his use of gothic typescript allows for far reaching irony. At one level gothic functions as a form of realism, as is the case with Werner Baeske's army reports and discharge letters. At the same time it offers an instant shorthand evocation of the past, like a translation of sepia into font: 'Es gab auch einige Tote: darunter den Bruder jenes Gastwirts [...], sowie [...] Andere, 𝔣𝔢𝔦𝔫𝔢𝔯 𝔷𝔢𝔦𝔱 am Mord unsres Vaters ebenfalls Beteiligte' [There were also some dead, among them the brother of the innkeeper, as well as others who at the time were also involved in the murder of our father] (*St*, 83). The use of gothic also reinforces the text's emphasis on the continuity of the state, whatever the government, so that script of the Wilhelmine period is gothic, just as official notifications under the National Socialists are (*St*, 256). The link of gothic with the state signals moments when official discourse is being quoted, and as with leitmotifs, the appearance of gothic then brings with it the associated critique of state power. It therefore comes as a visual surprise to see John F. Kennedy's slightly adapted words in gothic: '𝔉𝔯𝔞𝔤𝔢 !𝔫𝔦𝔠𝔥𝔱, 𝔴𝔞𝔣 𝔨𝔞𝔫𝔫 𝔡𝔢𝔯-𝔖𝔱𝔞𝔞𝔱 𝔣ü𝔯 !𝔇𝔦𝔠𝔥 𝔱𝔲𝔫; 𝔣𝔯𝔞𝔤𝔢 𝔡𝔦𝔠𝔥, ?𝔴𝔞𝔣 𝔨𝔞𝔫𝔫𝔣𝔱 𝔡𝔲 𝔣ü𝔯 !𝔡𝔢𝔫-𝔖𝔱𝔞𝔞𝔱....𝔱𝔲𝔫' [Ask !not what the-state can do for !you, ask ?what you can do for !the-state] (*St*, 88). Here, gothic signals the exploitation of the apparently democratic US government of its people, and its hypocrisy as a slave-owning nation.

The association of gothic with the voice of those in authority, with official documents and with German-ness, confers a cartoonish quality to its use that elicits unintended humour. When the workers at the orphanage say to Georg, '𝔇𝔢𝔦𝔫𝔢 𝔖𝔱𝔯𝔞𝔣𝔢 𝔦𝔣𝔱 𝔫𝔬𝔠𝔥 𝔩𝔞𝔫𝔤𝔢 !𝔫𝔦𝔠𝔥𝔱 𝔷𝔲𝔢𝔫𝔡𝔢' [your punishment is by !no means over yet] (*St*, 50), the gothic tips the threat into caricature; it adds a level of visual hyperbole that produces echoes of 'we have ways of making you talk'. Similarly, when the army officer screams out '𝔄𝔞𝔞𝔞𝔞𝔠𝔥 !𝔗𝔲𝔫𝔤 :𝔙𝔬𝔯𝔴ä𝔯𝔱𝔣-!𝔐𝔞𝔯𝔣𝔠𝔥' [Aaaaaten !tion :Forward-!March] (*St*, 149), the gothic transforms the order into a stereotype of handlebar-moustached militarism. At such moments it is difficult not to be reminded of *Asterix in Gaul*, with its use of gothic script to encapsulate the stereotype of German national character. And as with any leitmotif, this association is then one that attaches to all its appearances. The comic-book dimension of his very serious use of gothic is also evident in Jirgl's orthography. His use of question marks, exclamation marks, and other idiosyncratic uses of punctuation and notation, is often reminiscent of the language of comics. This is particularly evident with exclamation and question marks, which placed in front of words, or even in the middle, dramatically stress their meaning and how they are read, punned or not.

The use of punctuation is often straightforwardly emphatic, such as when Georg is being taken to the accident and emergency clinic: '!Loslos !Notaufnahme !Diensthabender Stationsarzt !Notfall !schnellschnell !sehrdringend' [!Gogo !Emergency admission !Doctor on duty !Emergency !quickquick !veryurgent] (*St*, 316). Frequently it is used to convey a particular intonation or how the speaker is conceiving of his or her statement: 'Du ?schweigst. [...] —?Steht Vernunft, wie Heute üblich, auch bei ?dir so ?schlecht zu-Kurs' [You ?remain silent. —?is reason so ?unpopular with ?you too, as is the norm nowadays] (*St*, 272). However punctuation is used, though, it lends an insistence to the text, or a hyperbolic dimension. So when Georg thinks about how to proceed with his story telling, question marks break up the sentence: '*?Wie nun weiter. Gar ?anfangen mit ?Erzählen: ?ich. Von ?Dingen u ?Schimären — von ?Lebenden u von ?Toten -*' [*?How to proceed. What ?even to start with ?Tell stories: ?me. About ?things and ?chimeras — about? the ?living and the ?dead —*] (*St*, 126). The use of punctuation as expressive form extends to body language, which is of course in keeping with Jirgl's aim of achieving a three-dimensional text-body. When Ralf and his father are looking for the old East/West border, we get a strong sense of gesture: '-Da-hintn — ungefähr hmm=da=da ? — ! : wo der Wald aufhört — ja [...] Ja — Odernee — N-Schtückchen weiternachrechtz — ! : da — !!: muß Diegrenze gewesn sein' [-Ovu-there — about hmm=there=there ? — ! : where the wood ends — yes [...] Yes — Orno — A-bit furthertotherite — ! : there — !!: mustuv been theborder] (*St*, 455). The most extreme example of this is when Dorothea wants to do Georg a favour by masturbating in front of him:

> Ich öffne mich (– – – – – zeige ihm mein Geschlecht –(,)– berühre es mit der einen Hand ;) ; – ; – ;=) während die andere die Spitzen meiner Brüste preßt : : Ich lasse mir Zeit – – (')
> Wir, der alte Mann u ich, schauen unverwandt mit festen Blicken einander an ' ' – ;– ;) – : ;) – :: – ::: – ;). (*St*, 484)
>
> [I open myself (– – – – – show him my sex –(,)– touch it with one hand ;) ; – ; – ;=) while the other presses the tips of my breasts : : I take my time – – (')
> We, the old man and I, look at each other steadily and with a firm gaze ' ' – ;– ;) – : ;) – :: – ::: – ;)]

This unusual representation of orgasm, however evocative some readers may find it, undoubtedly has a ludicrous dimension. The accumulation of colons, semi-colons, dashes, and parenthesis looks like a string of emoticons rather than a carefully fashioned alphanumerical code, culminating in a wink. The masturbation scene is an extreme example of what pervades the whole text: the persistent deployment of punctuation injects a comic-book brashness and a social media frivolity that becomes rather comical.

Unintended comedy also arises out of the relentless negativity of the text, which at times tips over into farce. This is the case for example, with Henry's pursuit and assault on his father, or the melodramatic plot twist of Henry conceiving his child in the same bed that he was incestuously conceived. And Henry's attempt to escape to the USA assumes ridiculous proportions: he abandons his job, bankrolls the Alaska trip for two unpleasant strangers, murders them on the basis of a mistranslation, successfully flees the combined police forces of two countries, and somehow smuggles the gun back from Alaska with which he then asks his wife to kill him. Dorothea's reaction when her husband suddenly appears in front of her mirrors the reader's: 'Beinahe hätt ich laut gelacht' [I nearly laughed out loud] (*St*, 487). Her near-laughter is only based on knowing he has evaded two police forces; the reader's is intensified by the whole unlikely tale, including the actual murder with its strong elements of panicked slapstick.

The unremitting awfulness of *Die Stille* generates its own absurdity, a process that is then intensified by the overall absence of empathy, a lack that is sometimes so excessive it is laughable. This is exemplified in Georg's response to seeing his son's crooked teeth, made in all seriousness: 'schon dafür habe ich ihn über-Allejahre verachtet' [for that alone I've despised him all-theseyears] (*St*, 125). The unintended comedy that is triggered here is reminiscent of those moments in Fassbinder's *oeuvre* where excess tips into the ridiculous, or in Sebald's, where the narrator's melancholy excess is incommensurate with what he observes. Yet whereas in these artists' work the comedy arising from excess is part of a wider aesthetic which sets a limit to melodrama or melancholy, in Jirgl's work it signals a moment where the rigid monologic composition of the text is exposed. In the middle of a discussion with his son about the family's history, Georg makes an incisive comment about Johanna's one-sided and narrow business view of life: '[es hat] durch solcherart 1seitigkeit genau=dieselbe unfreiwillige Komik wie jedwede andere Welt-Anschauung, die ihre Dioptrien nur auf die 1=1zige Lehre 1stellen will' [it is so 1sided that it has precisely=the same unintentional comedy as every other world-view that focuses its dioptres short-sightedly on its 1=only lesson] (*St*, 235).

The 'unfreiwillige Komik' of *Die Stille* is a symptom of the one-sidedness of his negating intent, into which all aspects of the novel are subsumed. Jirgl's monologic voice recalls Dieter Wellershoff's warning about irony, that it is only creative if it does not atrophy into a posture: 'Dauerironie ist nur eine neue falsche Identität, die die eigene Leere unter der fadenscheinigen Maske angeblicher Reflektiertheit verbirgt' [Persistent irony is merely a new false identity that hides its own emptiness beneath the flimsy mask of alleged reflexivity].[39]

Volker Koepp

If in Jirgl's novel comedy is an integral part of the relentless negativity, in Volker Koepp's films it belongs to a strategy of persistent affirmation. Koepp's documentaries are not particularly comical. Nevertheless, he sees comedy and laughter as an integral part of how people speak of themselves and their lives and admits to being amazed by how amusingly people relate all manner of things that are not amusing. And, in a remark that serves as a comment on his own creativity, he considers it ideal for art of any sort if it can maintain its balance between tragedy and comedy.[40] In Koepp's films, this notion of balance appears initially to be ethically important: working with real subjects, many of whom have experienced devastation and loss, comedy risks tipping into ridicule, and *Schadenfreude* quickly functions as form of humiliation. However, the balance, combined as it is with Koepp's determination to be positive, tames comedy and deprives it of its critical potential. In a structural inversion of Jirgl's deployment of comedy to depict a world in which everyone is a villain, in Koepp's documentary world, comedy helps persuade us that no one is a villain.

In Koepp's most autobiographical film, *Berlin — Stettin* (2009, henceforth *B-S*), he tells the story of his life, the geographical moves he has made, and his development as a director. As with all autobiographical accounts, Koepp crafts a persona, and the film ends with two telling scenes that reveal how he would like to be seen. The first of them takes place in contemporary Szczecin, the town of Koepp's birth, and affirms his identity as a *Vertriebener*. The return to his birthplace is made in the company of two Polish families who themselves embody different types of migration and shifting borders. Pavel's family lives in Barlinek, formerly the German town Berlinchen. His grandmother was born on the eastern fringes of Europe, was taken to Siberia during the war, and was then resettled in Poland once it ended. His grandfather worked as a slave labourer in Germany during the war, was imprisoned in Dachau and returned to Poland after the war. Aleksandra's family lives in Szczecin and, looking to the future, the members anticipate being separated through economic migration within the EU.

For Koepp to be in the company of these Polish families when he refers to his birthplace is significant, for it is a gesture which sets him apart from any nationalistic identification. He effectively distances himself from the discourses of the *Vertriebenenverbände* and their conservative coupling of ethnicity and national identity. Instead he situates himself within a wider group of Eastern Europeans who have at a personal, familial, and local level, lived with a legacy of uprootedness. For them migration continues as a current reality, but they do not politicize this experience. Such positioning renders ethnicity and national allegiance irrelevant, for what is at stake is not the cause of forced or voluntary migration but the individual's story. The scene is also telling in that the brief references to expulsion and slave labour are non-accusatory to the Germans. Rather, they become the backdrop for a cautionary tale about Polish nationalism when Aleksandra expresses concern about the intolerance of Poles towards foreigners (*B-S*, 1:05:10). In contrast, these two families represent openness and tolerance, for they speak German and look forward to a European future. Furthermore, by asking Koepp about his origins, they establish a dialogue and demonstrate the possibility of harmony in the present despite the atrocities and injustices of the past.

The final scene of the film, following directly from the Szczecin location, is a montage of four brief sequences from Koepp's GDR documentaries of the 1970s and 80s. The first is of an old man who, walking along the street, looks into the camera and breaks into a wide smile. The next is of Elsbeth, a key protagonist of the Wittstock films, who after looking sullenly into the camera suddenly bursts out laughing. The third is of the girls in the Wittstock factory at a party at which a much younger Koepp is called in front of the camera and given a present. And finally we are shown a very funny episode of Karin the welder repeatedly trying and failing to close the bonnet of a Trabi car.

In the juxtaposition of these two final scenes Koepp offers a microcosm of his central concerns as a filmmaker. In his explorations of the eastern territories he encourages individuals of different ethnicity, class, and age to tell their own stories. Their experiences form part of the wider collapse of multicultural communities, of the thriving Czernowitz where Romanians, Ukrainians, Germans, Jews lived side by side, or of East Prussia where Germans, Poles, and Kashubians did. The melancholy or nostalgic yearning for this lost time is, though, offset by an intense humanity and interest in individuals. Many of the characters recount experiences of violent dispossession, genocide, death of immediate family, and abandonment, but they are mostly not bitter or accusatory. Furthermore, the destruction of multicultural communities is viewed from the perspective of an expanding Europe, which offers new opportunities for transnational harmony and the breakdown of ethnic divisions. And as is clear from the final scene of Berlin — Stettin, Koepp's fascination with his subjects extends to his eye for laughter and comedy.

'Volker, say "Action"'

The comedy double act is a recurring feature of many of Koepp's films. The most well-known is the pairing of Herr Zwilling and Frau Zuckermann in the film of that name (*Herr Zwilling und Frau Zuckermann*, 1999, henceforth *HZuFZ*). Their interaction was fundamental to the film's success: it was nominated for the Best Documentary category at the 1999 Berlinale, and won the Grand Prix at the Nyon Visions du Réel in the same year. When Koepp shot the film, Rosa Roth Zuckermann and Matthias Zwilling belonged to the last 'few specimens [...] of old Czernowitzers still speaking German', themselves members of the small Jewish community of present day Chernivtsi.[41] In 1977 there were only three remaining German-speaking Jews, of whom Herr Zwilling, born in 1929, was the youngest.[42] Frau Zuckermann was born in 1908. The film portrays the two as close friends: Herr Zwilling visits Frau Zuckermann every evening from six until ten. They eat together, speak German, and read German papers.

The comedy generated by Frau Zuckermann and Herr Zwilling arises from the strong contrasts between them. Frau Zuckermann is small and plump, whereas Herr Zwilling is taller and thinner and cuts a somewhat dour figure particularly when he wears his overcoat and hat. She is spirited, dynamic, decisive in her movements, humorous, and positive. He is lugubrious, doleful, long-faced, and possesses a gloomy outlook. Frau Zuckermann recognizes and enjoys the contrast between them, and when interviewed alone, she describes him as her fearless knight with a sad face and beyond reproach (*HZuFZ*, 1:38:06). Their routine, in her words something of a comedy routine, is well established: '[Er] kommt seit sechs Jahren zu mir ins Haus und j-e-d-e-n Abend mit einer Hiobsbotschaft. Jeden Abend muß ich ihm ausreden, daß das Leben weitergeht' [He's been coming to visit me at home for six years and e-v-e-r-y evening he brings bad news. Every evening I have to persuade him that life carries on] (*HZuFZ*, 15.00). Koepp uses the differences between his two protagonists to structure the film. We see their two very contrasting modes of teaching: Frau Zuckermann's enthusiasm is uncontainable, whereas Herr Zwilling, dressed in a white laboratory coat, guides his students through the year 'mit Ach und Krach' [by the skin of their teeth] (*HZuFZ*, 16.02). Yet Herr Zwilling too is well aware of the interplay between the two of them. He agrees that they are optimist and pessimist, and is amused by his role: 'Ich bin leider ein Pessimist, der fast immer Recht hat' [Unfortunately I'm a pessimist who's nearly always right] (*HZuFZ*, 17:20). He plays his gloomy comic foil to Frau Zuckermann's positive outlook, describing the dire economic state with some satisfaction, saying with grim humour: 'Neunzig Prozent leben vom Gehalt, der nicht ausgezahlt wird' [Ninety per cent live off salaries that aren't paid] (*HZuFZ*, 2:04:14).

The double act played out by Herr Zwilling and Frau Zuckermann, although it arises out of a real difference in their personalities and outlooks, is nevertheless one that they are aware of and enjoy. Most of the comic double acts do not unfold with the same degree, if at all, of knowing participation, which can then itself contribute to the comic effect. *Uckermark* (2002, henceforth *U*) opens with a five-minute sequence in which Adolf-Heinrich von Arnim speaks almost non-stop, and with great passion, about the virtues of a proper rail network. He speaks at length about his successful fight to increase the number of trains along the branch line (up from one to eight or nine in each direction), the connections as they existed in 1923, the importance of establishing effective bus connections (which are not yet what he would wish them to be), the need for investment in the railway infrastructure (after one hundred years of simply taking), and the crucial role of the transport network: 'das Netz, das muss funktionieren! Anschluss muss sein!' [the network must function! There must be connections!] (*U*, 3:56). Frau Albert, in the meantime, the reticent young woman who operates the old Wilhelmine signalling equipment from 1907, is always in the frame, standing with a deadpan expression except when he addresses his remarks to her or solicits a response. They are an incongruous pair: the urbane aristocrat and the provincial worker, the articulate man and the woman of few words, the old activist and the passive employee. Indeed, in his enthusiastic bearing, von Arnim seems more youthful than she: 'Ich bin 84, ja, aber ich hab' noch einiges vor mir' [I'm 84, but I still have quite a lot ahead of me], he says, adding that he is newly married (*U*, 2:43).

Frau Albert's on-screen reserve forcefully offsets von Arnim's animated soliloquizing and opens up a space for seeing the comic side of von Arnim's eagerness. This is further reinforced by von Arnim's wife, who corrects his version of how they met on a train: for him they entered into a nice chat, for her he interrupted her reading, ignored the fact that she said he was disturbing her, and insisted on a conversation (*U*, 1:14:05). Later in *Uckermark*, von Arnim's loquacious optimism signally misses the point that another interlocutor, the young man Marcel, is making. Upon mention of the difficulties Marcel sometimes encounters because he has longer hair than others at the bus stop, von Arnim is disbelieving: 'Ich finde nichts so unwichtig im Leben wie die Länge der Haare' [There's nothing in life I consider as unimportant as the length of someone's hair] (*U*, 1:28:41). Even when Marcel tactfully explains that political orientation is the issue, that these are people who would happily return to 1945, von Arnim comically fails to grasp that it is neo-Nazi skinheads that are being talked about with an unintended non sequitur: 'Das mit der Haarlänge, das ändert sich doch dauernd' [But the thing about hair-length is that it's constantly changing] (*U*, 1:29:20). He offers proof: in his lifetime he has changed the length of his hair at least ten times.

In contrast to the double act that generates comedy through differences, the two old farm workers in *Uckermark* are similar in background and outlook. Visual comedy is initially established through filming the men head on, with a still and unflinching camera. The old men sit next to each other: one is plump, and his physique is unflatteringly emphasized by the direct frontal shot on his groin; the other is scrawny. Both wear similar hats, and together they are a gloomy, Laurel and Hardy-esque pair. There is nothing funny about what they say, for they circle around their memories of disempowerment, their repeated experience of having stock and land taken from them, first after the war, then through collectivization, finally after reunification. Yet the way in which they egg each other on to speak lends a comic edge to the scene, for they enact many of the routines of a double act. One repeats and reinforces what the other says: '"viele sind nach Canada", "ja viele von hier nach Canada"' ['lots have gone to Canada', 'yes, lots from here to Canada'] (*U*, 53:40), and they constantly affirm, with repeated 'ja' or 'ja, ja', what the other has said. They bicker mildly like an old married couple, disagreeing about whether to relate certain events: '"Ich möchte was sagen, aber ich werd' mal lieber still sein". [...] "Es ist die Wahrheit". "Ach, und wenn's die Wahrheit ist" ['I want to say something, but it's better if I keep quiet'. 'It's the truth'. 'Oh, so what if it's the truth'] (*U*, 1:19:00). When they are finally persuaded to speak, they then bicker about what point in the past things started to go wrong.

The unflinching camera in this scene points towards its role in contributing to comedy, largely through the characters' response to it. Their response to being filmed varies, and Koepp plays with their reactions, which range from ignoring it, through playing up to it, to embarrassment. Herr Zwilling behaves as though there is no camera there, waiting for instructions to begin talking even though he is already being filmed. In contrast, Harvey Keitel's training as a film actor is evident in *Dieses Jahr in Czernowitz* when he says to the director, 'Volker, say Action' (2004, henceforth *DJiC*, 11.40). The Jewish men on the Brighton Beach Boardwalk need no direction as they enter an amused hide and seek with the camera, taking charge of their own visibility (*DJiC*, 34.00).

It is also people's embarrassment at being filmed that is amusing, such as when in *Pommerland* the couple Halina and Janek stand in front of the camera saying nothing until out of embarrassment they suddenly put their arms around each other and grin (2005, henceforth *P*, 39.40). Koepp's use of long takes results in some funny scenes. At the start of *Uckermark*, he asks two men about the old machines they are restoring for a museum. One man is fat and informative, telling Koepp all about the project, the other is thin and utterly silent, not quite sure where to look throughout the whole three-minute sequence, his permanently raised left eyebrow drawing attention to his discomfort. We then see the two men again, lined up with four further colleagues in front of the unmoving camera in a style that is visually reminiscent of Fassbinder's *Katzelmacher*. Again, the fat man does the talking, while the other five stand in edgy silence. The thin man only mutters something to his neighbour when he thinks he is off camera, but as the camera finally pans across the line-up, he realizes he is being filmed and hastily becomes taciturn and unsmiling again. Later in the film the von Hahns are standing at the front door of their manor house, talking earnestly about agricultural management, when Frau von Hahn's mother enters the shot through the door. When she realizes that filming is taking place, she hides in the porch until her daughter asks her out. But the dog keeps howling from behind the door (*U*, 23:50).

Central to the films' comic moments are the characters themselves, their idiosyncrasies, their own sense of humour and their interaction with others. This is evident with Koepp's stars, like Frau Zuckermann, Herr Zwilling, and von Arnim, but is also the case with minor characters. In *Herr Zwilling und Frau Zuckermann* an enthusiastic but not altogether practical orthodox Jew helps another, more efficient man with a maintenance task. Various ladders are brought in and moved around, the bimah is shifted, and considerable concern is expressed because the ladder must extend above the bimah. The orthodox Jew gives the impression of wanting to oversee proceedings, whereas the other man gets on with it. Further slapstick ingredients are added by the intrusive ringing of a telephone and an abrupt conversation held by the orthodox Jew on an incongruous and huge brick of a mobile phone. Finally we see what the operation was about: a fluorescent, number 9-shaped bulb replaces the number-8 for the Jewish New Year and the orthodox Jew looks very pleased with himself. In *Memelland*, the old ornithologist cuts an amusing figure (2008, henceforth *Me*). Dressed in what appear to be rather ill-fitting military or pseudo-military fatigues, his high-waisted trousers drooping from under the belt, he starts speaking in heavily accented and broken German, adding gestures to further elucidate what he is saying. Director of the ornithology station since 1974, he refers to the birds as though they are people. And in the same film, we are introduced to three formidable old sisters, who still work their land despite being at least in their seventies. The three brothers they employ to help with the hay, themselves no longer young, fall far short of the sisters' standards. Edith tells one of them, who has momentarily paused, to keep going, to which he responds that he needs a break. 'Du machst doch gerade eine' [Well you've just had one] she retorts (*Me*, 1:14:07).

Children are major actors in Koepp's film, for he is fascinated by their apparent artlessness in front of the camera and the sheer funniness of their expressive behaviour. In *Schattenland* (2005, henceforth *Sch*) we see them bored in the classroom: biting nails (*Sch*, 28.13), rubbing a rubber on the face (*Sch*, 28.26), or swinging on a chair (*Sch*, 28.33). Later, a group of girls, giggling and laughing throughout, tell us about the local area and we soon realize that their hilarity is fuelled by the off-screen group of boys, who are too embarrassed to be filmed and are hiding behind a tree. In *Pommerland* the children rush out of school and jostle wildly and playfully to maintain their position in front of the lens, the shot ending just as one plaited girl, a skilled pusher, turns and gives a particularly disdainful look at another (2005, henceforth *P*: 2.32). *Holunderblüte* is a film that concentrates solely on the children of the Kaliningrad exclave (2007, henceforth *H*). One of its stars is a delightful chatterbox who is adept at playing up to the camera and whom we first see in a comic double act with his stolid sidekick. The chatterbox speaks about himself with unrestrained eagerness, a constant grin, and barely pausing for breath. He is unimpressed by his friend's ponderous narration and makes his boredom clear by pulling a face when he notices that the camera is on him. His charisma is rewarded by a later solo performance, at which with his enthusiastic and almost non-stop talking he is determined to keep the camera focused on him. He reads aloud from one of his books, stopping abruptly as he notices that the camera is panning away to the waving reeds (*H*, 1:13). He wonders what else he can say, contorting his face to think hard (*H*, 1:13:16), offers a long and heartfelt monologue about friends, concludes 'Das ist alles' [That's all] (*H*, 1:14:35), immediately starts talking about animals, finishes again with 'Das ist alles' (*H*, 1:15:29), only to continue talking about a cow.

Individual idiosyncrasy is also manifested in people's faces. The long comic tradition that centres on physiognomies and appearance cannot be ignored when watching Koepp. His emphasis on interviewing people from a range of socio-economic backgrounds results in an impressive array of features and expressions that challenge the aesthetic norms and beautiful images of commercial visual culture, occasionally tipping into the unusual or exaggerated. In the opening scene of *Herr Zwilling und Frau Zuckermann* the camera pans across the group of musicians, and the quirky *Zigeunermusik* is an apt accompaniment to the quirky faces. In *Schattenland* the old man who guides us round the ruined castle proffers a huge grin, one side of his mouth a toothless hole, the other with a few remaining teeth clinging on (*Sch*, 4.39). Yet it is not only distinct physiognomies that may be funny. Appearance more generally can become amusing if it seems to conform to stereotype. Part of Herr Zwilling's own comic effect is the fact that he looks so lugubrious; Harvey Keitel not only looks like the film star he is with his flowing batik scarf on the streets of Czernowitz, but at the same time he also conforms to the type of gauche American tourist abroad; the two alcoholic women in *Holunderblüte* are comic, however sad, caricatures of a pair of drunks, bickering over a bicycle and profoundly insulting each other with evocative phrases.[43] And, fitting with an archetypal stereotype, albeit one that does not rest on appearance, the tractor-driver's wife in *Schattenland* ran off with the postman.

'The Goodness in Humans'

As is evident from Sebald's work, the generation of comedy from individuals' idiosyncrasies lends itself to satire and the possibility of social critique. Indeed, in Koepp's films the potential for criticism is also given structurally in the juxtaposition of very different class and status. Aristocratic voices are heard alongside employees, labourers, or the unemployed. West Germans, or those who have accrued wealth in Western Europe, appear next to those who have never left their villages. We see the excitement of restoring the old family home and setting up business as well as the suffering of confiscation and entrenched poverty. There are rare episodes when such juxtaposition of differences hints at critical social commentary. How these moments occur but are then effectively subsumed into a wider mood of affirmation can be seen particularly well in *Uckermark*. Here the von Hahns exemplify the return of the ancient aristocracy, re-claiming the lands they lost in 1945. There are moments when we wonder whether aristocratic superiority and sense of entitlement are being lampooned. Gräfin von Hahn and her mother host a coffee afternoon for former employees of the estate, an event at which we hear snippets from their working lives in the GDR, including collectivization. The wealthy landowning Gräfin von Hahn, née von Arnim, impervious to differences imposed by class and the wall, remarks to one of the women of her mother's generation, 'Sie haben das selbe Schicksal wie wir, auch Flüchtlinge' [You share the same fate as us, also refugees] (*U*, 47:19). At a later private social event, one of the von Hahn's guests remarks with surprising conviction and lack of irony: 'die Preussen sammeln sich jetzt hier wieder, das ist ganz gut' [The Prussians are gathering here again, that's very good] (*U*, 1:17:35). How good is perhaps relativized by the women on an unemployment work scheme searching for archaeological remains. These are women for whom the *Wende* brought unemployment and disempowerment when female cement workers were made redundant. The GDR, which for the von Hahns is an interruption in the continuity of history, was for these women a pleasant, calm time (*U*, 1:10:00) that gave them a strong sense of community.

A further dissonant voice in *Uckermark* is that of the actor and director, Fritz Marquardt. Also expelled from his birthplace, he speaks of his allegiance to Communism as part of the post-war desire for radical change from National Socialism (*U*, 1:31:15). His allusion to the Nazi period and the desire for change is in stark contrast to the negative view of the GDR and collectivization expressed by both the von Hahns and the two old men, who see it as a violent imposition and aberration, albeit in different ways. Indeed, Marquardt is adamant that the reunification represents an absolute restoration (*U*, 1:31:50), an ironic reversal of the Communist monument celebrating the transition of 'Junkerland in Bauernhand' [Junkers' lands in farmers' hands]. The historical shifts from pre- to post-1945, and then post-1989 are for Marquardt like shifts through different dramatic genres. In answer to Koepp's question, 'komisch mit der Geschichte, nicht?' [history's a funny thing, isn't it?], his response forms the last words of the film: 'Ja, ja. Ein Mal als Tragödie, und dann als Komödie, und dann: Tragikomödie' [Yes, yes. First it's tragedy, then it's comedy, and then: tragicomedy] (*U*, 1:42:00).

Koepp asks a leading question in which he describes history as quirky, and Marquardt's answer plays into his hands. History shifts from the realm of political and social responsibility and conflict and finds resolution in a compromise artistic genre: a bit of tragedy here, a bit of comedy there, and a balanced synthesis in tragicomedy. This drive for coherence exemplifies Koepp's films, which achieve harmony through their emphasis on the organic relationship of individuals with their home, normally rural. Beautiful landscapes are central to Koepp's films. Individuals are firmly located in their surroundings; they speak to the camera against a background of their home or their workplace. Interior shots are set within a wider, rural context: the countryside is either just outside, or the city, as with Czernowitz, is shown only after shots of the surrounding landscape. Thus human habitation is visually posited as arising out of the land and the aesthetic focus on the timeless, unchanging countryside is frequently reinforced by voice-overs that summarize the momentous events of migration, invasion, and wars, all of which have been survived by the enduring landscape. As Peter Braun suggests, the landscape becomes a medium of memory rather than simply a place to live.[44] Individuals themselves are victims of larger forces beyond their sphere of personal responsibility, and trauma and suffering are part of humanity's lot in the *longue durée* of nature, and are thereby removed from the realm of political scrutiny. Claims to the land may change, but nature persists: in *Kurische Nehrung* the camera lingers on the plaque of the ornithology station, with its Russian plaque of 1956 and its German plaque of 1901 (2001, henceforth *KN*, 11:17). The birds and their environment represent continuity, not rupture. As the director of the ornithology station in *Memelland* asserts, whoever was in power, be they Communists, Bolsheviks, Catholics, or Protestants, his nightingales carry on singing for all (*Me*, 1:25:05).

Landscape functions as a counterpoint to the cruelty of history, as Stefan Reinecke writes, and Koepp's poetic gaze is not suited to criticism.[45] But it is rather the landscape in relation to the people who live in it that counters history's cruelty and it is the focus on individuals that is key to Koepp's avoidance of satire and social criticism, as well as ridicule. Koepp's delight in the *comédie humaine* forms part of a wider affirmation of his subjects, whom he accepts on their terms. He films people in their own context, and invites them to talk about what is important to them, encouraging them to speak while carrying out their normal activities.[46] His intense interest in people, in their stories and histories, leads Rainer Rother to describe his work as 'filmische Liebeserklärungen' [filmic declarations of love]. This devotion is also identifiable in moments of portraiture, influenced by photography and art, when the camera lingers on people's faces either before or after they speak.[47] The complementary visual modes of portraiture and landscape, both of which invite contemplative viewing, formally represent the bond between land and inhabitants that transcends temporary change. Thus, although Marquardt's critical views on restoration are voiced, and he, like most characters, is empathetically presented, the overall emotional tenor of *Uckermark*, as with the other films, is on the importance of restoration as a reassertion of the *longue durée* of belonging and against the forces of modernizing homogenization. Von Arnim refers to the twenty-two generations of his family who have lived in the Uckermark, and Graf von Hahn emphasizes the relationship of the aristocratic families with their land, seeing their re-acquisition of the estate as a continuation of a time that was interrupted (*U*, 18:13). In terms heavy with spiritual resonance, he describes their deep identification with the landscape (*U*, 1:00:00).

The possible political provocation of these aristocratic claims is first of all sidestepped precisely because of the focus on the individuals. The women on the unemployment scheme agree that the von Hahns are normal, nice people (*U*, 1:09:15), and the director of the fodder production works admits that not all von Arnims are the same and this one is not a typical capitalist (*U*, 42:26). But the vision of restoration as something that promotes historical and social continuity also tallies with Koepp's own vision. However, restoration is not unconditional. He is fascinated by those people who are committed to sustaining the rural economies and communities of the increasingly depopulated and often impoverished areas of Eastern Europe. Crucially too, he insists on the historical multi-ethnic and multi-linguistic make-up of these areas, and restoration therefore encompasses those who participate in or work towards multi-ethnic interaction and co-habitation. Von Arnim and the von Hahns conform to his positive vision through their contribution to the local economy and agriculture. In *Schattenland* it is Poles who are concerned to remember the multi-ethnic past. One couple is reconstructing the old wooden houses which were deserted after 1945 and they remind us of the time when the population spoke Polish and wrote German (*Sch*, 1:03:30). They also contribute to the restorative vision by belonging to a group campaigning against the cutting down of old trees, and the group is in turn a home for multi-ethnic interaction: one member was born in Brandenburg, worked as a foreign correspondent in Poland, and now lives in Masuren and sees her national identity as German and

Polish. This vision of multi-ethnic harmony combined with historical continuity is again emphasized by the three young students from Warsaw: Gildas is Polish but was born in France, Irina is from Vilnius, and Marciek describes himself as born in Pomerania, once Prussian. Irina feels at home in Masuren because the smells are like those of her grandmother's home in Lithuania.

The Bartosiewicz family in *Pommerland* exemplify positive restoration, their credentials confirmed by their friendship with von Arnim who makes a re-appearance in the film. Both Bartosiewiczs left Poland in the 1980s, she left to live and study in Germany, he to live in England. They have now moved back to Poland, have bought an estate in Pomerania, and are restoring the house and working to make the estate a thriving agricultural concern. Their commitment to the land takes on ethical overtones when Frau Bartosiewicz remarks, 'wir kommen von dem Reichtum und machen hier unseren Werk' [we have come from wealth and are doing our work here] (*P*, 18:50). Their devotion is emphasized by the fact that there will be no profits from the farming for at least another two or three years. The positive vision of a future where different language communities can live together harmoniously is constantly to the fore. The Bartosiewiczs and von Arnim are delighted that with the accession of Poland to the EU, the Oder-Neisse line has been made redundant, but Frau Bartosiewicz nevertheless wants to uphold history and not forget that the Germans lived here for centuries. She likes the Germans very much (*P*, 22:56) and is full of admiration for their building skills (*P*, 45:42).

Crucially, Frau Bartosiewicz not only epitomizes Koepp's vision of positive restoration but she also articulates another of his profoundly held values: a commitment to reconciliation. For in addition to preserving traces of the German past in Poland, she is sanguine in her response to the atrocities of war. Her grandfather spent three years in Auschwitz and was subjected to medical experiments by Mengele. He survived, but never taught his children to hate. She feels that the Poles too were no angels, and that on both sides there were such experiences, including deeds perpetrated by Poles that were utterly cruel. Such cruelty notwithstanding, she is utterly optimistic: 'Das Gute in den Menschen [wird] gewinnen' [The good in people will win out] (*P*, 1:08:00). The appearance of the gentle Louise Hedmainska, a German born in Pomerania in 1925, illustrates the point that Germans also suffered. But unlike the resentment associated with much of the discourse around the collective punishment of ethnic Germans, she too speaks without rancour of her internment in a Russian camp at the end of the war. She expresses no sense of injustice that she was forced to work in Poland in the same way the Poles had been forced to work in Germany. She admits that life was hard as the only remaining German, but she married a Polish man and was happy with him. She expresses no bitterness and has never regretted not moving to Germany (*P*, 52:56).

Figures like Frau Zuckermann and Louise Hedmainska demonstrate the ability to narrate the suffering of the past and yet be reconciled to the present. But present hardship too is borne with equanimity, if not goodwill. The films gravitate towards workers, the poor, and those who live with the threat of impoverishment, who seem positive about their circumstances or determined to make the best of them, and who are rarely shown to be resentful, angry, or politicized. In *Kurische Nehrung* the Russian fisherman and his wife from the Kaliningrad exclave are the opposite of the Grimm Fisherman and his Wife, happy in their simple but good life. *Holunderblüte* offers some of the most moving examples of such an affirmative outlook by showing children living in extreme poverty playing and caring for each other. One family of ten children, whose parents we never see, live in slum conditions, but they do not complain and we see them playing together in different ways throughout the year. The children are able to find joy and they look forward to a better future of completed education and a job. They typify the heroes of Koepp's films, people who in large or small ways are positive in the face of adversity.

Koepp is drawn to people who fit his wider humanitarian striving for coherent community in which difference does not lead to conflict and suffering does not result in antagonism and a perpetuation of strife. His optimistic vision, his emphasis on landscape and belonging, and the freedom he gives his subjects to recall their memories unchallenged, has resulted in some forceful criticism. Thus Andrea Becker writes of *Kurische Nehrung*: Koepp 'imaginiert sich einen im günstigsten Fall unpolitischen Heimatfilm zusammen' [has created for himself what is at best an apolitical *Heimat* film].[48] Urs Richter concurs, considering the film nostalgic.[49] There are, of course, differences between Koepp's films, and *Kurische Nehrung* is certainly a film in which the combination of the landscape and the positive outlook of the subjects produces a strong sense of nostalgic yearning: 'damals war das schön' [in those days it was lovely] (*KN*, 3:30). Koepp admits that the film was a type of break after the intense discussions with Herr Zucker and Frau Zimmermann, but these characteristics are nevertheless not untypical.[50] Yet as Ginette Vincendeau and Richard Dyer argue in their discussion of heritage films, the nostalgia with which they approach the past need not reduce them to ideological vehicles of the present, for they may nevertheless convey 'the contradictoriness of the past itself'.[51] Lutz Koepnick is less generous in his characterization of heritage films as producing 'usable and consumable pasts, [...] history as a site of comfort and orientation',[52] but he praises *Herr Zwilling und Frau Zuckermann* for refusing to simplify history: it 'understands the public and the everyday, history and memory, in terms of a dialectical relation — one unthinkable without the other; one dependent on the other'.[53]

There is an interesting contrast to be drawn here with the way in which individuals are presented in Guido Knopp's popular documentaries. Here, those who lived under National Socialism and through the Second World War and who offer their memories as testimony, are filmed against a black background and are intercut with original film footage or photographs from the period. This has the effect of divorcing them from the contemporary context, of presenting their accounts from a space that is not impinged upon by their current situation. The impersonal and apparently neutral space removes them from the interference of subjective positioning, and frees them to remember the past as if objectively. At the same time, their accounts are presented as filling in a blank: their versions of events do not relate to other accounts or interpretations of history, but are unmediated witness statements that seem to arise spontaneously and authentically from the recesses of memory.[54] In contrast, Koepp's protagonists are rooted in a specific location and their memories arise out of the experiences of that place and its historical traces. Thus his films inevitably also become a comment on the present.[55]

The dialectical relationship between the past and present that permeates the films means that their idealistic vision is not simply directed at the past in the form of nostalgic melancholia but encompasses the present. The present is thus not devalued by reference to the past through a melancholic lens of decline, but remains as the optimistic starting point from which the past, including past suffering, is remembered. For this reason Tim Bergenfelder suggests that Koepp's multicultural vision is not idealistic for it accepts 'that neither then nor now was this multiculturalism without its problems, frictions, and mutual suspicions'.[56] Yet for all that Koepp's films demonstrate the interaction of the past and the present and make explicit the subjectivity of people's narratives, their coherence is premised upon a yearning for a harmonious multi-ethnic and multi-lingual modern Europe. This emotional coherence is dependent upon featuring people who either exemplify such a society by virtue of their background, or who articulate the desire for reconciliation and harmony. Thus Frau Zimmermann becomes the figure of reconciliation par excellence, telling Koepp that had anyone told her fifty years ago that she would offer a German her hand, she would have killed him (*HZuFZ*, 22:40).

Along with generally selecting people who share his outlook, Koepp also depends on a strategy of exclusion for reinforcing his vision of harmony and absence of conflict. As Reinecke observes, although his work is full of violence, expulsion, and death, there are almost no portraits of perpetrators.[57] So when Peter Braun suggests that Koepp's ethnographic interest in declining or eradicated communities is a form of collective mourning that is negotiating what should stay in or out of the emerging 'European cultural memory', it is clear that only the good can stay in.[58] To draw on the language of melodrama, there are very few villains in Koepp's work and they are usually off-screen. They are also, most obviously, those who actively oppose reconciliation and multiculturalism. In *Uckermark* we hear in passing of the skinheads, in *Berlin — Stettin* the Jewish woman speaks of the encroaching violence of the radical right, and in *Pommerland* Frau Bartosiewicz speaks of Frau von Mach, a member of the family that owned the estate before 1945. Sixty years later von Mach is still not reconciled to the fact that the house is no longer theirs. Other off-screen villains include those who undermine a holistic, environmentally inclusive vision of restoration: the agency responsible for cutting down the avenues of trees in *Schattenland*, for example, or the wind-farm lobby which uses the EU definition of 'uninhabited' to cover the Uckermark with wind turbines without consulting its population (*B-S*, 53:12). The modern city, urban communities, and industrial development simply do not figure.

Holunderblüte offers an extreme example of off-screen wrongdoing. Children are the innocent victims of the endemic alcoholism of the region, the apparent unavailability of parents to their children, and of poverty. The ten siblings see their father at occasional weekends and report that most adults are alcoholics. This seems to be confirmed by the young woman Ljuda, who tells us that her parents are alcoholics, her three brothers are in care and that only she visits them. Adults are not given screen time and they are not given a voice, rather they are cast as part of the background of decline and degeneration, symbolized so starkly in the images of neglected Gothic churches and derelict 'German' houses. Adults in the film are both derelict and neglectful and as such also represent the devastating Soviet governance. The once productive husbandry of the land and flourishing culture is explicitly described as German, whereas Koepp ascribes its destruction to the Soviet army and collective farming (*H*, 30:50). Now wide expanses of land have returned to wilderness, the population is without work and impoverished, and average life expectancy of fathers is fifty-five years. The hasty glossing over of the war underpins the contrast between the evocation of a better, German time, and post-war Russian control, between a multi-ethnic past before the last Germans were driven out and a mono-cultural present after people from the Soviet Union were brought in (*H*, 3:35).

This film is unusual in establishing such a stark juxtaposition between a lost German past and a debased Russian present, so in *Kurische Nehrung* the very positive Kaliningrad Russians are presented with typical empathy. The film is typical, however, in its disavowal of the National Socialist past and Nazi perpetrators. Clearly an awareness of German atrocities carried out under Nazi rule is not absent from all of Koepp's films. In *Herr Zwilling und Frau Zuckermann*, Frau Zuckermann explicitly evokes German responsibility by commenting that she never thought she would speak to a German. In *Dieses Jahr in Czernowitz*, Leon Botstein describes how from his Jewish class in Lodz only his mother and one other child survived the Holocaust, and that his father's whole family was murdered. Both films convey powerfully the destruction of the flourishing Jewish community in Czernowitz by anti-Semitic race laws and genocidal policies, a process that was a microcosm of the genocide. Norman Manea recalls his deportation to Transnistria at the age of five, a hellish experience and one that he sees as an attempt at total destruction of the Jews (*DJiC*, 1:26:05).

Yet crucially, German perpetrators are not the subjects of the two films, leaving undisturbed the ability of a German audience to identify with the Jewish victims, or with those who, whether Jewish or not, are in search of a *Heimat*. In *Herr Zwilling und Frau Zuckermann* it is the Russians who sawed off the points of the Star of David in the Jewish House, and it is the economic stagnation of contemporary Ukraine that is making life so hard. Frau Rosa, the one remaining Jew in her village, describes Romanian villagers murdering the Jews. In *Dieses Jahr in Czernowitz*, Germany and Austria are benevolent countries for Jews: Eduard Weissmann plays and teaches cello in Berlin and the sisters Evelyne Mayer and Katja Rainer live in Vienna. Germany is also a country of culture and love: the young Ukrainian student Tanja Kloubert studies German and once she has graduated marries a German and leaves to join her husband there. The interview with Johann Schlamp, the ninety-year-old German from Czernowitz, presents the figure of the 'good German' who can be understood as a victim: he recalls how he disliked the wave of anti-Semitism that emanated from Germany (*DJiC*, 1:07:03), which was why he did not move to Germany with other Germans. He was sentenced to three years' of labour camp by the Russians and then served six until he was released.

Another good German who is old enough to have witnessed the wave of anti-

Semitism is the humane and sympathetic von Arnim. Unlike Frau Zimmermann and Herr Zucker, for whom the experience of violence is central to their narrative, we hear nothing of von Arnim's life under National Socialism, but rather anecdotes of his youth when he was on his beloved train network to Hinterpommern, of his post-*Wende* commitment to the area or of his similarity to Fontane's Stechlin. His past is not probed, and he is therefore able to serve as an unambiguous figure of positive continuity. No mention is made of his active service in the 3rd Panzer Division and his participation in the invasion of France and the Soviet Union, that he completed his legal training following a severe injury in 1941 and then worked gathering intelligence in the 'Fremde Heere Ost' until the end of the war. German aggression is similarly skirted over in the discussion between von Arnim and his cousins, the von der Marwitzes. Friedhelm describes the family's flight westwards in 1945 that was planned with military precision by his father (*P*, 1:14:10). Again, the emphasis is on continuity, love of the land, and commitment to its proper husbandry. The von Marwitzes are interviewed on their family estate at Wundichow. Their sense of belonging is symbolically and visually reinforced by cutting straight to a scene in which Friedhelm shows us a photograph of his grandfather, Kavalriegeneral Georg von der Marwitz, escorting the German Empress on her horse. There is no mention of National Socialism or of the family's relationship to the regime.

'Shall I Laugh?'

The degree to which Koepp uses his eye for comedy to consolidate his positive vision of reconciliation and restoration and to counter the melancholy awareness of loss, is evident in three episodes, each of which in different ways exposes his desire for harmony and avoidance of conflict. It is the explicit reference to something funny or to laughter that proves so revealing in these examples. The first of these involves his interaction with the two gloomy, Laurel and Hardy-esque Uckermark farmers. The scenes focusing on the pair are wrought with comic tension for the viewer, who is caught between the painful events that they relate and the darkly humorous relentlessness of their dourness. This tension is both articulated and finds release when Koepp asks them: 'und gibt's garnichts lustiges?' [and isn't there anything funny?] (*U*, 52:47). In a subsequent scene he tells them: 'ihr guckt ja so ernst' [but you look so serious] (*U*, 1:18:54). In both cases the gaunt man laughs, responding 'was soll's lustiges geben?' [what is there to laugh about?]. The effect of Koepp's intervention is twofold. By provoking some laughter and taking the edge off the men's bitterness, they come across as more empathetic. It facilitates a more sympathetic response on the part of the viewer, offering us a salve to their suffering. The exchange also, however, serves to emphasize Koepp's desire for a reconciliatory vision, for he tries to steer the men away from their sense of injustice and to encourage them to be positive in some way.

In a painful scene in *Herr Zwilling und Frau Zuckermann*, Frau Rosa, the sole surviving Jew of her village, sits in the eatery run by her close friend. As though second-guessing Koepp, she asks him, 'soll ich lachen?' [should I laugh?], to which he responds with an enthusiastic 'gerne' [please do]. She laughs on demand, and this triggers her rather jolly friend into laughing too. But the viewer is discomforted by Rosa's put-on laugh, and by her subsequent remark: 'so traurig ist mein Lachen' [my laughter is so sad] (*HZuFZ*, 1:03:02). Her comment is well illustrated by the following sequence in which we see Rosa's despairing visit to her father's overgrown grave. This is a rare example of laughter demonstrably failing to be aligned with an optimistic vision. It is also a moment when the explicit attempt to conform to what she rightly perceives to be Koepp's expectations lays bare a vital element of his structuring vision.

The final example of where Koepp tries to propagate his view of restoration and multi-cultural harmony is in his interview with the Lithuanian woman who works in the amber museum in *Kurische Nehrung*. Referring to the border that divides the Curonian Spit between the Kaliningrad Exclave and Lithuania, he rather suddenly asks her: 'Aber dass es so 'ne Grenze gibt ist ja komisch, nicht?' [But it's funny that there's such a border, isn't it?] (*KN*, 28:53). Taken aback, she responds: 'Aber warum komisch? Das ist [*sic*] zwei verschiedene Länder. [...] Vielleicht ist es gut, alle haben ein bißchen' [But why is it funny? They're two different countries. Perhaps it's good, then everyone has a bit]. In this exchange, what Koepp finds funny or odd, the unnatural division of the land into borders that effect a radical separation, is brushed off and relativized by the incredulous woman, for whom nothing could be more normal than a border.

Conclusion

Koepp and Jirgl both refuse the discourse of collective German suffering. Koepp's fascination with individuals' stories makes the point that people of all ethnicities experienced war and violence, and Jirgl emphasizes the whole range of cruelty and abuse that the German state, and Germans, inflict on other Germans and themselves. Both are also linked through the marked way in which the question of responsibility for violence and atrocity is neutralized in their work. In Koepp's films this is done through his emphasis on reconciliation and restoration, and through banishing those to off-screen who do not comply with his vision. Furthermore, individuals inhabit a landscape to which history happens, just as borders are arbitrarily erected upon it. In Jirgl's *Die Stille*, history is reduced to a state of perpetual war in which all individuals are on the spectrum of reprehensible, all people are condemned by the cycle of violence to further violence, so an exploration of responsibility is futile. The two artists structurally mirror each other in their approach to the particular and the universal. Koepp focuses on the specific and consequently loses sight of the universal: in his case he refuses political or structural analysis of events, sublating potential conflict into a wider collective of positive humanity. Jirgl reduces individuals to ciphers of universal violence and suffering, excluding any possibility of them finding unique and specific access to happiness.

The work of both Koepp and Jirgl is fundamentally monologic despite the central role of dialogue and interviews. Koepp selects his interviewees and stars to articulate the goodness and resilience in humanity, and Jirgl places characters, plot, and form in the service of what he sees as a politics of negation. (And, following Adorno, what we might rather see as committed than autonomous art.) Both men use comic devices to underpin their outlook rather than as part of a critical engagement with their material or mode of representation. Koepp's taste for the comic complements rather than challenges his melancholy sense of loss, for he uses it to advocate his wider vision of a restoration of what was, not least through the continuity offered by the landscape. Jirgl's pervasive *Schadenfreude* contributes to a representation of suffering that precludes its privileging as redemptive, but it also helps counter the drift towards melodrama that results from the undiluted horrendousness of the family drama. It is in moments when the comic underpinning is shaken that the monologic trajectory of their work is exposed: in Koepp's case when his interlocutors challenge his desire to look on the funny side, and in Jirgl's when the reader cannot help but do so in the face of his hyperbolic awfulness.

The ethical implications of each author's monologic approach are, though, very different. If Koepp's forgiving comedy has no critical bite, this may well stem from the fact that his films are documentaries. In his case *Schadenfreude* would function as ridicule. For Jirgl, the comic effects of *Schadenfreude* might be defended as a form of critical bite, but no one is at risk of harm: fictional characters exist on a different ontological plane from real subjects. However, the kindly toothless grin of Koepp's *oeuvre* brings with it a certain complacency towards questions of cause and responsibility. In answer to the question of whether documentary film about real people can afford to ridicule its subjects, one might respond that ridicule is not the only form that critical comedy can take. It is a question indirectly taken up by Ruth Klüger, whose memoirs, like Koepp's documentaries, do not have the protective layer of a fictional framework, yet make ample use of biting humour.

Notes to Chapter 4

1. Reinhard Jirgl, 'Schlußwort für einen "Nachlaß zu Lebzeiten"', in *Reinhard Jirgl: Genealogie des Tötens* (Munich: DTV, 2003), pp. 815–33 (p. 822).
2. Volker Koepp, in interview with Rainer Rother, 5 May 2006, *Schattenland*, in 'Volker Koepp Kollektion' (Edition Salzgeber, 2010), 49:57–50:55 [on DVD].
3. Helmut Schmitz, *On Their Own Terms: The Legacy of National Socialism in Post-1990 German Fiction* (Birmingham: University of Birmingham Press, 2004), p. 2.
4. Ahonen, p. 1.
5. Ibid., pp. 266–67.
6. Ibid., p. 274.
7. Ther, p. 344.
8. Graham Jackman, 'Introduction', *German Life and Letters*, 57, 4 (2004), 343–53 (p.345).
9. Ahonen, p. 278.
10. Moeller, p. 48.
11. For a fuller discussion of German victimhood see 'similar feelings' in the Introduction.
12. Reinhard Jirgl, *Die Stille* (Munich: DTV, 2009), p. 223. All further references will be given in parentheses with the abbreviation *St*.
13. Reinhard Jirgl, '"Das Gegenteil von Spiel ist nicht Ernst, sondern Wirklichkeit!"', *Text + Kritik*, 189 (2011), 80–85 (pp. 81–82); *Gewitterlicht: Erzählung/Das poetische Vermögen des alphanumerischen Codes in der Prosa* (Hannover: Revonnah, 2002), p. 66.
14. Helmut Böttiger, 'Buchstaben-Barrikaden: Von Reinhard Jirgls Anfängen bis hin zu *Die Stille* — ein in sich stimmiger ästhetischer Kosmos', *Text + Kritik*, 189 (2011), 14–24 (p. 22).
15. Ibid., p. 24.

16. The hundred sections are grouped into forty-five chapters, with each chapter representing a page of the photograph album, so that Chapter 1, with two sections, represents a page with two photographs. A further compositional feature is the relationship of the section size to the size of the photograph: 'die Gestaltung der einzelnen Blöcke [orientiert sich] nach Angaben des Schriftstellers an genau der Zeichenmenge, die sich aus den Abmessungen der vom Textweltenschöpfer durchnummerierten Fotografien ergibt' (Dieter Stolz, '"45 Seiten aus dickem braunem Velourspapier beklebt mit 100 Mal geronnenem Tod": Reinhard Jirgls Roman *Die Stille*', *Text + Kritik*, 189 (2011), 57–68 (p. 61).
17. Ibid., p. 58.
18. Katrin Hillgruber, 'Berge, Meere, deutsche Giganten', *Frankfurter Rundschau*, 16 March 2009, <www.fr-online.de/literatur/-die-stille-berge-meere-deutsche-giganten,1472266,3085124.html> [accessed 3 September 2012].
19. See, for example, Reinhard Jirgl, *Abschied von den Feinden* (Munich: DTV, 2010), pp. 325–28.
20. Reinhard Jirgl, 'Die wilde und die gezähmte Schrift: Eine Arbeitsübersicht', *Sprache im technischen Zeitalter*, 42 (2004), 296–320 (p. 313).
21. Arne De Winde, 'Das Erschaffen von "eigen-Sinn": Notate zu Reinhard Jirgls Schrift-Bildlichkeitsexperimenten', in *Reinhard Jirgl: Perspektiven, Lesarten, Kontexte*, ed. by David Clarke and Arne De Winde (Amsterdam & New York: Rodopi, 2007), pp. 111–49 (p. 123).
22. Jirgl, 'Die wilde Schrift', p. 306. See also De Winde, 'Das Erschaffen', p. 125.
23. David Clarke, 'Einleitung', in *Reinhard Jirgl*, ed. by Clarke and De Winde, pp. 7–12 (pp. 8–9).
24. Erk Grimm, 'Die Lebensläufe Reinhard Jirgls: Techniken der melotraumatischen Inszenierung', in *Reinhard Jirgl*, ed. by Clarke and De Winde, pp. 197–226 (p. 207).
25. For contributions to this discussion see Harald Welzer, 'Schön unscharf: Über die Konjunktur der Familien- und Generationsromane,' *Mittelweg*, 36, 1 (2004), 53–64; Timm Menke, 'Reinhard Jirgls Roman *Die Unvollendeten* — Tabubruch oder späte Erinnerung?', *Glossen*, 8 (2004), <http://www2.dickinson.edu/glossen/heft20/menke.html> [accessed 14 October 2014]; Stuart Taberner, 'Literary Representations in Contemporary Literary Fiction of the Expulsions of Germans from the East in 1945', in *A Nation of Victims?*, ed. by Schmitz, pp. 223–46 (pp. 235–36); Elizabeth Boa, 'Lost *Heimat* in Generational Novels by Reinhard Jirgl, Christoph Hein, and Angelika Overath', in *Germans as Victims in the Literary Fiction of the Berlin Republic*, ed. by Stuart Taberner and Karina Berger (Rochester, NY: Camden House, 2009), pp. 86–101; Bill Niven, *Representations of Flight and Expulsion in East German Prose Works* (Rochester, NY: Camden House, 2014), pp. 171–93.
26. Fassin & Rechtman, p. 284.
27. See also Niven, *Representations of Flight*, p. 173.
28. 'Gotzverdammten' puns with Gott/Götze [God/idol], thus suggesting that corporations are the new idols that deserve damnation.
29. Jirgl, 'Das Gegenteil von Spiel', p. 82.
30. Frances L. Restuccia, *Amorous Acts: Lacanian Ethics in Modernism, Film, and Queer Theory* (Stanford, CA: Stanford University Press, 2006). See particularly Chapter 1, 'The Paradox of Lacanian Ethics', pp. 1–27.
31. Lacan, *The Ethics of Psychoanalysis*, p. 189.
32. Ibid., p. 267.
33. Restuccia, p. 15.
34. Jacques Lacan, *Television: A Challenge to the Psychoanalytic Establishment*, ed. by Joan Copjec, trans. by Denis Hollier, Rosalind Krauss, and Annette Michelson (New York: Norton, 1990), p. xxx.
35. Heiner Müller, *Gesammelte Irrtümer: Interviews und Gespräche* (Frankfurt a.M.: Verlag der Autoren, 1986), p. 115.
36. Here the pun is with 'Unfall' [accident] and Phallus. 'Verkehr' [traffic] can also refer to intercourse.
37. Jirgl, 'Das Gegenteil von Spiel', p. 85.
38. Ibid., p. 81. It is interesting to note in this respect that both Arne De Winde and Karen Dannemann agree that Jirgl's writing practice suggests that it is as though he is not writing separate novels but one monolithic work. See Arne De Winde, '"Das hatte ich mal irgendwo gelesen": Überlegungen zu Reinhard Jirgls Essayismus', *Text + Kritik*, 189 (2011), 86–97 (p. 86).

39. Dieter Wellershoff, '*Schöpferische und mechanische Ironie*', in *Das Komische*, ed. by Wolfgang Preisendanz and Rainer Warning (Munich: Fink, 1976), pp. 423–25 (p. 424).
40. Volker Koepp, in interview with Rainer Rother, 5th May 2006, *Schattenland*, 20:40 [on DVD]
41. Rosa Roth-Zuckermann, quoted in Marianne Hirsch and Leo Spitzer, *Ghosts of Home: The Afterlife of Czernowitz in Jewish Memory* (Berkeley: University of California Press, 2010), p. 18.
42. Mathias Zwilling, quoted in 'Nur die Alten bleiben: Auf den Spuren jüdischen Lebens in der heute ukrainischen Stadt Czernowitz', *Die Zeit*, 24 October 1997, <http://www.zeit.de/1997/44/Nur_die_Alten_bleiben> [accessed 7 November 2011].
43. For example, 'Du schreckliches Buchenwald, du' (lit. 'You terrible beechwood!') (*H*, 18.50).
44. Peter Braun, 'Von Europa erzählen: Über die Konstruktion der Erinnerung in den Dokumentarfilmen von Volker Koepp', in *DDR — erinnern, vergessen: Das visuelle Gedächtnis des Dokumentarfilms*, ed. by Tobias Ebbrecht and others (Marburg: Schüren, 2009), pp. 71–91 (p. 71).
45. Stefan Reinecke, 'Das Land, das einfach verrostete', *TAZ*, 28 January 2010, p. 15.
46. Koepp, interview with Rother, 26:30.
47. Ibid., 32:45.
48. Andreas Becker, 'Zeig doch mal die Deutschen', *TAZ*, 12 (2001), p. 26.
49. Urs Richter, 'Und Sonntags Krähensuppe', *TAZ*, 3 (2001), p. 15.
50. Koepp, interview with Rother, 54:20.
51. Richard Dyer, 'Nice Young Men Who Sell Antiques — Gay Men in Heritage Cinema', in *Film / Literature / Heritage: A Sight and Sound Reader*, ed. by Ginette Vincendeau (London: BFI, 2001), p. 48.
52. Lutz Koepnick, 'Reframing the Past: Heritage Cinema and Holocaust in the 1990s', *New German Critique*, 87 (2002), 47–82 (p. 51).
53. Ibid., p. 75.
54. See for example Guido Knopp's *Die Große Flucht* (Munich: Universum Film, 2004) [on DVD] in which these techniques are further dramatized through the use of extra-diegetic music, frequent cuts, and the use of contemporary shots of landscape to intensify the 'Modus des emotionalen Nacherlebens', to use Assmans's phrase. See Assman, *Der lange Schatten der Vergangenheit*, p. 194.
55. Peter Braun, 'Landschaften mit Geschichte: Über die Dokumentarfilme von Volker Koepp', in *Die Medien der Geschichte: Historizität und Medialität in interdisziplinärer Perspektive*, ed. by Fabio Crivellari and others, (Constance: UVK, 2004), pp. 351–77 (p. 363).
56. Tim Bergfelder, 'Shadowlands: The Memory of the *Ostgebiete* in Contemporary German Film and Television', in *Screening War: Perspectives on German Suffering*, ed. by Paul Cooke and Marc Silberman (Rochester, NY: Camden House, 2010), pp. 123–42 (p. 135).
57. Reinecke, 'Das Land, das einfach verrostete'.
58. Braun, 'Von Europa erzählen', p. 73.

CHAPTER 5

Ruth Klüger: Comedy and *Ressentiment*

'Darf man sich gut unterhalten bei einem Film über den Holocaust?' [Should you enjoy a film about the Holocaust?].¹ Adapting Ruth Klüger's question, one could also ask whether one may enjoy reading the memoir of a woman who survived Theresienstadt, Auschwitz, and Christianstadt (Groß-Rosen). As Klüger herself points out, part of the enjoyment is derived from the fact that she is a survivor: her story thus lends itself to being read as one with a happy ending, whatever the impact of persecution, ghettoization, slave labour, near death, and the murder of her father and brother is on *weiter leben*.² She describes the challenge in writing about her escape without letting the reader heave a sigh of relief, since the survival stories of ten thousands do not help the millions murdered. Our enjoyment at the fact that the inevitability of genocide has in fact been avoided is the product of a 'Trick emotionaler Algebra' [trick of emotional algebra] (*wl*, 141). Klüger is right that the effect of this trick is a powerful one, and in their reception study Stephan Braese and Holger Gehle demonstrate how in Germany identification with one side of the algebraic equation has contributed to the success of *weiter leben*.³ Nevertheless, Klüger does a lot to interfere with any simple generation of pleasure based on identification and as a result the enjoyment elicited by her memoirs is complex. Her narrative is an interweaving of her memories and experiences with her highly reflexive and emotional responses to them, including direct engagement with discussions around questions of Holocaust representation, memorialization, memory, and feminism. The intellectual and emotional complexity of her writing is fundamental to the increased attention her work is receiving academically.

One aspect of Klüger's writing that both contributes to and challenges our enjoyment of her texts is its comedy. Her use of humour, the role it plays in her autobiographical works and how her discussions of comedy in her critical essays help us to understand her memoirs, has received little critical consideration. Some critics comment in passing on her subtle humour, her intelligent wit, or the often-funny dialogue, but these points are not developed.⁴ This is perhaps not surprising in view of her assertion in *unterwegs verloren* that she does not write 'Witzbücher' [joke books].⁵ Nevertheless, even if her memoirs are not joke books, it is by no means the case that their comedy is always unintended, for, as Klüger writes in *Frauen lesen anders*, she did not want her account of war and imprisonment to be 'ganz witzlos' [utterly humourless].⁶ Perhaps one of the reasons for the critical reticence in considering Klüger's humour is that it is so often inseparable from another characteristic of her writing: 'Wut' [anger], 'Schonungslosigkeit' [ruthlessness], and 'die Kühnheit zu schreiben, wie ihr der Schnabel gewachsen ist' [boldness to write exactly what she thinks].⁷ Thus Klüger aggravates the moral anxiety that attends the question of how far we may enjoy Holocaust representations. Not only does the bringing together of comedy and the Holocaust anyway concentrate that anxiety, but her comedy is not conciliatory: it can be biting in tone, and, conversely, her uncompromising tone can often become comic.

The anger and bite that are a characteristic of Klüger's writing point to a further challenge of her work: the tactlessness of *ressentiment* [resentment]. In his *Zur Geneologie der Moral*, Nietzsche is scathing about *ressentiment*. He argues that it is fundamental to a reactive morality, one that is based upon the spiritual revenge of the priestly castes, including the Jews, against the naïve, but strong, free, and active morality of aristocratic peoples. Whereas decent, aristocratic morality stems from the strength to say 'yes', slave morality, driven by *ressentiment*, rests upon the need to say no and to negate the other.⁸ However, the strength of *ressentiment* is its creative potential, resulting in the triumph of slave morality in the form of Christianity in Europe, which has successfully persuaded humanity that weaknesses, such as humility, obedience, and pity, have become the highest virtues.⁹ In the post-war context Jean Améry takes a particular position on Nietzsche's view of *ressentiment*, both recognizing its negative effect in shackling the individual to his past and also picking up on its creative moral potential: it is through *ressentiment* that injustice is not forgotten with time.¹⁰ But *ressentiment* is no benevolent force, for Améry describes the exploration of his own *ressentiment* as neither a pleasant undertaking nor a tactful one.¹¹ His description resonates with much in Klüger's work, though in her case *ressentiment* is inseparable from the role that comedy plays in her memoirs.

Before focusing on her memoirs I shall consider the conceptual framework that Klüger establishes in her essayistic work, as well as the particular tone that characterizes them. For Klüger's concern with the relationship of fiction and history, of the nature of truth in fiction and her association of comic modes with an absence of empathy, raise interesting questions about the function of comedy in her own 'subjective history': the fact that Klüger's comedy is not contained within a fictional framework intensifies the ethical disquiet concerning both what the reader may find amusing and what Klüger constructs as humorous. It is with Klüger's insistent self-positioning as a historian that this exploration of her comedy will start.

Uncompromising Borders

When it comes to autobiography Klüger's aim is to be uncompromising in insisting on the sharp division between fact and fiction (*GW*, 218). Although she points to strong overlaps between autobiography and historical novels, she is clear that her memoirs are not novels: she wishes they were, for then she would not have actually experienced what she depicts. Rather, they are historical (*GW, 145*), for as she writes, 'Autobiographie ist Geschichte in der Ich-Form' [autobiography is history in the first person] (*GW*, 86). She is a witness to events, hence in a position to tell the truth about them or not, unlike fiction which cannot be likened to a witness statement. Even though witnesses may be unreliable and historians cannot be objective, an autobiographer nevertheless bears a specific responsibility to be truthful. So just as the police expect a witness to be able to tell the difference between real events and imagination, readers expect a history book to follow different rules from novels. It is for this reason that she is unhappy with Amos Oz's view that readers should not ask whether Oz has experienced exactly what he depicts, but whether they can empathize with what they read (*GW*, 146). As Karolin Machtans argues, for Klüger the autobiographical project is referential, and she, as author, exists as subject outside the work.[12] Language too is referential and the language of autobiography, as history, refers to unchallengeable facts: '[d]ie historischen Fakten sind wie Stonehenge' [historical facts are like Stonehenge], so whatever interpretation is offered, the facts remain (*GW*, 92). Klüger points to her own experience as a reason for her concern with the relationship between fact and fiction and her tone is dismissive when she refers to the '[h]ochkarätige moderne Theorien' [high-carat modern theories] which attract lazy readers and which do not care for the difference between the two (*GW*, 218).

Klüger's uncompromising stance on autobiography's status as history on occasion slides closer to assertion than argument. Thus she likens autobiography to a border village between the states of History and Literature, where two languages are spoken, but where the village must belong to one or other state. This analogy is evidence enough for her to declare that autobiography is clearly on the side of history, without acknowledging either that some border disputes do not get resolved, or that the intellectual debates around autobiography are perhaps not best settled by claims of territorial ownership, or that in the logic of this analogy, autobiography could just as clearly end up on the side of fiction (*GW*, 86). Klüger's comparison here is indicative of her general approach in her essayistic work. She presents her views without engaging with the theoretical and literary critical scholarship that explores the relationship of autobiography to fiction, be that, for example, Paul Ricoeur or Jacques Derrida.[13] Or, in examples that spring from her expertise in theatre, she effectively ignores Bakhtin by asserting that drama is the most objective genre, and dismisses all analyses of the importance of the camera when she claims that theatre and film have in common that the actor stands in place of the narrator (*GW*, 85 & 190). Machtans argues that Klüger's choice of the essay form, and her eschewing of all but the very necessary footnotes, is part of her wider intellectual and feminist project which emphasizes the subjectivity of interpretation as well as the context of the author for that interpretation. In her view an essay explores its subject without making a claim to be a general truth.[14]

The essays combine, then, the paradox of any opinion piece, that it is both subjective yet the author assumes the authority to express a correct view. In Klüger's case she places particular value on the authority of the author, and, more specifically, the author as witness. She seems reluctant to allow witness testimony to be subjected to critical scrutiny. When referring to police witnesses, she does not allude to cross-examination in court, and she is critical of the craze for recording oral testimony because it reduces the individual from being a witness to being raw material. She objects to the fact that the witnesses' capacity to differentiate events from memory is put into question, and with it their identity as thinking, rational individuals (*GW*, 59). Thus Klüger constructs the autobiographer as a witness whose relationship to events and to memory is fundamentally unproblematic. What results is a tension. On the one hand Klüger asserts her position as witness with a particular moral responsibility to represent reality truthfully. She draws on the authority of her experience to comment, voice opinions, and engage in debates, sometimes with a marked vehemence that has the ring of prescription about it. Her tone means that she occasionally seems to slip into using the verbal equivalent of the wagging finger against which she warns in discussions about the Holocaust (*GW*, 218). On the other hand, her subjective voice is consistently evident and further emphasized by her references to those who differ in their views, Oz being a prime example. Her uncompromising assertions function as provocations to the reader to react and to think about the relationship between interpretation and context. The challenge she sets her German readers in *weiter leben* is thus also one she makes to the readers of her essays: 'sucht die Auseinandersetzung' [seek debate] (*wl*, 142).

Comedy in Context

The tension between authority and subjectivity is one that is fundamentally interwoven with Klüger's conceptualization of the boundary between fact and fiction, or context and fantasy, and the relationship of each to truth. Klüger is adamant that there exists a fundamental difference between fact and fiction, remarking that a death enacted on the stage moves the audience, whereas the real death of the actor would horrify it. Similarly, it is the fictional or mythological frame that allows women to enjoy an erotic frisson when looking at the painting of the 'Rape of the Sabine Women' despite its typical objectification of women. Such enjoyment is possible in a way that an illustration of the same scene in the daily newspaper would not be (*Fla*, 101). She argues that no novelist need be confined to real events but that a historian can take fewer liberties with those events than a writer of fiction (*GW*, 84).[15] Yet the freedom that fiction has in its treatment of events does not mean that it cannot incorporate lies. Klüger outlines two different types of aestheticization of the real. The first is a search for truth based on fantasy and empathy, an attempt to interpret events in such a way that is thought provoking. The second involves conforming to the purported limitation of the public and is kitsch (*GW*, 61). All aestheticization involves a transformation of the real, thus, for example, caricatures must maintain enough of the original to be recognizable as caricature. But a lie insinuates itself when fantasy is presented as truth and this lie is by definition kitsch.[16] An author must indicate aesthetically that a transformation of reality into fiction has occurred, otherwise the result is kitsch: when 'das bunte Spielgeld eines Wunschtraums dem Publikum als bare Münze angeboten [wird]' [the colourful toy money of a fantasy is presented to the public as hard cash] (*K*, 89).

Klüger is a keen defender of literature as an attempt to find what she calls a 'rhyme' with reality, as that which supplements it (*GW*, 218). In historical fiction particularly it is not possible to draw clear lines between fact and fiction, and it is the reader who must decide in each case whether to accept what fiction has to offer. Nevertheless, the fluid line between history and fiction is one that should be respected in the contract between author and reader, or director and viewer. If the choice of material is historical, then authors and directors effectively promise their readers to adhere to facts, and any breaking of this contract becomes cannibalization of history, and with it kitsch (*GW*, 85,92). Crucially, therefore, a fictional framework is not an excuse or a licence to represent reality unconditionally: lies are both possible and dangerous. It follows from Klüger's argument that comedy, as one of the devices of aestheticization, can belong either to a search for truth or can facilitate kitsch, depending on whether or not it is part of wish-fulfilment masquerading as reality, or reality's reflective supplement. In her essayistic work, however, although the question of artifice and comedy's potential as play is hinted at in relation to jokes, overall Klüger's concern with historical context leads her to articulate a certain reticence towards comedy, and she links it to oppression, cruelty, and a lack of empathy.

In her discussion of jokes, Klüger describes them as verbal artefacts, and as such a simple form of literature. Like literature, one of their functions is to free repressed layers of emotion (*GW*, 39). This is why risky or controversial jokes, like racist jokes, disturb us morally even if they are narrowly funny in the sense that they provoke our laughter through unexpected twists. In this brief reference to jokes, Klüger points to their artifice, which in the context of her wider discussion of fiction and kitsch would seem to suggest a positive evaluation. Elsewhere in her essays she discusses the shock of pornographic writing, concluding not only that pornography is more honest than kitsch, since its aim is explicit (*GW*, 48), but that we can deal with the shock of pornography when certain borders are upheld: between fantasy and reality and between 'Identifikation und der durch die Kunst (oder zumindest Künstlichkeit) des Werks vermittelten Distanz' [identification and the distance that is mediated through art (or at least through artifice)] (*Fla*, 101). The constellation of shock, evident artifice, targeted response, and distance is one that well describes jokes, and in this respect Klüger's point seems to resonate with Christie Davies's analysis of jokes. Davies seeks to refute theories that identify the content of a joke with the beliefs of the teller by examining ethnic jokes and their contexts and showing the sheer variety of ways in which they are used and responded to. He distinguishes jokes from other types of humour or put down: as highly structured set pieces they do not require a real victim, whereas wit and anecdote, with their relationship to spontaneity and sociability, come closer to verbal aggression than jokers with set pieces. Although jokes play with superiority and disparagement, this may or may not coincide with a reality. Thus, for example, he points to the fact that there were very few jokes about Japanese or Japanese Americans during World War Two, whereas the 'stupidity jokes' in North America related to two groups not in serious conflict with anyone.[17]

A joke is a self-contained text that plays with superiority and disparagement through a temporary creation of illusion or 'deception by agreement', it does not intrinsically describe actual relations: it may or it may not and so cannot be reduced to a serious statement. Because a joke is funny and not persuasive it is the form of humour least equipped for serious purposes.[18] Davies argues that the malicious use of jokes is not a property of the joke itself but of its frame, and even then a joke has little significant political impact in the face of ideologies that shape belief systems. Specifically in relation to jokes about anti-Semitism, he points to the lack of evidence that Jewish jokes contributed to persecutory and genocidal anti-Semitism, as they were insignificant compared to material and ideological factors, and who controlled the use of force:

> The very terms and phrases used to assert the consequences of jokes, such as 'inter-connections', 'reproducing the social order', 'perpetuating stereotypes under relaxed conditions', indicate an inability to ask the question 'how much?' [...] Jokes may have had a *tiny* net effect in promoting or in retarding anti-Semitism, depending on where the balance lay between the humanising impact of Jewish jokes and self-mockery so disliked by anti-Semites and the use of jokes in a brutal way by the Jews' enemies.[19]

Yet Klüger's assessment of jokes as verbal artifice and her recognition that they can be 'narrowly funny' does not translate into a willingness to evaluate them as temporary, funny deceptions divorced from context. On the contrary, she presents a sustained and vehement refusal to interpret any cultural production as a 'moral holiday' despite her recognition in theory that distance between fantasy and reality can be sustained. So, despite claiming of film that every child knows the difference between images and reality, she also argues that film audiences find it hard to separate film actor from role (*GW*, 63 & 175). Despite pointing to the difference between a staged death and a real death, and to reading as an activity that helps sustain distance, she also argues that there is a danger in the representation of Jews: 'Phantasiejuden [werden] für fotografierte Menschen gehalten' [Fantasy Jews are taken to be photographed people] (*K*, 108). She sees this danger realized in the example of Wilhelm Raabe's *Der Hungerpastor*, an extremely popular novel that caused considerable damage to the minds of its readers.[20] Literary texts perpetuate and contribute to anti-Semitic and misogynist attitudes when they depict Jews and women as stereotypes, and their status as fiction is not enough in itself to remove them from complicity in entrenching damaging views. Thus in her study of the representation of Jews in post-war German literature, she argues that there is a persistent pattern whereby Jewishness is described with either sentimentality or brutality, deteriorating into either kitsch or pornography (*K*, 36). Amongst others, she criticizes Günter Grass for the clichéd figure of Sigismund Markus as the unattractive Jewish man lusting after the Aryan woman (*K*, 23), and Fassbinder and Zwerenz for using the character of the rich Jew for perpetuating stereotypes rather than for challenging taboos (*K*, 32). It is precisely text-immanent criticism and evaluation of literature based purely on aesthetic considerations that can serve prevailing attitudes by divorcing content from wider debates (*Fla*, 85).

Klüger's view that members of minorities suffer from the stereotypes made of them (*K*, 48) encompasses caricature and satire. Although the satirist does not reproduce reality he chooses the traits that seem to him to be significant, and is therefore responsible for the meaning that is generated.[21] It is for this reason that she is scathing in her condemnation of Martin Walser's satirical novel, *Tod eines Kritikers*. She regards the novel as fundamentally anti-Semitic, since the corrupt and lecherous critic who ruins German writers' careers is Jewish, or considered such. At the same time the society in which he lives is both represented as free from anti-Semitism and anti-Semitism is not thematized. Walser's claim that the murder of a Jewish critic is in the imagination of a fictional protagonist further fuels Klüger's ire, for she views it as his attempt to ignore German history: the imagined murder of a Jewish critic in a novel that Walser explicitly links with the humiliation of Germany's defeat in 1945, cannot simply be bracketed out from Germany's past. For Klüger the plea that the novel is a comedy or a farce is no defence: 'Als ob Komödien und schlechte Witze nicht seit eh und je besonders beliebte Vehikel der Verhöhnung gewesen wären!' [As though comedy and bad jokes haven't always been much loved tools of humiliation!].[22]

The relationship between fantasy and context is complex and political, as Klüger's discussion makes evident. Yet the complexity she invokes is sometimes flattened out by the dynamics of polemic: her own experience provides the critical perspective from which to insist on the political importance of understanding the relationship of fantasy and context, but it also fuels her adoption of an authoritative voice that resists ambiguity. So on the one hand Klüger offers an important challenge to Davies's analysis of ethnic jokes by raising the question of how far culture contributes to discourses that then facilitate the imposition of persecutory economic and political policies. On the other hand she seems unwilling in practice to entertain the possibility that apparently un-complex texts can result in ambivalent, conflicting, or even unpredictable responses. As Steve Neale argues in his detailed analysis of propaganda and Veit Harlan's *Jud Süß*, both a text's mode of address and its place within the social apparatus is crucial to the meaning it generates, and the two do not always cohere. The response to *Jud Süß*, with the stereotyped figure of Oppenheimer becoming the object of desire of many non-Jewish German women, demonstrates that stereotypes do not function within a simple intention/effect relationship.[23] But Klüger's political and ethical aversion to stereotypes and caricature, combined with the position of subjective authority that she assumes, puts her in a position of recognizing the dangers while reducing readers and spectators to passive recipients of ideology. To put it at its most extreme, she may have got fed up with the 'Schönheits- und Hoheitsgetue' [to-do about the Great and the Good] of other classics and enjoy Grimmelshausen's casual way of treating violence, torture, rape, and murder (*Fla*, 187), but others are in danger of mistaking a character in a novel for a photograph.

The harm that Klüger ascribes to satire or bad jokes is in keeping with a more general association that she makes in her essays between comedy as a mode of representation and a lack of empathy. Thus she refuses for Shylock the possibility of empathy that results in catharsis, since the play is a comedy and he is its villain. Any attempt to portray him sympathetically can only result in sentimentality. Similarly, in her analysis of *Penthesilea*, Klüger argues that Kleist presents us with two views of the behaviour of Penthesilea and Achilles, one tragic, the other comic. The defining difference between such different responses to the same events is the presence of empathy: whereas empathy provokes fear and pity in the viewers, its absence leads to alienation and laughter. Within the play, she argues, it is the Greeks whose reaction represents comedy as they defend themselves from what they see, shaking their heads in disbelief, and narrow-mindedly demonstrating a lack of sympathy and understanding (*Fla*, 145). In contrast, the empathetic Amazons show horror and pity and effectively become a tragic chorus. Klüger again draws attention to the absence of empathy as a characteristic of comedy when she discusses Kleist's anecdote of the twelve blind men and the pig. The spectacle of the blind men attempting to club the pig, and in the process hitting each other, is laid on for the amusement of Emperor Maximilian and other onlookers, and it clearly demonstrates that 'Grausamkeit ist Belustigung' [cruelty is entertainment] (*K*, 198). Indeed, she suggests that Kleist may, in recounting the episode, be pointing to the true source of humour.

Klüger's essays make clear the importance she places on taking seriously the experience of harm and the harm that literature can do by being complicit with hegemonic and persecutory forces. Her insistence on context, on a clear understanding of literary lies, and on autobiography as history, is informed by the harm done to her as Jewish and female. At the same time, the essays demonstrate how centrally her writing is characterized by a highly subjective but also assertive tone, one that often derives its authority from experience and anecdote. Her tone betrays her pleasure in polemic, but can result in the emotional tenor of her writing seeming more prescriptive and judgemental than what she actually writes. The obdurate resonance of her tone is not one that obviously seeks or evokes empathy and it is then perhaps slightly surprising that lack of empathy is a reason for her suspicion of comedy, which she even posits as having its origin in cruelty. When approaching her memoir in the knowledge that she wished to write it 'not without humour', there are therefore interesting questions to be asked. One relates to the intersection of comedy, lack of empathy, and autobiography as history: against whom is the comedy directed, and does it matter that the people are, in Klüger's own terms, real? Another stems from her understanding of the comic aesthetic: what is the purpose of her wit if comedy is a defensive strategy that precludes comprehension? And, related to this and to the polemic tension of subjectivity and authority: if the forceful, even aggressive articulation of her point of view itself tips into comic hyperbole, does comedy, quite contrary to her association of it with alienation and lack of empathy, in fact allow her to articulate *ressentiment* while yet eliciting empathy from the reader?

Malicious Half-Tones

In *weiter leben*, Ruth Klüger articulates her profound ambivalence towards Austria, and towards Vienna in particular. She has no friends or relatives left in the country and Vienna is both alien and familiar. She describes the city as 'heimatlich unheimlich' [uncannily familiar] and to its very core 'judenkinderfeindlich' [hostile to Jewish children] (*wl*, 68). Yet it is Austrian literature that still speaks to her more intimately than any other and in a very particular way: 'im bequemen Tonfall einer vertraut hinterfotzigen Kindersprache' [with the comfortable intonation of a familiarly underhand children's language] (*wl*, 66). In *Landscapes of Memory* she describes this ribald or indecent dimension of Viennese German entailing 'a sense of humor that Germans often don't get, and a wealth of malicious half tones that would be obscene in any other tongue'.[24] Although she is at once hooked on the language and does not like it, she again emphasizes the 'insolent humor and [...] aggressive, colorful verbiage' of Viennese German when referring to New York English, which in her view shares the same qualities (*LoM*, 249). The combination of humour and aggression is a notable characteristic of Klüger's writing and is far from accidental. As she says of Grimmelshausen's Courasche: 'Ihre Skrupellosigkeit wirkt befreiend, ihr Witz macht das Schlimme erträglich' [Her lack of scruples is liberating, her wit makes terrible events tolerable] (*Fla*, 189).

Weiter leben is punctuated by insolent humour, irony, and surprising, funny turns of phrase. The adults seek to keep the terrible news of death and persecution of Jews from the children, but Klüger's choice of verbs betrays a certain cheek: she uses 'zum besten geben' [entertain] to suggest a sense of theatricality and entertainment when they tell each other bad news at the table (*wl*, 9), and 'endlos [...] quatschen' [endless blather] to describe their response to anti-Semitism (*wl*, 14). Her colourful language leads to witty images and juxtapositions. She describes herself as someone who easily drops things, be that breakable objects or love affairs (*wl*, 9), and who as a child forgot all her English with a thoroughness that would have made Penelope proud because her teacher was a Nazi sympathizer (*wl*, 17). When describing the increasing pressures on family relations as a result of persecution she drily points out that more crockery breaks during an earthquake (*wl*, 56), and she describes German post-war anti-Semitism bubbling along under the surface like a stew in a good quality cooking pot (*wl*, 196). Later in the USA, she sheds her prejudices against baptised Jews quietly and secretly, as she would shed a pair of laddered tights under the table (*wl*, 249). Her family is presented in terms of Austrian literature, with her brother figuring as a child of a Schnitzler novella with traits of Werfel and Zweig thrown in, and her father as coming from a poor family more typical of Joseph Roth (*wl*, 21). It is particularly her brazen tone and uncompromising remarks that inject humorous half tones into her narrative. Her mother is yellow as a lemon from jaundice, Auschwitz has become a place for 'Geländerbewahrer' [site-custodians], psychological rules are 'wackelig' [wobbly], and post-war New York psychoanalysis is little more than 'Wiener Wald- und Wiesenpsychoanalyse' [psychoanalysis of the Vienna Forest-and-Fields school] (*wl*, 84, 139, 73, & 240).

Humorous half tones are also present in the way Klüger recounts certain events or scenes, even when what she is depicting is disturbing. The autobiography begins with the reference to death as the all-pervading secret, which intensifies the comic grotesqueness of Klüger's first encounter with a corpse: her grandfather's speaking parrot which is butchered in front of her by an 'überzüchteten, überkandidelten Drahthaarterrier' [overbred, affected, wire-haired terrier] (*wl*, 40). She describes her visit to her cousin Hans, whom she wants to ask about his experience of being tortured in Buchenwald as a boy. She draws a darkly comic picture of their meeting, describing the living room as 'so kleinkariert, wie es eigentlich nur den englischen Kleinbürgern gelingt, häßlich zu wohnen' [petty-minded and ugly in a way that really only the English lower-middle class succeed at]. Klüger is so bored by banal small talk that she cannot sit still, leading Hans to ask their other cousin, Heinz, whether she suffers from haemorrhoids. She, the well-trained academic, who knows how to ask her precise questions about Hans's past, is contrasted with the others in the petit-bourgeois room who only want their peace and hastily leave (*wl*, 10–11). This episode certainly seems to confirm Klüger's later assertion that her upbringing emphasized 'Skepsis und Widerspruch' [scepticism and dissent] (*wl*, 227), qualities that can give her writing a strong satirical edge and which expose conformity. At the very start of *weiter leben* she conveys her Viennese family's social aspirations in the ironic aside about the living room: 'eigentlich sagten wir "Salon"' [actually we called it the 'drawing room'] (*wl*, 9), and in *Landscapes of Memory* she seems amused by her grandfather's 'writhing' embarrassment when little, but uncircumcised, Heinz is playing naked on the beach. Further irony is added to this scene by the knowledge that the 'shameful piece of skin' helped him pass as a Catholic and survive the war in Hungary (*LoM*, 4). Later in New York the pretentions and hypocrisy of her 'real American' relatives are ruthlessly exposed. The ghastly Thanksgiving dinner at which she and her mother are lectured and condescended to seems aptly symbolized in the raw sticks of celery that are served as the starter. Klüger sits listening to her father being insulted, unable to conjure up the anticipated enthusiasm for a vegetable that consists of 'faserigen, wahrscheinlich unverdaulichen, auf jeden Fall unappetitlichen grünen Stengeln' [stringy, presumably indigestible, but at any rate unappetizing green stalks] (*wl*, 229). The celery is in fact much like the family. Also in New York, Klüger is scathing about the fat women who pay her mother a dollar an hour to massage away their American lard (*wl*, 226).

Klüger's comic undertones are not limited to social and family mores. They are present in her account of her encounter with the civilian overseer in Christianstadt. She starkly juxtaposes the chatty fatty, who eats his *Schmalzbrot* while asking lots of questions and telling her about the German children who are being called up, with the starving girl intent only on getting his food (*wl*, 157). In a highly dangerous situation, Klüger, her mother, and Ditha are arrested by a military policeman after they have escaped from the forced march. The comedy in this situation is generated by the apparent incongruity of the situation. Klüger's mother decides to put on airs, as the young Klüger sees it, conversing with the policeman about culture and music in order to convince him that they are from the higher echelons of society. In the absence of his boss, and the uncanniness caused by his peculiar catch, the man releases them. Klüger recounts how much the three of them laughed during their escape, remarking that 'Gefahr ist ein guter Nährboden für Komik' [Danger is fertile ground for comedy] (*wl*, 174). She reinforces this point when she tells of her experiences of being bombed by the allies in Straubing. Taking refuge with the farmer's family in the cellar, and in terror for her life, she finds the sight of the farmer popping up from behind a barrel between bombs funny: 'Komik gedeiht, wie gesagt, bei Gefahr' [As I said, comedy thrives when there's danger] (*wl*, 189).

Klüger's sense of humour persists in *unterwegs verloren*. She is amused by the matching names of Professor Schneider and Mr Taylor and shows her own comic verve by calling one of her cats Golda Miau (*uv*, 17 & 26). She describes her own very pleasurable encounter with marijuana at the age of forty, and conjures the scene where the rather shocked and censorious Percy caught her smoking it (*uv*, 99). There is a similar moment of fleeting incongruity and momentary amusement when we hear how the ageing Klüger and Ditha giggle together (*wl*, 175), that she and Maria recommend each other diets (*uv*, 122), and of Klüger's love of Blackjack in the cruise ship's casino (*uv*, 234). With gently self-deprecating humour she describes the rather tedious process of ageing, and how glad she is that with the effort of getting two legs out of the bath humans do not have a third. Decrying the boredom of washing and tooth-brushing, she considers it no bad thing that the end is approaching, though, with an ironic reference to German Romanticism, admits that this thought is not romantic enough to qualify as 'Todessehnsucht' [yearning for death] (*uv*, 146). Generally her humour is ironic, acerbic, and, true to her Viennese German, even malicious. When responding to questions about whether she really did throw red wine in a colleague's face, she shakes her head: 'Es war leider nur Weißwein' [Sadly it was only white wine]. She also advises against slapping, for not only may the man hit back, but he is probably unappetizing, so best to avoid touching him (*uv*, 54–55). The colleague who provoked her anger did so by spreading rumours that she had made anti-Semitic remarks, an accusation that is a fundamental attack on her identity and experiences as Jewish, an identity on which she dryly comments: 'In dieser Haut läßt es sich gut leben (wenn man nicht gerade gehäutet wird)' [I feel comfortable in my skin (if I'm not in the middle of being skinned)] (*uv*, 58). She challenges orthodoxy, mocking the much-admired Ivy League universities for offering different types of perversity alongside their top academics (*uv*, 59). She makes fun of sanctimonious attitudes to literature, claiming that it is gossip on a large scale, consisting as it does of love affairs, dramatic deaths, betrayal, courage, and cowardice. She then makes fun of literary critics for demanding that students make snooty interpretations of that gossip (*uv*, 53).

Often Klüger's irony is understated. She describes how depressed she was about the future of the world when reading her father's copy of Spengler's *Untergang des Abendlandes*. But when she reached a casual anti-Semitic remark about a Jewish General, her faith in Spengler evaporated and that in the western world was restored (*uv*, 48). Klüger is equally dry on the subject of the afterlife, of which she does not think very much (*uv*, 15), on her inability to breastfeed — she was not calm enough to be a cow (*uv*, 84–85) —, and on ending up married: 'Irgendwie erwartete ich, daß [meine Mutter] wieder heiraten würde, was auch geschah. Andere erwarteten von mir, daß ich heiraten würde. Was ebenfalls [...] geschah' [Somehow I expected my mother to marry again, which is what happened. Other people expected me to marry. Which also happened] (*uv*, 19). Nine years later, when she leaves the marriage, she feels as though she has fallen out of the freezer to defrost (*uv*, 85). Yet the brazenness of her irony is undoubtedly one of the things that makes it amusing. Paraphrasing Freud, she mocks money as being 'sublimierte Scheiße' [sublimated shit] (*uv*, 46), and it therefore comes as little surprise when she is unimpressed by the argument of non-smokers that giving up smoking will mean she can save money for something nice. For a smoker as she then was, a year's supply of cigarettes would be exactly the right investment (*uv*, 97). In an unabashed diagnosis of her relationship to Germany and Austria, she describes the way that remaining examples of a species hunted to near extinction are particularly cared for. Jews, like whales, are a protected species, and there is a tendency in Germany to collect them. This, however, raises the question of what to do with them once you have them: 'Umbringen kann man sie nicht mehr, das ist vorbei. Man hütet sie' [They can't be murdered any more, that's finished with. They are looked after] (*uv*, 215).

Discrepancies in Perception

Klüger's comedy is not always obvious, nor is her irony always responded to in kind. In the film *Das Weiterleben der Ruth Klüger*, Klüger remarks on the difference in how audiences respond at readings of her memoirs.[25] American students are less reserved in their response to her story, and if something humorous is described, they laugh more easily. This in contrast to Germany, where they do not laugh at all, and to Austria where they also do not laugh but where there is even more resistance to the possibility that they may have been guilty (13:24). Closer to home too her sense of humour is not always appreciated. As a girl she found the repetition of 'tor' in the door sign 'Doktor Viktor Klüger' amusing, and is amazed that the adults do not (*wl*, 26). She also finds the compliment paid to her mother that the new yellow star matches her blouse funny; not so her mother (*wl*, 50). The discrepancy in perception underlying the different responses, that in the case of the door sign she ascribes to the gulf between children and adults, is also present when her attempt at a joke with her son Percy falls flat: 'der Witz wurde nicht mit der gebührenden Ironie aufgenommen' [the joke was not taken with the right irony] (*uv*, 46).

Two distinct characteristics of Klüger's writing open up space for comedy, a space that fosters its ambivalent tone and effect. The first is the combination of the strong and evocative images that her prose conjures with the reflexivity of her writing. Much of the comic effect of the scenes cited above arises from their intense visual representation and vivid physicality. This nudges some scenes towards situation comedy or even lends them a hint of slapstick. Crucially, however, the scenes' vividness incorporates the dual perspective of the Klüger who is participating in the events with that of the narrating, and frequently commenting, Klüger. Scenes combine the interiority of Klüger's emotional responses and direct impressions of the experience as an actor in the scene with the exteriority of the retrospective look. This narrative interlacing of a double perspective establishes a distance and sustains a space that generates a degree of comedy even if it was not present for the participants at the time, as is the case with the parrot. Furthermore, the vivid but also distanced gaze on a scene grants the reader the freedom to perceive a comic dimension even when there is no indication that the narrating Klüger does. Thus when the young Ruth goes to the cinema to watch *Snow White*, it is darkly funny that the most expensive box seat she selects in order not to be noticed, is precisely the seat that places her next to the enthusiastic Nazi, the baker's daughter from next door (*wl*, 46–47). More controversial perhaps is the central selection scene at Auschwitz for the work transport. Her mother has been selected for the transport, Ruth has been rejected, and they both stand bickering in the road beside the barrack.

This bickering takes on ludicrous proportions, so incongruous does it seem in the life or death situation that the mother should be snapping at her daughter 'Hör doch endlich zu' [will you listen to me!] (*wl*, 131), with Klüger seemingly still indignant that her mother took no notice of her counter-arguments. Yet as Klüger remarks in *Landscapes of Memory* about Hans's anger at the English rabbi who objected to his choice of a gentile wife, it is 'incongruous, and therefore amusing' (*LoM*, 5).

The second characteristic of Klüger's writing that both facilitates and complicates its comic dimension is the distinctive combination of irony and directness. Klüger's candid response to the situations and people she describes is not necessarily comic in itself. Her judgements can seem arbitrary and unforgiving, as when on her visit to Hans she accuses his wife of not having taken on board the fact of his torture, reinforcing her own position as someone who is breaking taboos by asking (*wl*, 11; *LoM*, 5). When her German doctor is delighted that she has recovered without his having operated on her, remarking that a doctor needs good fortune, she rather harshly comments: 'er schmückt sich mit meinem Glück' [he's adorning himself with my luck] (*wl*, 274). And when as a young woman she visited relatives in Canada, she refused to accept a gift of a jumper because she wanted either family or nothing (*uv*, 43–44). But Klüger's directness can become comic because the 'malicious half-tones' of her irony interact with her directness in such a way that the boundaries between the two are blurred. This may, as with Percy and German audiences, have the effect of her intended wit or irony not being recognized, but it also has the opposite effect. Klüger's blunt honesty and candid judgements can assume a comic dimension of their own without obvious intention on Klüger's part: half-tones work both ways. Thus the cumulative effect of her remarks and her uncompromising tone can tip into hyperbole, with echoes of Thomas Bernhard's comically relentless fury, and the reader starts to find something amusing that Klüger maybe does not.

One example of this is the extraordinary Gisela, the German wife of a Princeton colleague. In her 'limited imagination' Gisela aims solely to domesticate all war experiences so that they sit easily with her German conscience (*wl*, 85), and she repeatedly makes shockingly complacent remarks about Klüger's concentration camp experiences. Thus Theresienstadt was not so bad, and although Auschwitz was terrible, Klüger was not there for long and had it relatively good: she could after all emigrate to the USA and was spared post-war Germany (*wl*, 93). Gisela is full of praise for an exile who holds nothing against any Germans (*wl*, 159), as though reconciliation is his to offer. Klüger is scathing about Gisela, whom she experiences as unmistakeably aggressive (*wl*, 86). Yet the audacity of Gisela's self-righteousness tips her towards comic stereotype, reflected in Pascale Bos's suggestion that she functions as a personification of the problems between Germans and Jews, and is a composite of several different people.[26]

Klüger's depiction of her relationship with her mother is the most pervasive, and is also a controversial example of how her 'aggressive, colourful verbiage' can assume a comic lustre. I am not suggesting that the relationship itself assumes such lustre, for Klüger's mother caused her profound suffering. In her memoirs Klüger experiences her mother as possessive, manipulative, and paranoid, and has had to cope with behaviour that has been damaging and demeaning for her. Her mother insists on putting paraffin in Ruth's hair to treat lice, and then ignores her pain, with the result that Ruth suffers bad burns to her scalp. She constantly belittles Ruth by claiming that she would have acted differently or by not taking her seriously. Thus when Ruth is almost reported for going to the cinema, her mother dismisses her, saying that there are worse things (*wl*, 49). Her mother claims that when she was a child she was braver than Ruth, could easily make up stories and poems, and knew more than her. She claims she would have hit the SS man back when Ruth did not, and that she can milk a cow (*wl*, 60, 164, & 172). Her possessiveness is such that Ruth feels treated like her possession, to the extent that she refuses to let Ruth go on the last *Kindertransport*, something for which Klüger says she has never forgiven her (*wl*, 64). In the USA, her mother seeks to make Klüger dependent on her financially, searches through her daughter's things, smells her underwear, and even at the time of writing examines her wastepaper (*wl*, 260). Her mother's jealousy of Klüger's new Hunter College friends drives her to insulting them as baptised cripples (*wl*, 256), and Klüger suspects that her mother's suicide attempt in 1955 is rooted in the fact that she is displaced by the birth of Klüger's first child (*wl*, 265).

These examples convey how difficult, oppressive, and debilitating Klüger's relationship with her mother has been. However, the representation of the relationship does at times assume a certain comic momentum. This arises from the context of Klüger's tone more generally, with its tinge of hyperbolic candidness, and then also from the palpable difficulty she has *not* to be negative about her mother. So her mother's description of her father as having humble origins is 'hochnäsig' [snooty], using spit to clean Ruth's face elicits the incommensurate response that it was 'zum Kotzen' [made me want to puke], and we are not surprised to learn that her mother feels at home in her small, ugly house near Los Angeles (*wl*, 28, 57, & 156). Klüger consistently casts her mother in a negative light. Her matter-of-fact barter of her wedding ring for bread is an opportunity for Klüger to remark that her mother only gets sentimental if she has an audience (*wl*, 90). When her mother publically questions a famous historian about Schorschi's death Klüger is suspicious that she is playing the role of suffering mother (*wl*, 94). She also suspects that the suicide attempt is precisely that, an attempt, intended to fail (*wl*, 265). And when her mother performs the feat of approaching a priest and getting false papers, Klüger ascribes her idea to megalomania despite recognizing it as the right thing to do. She thinks her mother goes alone in order not to feel inhibited in her dramatization of events: '[d]enn sie hat immer gern und ohne Not gelogen' [since she has always enjoyed lying, even when there was no need] (*wl*, 179–80). Indeed, her mother is not to be trusted: she 'biegt sich die Welt zurecht' [she twists the world to suit herself] and her language is fundamentally manipulative, used according to which role she is playing (*wl*, 34, & 255–56).

The persistence of Klüger's negativity introduces a certain comic predictability. Even when, as is the case with the priest, her mother does something impressive or that is vital to their survival, Klüger is quick to set herself apart or have the last, often vehement, word. Thus the time in Straubing when her mother is hospitable and good to everyone is the time that Klüger loves and respects her the most, but she is also quick to point out that they do not see much of each other (*wl*, 206). Klüger hastily differentiates herself even if she recognizes her mother's generosity, as is the case when her mother responds with a pragmatic, humane gesture to the old woman who urinates in her lap. Although this is a rare occasion when her mother is a role model, nevertheless Klüger felt her mother should have been thoroughly indignant (*wl*, 110). While Ditha has always believed that Klüger's mother saved her life by adopting her in Auschwitz, and Klüger praises it as the best thing her mother did, she nevertheless rather subtly shifts Ditha's emphasis from her mother to the small family unit as what was crucial (*wl*, 156). The starkest example of this relates to the fact that her mother was right in her assessment of the extermination camp, right to persuade Ruth to go through the selection a second time, and right to advise her to say she was fifteen. Klüger concedes this, but ascribes her mother's life-saving approach to Auschwitz wholly to her mother's profound paranoia, arguing that it was the 'Zwangsneurotiker, die [...] in Auschwitz am ehesten zurechtkamen' [obsessional neurotics who were the first to cope] (*wl*, 129). In a move that deflects credit going to her mother, Klüger proceeds to describe her paranoia as a latent madness that she carries around with her, claws ready to strike. It is a predator that Klüger would not want to carry inside her even if it could save her life in the next extermination camp (*wl*, 129).

This assertion, suggesting as it does that periodic attacks of paranoia are worse than the threat of extermination, is extreme and pushes at the boundaries of credibility. But the dark comedy generated by the persistent negativity signals that Klüger's representation of her mother is more than that: it is also fundamentally about her own response to her mother and the part she plays in the dynamic of the relationship. Klüger draws attention to her own participation in the dynamic by referring to the 'gegenseitig[e] Mutter-Tochter-Neurose' [mutual mother-daughter neurosis], and how deep-seated and persistent it continues to be. Yet Klüger admits: 'die Erkenntnis [hilft doch] keineswegs darüber hinweg' [knowing about it by no means helps get over it] (*wl*, 59). So after admonishing her mother for her use of birthday gifts as a tool for emotional manipulation, Klüger admits to being no different, for she rejects gifts from her mother as a means of keeping her distance (*wl*, 59). Similarly, her deep-seated suspicion of her mother makes her wonder whether the madness is her mother's or her own (*wl*, 266). Thus, importantly, Klüger situates herself within her candid yet often ironic frame. *Ressentiment* becomes *Ressentiment* with a comic touch, a shift that alters the ethical tenor of both.

Comedy and Derision

In her open letter to Walser, Klüger refers to the use of comedy as a vehicle for derision. In her memoirs too she makes evident the link between comedy and cruelty that she sees exemplified in Kleist's tale. She recounts two episodes of wilful humiliation of camp prisoners, presumably amusing for the guards involved. In one, a woman has to endure *Appell* [roll call] in the freezing winter dressed only in an old evening dress, and in the other a guard walks up and down along the barbed wire fence in front of the starving prisoners with a piece of bread at the end of his stick, encrusted with dirt (*wl*, 121, 143). These are extreme examples of *Spottlust* [the enjoyment of mockery], and do not fit within the norms of what is held to be comic. But they point to those disturbing aspects of comedy that construct an object for others' amusement, including jokes that are made at someone's expense. At a more elevated end of the spectrum than the camp guards' fun at the prisoners' cost is the 'muse of history [who] has a way of cracking bad jokes at the expense of the Jews'. Klüger's particular example is Theresienstadt, which was built by Emperor Joseph II, who was 'revered by Austrian Jews for emancipating them' (*LoM*, 76). At the more intimate end is her grandfather's joke, when, in the company of his daughters, he says to his dog with 'playful sombreness': 'You are the only one around who'll be able to say kaddish for me' (*LoM*, 24; *wl*, 25). For Klüger this is no joke but a humiliation for her mother.

The fact that her grandfather meant it as a joke, but Klüger refuses to accept it as such, points again to the 'discrepancy in perception', which is also at the centre of her anecdote about the American air force pilot. The pilot recalls his experience of attacking a man on the ground, hunting him back and forth like an animal, until 'lachend und "bewundernd"' [laughing and 'impressed'] he rewards the man's stubborn fight for survival by giving up the chase (*wl*, 194). The pilot's privileged point of view allows him to view the chase as an amusing game, whereas for the man running for his life it can be no game for he is reduced to being a victim. Klüger's censorious response to these examples clearly rests on the unequal power dynamic of those involved, which dictates that any amusement derived necessarily has a butt or a victim. Yet her powerful sense of injustice in these examples begs the question of how far Klüger's own ironic or insolent humour constructs a butt and whether she is herself exploiting the very modes of instrumentalizing humour that she criticizes elsewhere. The farmer popping up from behind the barrels between bombs is also a man in fear of his life who has been transformed after the event into an anecdote. One might ask whether her directness, the uninhibited tone with which Klüger presents scenes and people in her memoirs with its tendency to hyperbolic comedy, slides others into the realm of caricature. In her description of her visit to Hans, for example, the less than flattering presentation of his family fuels disquiet that the humour of the scene is derived at their expense. Her American family, Gisela, her Ivy League colleagues, the Germans who are so thorough in facing up to the past (*LoM*, 67), all are the objects of her biting ironic tone. Are they, then, the humiliated butts of an ironic joke on Klüger's part, with her malicious half-tones themselves approaching a form of *Spottlust*? This question is particularly acute in view of Klüger's insistence that her autobiographical writings are history, the potential for harm acknowledged in her attempt to keep *weiter leben* from her mother, and the fact that she changed the names of many of the figures.

There are three key reasons why Klüger's comedy does not simply replicate structures of humiliation. First is the fact that she is present in the scenes she describes or implicated in the comedy. Thus, in the bombing scene her life is just as much in danger as the farmer's, and in the parrot scene she as a girl is bawling but as an adult she can see the funny side. In the scene at Hans's house, although Hans, his family, and his house are characterized as tediously petit-bourgeois, she also casts herself in the role of the impatient intellectual who gives the impression she is suffering from piles. Here, as in many scenes, she is part of what is amusing and humour does not rely on an asymmetric power dynamic. And crucially, as in the case of her representation of her mother, it is the quality of excess and hyperbolic criticism that draws attention not only to the content of the scene but her emotional relationship to her memories. Her responses are thus often both the trigger for, and included in, the comedy produced by the malicious half-tones.

Secondly, and following directly from the fact that her tone is so distinctly part of what we respond to, Klüger's hyperbole is part of a wider aim to solicit a critical response, including to her own views. Comedy forms part of her challenge to her readers to offer a critical, engaged response. She makes use of what she sees as the qualities of comedy, a lack of empathy and alienation, to facilitate this aim. Thus, for example, despite her presentation of Hans's family as stereotypes of their class, the very bluntness of her views is a provocation to the reader to maintain a critical distance, further reinforced in this case by her blunt admission that she is indifferent to family relations (*wl*, 12). She demands of her German readership: 'Werdet streitsüchtig, sucht die Auseinandersetzung' [Become argumentative, seek out debate] (*wl*, 142). The reader is encouraged to cultivate her own perspective on what she is reading, encouraged to be an interlocutor and not succumb to the pose of listening to Klüger's experiences with 'einer Art Ehrfurcht' [a type of reverence] (*wl*, 112): reverence keeps the reader at a distance and can all too easily turn to revulsion. Klüger actively counters an ingratiating response to her work that finds it 'shattering' (*wl*, 201) and her honesty about her own directness and judgements is part of a provocation which forecloses on such awe. She invites the reader's criticism by pointing out that she is impatient (*wl*, 9), honestly recounts Anneliese's criticisms of her that she bears grudges (*wl*, 254 & 278), and openly questions herself when she senses that she is assuming a position of moral authority. When she catches herself being critical of her mother's decision to lie about her age and have her tattooed number removed, she asks '[w]arum war ich so doktrinär?' [why was I so doctrinaire?] (*uv*, 20). She has doubts about her sentence which starts 'wer je frei entschieden hat' [anyone who has ever been free to decide] because of its claim to universal authority based on 'I know something you don't know' (*wl*, 167).

The freedom she promotes in her readers is allied to her persistent resistance to being told how to remember, represent, or respond to her experiences. Thus Klüger cannot forgive Hans's mother for her treatment of her as a girl, even though she knows that the aunt was murdered in the gas chambers: 'it is not in our power to forgive: memory does that for us, and when memory refuses, the honeyed words that are meant to convey what we sincerely think we ought to feel turn sour with hypocrisy' (*LoM*, 9). She rejects the moral prescriptions of what writing after Auschwitz should be, arguing that the expectations of what is allowed or what should be written turn the issue into a burning bush, sacred ground that can only be trodden barefoot and with subservient humility (*wl*, 127). Similarly, she resists pressure from others to show, hide, or remove her Auschwitz tattoo as they think is right, rather than according to what she wants, which varies over time: '[w]arum die Vorschriften, die doch, wie jede Form von Zwang, suspekt sein sollten?' [why the regulations, which should anyway be suspect, like any form of compulsion?] (*wl*, 237). It is then not surprising that her closest friend, Maria, former member of the *Bund Deutscher Mädel*, the girls' wing of the Nazi party youth movement, is someone with no principles and who is consequently immune to any ideology (*uv*, 124). Klüger's scepticism about moral prescription also lies behind her greater forbearance for the moral indifference of the Viennese regarding open anti-Semitism, which, she argues, is 'gemäßer als die deutsche Prinzipienreiterei, die oft in Selbstgerechtigkeit ausartet' [more appropriate than the German insistence on principle, which often degenerates into self-righteousness] (*uv*, 205).

Klüger's dislike of self-righteous moral prescription is encapsulated in her ironic response to Celan's poetry. She bluntly, and very funnily, points out that no one really knows what it is about, and that some experts claim the poems are about Jewish history, others that they are about language problems. She recounts how on the occasion when she composed a harmless parody of one of his abstruse works, she shocked people she had never shocked before: 'Über Gott und Goethe darf man lästern, der Autor der "Todesfuge" ist unantastbar' [One can be nasty about God and Goethe, but the author of 'Death Fugue' is untouchable] (*wl*, 127–28). But his untouchable status is not because he is a good poet, for so was Goethe. Klüger's willingness to challenge orthodoxy thus extends to survivors or their poetry: neither inhabits a special status. She too does not wish to silence her audience (*wl*, 72). Thus comedy, both caused by her uninhibited personal judgements, and drawing attention to and provoking a response to the subjectivity of her writing, can be understood as a key aesthetic strategy. It is fundamental to her attempt to disrupt existing power formations by demystifying Holocaust survivor accounts and fashioning an equal discussant of her reader.

The third reason why Klüger's insolent comedy resists the humiliating *Spottlust* of which she is so critical is political. All three of her memoirs are dominated by her position of having to fight for survival and for recognition as a Jew, as a woman, and as both. Within the wider economy of her narrative, therefore, there is no scope for the comic aspects of her writing to be cast as morally questionable mockery or caricature, for they are part of her struggle against murderous or oppressive practices. The objects of her bite cannot be victims of tendentious humour, for they are complicit with the discriminatory or persecutory structures that have oppressed her. Her comedy is a priori justified by being embedded within a context in which she is or has been disempowered. Even Klüger's encounter with Hans, another survivor, is framed as a two-fold power struggle, the first of which is her retrospective fight against the family power structures that upheld the lies of the adults when she was a child. Her precise questions to Hans now are a late recompense for the taboo around death that kept her in a position of ignorance as a girl. Against this background the disquiet of Hans's wife and Heinz because Hans must once again retell his torture experience re-enacts the old structures and serves as an emotional justification of their caricatured presentation. Secondly, and more broadly, Klüger's questioning here, however tactless, becomes part of her assault on the gendered possession of knowledge. She describes her need to acquire ever more information about the Holocaust and the war as part of her belief in the adage 'knowledge is power', a power that has hitherto largely belonged to men (*wl*, 12).

Klüger's malicious half-tones are part of her political counter-attack and she thus feels justified in enjoying her cheek and irony. She explicitly remarks on how amused she is by her own audacity when she drily puts down an old Princeton colleague (*uv*, 68). And in Göttingen, after having a considerable sum of money stolen by a bank official, she has little patience with the lawyer who expresses surprise that such fraud could happen in Germany. Klüger positively thrives on her response to the provocation, giving free reign to her biting remarks about German honesty. She rebuffs the lawyer with the caustic, and very funny, remark about the purported honesty of Germans: 'mein Konto sei eben arisiert worden' [my account was simply arianized]. She then comments with huge satisfaction, 'manchmal blühe ich geradezu auf, wenn ich boshaft sein kann' [sometimes I really flourish when I can be malicious] (*uv*, 190). Her pleasure at how scathing she can be is related both to her identity as a Jew and as a woman and she has no qualms in asserting her right to use a misogynist stereotype to her own advantage. So if *Die Welt* newspaper refers to the 'Bissigkeit der Frauen' [how biting women are] the consequences are evident: 'wenn ihr sogar in der Zeitung Bisse proviziert, wundert euch nicht, gebissen zu werden' [if you go as far as provoking bites in the newspaper, don't be surprised when you get bitten] (*uv*, 191). Being snide, and the comedy generated by it, is not only acceptable when it is part of the long fight against the institutions of anti-Semitism and misogyny, it is necessary. Teeth are part of the arsenal of an underdog.

The pleasure that Klüger displays gives an important signal to the reader that her irony is there to be enjoyed, though, as has been discussed, she is also well aware that her humour is often overlooked or received differently by different audiences. It is this aspect of Klüger's tone that Stuart Taberner overlooks when he refers to two distinct voices in her writing, one characterized by 'bluster, belligerence and self-absorption', the other 'more discursive, allusive and adept'.[27] He suggestively proposes that Klüger's display of anger, in view of the conventional prohibition on women articulating fury, can be read as 'subversive cross-dressing, as a challenge to the male prerogative to rant'. However, he argues further that the fact that Klüger feels she must have a point to her rant 'may already undercut true rant's sovereign claim to not care about what others think'.[28] As a result, her efforts to assert her importance 'appear only to confirm that women — and Jews, of course — can never truly belong'.

A number of points are important here. The first is that Klüger does indeed have a point to her rant, more than one in fact; it is not that she feels she must. Secondly, the privileging of 'true' rant as not caring what others think itself reinforces the hierarchies of power against which Klüger writes; sovereign claims are, after all, made by those who inhabit positions of power. Thirdly, how far Klüger's tone is understood only as belligerent, and its comic dimension overlooked, is probably inseparable from the degree to which a reader feels implicated in the criticism. Her anger against and public exposure of the misogyny of academic institutions is potentially less likely to be perceived as bluster and self-absorption by female readers. Finally, the apparent confirmation that women and Jews can never belong is symptomatic of Klüger's experience and of the resentment she carries because of her experience.

Jean Améry refers to himself and those like him as Shylocks, cheated of their pound of flesh.[29] Klüger had her flesh and blood violently taken from her and was then punished for it: the lives of her father and brother cannot be given back to her, and for most of her life she has been haunted by them. She has also less literally been cheated of her pound of flesh in the sense that Améry refers to: that with the passing of time the world forgives and forgets and the victims must come to terms with their anger.[30] The passing of time and healing of wounds is 'natural', but it is also '*antimoral*', and Améry claims the right as a human not to accept what is deemed natural.[31] Importantly, he rejects the ethically elevated suggestion that the survivors internalize their suffering and he effectively refuses any redemptive Christian injunction represented by Portia's demand 'Then must the Jew be merciful' (*The Merchant of Venice*, IV.I).[32] In an inversion of Nietzsche's damning view that the man of *ressentiment* is 'neither sincere, nor naive, nor honest and forthright with himself. His soul squints', Améry links *ressentiment* with those who witnessed the 'union of the brute with the subhuman'.[33] It is in this capacity that *ressentiment* becomes valuable as the 'emotional source of every genuine morality'.[34] Nevertheless, Améry recognizes its dangers, acknowledging that *ressentiment* nails individuals to their destroyed pasts while demanding that the past be undone. Thus *ressentiment* 'blocks the exit to the genuine human dimension, the future'.[35]

Just as Améry points to *ressentiment*'s moral force, Vladimir Jankélévitch argues in 'Should We Pardon Them?' that *ressentiment* 'can also be the renewed and intensely lived feeling of the inexpiable thing; it protects against a moral amnesty that is nothing but shameful amnesia; it maintains the sacred flame of disquiet'.[36] He too refuses to countenance the acceptance of time's ameliorating effect on memory, '[b]ecause this agony will last until the end of the world'. Yet, as he himself points out, in his work *Forgiveness*, '*the answer to the question, Must we pardon? seems to contradict the one given here*'. In *Forgiveness*, as though in response to Améry's claim that *ressentiment* demands the past be undone, Jankélévitch argues that by the 'grace of forgiveness, the thing that had been done has not been done'.[37] Forgiveness is not blind, however, and if 'the guilty person is fat, well nourished, prosperous, and takes advantage of the economic miracle, then forgiveness is a sinister joke'.[38] The act of grace is only meaningful if the criminal works towards 'desperate remorse' and then forgiveness 'forgives everyone for everything for all times'. By using the language of grace Jankélévitch invests forgiveness with profound moral value, further privileging it by seeing the refusal to forgive as a sign of pride, and the person who refuses to forgive as seeing himself as 'above sin', of 'being infallible'.[39] Indeed, entrenched unforgiving is akin to the Hell of despair.[40] However, Jankélévitch fundamentally refuses to posit forgiveness as a final resolution to what is unforgivable. For forgiveness is aligned with the absolute of love and the unforgivable with that of justice, and the synthesis of the two absolutes is impossible. Furthermore, what is both a second refusal of the possibility of sublimation and a riposte to Saint Paul, Jankélévitch insists finally that 'where grace overflows, evil overflows in response': 'No! there is no last word'.[41]

The work of Améry and Jankélévitch helps understand Klüger's complex negotiation between *ressentiment* and memory on the one hand, and conciliation on the other. Her exit to the future has not been blocked. On the contrary, her memoirs demonstrate her capacity for forming close relationships throughout her life, for fighting to develop a successful career, and for negotiating a dialogue with German culture and Germans on her own terms. She even reaches the point where she has her Auschwitz tattoo removed, for she no longer owes it to the memory of her brother, whose biblical three score years and ten would by then have been reached had he lived. But although Klüger's exit has not been blocked, it is also impossible for her to leave the past: 'Je älter ich werde, desto deutlicher wird es, daß die Jugenderlebnisse nicht die geringste Absicht hatten, sich aus der Psyche zu entfernen' [The older I get, the clearer it becomes that my childhood experiences don't have the slightest intention of leaving my psyche] (*uv*, 235). Nor does she wish to, since the memory of suffering is valuable: 'eine Art Schatz, ein Besitz, und wer ihn uns entreißen will, macht uns ärmer' [a type of treasure, a possession, and whoever wants to tear it away from us, makes us poorer] (*GW*, 54). The tone of much of Klüger's work is part of this treasure, for it is a sign of *ressentiment* as a form of witnessing. Her *ressentiment* is inseparable from her moral position and it also fuels her often-uncompromising judgements on the world and her tactlessness. As Améry writes, the expression of resentment entails a 'Mangel an Takt' [lack of tact].[42]

Yet the comic aspects of Klüger's work add a further dimension to this *ressentiment*, for they open up a movement between *ressentiment* and conciliation. In one way it can be understood as an important counterweight to resentment, evidence of her exit to the future. The 'retroactive rancour' is tempered by the desire to be heard and appreciated. She is, after all, pleased when her audience enjoys her writing, including the funnier bits. Comedy tempers the rancour, even though, as has been discussed, Klüger's comedy is far from gentle. It does so by adding to the pleasure of reading, and, furthermore, it humanizes the anger. Her wit frees the reader to take pleasure in her tone and not experience it solely as an attacking polemic. Witty resentment is more attractive than simply expressing a grudge, however justified it is. Furthermore, and crucially, while facilitating the concurrent articulation of *ressentiment* with conciliation, her comedy defends against any emotional drift to either 'absolute'. The comedy forecloses on either an emotional sublimation of the two (which could only take the form of kitsch), or on entrenchment in either. Klüger's malicious half tones and her enjoyment of irony belong to the comedy that does not promise a happy ending but which holds together incompatible perspectives and allows resentment to jostle against conciliation.

In her work on trauma and mourning, Clara Mucci echoes Jankélévitch's coupling of grace with forgiveness. She argues that forgiveness is vital as 'a symbolic act, issued from the intrapsychic mind towards parts of the Self, and only as a secondary consequence might it be directed towards the perpetrator in reality'. But this gesture towards a perpetrator is 'absolutely irrelevant for healing and forgiveness to take place'.[43] Yet forgiveness is like grace in that it cannot be achieved by will: 'in other words, it is out of the subject's control'.[44] Klüger does not speak of grace in relation to forgiveness, but she does link it to the gift of 'die reine Tat' [the pure deed] (*wl*, 135): the free and spontaneous act of the prisoner who risked her life by helping the girl Klüger through the selection. This 'Gnadenakt' [act of grace] represents goodness because it is done freely, remains inexplicable, is unearned, and given 'aus heiterem Himmel' [out of the blue] (*wl*, 132).

Imre Kertész radically develops the notion of grace as something that is bestowed independent of individual striving or actions when he presents the 'state of grace' as the freedom from the burden of individuality that is common to victim and executioner. The provocation of his statement forms the starting point for the final discussion on perpetrator justice and trauma.

Notes to Chapter 5

1. Ruth Klüger, *Gelesene Wirklichkeit: Fakten und Fiktionen in der Literatur* (Göttingen: Wallstein, 2006), p. 61. Further references will be given in parenthesis with the abbreviation *GW*.
2. Ruth Klüger, *weiter leben: Eine Jugend* (Munich: DTV, 1999). Further references will be given in parenthesis with the abbreviation *wl*.
3. Stephan Braese and Holger Gehle, 'Von "deutschen Freunden": Ruth Klüger's *weiter leben. Eine Jugend* in der deutschen Rezeption', *Der Deutschunterricht*, 47, 6 (1995), 76–87.
4. Irene Heidelberger-Leonard, *Ruth Klüger, weiter leben: Eine Jugend* (Munich: Oldenbourg, 1996), p. 47; Hans Joachim Kreutzer, 'Die Auschwitznummer nicht verdecken: Ruth Klügers Erinnerungen — eine Einladung zum Streiten', in *Erläuterungen und Dokumente: Ruth Klüger weiter leben*, ed. by Sascha Feuchert (Stuttgart: Reclam, 2004), p. 140; Heidi Gidion, 'Im Parlando-Ton und lakonisch', in *Erläuterungen und Dokumente*, ed. by Feuchert., p. 144.
5. Ruth Klüger, *unterwegs verloren: Erinnerungen* (Munich: DTV, 2008), p. 56. Further references will be given in parenthesis with the abbreviation *uv*.
6. Ruth Klüger, *Frauen lesen anders* (Munich: DTV, 1997), p. 190. Further references will be given in parenthesis with the abbreviation *Fla*.
7. Kreutzer, 'Die Auschwitznummer nicht verdecken', p. 140; Sigrid Löffler, 'Davongekommen', in *Erläuterungen und Dokumente*, ed. by Feuchert, p. 146; Marcel Reich-Ranicki, 'Vom Trotz getrieben, vom Stil beglaubigt. Rede auf Ruth Klüger aus Anlaß der Verleihung des Grimmelshausen-Preises', in *Erläuterungen und Dokumente*, ed. by Feuchert, p. 155.
8. Friedrich Nietzsche, *Jenseits von Gut und Böse: Zur Genealogie der Moral. Kritische Studienausgabe*, ed. by Giorgio Colli and Mazzino Montinari (Munich and Berlin/New York: DTV/de Gruyter, 1988), pp. 270–72.
9. Ibid., p. 281.
10. Améry, *Jenseits von Schuld und Sühne*, pp. 128 & 133; *At the Mind's Limits*, pp. 68 & 72.
11. Améry, *Jenseits von Schuld und Sühne*, pp. 119–20; *At the Mind's Limits*, p. 63.
12. Karolin Machtans, *Zwischen Wissenschaft und autobiographischem Projekt: Saul Friedländer und Ruth Klüger* (Tübingen: Niemeyer, 2009), p. 151.
13. Indeed, Machtans comments on the way in which Klüger loses sight of the fact that Derrida's writing is, in part at least, a response to the Holocaust and the questions it posed to traditions in Western philosophy. See Machtans, p.152, n. 73.
14. Machtans, p. 147.
15. Ruth Klüger, '"Siehe doch Deutschland": Martin Walsers *Tod eines Kritikers*', in *Erläuterungen und Dokumente*, ed. by Feuchert, pp. 157–63 (p. 158).
16. Ruth Klüger, *Katastrophen: Über deutsche Literatur* (Göttingen: Wallstein, 2009), p. 13. Further references will be given in parenthesis with the abbreviation *K*.
17. Davies, p. 211.
18. Ibid., p. 204.
19. Ibid., p. 224.
20. Klüger, '"Siehe doch Deutschland"', p. 162.
21. Ibid., p. 159.

22. Ibid.
23. Steve Neale, 'Propaganda', *Screen*, 18, 3 (1977), 9–40. For a fascinating discussion of *Jud Süss* and its harnessing and releasing of desire in relation to stereotypes, see: Linda Schulte-Sasse, 'The Jew as Other under National Socialism: Veit Harlan's *Jud Süss*', *The German Quarterly*, 61, 1 (1988), 22–49; Marcia Klotz, 'Epistemological Ambiguity and the Fascist Text: *Jew Süss, Carl Peters*, and *Ohm Krüger*', *New German Critique*, 74 (1998), 91–124; Valerie Weinstein, 'Dissolving Boundaries: Assimilation and Allosemitism in E.A. Dupont's *Das alte Gesetz* (1923) and Veit Harlan's *Jud Süß* (1940)', *The German Quarterly*, 78, 4 (2005), 496–516.
24. Ruth Klüger, *Landscapes of Memory: A Holocaust Girlhood Remembered* (London: Bloomsbury, 2004), p. 63. Further references will be given in parenthesis with the abbreviation *LoM*.
25. Renata Schmidtkunz, *Das Weiterleben der Ruth Klüger* (Falter Verlag, 2012) [on DVD].
26. Pascale R. Bos, *German-Jewish Literature in the Wake of the Holocaust: Grete Weil, Ruth Klüger, and the Politics of Address* (New York: Palgrave Macmillan, 2005), p. 83.
27. Stuart Taberner, *Aging and Old-Age Style in Günter Grass, Ruth Klüger, Christa Wolf, and Martin Walser: The Mannerism of a Late Period* (Rochester, NY: Camden House, 2013), p. 105.
28. Ibid., p. 106.
29. Améry, *Jenseits von Schuld und Sühne*, p. 138; *At the Mind's Limits*, p. 75.
30. Améry, *Jenseits von Schuld und Sühne*, p. 148; *At the Mind's Limits*, p. 81.
31. Améry, *Jenseits von Schuld und Sühne*, p. 133; *At the Mind's Limits*, p. 72.
32. William Shakespeare, *The Merchant of Venice* (Oxford: Oxford University Press, 2010), p. 73
33. Améry, *Jenseits von Schuld und Sühne*, p. 127; *At the Mind's Limits*, pp. 67–68.
34. Améry, *Jenseits von Schuld und Sühne*, p. 148; *At the Mind's Limits*, p. 81.
35. Améry, *Jenseits von Schuld und Sühne*, p. 128; *At the Mind's Limits*, p. 68.
36. Vladimir Jankélévitch, 'Should We Pardon Them?', trans. by Ann Hobart, *Critical Inquiry*, 22, 3 (1996), 552–72 (p. 572).
37. Vladimir Jankélévitch, *Forgiveness*, trans. by Andrew Kelley (Chicago: Chicago University Press, 2005), p. 164.
38. Ibid., p. 157.
39. Ibid., p. 161.
40. Ibid., p. 162.
41. Ibid., pp. 163 & 165.
42. Améry, *Jenseits von Schuld und Sühne*, p. 120; *At the Mind's Limits*, p. 63.
43. Mucci, p. 221.
44. Ibid., p. 211.

CHAPTER 6

Edgar Hilsenrath and Jonathan Littell: Perpetrators, Comedy, and the Fantasy of Justice

As part of Imre Kertész's scepticism about Adorno's 'moral stinkbomb', he launches his own anti-Holocaust-piety rocket: the state of 'grace' (*DK*, 130). His work explores the notion of the step-by-step movement towards Auschwitz, which might have occurred differently at any point, and how the easy step into violence can occur under certain 'states of affairs'. In *Fiasco* the old boy ponders the motives of Ilse Koch and describes the way that Buchenwald was created by one state of affairs, which in turn created many others, including the specific context that created Koch herself. The ever-determining state of affairs makes her individuality increasingly insignificant, and therefore also possible that her role as camp commandant's wife 'could have been filled by essentially *anybody* else with similar feelings and actions' (*Fi*, 51). Whatever her motives, those of a sadist or of a 'more complex being', the cumulative states of affairs mean that systematized murder cannot be the stuff of tragic representation. There is no place for the extraordinary individuals on whom tragedy depends in standardized processes of mass murder, and furthermore the violent world of totalitarianism is circumscribed by historical time and cannot belong to the infinite perspective of tragedy. The question of tragic representation is also relevant in relation to the victims of mass atrocity, whose fate is neither their own nor individual. At the end of *Fateless* György describes the way in which Auschwitz happened 'step by step' and that each minute might have happened differently. Like the cumulative 'state of affairs', each step contributes to a given and at one level impersonal fate: 'It had not been my own fate, but I had lived through it'. (*F*, 259) At the same time as being impersonal, however, everyone takes the steps that enable that fate to occur, and in this sense everyone is on a level, if not called to account, then implicated. This is one of the reasons why for Kertész Auschwitz is a universal human experience and not limited to the victims, as is the failure it represents (*DK*, 108).

The way in which the 'state of affairs' reduces individuality and results in the exchangeability of fates assumes its most provocative manifestation in Kertész's equation of executioner and victim. Both share the same state, variously described as 'grace', '*fatelessness*', or even 'happiness': 'the essence of both roles is a complete release from the burden of personality' (*DK*, 131). In his story 'I, the Executioner' and in his self-interrogation, Kertész suggests that one cannot know beforehand who will strike a defenceless prisoner in the face, the 'first and decisive step, from which there is no turning back' (*DK*, 129). The step results 'solely from the situation, which commands the terrain like a foreign power' (*DK*, 130–31) and within which 'your "existence has gone to sleep"' (*DK*, 129). As Kertész's questioning alter-ego remarks, this understanding of the step into violence means that '*it would be impossible to call any mass murderer to account*', to which Kertész responds that as a writer he is 'not concerned with calling people to account but with accurate portrayal' (*DK*, 129).

It is interesting to consider Kertész's provocative remarks in relation to two novels, each of which strains expectations of Holocaust representation in its exploration of perpetrator responsibility and justice. In contrast to the dominant cultural focus on victims of Nazism, or more generally on suffering caused by the violence of the war even across generations, Edgar Hilsenrath's *Der Nazi und der Friseur* and Jonathan Littell's *The Kindly Ones* present the point of view of perpetrators.[1] Both novels play with the notion of calling the perpetrator to account through the device of fictional memoir. By recounting their versions of events, both mass murderers explicitly and implicitly raise questions about the nature of justice in relation to their own agency, or, in Kertész's words, to their position within 'the situation'. The protagonists point to circumstances within which they figure as victims, which, along with their symptoms of trauma, challenge us to recognize their common humanity and also evoke the problematic equation of perpetrator and victim. Both novels too play with the notion of accurate portrayal in their interrogation of justice and culpability, with the protagonists functioning as anti-realist narrative devices within a wider strategy that draws upon comedy. *Der Nazi und der Friseur* is self-evidently a comedy, but is included in this study for the provocation it represents and the crucial issues it raises in conjunction with *The Kindly Ones*. The novels draw on comic devices or structures to undermine representative modes that promise redemption: both depend on the figure of the picaro, or rogue, and this is combined with fairy tales in *Der Nazi und der Friseur* and tragedy in *The Kindly Ones*. But whereas Hilsenrath's novel confounds realist conventions from the outset, Littell combines comic structures with a realism so detailed that it blurs the boundaries of fiction. By thematizing justice and yet drawing on comic devices, the novels stage the fantasy of justice and enact its ambiguity. In fiction, justice is sought in the fantasy of divine retribution and the physical justice of trauma symptoms. But the fantasy of justice remains precisely that: the frustrated desire for redemptive narratives.

The novels have as their narrators violent SS men who participate actively in the Jewish genocide. There are some marked similarities between the two. They tell their stories from a position of safety, having escaped persecution by assuming a false identity at the end of the war and leaving Germany. Max Schulz and Max Aue are members of *Einsatzgruppe D* until 1942, before assuming further 'administrative' roles in the implementation of the Nazi race and genocide policy: Schulz is transferred to the concentration camp 'Laubwalde' and Aue manages policy on Jewish slave labour, including the deportation of Jews from Hungary. Both narrators at points address their reader directly, inviting complicity with their view. The two Maxes also each have a twin, Aue a real one in his sister Una, and Schulz in the figure of Itzig Finkelstein, who is born next door just two minutes and twenty-two seconds after Schulz. The idea of the twin extends into that of the double or doubling, particularly in association with the relationship of Germans and Jews. Finally, each of the men is linked with sexual violence and perversion, albeit very differently. Schulz is a victim of rape and abuse from infancy, and the homosexual Aue, who has had a failed incestuous relationship with his beloved twin sister and unknowingly fathered twins with her through rape, is characterized by extreme sexual fantasies.

Der Nazi und der Friseur

Given the overlaps between the two novels, it is somewhat surprising that Hilsenrath is so adamant that there are no similarities at all between the two Maxes. For him, Aue is a realistic figure and *The Kindly Ones* is more like an autobiography, whereas his own Schulz is a fictional person. 'Ich habe eine Groteske geschrieben und Littell hat einen ganz realistischen Roman geschrieben' [I wrote a grotesque novel and Littell has written a very realistic novel].[2] Nevertheless he is right that his novel departs from narrative realism. It is a blackly comic story of how Schulz, neglected by his mother and continuously raped and beaten by his stepfather, grows up best friends with his Jewish neighbour Itzig Finkelstein. Schulz completes his apprenticeship with Chaim Finkelstein, the famous barber, but with the rise of Nazism becomes a member of the SS. In order to escape persecution as a war criminal after the war, Schulz adopts the identity of his friend Itzig, whom he killed in Laubwalde, along with Chaim and Sara Finkelstein. He emigrates to Palestine where he fights for the establishment of an independent Israel before becoming a successful barber and respected member of the community. It is grotesque, brazen, shocking, and very funny, and, by combining an explicitly comic aesthetic with the point of view of a perpetrator, it brings together two already controversial modes of representing the Holocaust. It challenges us to wonder whether the novel is a bad joke and who ends up being the butt of the humour.

The publishing history of *Der Nazi und der Friseur* has commonly been held to reflect the anxiety around Holocaust humour and in particular the 'paralysing effect of the cultural climate in postwar Germany'.[3] Hilsenrath's first novel, *Nacht*, was published in Germany in 1964, but in an edition of only 1250 copies it was effectively repressed. This was due to its uncompromising depiction of survival in a Jewish ghetto, and the fear among German editors that it could fuel anti-Semitic tendencies in Germany. The German reception of *Nacht* was in marked contrast to its positive reception in the United States.[4] Against this background, Hilsenrath wrote *Der Nazi und der Friseur* in German in 1968, and authorized the American translation that was published by Doubleday, New York, in 1971. It was then published in Italy in 1973, France in 1974, and the UK in 1975, and finally in the original German by the small publishing house of Helmut Braun in 1977. Publication in German followed rejections by over twenty-five German publishers despite global sales of over one million copies of the English version along with positive reviews, and according to Helmut Braun was because the novel offended against expectations of Holocaust writing (*DNuDF*, 472). This view echoes Hilsenrath's own, when he reported that his 'German Agent [...] told me: "German publishers are afraid to print this book"'.[5]

Yet more recently Patricia Vahsen has cast doubt on whether it was fear that lay behind the rejections, considering it more likely that the publishers were concerned about sales and did not assume that the German reading public would be receptive to the book. GDR publishers were similarly uninterested in Hilsenrath's first two novels.[6] Indeed, the novel's reputation for being controversial has not been sustained by its reception, which has generally welcomed its contribution to Holocaust representation. Vahsen discusses in detail the positive reviews it received globally both in relation to the appropriateness of the grotesque humour for depicting its subject matter and in the way it challenges philo-Semitic attitudes.[7] Gert Sautermeister argued the opposite, expressing strong criticism of *Der Nazi und der Friseur* as a novel that exemplifies post-modernism and an entertainment industry that has abandoned moral criteria in favour of easy pleasures and a lack of ethical concern.[8] Largely, however, the academic reception has welcomed Hilsenrath's approach. Hans Otto Horch argues that *Der Nazi und der Friseur*'s satire functions as an enlightening critique of language and exposure of inhuman behaviour, and Claude Conter is representative of the wider critical mood in his praise of the novel's multi-layered unmasking of clichés precisely by drawing on them so heavily.[9]

In *Der Nazi und der Friseur* the grotesque satirical comedy both enables provocative issues and comparisons to be made and yet contains their potential for disturbance. This tension is played out through Max Schulz's double role as character and comic narrative device, which is made evident to the reader from the outset. Here Schulz is presented as heir to Oskar Matzerath, the protagonist of Günter Grass's *Die Blechtrommel* of 1959, for like Oskar, Schulz is able to comment on events from birth, although he is unable to explain why: 'Ich kann es Ihnen beim besten Willen nicht sagen' [I can't explain it for the life of me] (*DNuDF*, 13). Both Grass and Hilsenrath draw on black humour and the picaresque tradition as a tool of criticism, although *Der Nazi und der Friseur* breaks a taboo that *Die Blechtrommel* does not 'by depicting a mass murderer with comic means'.[10] The textual movement between Schulz's dual roles as character and device is particularly significant in relation to the text's treatment both of perpetrators and victims and of guilt and justice.

The Pleasure of Flinching

The fundamental comic conceit of *Der Nazi und der Friseur* is an extended play on the theme of mistaken identity and it is from this that the novel's satirical critique flows. Nazis and the hypocrisy of German morality are among the many targets of ridicule, some of which are more provocative than others. At the heart of the book is the derision of Nazi racial ideology, which is achieved through the play on mistaken racial identity. Schulz the Aryan looks like a caricatured *Stürmer* Jew, with black hair, bulging eyes, hooked nose, and thick lips, whereas the Jewish Itzig Finkelstein is blond and blue-eyed and looks like a model Aryan (*DNuDF*, 31–32).

The arbitrariness of Nazi race categories and the ludicrous processes of 'proof' are lambasted through Schulz's inability to confirm who his own father is and his Polish stepfather Slavitzki's oath that he is a real German: 'wenn ein echter Deutscher einen Meineid schwört, dann ist das ein echter Meineid' [when a real German takes an oath, then it's a real oath] (*DNuDF*, 45). Beyond the obvious satirizing of the Nazis, wider German moral and cultural aspirations are exposed. Running through the novel is the frequent juxtaposition of the moral aspiration of the Germans to 'Anständigkeit' [decency] and the murderous immorality that underlies it. Schulz's mother, a cynical prostitute who stands by while her son is raped by her lover, sees herself as a decent woman. Frau Holle, appalled by the iniquity of the black market, proof in itself that the German farmers are really Jews, invokes Hitler as the moral saviour: 'wenn der Führer das wüßte!' [if only the Führer knew!] (*DNuDF*, 97). Artisanship and learning a proper profession contribute to living a decent life, and Itzig Finkelstein is fond of quoting the adage: 'Handwerk hat goldenen Boden' [A craft has a golden foundation] (*DNuDF*, 37). With echoes of the mocking signs hung in Auschwitz, Schulz the Nazi is true to this moral platitude. In his case, the ability to re-establish a decent life for himself by practising the decent craft of barber really does have a golden foundation, for it is funded with gold taken from the corpses of murdered Jews (*DNuDF*, 180–81).

The moral insincerity of many Germans is also ridiculed through the grotesque incorporation of *Märchen*, or fairy tales, into the novel. *Märchen* make their appearance through the figure of Frau Holle, who in the Grimm brothers' tale is the otherworldly mother who rewards the dutiful stepdaughter and punishes the lazy daughter. In the novel she is transformed into a one-legged widow, rape victim, and occasional prostitute, but her role as rewarding or punishing mother is projected onto the figure of Veronja. Veronja, an old Polish woman living in the snowy forest, first saves and then punishes Schulz for his murderous deeds. To this extent, the moral universe within which transgression is duly punished is sustained. However, Veronja doubles as the witch in *Hänsel und Gretel*, the 'Menschenfresser' [man-eater] (*DNuDF*, 146) who lives in an enticing hut in the middle of the forest, which apparently offers safety. Like Hänsel in the tale, Schulz is imprisoned in order to feed the old witch's appetite, which in Veronja's case is an insatiable sexual need. Also like Hänsel, Schulz finally escapes to a new life after killing the witch and burning her head in the oven.

Hilsenrath's play with *Märchen* functions critically at various levels. As Peter Arnds points out, fairy tales, with their profound association with German language and culture, became a 'prime vehicle in supporting [Nazi] Aryan policies'.[11] But for the same reasons the fairy tale also became central to post-war writers' responses to National Socialism and the genocide, and to their re-evaluation of German national identity. The satiric distortion of the tales in the novel has as its butt both the Nazi exploitation of the fairy tale, and that of the post-war writers who reclaimed it in the service of the 'reconstruction of a humanist culture'.[12] Schulz's rebirth deep in the forest not only recalls the Nazi promise of rebirth, but that of *Stunde Null* [zero hour] and the Federal Republic of Germany's attempt to break with its past. Max's transformation into Itzig thus offers a critique of Nazism as well as a threefold ironic critique of trends in post-war Germany: of Holocaust denial and the repression of guilt; of the self-refashioning of Germans as victims; and of post-war philo-Semitism.[13]

The criticism sustained by comedy is not limited to the puerile morality and nationalist ideology of the Germans. The Nazis determine what Jews look like, but Jews themselves reinforce the same racial stereotypes. Once Schulz adopts Itzig's identity, his looks are guarantee enough for him to be immediately recognized as a fellow Jew and receive compensation. Conversely, as an apparently recognizable Jew, Schulz becomes the victim of anti-Semitism in both its hostile and philo-Semitic forms. Racial hierarchies are not the prerogative of Nazi ideology, and in Israel differences quickly emerge between Jews along lines of origin and ethnicity. Frau Schmulevitch introduces a system into the seating order of her barber's shop, with Jews ranked as follows: Germans at the top, followed by other West European Jews, Russians and Lithuanians, other East European Jews, Romanians, the Yemenites, and finally all other oriental Jews (*DNuDF*, 413). Such racism is not surprising in view of the susceptibility of the Jews in Israel to grand rhetoric, which is demonstrated in their response to Schulz's speech in the barber shop. He has learned his trade from Hitler's speech in Wieshalle in 1932, an occasion when Hitler preaches his message to an enraptured crowd at the Ölberg [Mount of Oil]. Although the Ölberg derives its name from the annual party thrown there by Meyer, the local cooking oil company, its evocation of the Mount of Olives is apt. Like Hitler, Schulz mesmerizes his audience, so with religious rapture they scream 'Amen!' (*DNuDF*, 369). In turn, Hitler's promises evoke the Sermon on the Mount: 'Selig sind die Starken, denn sie werden das Erdenreich besitzen' [Blessed are the strong, for they shall inherit the earth] (*DNuDF*, 56). Common to all three speeches is the appeal to a perfect future that contributes to the next cycle of violence. Christianity is a cause of anti-Semitic violence, albeit unintended: the crucified Christ feebly weeps as Jews are herded by mistake into a Christian graveyard to be murdered: 'So hab ich das nicht gemeint' [That's not what I intended] (*DNuDF*, 77). Christ is promptly shot by Schulz for interfering. Nazi genocidal violence then leads to the violence of establishing the Promised Land in Palestine. As Schulz points out to Jankl Schwarz, notorious leader of a Zionist terrorist group, if the Arabs do not wish to sit on Jewish benches, it will be a problem. In all three cases the vision of a better future for a self-identifying group is caricatured as dangerous.

Schulz, then, can become a respected Israeli citizen not because he changes his ways, but because his ways are perfectly suited to another rebirth and another round of nation building. The *Exitus*, the ship carrying the cargo of Jews to Palestine, is aptly renamed the 'Auferstehung' [Resurrection] as it approaches land, which quickly becomes an ironic comment on the ways in which a resurrection is a revitalization of what has been. He moves comfortably from being a committed Nazi to being a committed Zionist, applying the skills he learned as a Nazi: injecting children (previously to murder them, now to keep them healthy) and fighting the enemy with German weapons. He need alter neither his nationalistic fervour nor his vocabulary, deploying words like 'Heimat', 'Volksfeind', 'Führerbeleidigung', 'Zersetzung' and 'Befehl ist Befehl' [Homeland, Enemy of the people, Insulting the

Leader, Subversion, an order's an order] (*DNuDF*, 365 & 391). His feelings make him a valuable advocate of Israeli nationalism as his promise of the 'Beherrschung der Welt' [conquering the world] (*DNuDF*, 368) demonstrates. Like Hitler, Schulz's rhetoric is persuasive, and he even convinces concentration camp survivors not to leave for the USA with his talk of the Jewish people's mission: 'Ich habe sie hypnotisiert' [I hypnotized them] (*DNuDF*, 419).

It is not surprising that Schulz should consistently draw parallels between his life as a Nazi and his life as a Zionist, between nation-building ideologies, the power of visionary rhetoric, and of racial stereotypes. It is a standard self-interested strategy to relativize the seriousness of his crimes and the culpability of the Germans. But more significant in terms of the novel's provocation is that Schulz's attempts at exculpation through *tu quoque* rhetoric cannot simply be ascribed to him as an unreliable narrator. The parallels established by Schulz are not limited to his retrospective confessional narrative but are also fundamental to the structuring of the text as a whole and the fact that he functions as a narrative device and vehicle for the grotesque narrative. As a result, the comparisons Schulz makes cannot be ascribed to him alone as a self-seeking narrator, but acquire the authority of the implied author. Schulz's challenge to discourses insisting upon the uniqueness of the Holocaust is sustained at the level of the text precisely through the devices of comic stereotyping and comparisons. It is also at this textual level that the boundaries between victims and perpetrators are shown to be contingent and blurred.

Comedy is central to *Der Nazi und der Friseur*'s criticism of moral hypocrisy, racism, and nationalism. At one level, though, the very grotesqueness of its comedy also limits the extent of its radical critique. By structuring the novel around stereotypes *Der Nazi und der Friseur* does, as Conter argues, expose how ludicrous they are. But extreme stereotypes are always ludicrous in their simplification, and the effectiveness of caricature resides in the exaggeration of isolated traits, not the depiction of mundane and contradictory norms. So while the conceit of the novel undoubtedly challenges moral cant, racism, and the complacent rigidity of the perpetrator/victim polarity, its sustained play with extremes lets the reader off the hook of implied criticism. The convinced Nazis in the novel are comically monstrous figures who enjoyably feed the reader's superiority, for even the shocking moments remain grotesque and enhance 'the pleasure of flinching'.[14] The persistent caricaturing upon which the novel's satire rests allows the reader to enjoy the comedy as though it were a discreet joke, and one which does not fundamentally implicate her as its butt, for the world it depicts remains fantastically unreal.

Laughing at Justice

Having said that, however, the novel's comedy plays a radical role in undermining the hope for justice and redemption. It does so not simply by depicting the impossibility of achieving justice commensurate to Schulz's crimes, but by toying with the humanizing discourses around trauma in order to confront the reader with her own need for redemptive narratives. Crucially, *Der Nazi und der Friseur* explores the ways in which the blurring of the simple opposition between perpetrator and victim serves a humanizing narrative by presenting the perpetrator's claim to be a victim, including being traumatized by his own deeds. But the credibility of Schulz's trauma is put into question both by his duplicitousness as narrator and through the comic inversion of fairy tales that sustains a sceptical questioning of perpetrator trauma.

The novel plays with the humanizing discourse of trauma and victimhood, in which the two are invested with ethical value, by showing Schulz to be a victim from the outset. He is raped by his stepfather Slavitzki at the age of seven weeks, and continuously sexually and physically abused thereafter. The rape is explicitly linked to his later being a mass murderer, for twice during the attack he refers to himself as an innocent baby who will become a mass murderer (*DNuDF*, 22). He joins the SA, the original paramilitary wing of the Nazi party, after hearing Hitler's speech specifically in order to escape the position of victim, telling himself: 'Du wirst den Hintern nicht mehr hinhalten' [You won't offer your backside any more] (*DNuDF*, 58). Thus he suggests that his later brutalization is a direct result of violence. Vestiges of Schulz's original humanity then become apparent in physical symptoms that reflect the horror of the murders he is involved in. He tells Frau Holle of his time in Russia: 'dort waren lange Gräben. — Und 1942... ja... da hatte ich einen leichten Herzinfarkt' [there were long graves. — And 1942... yes... I had a mild heart attack there] (*DNuDF*, 122). Later he explains to Veronja that the heart attack was a result of the killings, which in 1942 he was not yet accustomed to: 'Ich war das nicht gewohnt... damals noch nicht... so viele auf einmal zu erschießen... und Frauen und Kinder... und die Augen [...] das war zuviel' [I wasn't used to it... not yet... to shoot so many all at once... and women and children... and the eyes [...] that was too much] (*DNuDF*, 158). The pauses in his story give the impression that he has difficulty recounting what he did, that he is emotionally overwhelmed and even traumatized by the memory of mass murder.

The emotional impact that the eyes of his victims have upon him has a parallel in the haunting presence of the six million dead Jews. Schulz makes periodic reference to the dead: they accompany the *Exitus* to Palestine, and he feels their company in the newly planted 'Wald der 6 Millionen' [Wood of the 6 million]. Here he cannot smell the scent of young trees, but instead a stench that turns his stomach, the smell of wet trousers and fear (*DNuDF*, 394). At his wedding he has a vision of the dead dancing with him, the sack filled with their gold teeth on his back. Their presence serves as a reminder of his role as mass murderer, a haunting guilty conscience that does not leave him. Schulz is very conscious of the effects of his acts on concentration camp survivors. Mira, his wife, was shot into a mass grave in the village of Wapnjarka-Podolsk, but managed to crawl out from beneath the corpses. She was then re-captured but nearly starved to death in a concentration camp, and as a result has become mute and an obese, obsessive eater. But many cannot recover from their experiences at all, as Schulz admits: 'Wir hatten sie fertiggemacht. Endgültig. Wir töteten ihre Seelen' [We did them in. Once and for all. We murdered their souls] (*DNuDF*, 419). In Mira he is directly confronted with the question of his own responsibility in Nazi crimes, for he may actually have been present at the mass shooting in Wapnjarka-Podolsk. Ostensibly he does not remember because he was present at so many mass murders and was never there for long: 'ich meine... in den kleinen und unwichtigen Städten... machten unsere Arbeit... [...] zogen dann weiter' [I think... in the little, insignificant towns... did our work... then moved on] (*DNuDF*, 382). But like the ellipses in his accounts of the mass murders, the apparent block to memory is reminiscent of traumatic repression, his trauma intensified by the possibility that he himself committed the atrocity against Mira.

Schulz's confession at the end of the novel offers the reader some moral comfort through the promise of justice and redemption. Schulz acknowledges the extent of his crimes and wants to hear what the commensurate punishment is. Wolfgang Richter, to whom he confesses, tells him there is none, for his crimes are too great, but as he dies Richter metes out a punishment of sorts: by telling Schulz that he will be judged by a higher authority, he successfully makes Schulz feel the fear that his victims felt before they died. This punishment is also not commensurate, but at least the text holds out the promise of divine judgement. The end of the novel thus offers a fantasy of redemption: the perpetrator has confessed and received a punishment of sorts, however inadequate. Furthermore, the perpetrator feels guilt and shows symptoms of trauma, both of which can be understood as evidence of his humanity; emotional and somatic evidence that he recognizes the immorality of what he has done. Finally, even if there is not open remorse, justice is served and the ethical universe is reinstated: Schulz's internal torment means that the perpetrator does not get away with it, and his guilt is testament to the natural moral order that demands that perpetrators should not be rewarded with happiness.

There is, however, a very different and more morally disturbing way of understanding Schulz. As J. P. C. Van den Berg argues, one question is unavoidable: '[ist] Max [...] tatsächlich *selbst traumatisiert* oder [wird] das erzählte Trauma nicht vielmehr nur im *nachhinein als Erzählung konstruiert*' [is Max really traumatized himself or is the trauma much more a story that is constructed retrospectively].[15] In this view, Schulz is concerned with little more than his own survival and social status, and this also governs his response to the past and its ghosts. So although he is justified in seeing himself as a victim of violent parental abuse, his reasons for joining the Nazi party remain unconvincing. It is when his German teacher, Siegfried von Salzstange, tells him that the people gathered to hear Hitler are all people who have at some point 'got it in the neck' (*DNuDF*, 51), that Schulz is offered a ready identity and starts to present himself as a victim. Clearly it is seductive to be part of a party that offers him, and others, the chance of acquiring power and redressing their grievances, but it is quite evident from his narrative that his is a consciously chosen path. He has an alternative: Schulz is a functioning adult and a skilled barber and has thus already acquired the means to escape a victim position. His role as perpetrator is neither determined by previous suffering nor relativized by it. As he repeatedly admits, he wants to be on the winning side whichever that is.

Similarly, the physical symptoms he suffers as a result of his participation in mass murder have little to do with trauma. Although he tells Veronja that his participation in mass shootings triggered his heart attack, he lets slip that at the time he thought his heart attack resulted from too much drinking and smoking. The fact that his continued fear of heart attacks is linked to too much sex confirms the suspicion that his weak heart has more to do with self-indulgence than his horror at inflicting violence. This view is consistent with the stomach-aches and diarrhoea that afflict him, but only at times when his own life is at risk: it is the imminent threat presented by the fall of Warsaw and not the order to kill the remaining concentration camp inmates that makes him feel ill (*DNuDF*, 135). Likewise, it is his fear of partisan reprisals that makes him defecate like the 'Untermenschen' [sub-humans] (*DNuDF*, 139). Looked at closely, Schulz's physical symptoms offer little support for his hints that inflicting violence has traumatized him. Indeed, his incomprehension of trauma is evident in his bemusement as to why survivors on the *Exitus* wake up screaming in the night, even though their persecution is over (*DNuDF*, 259). This rightly makes us sceptical of what might be read as the textual symptoms of trauma, the points when Schulz seemingly struggles to narrate and that conform so neatly to the cliché of the incursion of trauma into language. The apparently emotionally laden pauses in his accounts of mass murder and his heartfelt reference to the victims' eyes are very specifically performances aimed at his audience. In the first example he is seeking a sympathetic hearing from Frau Holle, and in the second he is desperately attempting to emphasize his vulnerability to Veronja in order to survive her life-threatening punishment.

Other examples too point to the apparently stylistic manifestations of trauma having more to do with feigned evasion and taunting. Schulz's dissimulation is inseparable from his narrative role as 'a prototypical picaresque pretender and debunker', which foils 'every attempt by the reader to obtain an unequivocal notion of the intentions of the narrator and the motivations of each narrative move'.[16] When Schulz first refers to the murder of Itzig Finkelstein at the start of Section 4, his narrative is characterized by the pauses and stalls that are noticeable at moments of emotional intensity. The whole section is addressed directly to Itzig, making Schulz's emotional investment even more intense. Asking Itzig if he knows his murderer, it is Schulz's overwrought narrative evasions that make the answer very obvious. Indeed, it is soon evident that the emotional exaggeration is part of his toying strategy: he taunts Itzig, not naming the killer, telling him 'Ich laß dich zappeln!' [I'll let you wriggle] (*DNuDF*, 244). He thereby also leaves the reader to wriggle in suspense at the end of his unsubtle narrative line. This moment of one-upmanship over his murdered friend betrays the extent to which Schulz is driven by concern over his own status and power. His pride and his need to be recognized as important are also central to another staged evasion: was he or was he not at the mass killing at Wapnjarka-Podolsk? The anxiety driving this question may stem from the realization that he attempted to murder his wife, but is just as convincingly coupled with his desire for recognition. He wants the name of Max Schulz to retain its notoriety and is concerned that it is no longer appearing in press accounts of the genocide: 'Ist der nicht mehr wichtig?' [Isn't he important anymore?] (*DNuDF*, 389).

It is Schulz's self-regard and his persistent worry about Max Schulz's status as a notorious perpetrator that casts suspicion on his final confession to Richter. Rather than being pleased by the discovery that Max Schulz was pronounced dead in 1947, an event that guarantees his safety as Itzig Finkelstein, Schulz is irritated and saddened by the fact that the death was only reported in one small provincial newspaper, for this confirms his status as unimportant small fry (*DNuDF*, 444). Provoked by inferiority and wanting to be cleverer than the authorities, he tells Richter his whole story and stages his very own war crimes trial. Similarly, his attitude to the spirits of the dead is also informed by the same urge for self-aggrandizement. However aware he may be that his new life is built upon the murder of others, the presence of the dead does not interfere with his successful new life, and their presence at his wedding provokes defiance: 'Nein! Mich kriegen die Toten nicht weich!' [No! The dead won't make me soft!] (*DNuDF*, 388). When he walks in the wood to converse with the dead, there is no doubt that he is aware of his past and that he does not deny responsibility for his actions. But there is no indication of guilt and remorse when he taunts them with the success of his, and other ex-Nazis', new life. As he vindictively tells the dead, these perpetrators live a good life, they have status and respect, and some are even in the government. Grinning and assuming messianic tones, Schulz goads the dead with the truth: 'Wahrlich, ich sage euch. [...] Sie [...] machen sich über Gott und die Welt lustig. Ja. Und auch über das Wort "Gerechtigkeit"!' [Truly, I say to you. They are making fun of God and the world. Yes, and of the word 'Justice'!] (*DNuDF*, 460).

The truth of Schulz's taunt is incontestable, for ex-Nazis did indeed evade justice and achieve positions of respect. As Friedrich Torberg observes, Hilsenrath offers proof, evident in many 'Nazi trials', that crimes that exceeded certain proportions were beyond the realm of human justice.[17] The reader is thus also subjected to Schulz's taunt, for he has the last laugh, challenging us to recognize the tenuousness of the link between the perpetration of atrocity and the 'appropriate' emotional response on the part of the perpetrator. There is no question for Schulz that he is guilty of crimes, but any feeling of guilt that may be in evidence, such as his worry about nearly killing his wife, has negligible impact on his living a good life. The few occasions when he might be displaying symptoms of trauma are little more than staged interludes or moments when he himself is threatened. Schulz is more terrified by the memory of the Polish forest, where he was surrounded by partisans intent on killing him, than he is by the memory of woods as Nazi killing fields. Thus the novel invites us to be wary of understanding perpetrator trauma as a testament to an individual's residual humanity by presenting Schulz's trauma, if it is to be believed at all, as a consequence of the existential threats to him, not as a consequence of the violence meted out to others.[18]

Thus, although trauma is a key theme of the novel as Van den Berg suggests, it is treated with fundamental scepticism. For this reason, the silences, repetitions, and contradictions of the narrative cannot be accepted as impressive expressions of Holocaust trauma as he proposes.[19] Indeed, the novel's grotesque humour ruthlessly confronts the reader with the question of whether 'humans are able to distinguish between good and evil' and with 'the potentially abysmal character of human nature'.[20] By so doing it also exposes the seduction that trauma has come to hold as an affirmation of fundamental humanity, reflected perhaps in Van den Berg's desire to locate 'ontological' trauma in Schulz's confrontation with unrepresentable otherness, or in Malkmus's suggestion that the picaro Schulz could in fact be the assumed identity of the deeply traumatized Itzig who suffers from 'severe survivor guilt'.[21] The search for redemptive narratives, of which the identification of trauma symptoms can become a part, is foiled in the novel not just by the confidence trickery of the picaro, but by Hilsenrath's grotesque integration of the *Märchen* form into *Der Nazi und der Friseur*.

In addition to criticizing constructions of national identity under the Nazis as well as in post-war West Germany, the novel's distortions of the *Märchen* also radically re-cast the conventional moral world that the genre supports. As highly symbolic and metaphorical explorations of transgression and moral order, and as tales depicting challenges that must be overcome in order to win the prize, fairy tales, like myth, can be adapted to specific historical situations while holding the lure of universal truths. Their political and ideological adaptability resides in their championing of those who are virtuous or weak against forces of cruelty and strength, with the implied reader constructed to identify with virtue rewarded. The triumph of wickedness is not entertained. However, as is clear in *Der Nazi und der Friseur*, Schulz could just as easily be the abused stepson Hänsel, the German woodcutter who saves the womenfolk from the lascivious hunger of the Jewish or Russian wolf, or the prince who finally wins Princess Mira after proving himself worthy in the battle against the British and Arab dragons. What he cannot be is the wolf or the witch, for in *Märchen* they get their come-uppance, and Schulz does not. When Bruno Bettelheim describes the manifold message of the fairy tale as one depicting inevitable struggle, 'but that if one [...] steadfastly meets unexpected and often unjust hardships, one masters all obstacles and at the end emerges victorious', he could be describing Schulz's life.[22] So far from being a fairy tale that helps 'neither the characters nor the reader come to terms with evil, understand evil or to emerge victorious',[23] the novel offers a very clear moral, succinctly conveyed through Schulz: 'Und werden die Schwachen und Wehrlosen nicht von den Starken überrumpelt, niedergeknüppelt, vergewaltigt, verhöhnt, in den Arsch gefickt? Zu gewissen Zeiten sogar einfach beseitigt? Ist es nicht so?' [And don't the weak and defenceless get overpowered, clubbed down, raped, scorned and fucked in the arse by the strong? Even sometimes simply done away with? Isn't that how it is?] (*DNuDF*, 24). Schulz knows this very well, steadfastly masters all obstacles, and undoubtedly emerges victorious.

The novel does not, therefore, systematically subvert the fairy tale, for it actually demonstrates how well the notion of 'struggle rewarded' and 'hurdles overcome' can be aligned to any number of contexts. It thereby offers the reader a very clear understanding of evil, but one that is based on an inversion, not subversion, of the *Märchen's* conventional moral paradigm. For this reason Hilsenrath's tale not only 'questions a model of story-telling which fulfils the reader's expectation that the bad will ultimately be punished', it also disturbs our wider desire for an ethical subject.[24] Thus, in addition to the theme of trauma, *Der Nazi und der Friseur* also undermines any expectation that a perpetrator feels shame. The novel exposes the gap between the reality of when shame is or is not felt and the anticipation or hope that shame be felt in response to moral transgression as evidence of an ethical subject. By understanding shame as both an emotion that is socially constructed through processes of introjection, and as an emotion of the self that also exceeds those social constructions, the motivation for committing extreme atrocities can be comprehended, as can the marked absence of shame amongst perpetrators for those atrocities.[25] Schulz feels no shame for the mass murders. The closest he comes to shame is when his SS comrades laugh at him for knowing the Finkelsteins, as a result of which he wants to cleanse himself (*DNuDF*, 439 & 441) and murders them. Purification here is associated with the avoidance of shame in front of the group, not atonement for an immoral deed.

In this respect Schulz is typical of those who participated in genocide. His behaviour exemplifies the intense shame culture that Thomas Kühne describes in the *Wehrmacht*, and which was crucial for facilitating participation in the genocide. On the one hand it guaranteed comradeship, power, and security. On the other, the fear of disgrace and the shame of being ostracized ensured soldiers' conformity to 'collective breaches of the norm'.[26] Kühne points to the fact that over and above similar mechanisms that are found in gangs and fraternities, the German situation was special in that the criminal breaches of norms were condoned by the state. The soldiers thus consolidated their identity in relation to a particularly strong and pervasive 'historically localized symbolic order'.[27] He emphasizes the historical contingency of shame cultures, but it is precisely as an emotion relating to one's identity, one that is felt as such a fundamental and traumatic assault upon the self, that it can be so potent in dictating immoral actions. It is for this reason, because the self by no means necessarily experiences such an assault if the action is carried out against others, that shame does not follow from transgression. One of *Der Nazi und der Friseur*'s most intense provocations is that Schulz recognizes his guilt, but feels no shame and shows no remorse. Indeed, he shamelessly demonstrates that justice belongs to the strong.

Schulz's taunt to the spirits of the dead that perpetrators are having a good laugh about justice also serves as a taunt to the reader. Despite Schulz's fear of a final judgement, and the novel's hope for one, the final invocation of God confirms the fiasco of human justice. The novel resonates with Kertész's statement that 'If Auschwitz was to no avail, then God has failed; and if God has been made to fail, then we shall never understand Auschwitz'. In his view God has been made to fail 'because the world order has not changed even after Auschwitz' (*DK*, 107). This is precisely Schulz's point when he refers to perpetrators who are respected and incorporated into the government. Schulz is not traumatized by inflicting violence and nor does he feel shame, for his identity was never put into question. Here is the cruel joke of Hilsenrath's novel: for the furies, whether they take the form of shame, conscience, or justice, it is a case of mistaken identity as they pursue the survivors more than the perpetrators.

The Kindly Ones

Graphic violence and sex are one of the reasons that Jonathan's Littell's novel *The Kindly Ones* is provocative, for the reader assumes the perspective of Max Aue and through his eyes witnesses the detail of all levels of genocidal atrocity as well as his sexual fantasies and practices. The novel is marked by its representational surfeit: it combines what might arguably be described as 'the splatter-aesthetics of contemporary action and horror films' with a voyeuristic and pornographic gaze to become 'symptomatic' of a contemporary 'culture of excess and consumption'.[28] As Petra Rau argues, it also reflects two specific wider cultural trends: the interest in violent perpetrators that has developed since the 1980s and the growth of 'dark tourism' that transforms history, including the Holocaust, into a site of 'morbid attractions'.[29] Representational surfeit characterizes its form too, with 894 pages devoted not just to sex and violence but also to the detail of National Socialist policy, politics, and socializing, all of which is then further superimposed on Aeschylus's *Oresteia* and the Oedipus myth.[30] Such formal excess has also been a cause of provocation, for it has blurred the boundaries between fact and fiction and has clouded the ability to evaluate the novel's moral significance. The novel is suffused with historical detail based on Littell's extensive historiographical research, yet is at the same time evidently fictional. This split is reflected in the figure of Aue, who is a realistic protagonist and first-person narrator on the one hand, and a narrative device on the other. In his guise as a narrative device he both offers unrealistically accurate insight into a historical period and a mythic re-working of Orestes's matricide. The novel thus invites the reader to assume the point of view of a perpetrator engaged in historically verifiable violence, directly feeding ethical anxiety around consuming and taking pleasure from the representation of violence.[31]

Edgar Hilsenrath criticizes the prevalence of facts in *The Kindly Ones*, condemning its literary qualities because it is a report and not a novel.[32] Hilsenrath's simplification misses the point. It is precisely because it is not just a report that many critics have voiced concern, since the text's unclear delineation of fact and fiction is variously seen to undermine historical accuracy, literary quality, and ethical integrity. Peter Kuon sees the documentary precision of the novel as its greatest strength, but also its greatest weakness aesthetically, for it results in a conflictual oscillation between 'reliable chronicler' (ethics) and 'unreliable autobiographer' (aesthetics).[33] Jeremy D. Popkin, who explicitly presents his view as that of a historian, eloquently outlines the problem posed by the apparent authenticity lent to the perpetrator by the novel's historical accuracy. Although as a creative novelist Littell is free to diverge from historical fact, 'the insertion of the fictional Maximilien Aue into the historical universe of the Holocaust would seem to impose at least some responsibilities on the author'.[34] There are, however, irreconcilable tensions. The mythic level of the novel, which seeks to confer universal significance on contemporary action, actually contributes to making Aue's behaviour untypical. In the face of the historical evidence, otherwise so 'diligently digested' by Littell, which demonstrates that mass murderers were generally fairly ordinary men, the novel revives 'the caricature of the Nazis as bizarre psychopaths and sexual deviants'.[35] For historians, the artificial construction of the text does not add to the understanding of the Holocaust, and so the merit of the book cannot be justified by claiming it provides readers 'with genuine insight into the mind of a Holocaust perpetrator'.[36]

The problems of blurring fact and fiction within the diegesis are, for some critics, further compounded by the nebulous relationship of the fictional 'I' of Aue and the authorial 'I' of Littell. Littell has never denied that there is some overlap between him and his character, saying that there was no hesitation in writing in the first person, that 'I've been in dark places a good part of my life' and that 'I based him mostly on myself'.[37] Indeed, both share a birthday of 10 October. But this is not tantamount to saying 'Aue c'est moi', for this would be 'reductive' and 'to exaggerate'.[38] Littell describes how the need to put himself in the perpetrators' shoes arose from his aim to find 'a voice that reveals the depths of the hell it describes', a voice that he did not find in 'empty' perpetrators' testimonies, nor could construct through a classic omniscient perspective. He started with himself and what he knew because through his professional life he 'had hung out with killers' in Bosnia, Chechnya, Afghanistan, and Africa.[39] For Littell this is not tantamount to closeness to the character, however, for the use of the third person would have involved greater proximity to the character: 'j'avais peur du "il" parce que le "il" était presque plus "je" que le "je". Le "je" me permettait une plus grande distanciation' [I was scared of the 'he' because the 'he' was almost more 'I' than the 'I'. The 'I' allowed me much greater distance].[40] So although Littell draws on himself and his experiences, he insists that Aue is neither a 'sociologically credible Nazi' nor even a 'plausible character'.[41] Rather, Aue becomes a means to 'ventriloquise historians',[42] observing and analyzing events even as he participates in them: 'I was always observing myself: it was as if a film camera was fixed just above me, and I was at once this camera, the man it was filming, and the man who was then studying the film' (*TKO*, 107).

Nevertheless, Kuon insists that Littell does 'far too little to establish an overall critical distance from the narrator's discourse'.[43] As a result, the perpetrator's point of view is invested with Littell's authority, and lent further credibility by the novel's historical accuracy. Despite agreeing that Aue's views cannot be ascribed directly to Littell, Dominick LaCapra is troubled by the question of whether Littell, even as implied author, '[identifies] with Aue, his admiration for bureaucratic efficiency, and his excesses'.[44] It is crucial to identify whether there is a 'significantly critical dimension' to the narrative, whether there are 'textual markers or procedures that provide the reader with critical distance that signals the way complicity with the first-person narrator be resisted, disrupted, or overcome'.[45] LaCapra concurs with Julia Kristeva's reservation that the lack of distance between the narrator and Aue makes it difficult to remain detached from his antisemitic universe.[46] Yet he still in fact points to very clear examples of possible alienation effects. These include the blatant implausibility of Aue's narration, the extremity of his sexual perversions, and the explicit mythological substructure. Nevertheless, for LaCapra, these potential alienation effects ultimately contribute to the novel's fundamental weaknesses: the implausible narrative does not develop our understanding of a perpetrator's motivation; Aue's perversion does not question the stereotype of the Nazi pervert; and the mythological substructure refigures history 'as a derivative of fate and myth (or of a fatalistic, transhistorical "theory")', such as Žižek's construction of psychoanalysis as a 'tragic account of a fatalistic death drive or a universal, annihilating "real"'.[47]

In what follows I suggest that the novel, despite its heavy debt to conventions of realism, is imbued with a sense of the comic absurd. This arises both out of the more realist dimensions of the novel that relate to the nature of National Socialism and from the intertextual references and structuring devices that play with comic and tragic genres. As with Hilsenrath's novel, there is an ongoing tension in the text between the two levels. At the realist level, Aue is both narrator of and character in his own narrative account, and intertextual allusions can be ascribed to his own self-presentation. At the level of structure, Aue is a device whose simultaneous relationship to the picaro and the tragic hero raises questions about representation and justice. In *The Kindly Ones* it is the marginal but niggling elements of comedy that remain disturbing as part of the novel's message that nothing has changed after Auschwitz.

National Socialist Circus Games

A defining characteristic of *The Kindly Ones* is its excessive detail. The relentless recounting of facts and amassing of details contribute both to a mounting sense of the absurd and to growing tedium. The number games in Aue's introduction set the tone for the obsession with detail and their contribution to creating a mood of a grotesque, absurd joke. Taking Hilberg's figures of the overall numbers of those killed on the eastern front, Aue works out that 13.04 people were killed per minute between 22 June 1941 and 8 May 1945. This can be further broken down into 'a dead German every 40.8 seconds, a dead Jew every 24 seconds, and a dead Bolshevik (Soviet Jews included) every 6.12 seconds' (*TKO*, 16). Counting the individual dead using a stopwatch becomes 'a good meditation exercise'. Aue's fixation on precise details and his concern with minutiae is typical of him and also of Nazi policy, where absurdity is generated from the juxtaposition of a fastidious and extreme concentration on detail with utter disregard for the practical human cost. Thus for over forty pages of the book, Aue is occupied with the problem of the *Bergjuden*, the Caucasus Jews who are so well integrated into the Kabard (Islamic) communities that these communities are not willing to tolerate them being murdered. The vexing question arises as to whether they are 'racially Jewish', originating from Palestine, or 'culturally Jewish' people of 'Caucasian, Iranian and Afghan descent' who have later converted (*TKO*, 296). If it can be determined that they are 'culturally Jewish', a view supported by the *Wehrmacht*, then they can be spared, since they present no threat to the German forces in a population that is otherwise peaceful. If they are categorized as 'racially Jewish', a position backed by the SS, then they should be murdered regardless of the local resistance it may provoke. Various experts present evidence based on their study of eastern Judaism, linguistics, ethnography, and cultural anthropology to representatives of the SS, the *Abwehr*, the military administration, the army headquarters (AOK) and the *Ostministerium*. Fundamental academic differences, based on extensive analysis of tiny nuances relating to the origins of language or shared customs, fuel equally fundamental differences between the official agencies. Utterly irrelevant to the discussion is the value of people's lives.

Another example of the absurd disjunction between meticulous theory and crass disregard for its human implications is the extended episode where Aue is put in charge of an 'interdepartmental study group' to solve the 'question of feeding in the camps' (*TKO*, 636–37). Aue is delighted to be able 'to contribute to the war effort and to the victory of Germany by other means than murder and destruction' (*TKO*, 637). In fact, these other means involve far-reaching calculations on how to improve the productivity of slave labourers while they are still alive. Aue has witnessed the extreme malnutrition and violent treatment of the inmates at Auschwitz, and the huge under-production and complaints from industry that results. The 'interesting discussion' (*TKO*, 623) on violence he has with Dr Wirths, the chief physician of the Auschwitz garrison, informs the further interesting discussions he organizes on questions of nutrition. These involve the experts analyzing calories, the proportion of protein in a meal and its relative importance compared to the vitamins and micronutrients, the equation of life expectancy to type of labour, and the additional calories that get lost in the natural selection of stronger inmates stealing from the weaker ones. The ludicrousness of Aue's research results from the polite, abstract number-crunching that is devoted to improving the victory of Germany precisely through ongoing murder and destruction: *Vernichtung durch Arbeit* [Extermination through work] (*TKO*, 656) that Eichmann advocates.

Aue himself unintentionally raises to the level of parody the intrinsic absurdity arising from the incongruity between a decorous obsession with policy detail and overwhelming murderous chaos. In the aftermath of the failed plot of 20 July 1944 to assassinate Hitler, and in the face of the allied advances, Aue is inspired by his reading of E. R. Burroughs's Martian adventures to develop policies to be implemented after the war. Taking his lead from both red and green Martians ('those three-metre-tall monsters with four arms and fangs'), Aue suggests to Himmler a celibacy tax and communal ownership among the SS elite. Himmler's response heightens the parody, for he is delighted by his 'useful research' and 'profound and necessary ideas' (*TKO*, 823–24). Readers familiar with Burroughs's complete works may be further amused by the fact that Aue looks to Martians as his preferred role models, rather than to the 'Zani', Burroughs's 1938 satirical representation of the Nazis in *Carson of Venus*. The Zanis, in order to 'keep the blood of Korvans pure', kill the Atorians, '[n]aturally, because they have large ears'.[48]

A sense of the absurd is not created solely through excessive detail, it also arises from the internal contradictions of Nazi policy, or idealism, and implementation. Whereas in theory Jews are racially distinguishable from Aryans, in practice, as is clear from the difficulties in defining the *Bergjuden*, there are difficulties: are Jews to be identified '[f]rom sight? By examining their noses? By measuring them?' or perhaps by asking them 'to drop their pants' (*TKO*, 40–41). The solution, asking Jews to identify and present themselves, causes Aue a sleepless night, because he worries about the 'unfairness' of murdering honest Jews. Even Aue is forced to recognize the 'comical misunderstandings' that result from the anti-Semitic fear of Jewish omnipotence: German officials are worried by the fact that the Hungarians place Jews near strategic targets, for if the Americans bomb these targets, 'that would prove that global Judaism was not as powerful as was thought' (*TKO*, 781).

Not surprisingly, the Americans do bomb the targets and do kill many Jews. Bizarre moral contortions are commonplace, reminiscent of the prim adages of the concentration camps: '*We must convey the impression that we are just*' (*TKO*, 90). Justice is a delicate matter of fine distinctions. An SS man who kills Jews under orders is one thing, an SS man who kills Jews to hide his corruption or for pleasure is quite another: 'that's a crime. Even if the Jew is to die anyway'. Legally, as Aue and the SS judge Dr Morgen admit, the distinction is 'hard to make' (*TKO*, 597). They are both more shocked by the fact that one corrupt Auschwitz nurse alone has managed to divert three fist-sized lumps of dental gold than the fact that the gold 'represents more than a hundred thousand dead' (*TKO*, 603).

There are constant examples of ironic juxtaposition between the claim to moral superiority of the Germans and the reality of their actions. Obergruppenführer Jeckeln outlines the 'sensitivity and delicacy' (*TKO*, 30) of the SS as Germans. These traits make them particularly critical of the Soviet law enforcers (the NKVD) as 'monsters' for massacring civilians (*TKO*, 35), the Ukrainian nationalist 'real savages' for their attacks on Jews (*TKO*, 53), and of those responsible for the dead Jews in the Dnieper river for not being '*gemütlich*' (*TKO*, 121). It is this sensitivity and appreciation of *Gemütlichkeit* that presumably triggers the men's anger when they are served blood pudding for lunch: a tasteless meal to give to those who have been murdering Jews all morning at Babi Yar. Russian cannibalism at Stalingrad reveals the Russians' 'true nature', and it therefore comes as a terrible shock when a German company kills and eats one of its war volunteers (*TKO*, 376). Although Aue is often the observer of such hypocrisy, thereby conveying a favourable impression that he, by being aware of it, is somehow better than others, he is fully implicated. When he complains to his sister Una that the British are killing innocent civilians by bombing German cities, she merely has to point out that the Germans have done just the same for him to become enraged: 'the difference seemed obvious to me, but she was [...] pretending not to see it' (*TKO*, 485). He is also very happy to accept Himmler's view of how 'ridiculous' it is for him, a 'perfect Nordic specimen, with perhaps just a touch of alpine blood', to be accused of murdering his mother and step-father: 'Only the racially degenerate nations, Poles, Gypsies, can commit matricide' (*TKO*, 743).

Central to the novel's focus on the absurd and 'interminable *National-Socialist circus games*', is the infighting of the various factions in their attempts to '[anticipate] the Führer's will' (*TKO*, 58). The obvious clowns in the circus are Göring and Goebbels, whose act involves Göring posting guards in front of his favourite restaurant to protect it from being closed, and Goebbels then organizing a '*spontaneous demonstration of the anger of the people*' (*TKO*, 442). The endless factionalism infects all aspects of Aue's experience. The *Wehrmacht* and the SS have different priorities, the *Ostministerium* is at odds with its gauleiters (*TKO*, 260), the idealist 'members of the Party' despise the venality of mere 'men of the party' (*TKO*, 474), Himmler is jealous of Speer's encroachment on SS autonomy, having already promoted Heydrich out of the way (*TKO*, 550), and Eichmann's investment in genocide is at odds with the *Wirtschafts-Verwaltungshauptamt* and with Speer's interest in maximizing manpower for the war effort. The relentless 'maelstrom of intrigues' (*TKO*, 760) is narrated at length and in great detail. Aue's language and style are mundane, dull, and literal, and his concern with reporting the minutiae of everything he does and observes aptly reflects his legalistic and bureaucratic outlook. The uniform, consistent march of details through one episode followed by the next undoubtedly adds to the credibility of the historical events, but it simultaneously contributes to the implausibility of the narrative as memoir and with it to our ability to identify with Aue. Furthermore, the overload of detail generates considerable tedium, as Aue relentlessly recalls one atrocity, followed by the minutiae of SS governance, followed by the next atrocity.

The Kindly Ones is based on extensive historical research and to that extent these absurd elements of the National Socialist circus, including the internal ideological contradictions and infighting and the ludicrous moral contortions, belong to the historical reality of National Socialism. Yet central to the novel's aesthetic is the excess of detail that at once contributes to a sense of the absurd and also induces tedium, both of which situate the novel in the tradition of anti-heroic war literature through showing the fog and boredom of war. The long-winded and tiresome narrative explicitly counters techniques of poetic condensation or metaphoric translation. So although at first glance Littell's novel might suggest the 'composite notion of blood, lust and the demon' which Kertész's old boy in *Fiasco* finds objectionable in certain aesthetic mediations of violence, its 900 pages soon confirm that '[c]umulative images of murder become just as lethally tedious and discouragingly tiring as the attendant work itself' (*Fi*, 46). Far from evoking notions of the sublime or of redemption, the novel emphasizes mass murder as an 'assembly-line operation' (*Fi*, 45), for which 'modern management techniques adapted to new requirements' (*Fi*, 554–55) are vital. This, the old boy suggests, is what has 'put paid to tragic representation. [...] Richard III wagers that he will be evil; the mass murderers of a totalitarian regime, by contrast, take an oath on the common good' (*Fi*, 45). In *The Kindly Ones*, the sense of the absurd and the unrelenting presentation of detail become vital for working against an aesthetic drift into myth and tragedy. In doing so, they complement those aspects of the novel that ostentatiously belong to the world of fiction and its play with genres, including comedy.

Sniggering up their Sleeves

In Kertész's *Fateless*, György Köves imagines that behind the careful planning of the way to the gas chambers, there are self-congratulatory gentlemen sitting in imposing suits and smoking cigars. In Littell's novel, the conspiratorial planners lurking in the background are the Aue family friends Dr Mandelbrod and Herr Leland. Herr Leland is a British born Germanophile, Dr Mandelbrod is, '[d]espite his Jewish-sounding name [...], like Minister Rosenberg, a pure German of old Prussian stock, with perhaps a drop of Slavic blood' (*TKO*, 448). Both men are influential industrialists, have supported and financed the Nazi party from the outset, and seem to exert a murky influence over the top-ranking Nazis, as members of the *Freundeskreis Himmler*. The conspiratorial air that surrounds them both, and particularly Mandelbrod as the one who intermittently meets with Aue, is reinforced by their eagerness to steer Aue's career, and by Mandelbrod's description of their role as being 'to stand by the Führer's side'. So powerful are they that they are not even answerable to the Führer, but to the 'immense space' that exists between the Führer's 'historic' decision to eradicate the Jews and the 'practical side of things' (*TKO*, 456). The impression of Mandelbrod as an arch conspirator is reflected in his ideological anti-Semitism which sees Jews as the true and deserving enemies of National Socialism because they, like the National Socialists, insist on the concept of the purity of the blood and of a chosen people.

Mandelbrod may not jump up and down when he has an idea of how to reduce the gap between the theory and practice of murdering Jews, but this hugely powerful figure is nevertheless well cast in the role of a Bond villain. Hugely obese, he sits 'like an enormous Oriental idol, placid, bovine, colossal' (*TKO*, 450) in a custom armchair mounted on a platform, regularly farting a putrid and nauseating stench. He surrounds himself with a harem of perfect, beautiful, and intelligent Nazi women who attend to his needs, and who offer Aue sex in order to bear perfect Aryan children. These Amazons too add to the comic ensemble by their physical interchangeability, so that Aue is in confusion about which woman has propositioned him. Mandelbrod also surrounds himself with a horde of cats, thus evoking the image of Ernst Stavro Blofeld, the evil genius intent on world domination. As Mandelbrod remarks in passing, once 'we've finished with the Russians, we'll still have the Chinese to contend with' (*TKO*, 454). Mandelbrod's evil genius and ability to pull strings behind the scenes is sustained until the end. Sitting with Leland in the midst of nineteen suitcases and the chaos of the Soviet assault on Berlin, he is waiting to be escorted to Moscow where the offer of their services has been accepted with interest.

As with any evil genius, Mandelbrod pops up periodically, apparently untouched by the chaos taking place around him. He is not the only character to turn up like this, indeed, the way in which certain figures appear intermittently, often in the most unlikely of places, is characteristic of the novel. Hohenegg, the Sixth Army's chief pathologist, first meets Aue on his way to Simferopol in the Crimea, then again in Pyatigorsk in the Caucasus, and then on the flight to Stalingrad, where he is going to study the effects of malnutrition on German soldiers. He next turns up working in Berlin, and at the very last bumps into Aue in the Führer's bunker, where he is Hitler's backup doctor. Hohenegg's appearances are still within the realm of the realistic, but those of Thomas Hauser become increasingly implausible. Thomas initially meets Aue when as an officer of the *Sicherheitsdienst* (SD) he intervenes to extract Aue from the charge of homosexuality with the suggestion that Aue join the SD himself. This sets the pattern for a friendship in which Thomas advises Aue on the best career moves, concerns himself with Aue's wellbeing, as understood by his outlook as a Nazi careerist, and normally manages to appear at Aue's side at critical moments. Thus, impeccably dressed, he is in a Stalingrad bunker to receive Aue when he arrives, he guarantees the wounded Aue's evacuation from Stalingrad by switching his 'untransportable' label with that of someone else, he rescues Aue from the advancing Red Army and leads him back to the German front, and finally he turns up to save Aue from being shot by the detective Clemens. As he says, 'As usual, I arrive just in time' (*TKO*, 974). Even after death he secures Aue's safety: Aue murders Thomas in order to steal the forged identity papers that confirm his identity as a Frenchman.

Thomas's appearances are always given a realistic framework, but their increasing improbability and eleventh hour timing, combined with Thomas's apparent invulnerability, mean that they cumulatively acquire a veneer of comedy. The uncanny nature of Thomas's unassailability is made explicit when Aue sees Thomas badly wounded by shrapnel. He watches how Thomas, 'his intestines spilled out of his stomach in long, sticky, slippery, smoking coils', inserts his hand into his wound to remove the still red-hot shrapnel, then re-inserts his own intestines before tying up the wound with a scarf. A few days later he shows no sign of injury and is even surprised to be asked how he is. The episode seems explicable only as part of Aue's fever-induced 'hallucinations and dreams' (*TKO*, 693), until months later, with a violent shock, Aue sees a huge scar on Thomas's belly. Thomas's mysterious invincibility emanates a demonic air, and he increasingly becomes a comic Mephistopheles who continuously drags Aue from the brink of death and tries to persuade him to enjoy the more hedonistic sides of being a successful SS man. He acts as a foil to Aue's earnest ruminations about what it means to be a committed National Socialist.

It is, however, through Aue himself that the novel tips definitively into being comically picaresque in structure. Aue presents his experiences in autobiographical form from the position of a later, regulated life. He travels from one adventurous episode to the next, narrowly escapes disaster each time, and, rising through the ranks, becomes the figure through whom Nazi ideology and practice is reflected. Like Woody Allen's Zelig or George MacDonald Fraser's Flashman, he pops up at key or exemplary events in the unfolding violence of war and genocide: he is present at the shooting of Jews into mass graves at Babi Yar, the gassing of Jews in the back of trucks, the final days of Stalingrad, Himmler's Posen speech, Auschwitz, the advancing Russian front, and the final days in Berlin and Hitler's bunker. He also encounters key Nazis, Himmler, Hitler, Heydrich, Speer, Bormann, Eichmann, Frank, and Höß, to name but a few. The separate episodes, and the situations within which Aue is placed, depend extensively on conventions of literary realism and historical reportage. However, the cumulative effect of the transitions from one episode to the next, each one involving a narrow escape from death, is to signal the implausibility of the narrative. This implausibility is crystallized in the moment when Aue bites Hitler on the nose, a moment when Aue most closely embodies the figure of the 'Schelm', the rogue who exposes the hypocrisy of society, which in this case is the scandalous discrepancy between Hitler's nose and the Aryan ideal.

Interestingly, though, there is a twist to the conventional picaresque trope of the lower class rogue who displays a canny intelligence and wit. Aue is from a bourgeois background, albeit through his mother's re-marriage, and is highly educated with a doctorate in law. He is, however, singularly lacking in precisely the quick-wittedness he needs to achieve his steady promotion and to extricate himself from tricky adventures. The picaresque structural devices whereby the rogue rises through the social strata (here the ranks of the SS and Nazi governance) as he successfully moves from one episode to the next, are effected by the involvement of others, usually Thomas. Aue the Picaro's success depends not upon his roguish wit, but is secured by the intervention of his Mephistopheles-like friend. The evident artificiality of the picaresque structure, which functions so effectively as a way of placing Aue in an unbelievably wide range of situations, is thereby uncoupled from the figure of the sympathetic and clever rogue. At the same time, the hint of the Faust myth that is introduced into the novel with Thomas does not confer metaphysical grandeur onto Aue. As narrator, Aue would very much like his story to assume such dimensions, as is clear from his pretentious opening appeal to the reader: 'Oh my human brothers, let me tell you how it happened'. He thereby immediately seeks to set himself up as Everyman, the representative figure in 'a bleak story, but an edifying one too, a real morality play' (*TKO*, 3). Gratifyingly for a female reader, women are immediately excluded from being told that 'this concerns you'. Whether this is because women have smaller super-egos, because their role in the Third Reich is less pronounced, because only men can represent a universal position, or because after his catastrophic incestuous relationship with his sister Aue prefers to avoid the term, remains unclear. Be that as it may, Aue casts himself in the central role of a morality play, potentially setting himself up as a would-be Faust.

This self-aggrandizing posture by the narrator is in itself an indication that the whiffs of Faust entering the novel at the margins do not function to bestow mythic stature on Aue and the Nazis. If Aue portentously hints at the myth, then the figure of Thomas as Mephistopheles comically casts doubt on its relevance for representing the reality of Nazi ideology and atrocity. Not only is Aue already a committed National Socialist before he meets his Mephistopheles, his pact with the devil brings him no worldly pleasures, no effective power despite his increasing rank, and no moment of happiness. It might be said that Aue is constantly striving for greater knowledge: he certainly sees himself as a bit of a philosopher among his Nazi peers, and periodically ruminates on questions such as death, the role of an individual in society, Kant's categorical imperative, and duty. Yet his apparent striving for knowledge is no more than the ongoing attempt to reconcile his already existing convictions with the murderous practices of Nazi policy. Thus he discusses with Eichmann how the categorical imperative is in sympathy with the *Führerbefehl* [Führer's order] (*TKO*, 566), how an extermination camp is 'a *reductio ad absurdum* of everyday life' (*TKO*, 622), and how the shifting signification of the stable signifier '*Endlösung*' [Final Solution] raises the question of whether 'there's really nothing but words' (*TKO*, 631). But when Aue is fundamentally challenged by a different view, such as Voss's fundamental refutation of theories of race, he falls back onto the certainties of faith: 'if you believed in a certain idea of Germany and the German *Volk*, the rest had to follow naturally. Some things could be demonstrated, but others simply had to be understood; it was also no doubt a question of faith' (*TKO*, 304). Undoubtedly Aue accumulates a certain type of knowledge: on all aspects of the Jewish genocide and slave labour, the corruption and in-fighting of the Nazis, and the conditions of war on the eastern front. The accumulating details of murder, slaughter, torture, atrocity, and abuse cause Aue anguish. However, this is not the anguish born of a tragic tension between the enlightened striving of man and moral clarity, as explored by Goethe, nor between the greatness of musical genius and the possibility of love, which is at the heart of Thomas Mann's version. In Littell's novel Aue is not the Faust he would like to be, and there is no pact with the devil because no bargain needs to be struck.

Thus the novel draws on picaresque devices as a comic signal of the narrative's implausibility while refusing Aue the role of sympathetic rogue. While Thomas has much more of the roguish intelligence associated with a picaro, his Mephistophelean air, combined with Aue's pretentious claim to being the centre of a morality play, introduces echoes of Faust into the text. But neither do the sympathetic characteristics of the picaro rub off on Aue, nor does he acquire the tragic grandeur of Faust, both factors that cast a significant light on another central structuring device and key intertext, Aeschylus's *Oresteia*. The parallels between the plays and the novel are evident: Aue murders his mother and stepfather in revenge for his mother symbolically killing his father by having him declared dead after he abandoned his family. However, his twin sister, Una (Electra), does not help him murder their mother, and the reminder by Thomas (Pylades) to Aue of the 'pledges sworn on oath' do not apply to the injunction to murder his mother, but rather encourage Aue to be a committed Nazi.[49] In a fundamental departure from the Orestes myth, Aue and Una had an incestuous relationship from which, unbeknown to Aue, twins have been born. The decisive invocation of the Eumenides in the novel's title means that the theme of incest also invokes the spectre of Oedipus's fate, and his need to appease the Eumenides when he steps on ground that is sacred to them in Sophocles's *Oedipus at Colonus*. Thus the themes of fate, guilt, and individual tragedy dominate the novel.

The question of justice is vital for understanding both the function of the *Oresteia* intertext and the significance of how it has been adapted. By invoking the Kindly Ones the novel conjures a crime that in its horror and its dimensions demands a justice that is itself 'terrifying to describe'.[50] Furthermore, by drawing on Greek tragedy, Littell presents a model of guilt and justice that emphasizes the deed, not the intention, awareness, or moral culpability of the individual involved in committing it. He confirms in interview the attraction of Greek morality, which took no account of intention or the reasons why an immoral act was carried out.[51] That Oedipus unknowingly killed his father and married his mother does not absolve him, or his descendants, of guilt. Similarly, the novel's title suggests that it is irrelevant whether Aue remembers murdering his mother and stepfather, or even whether he was not of sound mind when he did it. Metaphorically, his denials evoke the denials of many perpetrators after the war who claimed they had no knowledge of atrocities. By invoking the Eumenides in its title, the novel draws upon an understanding of justice that insists upon the absolute nature of the perpetrators' transgression and that allows of no mitigating circumstances, least of all forgetting or denial.

Greek justice would seem to be served in the physical symptoms Aue suffers as a result of participating in extreme violence. Even as he rationalizes the need for annihilation of the Jews, he is plagued by diarrhoea and vomiting. Aue believes that his retching and vomiting began in Zhitomir (*TKO*, 142–43), and during his time in the Ukraine it then becomes a near daily occurrence (*TKO*, 167). He chooses to witness numerous mass executions and observes how he stops feeling much (*TKO*, 178). Nevertheless, his somatic responses, including repeated disturbing dreams, persist through his time in the Caucasus (*TKO*, 241 & 305), when his work takes him to Auschwitz (*TKO*, 620 & 789), and as the Red Army approaches Berlin (*TKO*, 860). They persist too into his current post-war family existence in France, where there is still a contrast between his reasoned claim that he feels no contrition or regret and did his work, 'that's all', and his physical ailments. He now suffers from constipation (*TKO*, 5) but still has the 'old problem' of having to vomit 'for no reason' (*TKO*, 8), which started in 1941. Thus, whatever justification or rationalizations Aue may offer for his deeds, he is pursued by physical debility. Here the Furies assume the guise of traumatic symptoms, including nightmares and emotional dissociation: 'Le fardeau dont Oreste se trouve délesté par le jugement de l'Aréopage, Aue le porte jusqu'à la fin de ses jours' [The burden from which Orestes is relieved by the judgement of the Areopagus is one that Aue carries until the end of his days].[52]

However, the fantasy of justice for the perpetrator that the notion of the Eumenides would seem to satisfy is frustrated at both character and textual levels. It is Aue, as first person narrator, who names them in the final line of his story, tying the Kindly Ones to his own suffering: 'The Kindly Ones were on to me' (*TKO*, 975). In the moment after murdering Thomas and securing his chance of escape and a new life, he suddenly feels 'the entire weight of the past', 'the pain of life and of inalterable memory', the cruelty of his existence and of his death to come. It is he who links his burden of knowledge and responsibility to the mythic figures and by so doing he places himself in the tradition of the tragic figures of Orestes and, more associatively, Oedipus. This is a crucial exculpatory comparison, for Aue shifts his murderous acts to the level of fate and necessity. Orestes's murder of Clytemnestra is an act that is justified in relation to the laws of filial piety and blood vengeance; it is encouraged by Apollo and offered in Homer's *Odyssey* as an honourable example of a son avenging his father's death. In Aue's case, his invocation of the Eumenides does not relate to his matricide, for this is something he not only denies, but cannot remember doing. Rather the matricide is overlaid with the genocide, which he opts to understand as a necessary deed. He describes his commitment to genocidal anti-Semitism in terms of 'submitting' to the necessity of terrible action rather than merely the fulfilment of duty. In his view, 'submitting' to necessity has the effect of transforming National Socialism into a 'living Law', and it lifts him from being a *Knecht* [slave] to becoming a man (*TKO*, 102). Thus Aue uses the language of tragedy, turning himself into the hero whose will must conform to the fate allotted him. The shallowness and opportunism of his self-aggrandizing comparisons is evident from his initial address to the reader, where, years later, he does not live in the torment of being pursued by the Furies, but admits to writing the memoir to see if he can still feel, or 'suffer a little' (*TKO*, 12). Nothing, then, has changed for Aue, since his solipsistic curiosity in his own emotions combined with 'passion for the absolute' is precisely what prompts him to watch several mass executions.

Aue's repression of matricide enables him to emplot his crimes as tragic necessity and not venal passion and it is clearly he who is attempting to give history the veneer of myth and tragedy. However, Aue's self-evident narrative function as a 'sweeping X-ray' co-exists and interferes with the framework of the fictional memoir.[53] Consequently, ascribing the underlying tragic intertext solely to Aue as author of his memoir does not fully address critical concerns that the novel overall elevates the SS man and the Nazi genocide to tragic proportions. Yet, as is the case with the examples of the picaresque and the Faust myth, the *Oresteia* intertext is treated in such a way that tragic emplotment is questioned rather than reinforced. Significantly, the avenging figures of the Eumenides more literally take the form of the comic duo of detectives, Clemens and Weser. Like Aue and Thomas, they are marked as implausible characters by their ability to pop up in unlikely and dangerous places just when Aue least expects them. In this respect they are loosely reminiscent of Hergé's Thompson and Thomson (Dupond and Dupont), and Aue refers to them as Laurel and Hardy (*TKO*, 753). Unlike these comic pairs, however, Clemens and Weser are effective and intelligent detectives, who doggedly search out evidence that locates Aue at the murder scene and exposes his cover-up. Their relentless pursuit of him is driven by their desire for justice and they offer a strong counter-voice to Aue's duplicity.

Yet Aue both kills the avengers, Clemens and Weser, and he escapes trial after the war by assuming a false identity. The novel radically departs from Aeschylus's play, in which Orestes stands trial for matricide, and, through the intervention of Athena, is acquitted. Thus in the very gesture of demanding absolute justice, and despite the sense that the past weighs upon Aue, the novel exposes any hope for justice as unattainable. Crucially, too, in Aeschylus's *Eumenides*, Athena intervenes to persuade the Erinyes to give up their desire for vengeance, and as a result they are transformed from their role as horrifying avengers to become Semnai, immortals who will be honoured by the Athenians. Thus the Erinyes are pacified, and it is in their pacified form, as Semnai or Eumenides that both Aue and the novel refer to them. For Aue the truth of the pacified Kindly Ones is exposed in his cynical moral posturing, his lack of regret, and absence of anything akin to torment. His constipation and vomiting, which are well managed, pacified even, with enemas, teeth-brushing, and a shot of alcohol, give him the excuse 'to complain a little' (*TKO*, 5). Or to complain just enough to evoke the language of perpetrator trauma and to alert the reader from the outset that he is burdened. The book's invocation becomes an ironic reminder that the Furies have indeed become kind from the perpetrator's point of view. Just as Max Schulz describes the perpetrators who live a good life, so Aue points out that not only many former colleagues are living peacefully, even in the Federal Republic, but that he too could have lived there claiming 'veteran's and disability benefits, no one would have noticed' (*TKO*, 11).

The Kindly Ones can thus be understood as offering a rejection of tragic catharsis and of redemption through justice, comparable in its scepticism to the commissioner in Kertész's *The Pathseeker*. The commissioner, who, it transpires, is a survivor of Buchenwald and Zeitz, dismisses *Iphigenia in Tauris* as 'cheating and lies set in blank verse'.[54] Goethe's play presents another version of how Orestes seeks to flee the Furies, by stealing the statue of Artemis from Tauris to bring back to Athens. In Euripides's version of *Iphigenia* as well as Goethe's, Orestes succeeds in his task, pacifying the Erinyes and bringing his exiled sister Iphigenia back with him. For the commissioner, however, the benevolent and forgiving outcome of Goethe's play represents 'what they want us to believe', and is a cover-up of real violence. In contrast, the commissioner presents his own version of the play, one that we suspect reflects the reality of his concentration camp experiences in the vicinity of Weimar. He describes a *mise en abyme* scenario: Iphigenia is raped by the king's soldiers in front of Orestes and his men, who are then hacked to pieces in front of her. After finally murdering her too, 'they all went to the theatre to watch the barbarian king exercising clemency on the stage as they, snug in the dress circle, sniggered up their sleeves'.[55] In the commissioner's version the familiar image of perpetrators enjoying culture at the end of a hard day's murdering is intensified into a scathing criticism of art's complicity in deceit. Art's aesthetic cover-up itself becomes a further source of satisfaction and amusement for the perpetrators.

Aue does not, following his involvement in mass murder, retire to an actual theatre to watch how art casts perpetrators in a benevolent light. He does, though, invert the theatrical metaphor by retreating into performing the role of a harmless lace producer to watch the benevolent response to perpetrators in the real world. He does not, as narrator of his account, offer a cover-up of violence, but he does want us to believe that he is a tragic figure even while making the claim that he acted as most others would. This is his way of sniggering up his lace sleeves. Littell, however, by drawing on comic structures and by linking the Erinyes both to comedy and the failure of justice, casts doubt on the appropriateness of tragedy for representing mass murder. The novel resonates with the theory articulated by B, the Auschwitz survivor in Kertész's *Liquidation*, that 'there were no tragic individuals anymore. [...] Man, when reduced to nothing, or in other words a *survivor*, is not tragic but comic, because he has no fate. On the other hand, he lives with an awareness of tragic fate'.[56] By depicting Aue as a picaro within a relentless and absurd regime, the novel shows us that Aue is not tragic, is if anything comic, but that he misappropriates for himself an awareness of tragic fate.

However, the novel stops short of concurring with Kertész's shocking equation of the victim and perpetrator in his reference here to a 'survivor' and elsewhere to the state of 'grace'. Fundamental to Kertész's assertion is the release from the burden of personality that occurs within totalitarian regimes that carry out mass murder. The torturer experiences this release in the moment he relinquishes his own fate by 'serving the order' (*DK*, 131), becoming, like the victim, a man without fate and thus also a 'survivor'. The notion that the victim and executioner inhabit the same state of grace is troubling, but one that seems to tally with Aue's point of view. He convinces himself that through his actions he is 'submitting to necessity', and he might even have read Kertész when he claims that in 'a State like ours, everyone had his assigned role: You, the victim, and You, the executioner, and no one had a choice, no one asked anyone's consent, since everyone was interchangeable, victims as well as executioners' (*TKO*, 102). After the war he desires to attain a state of grace, and to '*strive for nothing except to strive for nothing*' (*TKO*, 12). Yet Aue's view is unsustainable within the terms of the novel, which depicts an unreliable perpetrator who wishes to fashion a tragic fate for himself, availing himself of the language of tragedy and necessity. Aue's own narrative betrays that he is clearly not a man who is 'reduced to nothing'. The only time he comes close is when he is in Stalingrad, which is also the point when he is furthest from being an executioner. He claims retrospectively that he had no choice in his actions and that 'nearly everyone, in a given set of circumstances, does what he is told to do' (*TKO*, 20). Yet his claims are belied by the novel's insight into the internal chaos and corruption of the Nazi party and the very varied space for manoeuvre this chaos opens up. The choices he makes are largely influenced by his own career ambitions and personal beliefs. This is precisely why, as Hohenegg points out to Aue, even if he recognizes that life is a joke, he suffers from this knowledge (*TKO*, 285).

The novel makes a more far-reaching rebuttal of the notion of Kertész's state of grace in relation to Aue as perpetrator. In Kertész's view, grace results from an act 'which does not ensue from the propensities, character, or individuality of the person concerned' (*DK*, 130). Yet over and above Aue's room for manoeuvre within a political and social system, he is persistently burdened by his propensities and desires. Aue obsessively loves his sister, his homosexuality threatens his career, and his extended enactment of his onanistic, masochistic, and violent fantasies in the face of the Red Army advance threaten his life. Aue's extreme non-normative sexuality and its explicit presentation have been subject to particular critical concern, not least because by linking perverse sexuality with violent and sadistic Nazism, Aue's status as a typical or representative perpetrator is undermined. Although this is of little significance at the level of Aue's unreliable and exculpatory self-narration, it is problematic in relation to Littell's claims about the novel and Aue's function as a narrative device for illuminating the motivation of perpetrators. Furthermore, the figure of Aue can be seen as playing into the sexualized fascination with Fascism that Susan Sontag discusses and that is perpetuated in films like Luigi Visconti's *The Damned* (1969) and Liliana Cavani's *The Night Porter* (1974).[57] Nevertheless, the distinct nature of Aue's sexuality, as well as the fact that it is interwoven with the novel's wider foregrounding of implausible structures and excessive detail, makes the graphic sexual descriptions serve a more interesting purpose than pornographic titillation.

Liran Razinsky argues that *The Kindly Ones* does not simply continue in the tradition of eroticized Nazism but reframes it as part of its exploration of 'flesh-witnessing'.[58] It is 'through an obsessive focus on bodily experience, remote from theory or textuality' that the body of the perpetrator becomes a witness of 'the event that defies description'.[59] However, such an extreme form of 'flesh-witnessing' must ultimately fail because Aue remains narcissistically the 'slave of bodily experience', which therefore remains incommunicable.[60] Yet ironically it is by demonstrating his enslavement to his body that Aue betrays the duplicitousness of his appeals to duty, necessity, and typical behaviour. Aue's sexual desires, a particular combination of heterosexual sibling incest and homosexual passivity, persistently mark him out as radically different. His sexuality is not depicted as being linked to his role as an SS officer other than the fact that the threat of blackmail over his homosexual encounters is what leads him to join the *Sicherheitsdienst*, the SS intelligence agency, in the first place. Indeed, his homosexuality causes him to refuse to conform to the Nazi ideal of establishing a family, despite direct pressure from Himmler, and for the same reason he refuses to impregnate Mandelbrod's Amazons. Aue is not a sadist. He takes no pleasure from murder or inflicting pain on victims, and is repulsed if he witnesses degrading sexual excesses, sadistic practices, and humiliation perpetrated on others by comrades, most of whom are 'normally' heterosexual. Aue's desires prevent him from becoming instrumentalized as a tool of the regime and he demonstrates quite clearly that duty has its limits.

Aue's sexuality belies Littell's claim to offer a typical example of a perpetrator. However, crucially it signals very clearly that over and above the choices open to Aue within a polycratic and increasingly chaotic regime, he is not 'reduced to nothing' as Kertész says, and cannot entirely subsume himself within the oath on the common good. This is not to say that the novel figures his sexuality as some sort of a site of resistance. The relentlessly detailed and solipsistically tedious depictions of his sexual fantasies and of their private enactment undermine any danger of affectively privileging his transgressive sexuality. What Littell's novel suggests is that the perpetration of atrocity does not involve the 'complete release from the burden of personality', but from accommodating one's personality enough to competing power structures and its demands that one's propensities can be overlooked. The novel resists the notion that the step into violence results solely from the commands of the situation (Kertész) or of duty and necessity (Aue), because it insists on desire as an inalienable element of agency. The position of the perpetrator and victim, over and above the chains of command, remains fundamentally asymmetrical. This is, perhaps, one way of understanding what Littell is driving at when he says in interview that perpetrators 'are the ones who are doing something and changing the reality'.[61]

Conclusion: Trauma and 'Trauma'

Der Nazi und der Friseur and *The Kindly Ones* use comedy to stage the question of our pleasure in Holocaust representation. However, *The Kindly Ones* is more radical in its disturbing effects precisely because comedy and comic devices remain less prominent. In *Der Nazi und der Friseur*, it is grotesque comedy that allows for provocative comparisons and radical criticisms to be made, but in the end it is comedy that also offers the security of unreality. The unsettling dimensions of the text that attach to the psychological motivations and moral ambivalence of the protagonist are contained by his concurrent function as comic narrative device. In *The Kindly Ones* the comedy is a more marginal aesthetic and does not invalidate those aspects of the novel that sustain psychological realism. At the same time, comic devices are an irritant, part of the novel's thematization of representation and the ways 'we have tried to explain fascist perpetration to ourselves in historiography, fiction and testimony'.[62]

Comic devices and structures in *Der Nazi und der Friseur* and *The Kindly Ones* serve to cast doubt on the relevance of tragic representation to the Holocaust and to undermine what Jaspers sees as its spark of transcendence and hope. By staging the failure of justice through comedy, they expose and challenge the reader's desire for a redemptive spark. They do this not only in relation to the theme of justice in its various guises, but also in their treatment of guilt and trauma. Through the confessions of the two unreliable picaros the novels invite us to reflect on questions of representation and also to be sceptical of the universalization and ethical privileging of trauma discourse. The uncoupling of trauma from moral responsibility through the developing clinical focus on symptoms rather than context means that even if perpetrators do not express remorse, signs of trauma are deemed to point to an underlying and persisting humanity.[63] Trauma is thus ethically privileged and to that extent mirrors tragedy in offering a burst of transcendence. Indeed, in Raya Morag's thought-provoking study of perpetrator trauma, she seeks to develop the link between trauma and morality into a new paradigm. She argues that victim trauma rests upon psychological registers, involving a fundamental threat to the individual's self and subsequent psychological disintegration. Perpetrator trauma in contrast 'lies in the profound moral contradictions challenging the perpetrators rather than in their psychological disintegration'.[64] The nature of the traumatic experience is not one of existential catastrophe but of participation in atrocity. The perpetrators' traumatic response is not disintegration but 'the perplexity of denial of wrongdoing', which 'induces them to reflect on fissures in their own integrity'.[65]

Although Morag clearly distinguishes between the traumatic experience at the root of victim and perpetrator trauma, her desire to extend the application of the word despite the fundamentally different states being described, reflects a broader shift into an undifferentiated usage that is tied up with the quest for ethical reassurance. Together, the novels invite us to reflect critically on perpetrator trauma in crucial ways: the extent to which physical symptoms connote trauma; how far perpetrator trauma relates to acts of atrocity or the perpetrator's own exposure to existential risk; the susceptibility of trauma discourse to sustain exculpatory narratives; and whether the notion of trauma is symptomatic of a secular search for redemptive narratives of which fiction is a part. The novels are, then, about trauma, the role of trauma discourse for moral self-fashioning, and its importance for satisfying a wider hope for justice and for a wider human redemption. The novels' comedy guards against a falling back on trauma as a sign of psychological justice done, for the hope of justice is also subsumed into their comic critique. Rau discriminates between Fascism as a historical phenomenon that is analyzed by historians, and 'fascism', which is its appropriation as a cultural fantasy.[66] Similarly the novels use comedy to signal the critical staging of the shift from trauma to 'trauma' if we understand by this the cultural and ethical appropriation of trauma as a part of an implicit redemptive narrative. They urge us to consider the relationship of trauma to 'trauma', and the way in which it functions as an ethical sop to the reality that, as both Maxes in own their ways point out, the world order has not changed after Auschwitz.

Notes to Chapter 6

1. Edgar Hilsenrath, *Der Nazi und der Friseur* (Munich: DTV, 2010); Jonathan Littell, *The Kindly Ones*, trans. by Charlotte Mandell (London: Vintage, 2010), first published as *Les Bienveillantes* (2006). References will be given in parenthesis with the abbreviations *DNuDF* and *TKO* respectively.
2. Edgar Hilsenrath, interview with Volker Dittrich, 26 March 2008, <http://www.yumpu.com/de/document/view/13081912/adie-wohlgesinntena-von-jonathan-littell-dittrich-verlag> [accessed 17 August 2013].
3. Anne Fuchs, 'Edgar Hilsenrath's Poetics of Insignificance', p. 183.
4. For a detailed discussion of the history see Patricia Vahsen, *Lesarten: — Die Rezeption des Werks von Edgar Hilsenrath* (Tübingen: Niemeyer, 2008), pp. 35–48; Susann Möller, 'Zur Rezeption: Philosemiten und Andere — die Verlagsstationen Edgar Hilsenraths', in *Edgar Hilsenrath: Das Unerzählbare erzählen*, ed. by Thomas Kraft (Munich: Piper, 1996), pp. 103–16 (pp. 103–09).
5. Möller, p. 110.
6. Vahsen, p. 52.
7. Ibid., pp. 82–90 & 116–21.
8. Gert Sautermeister, 'Aufgeklärte Modernität', pp. 227–42.
9. Hans Otto Horch, 'Grauen und Groteske: Zu Edgar Hilsenraths Romanen', in *'Wir tragen den Zettelkasten'*, ed. by Stüben and Woesler, pp. 213–26, (p. 224); Vahsen, p. 250; and Claude Conter, *Literatur und Holocaust* (Bamberg: Otto-Friedrich-Universität Press, 1996), pp. 22 & 18.
10. Anne Fuchs, *A Space of Anxiety: Dislocation and Abjection in Modern German-Jewish Literature* (Amsterdam & Atlanta, GA: Rodopi, 1999), p. 165; see also Andreas Graf, 'Mörderisches Ich: Zur Pathologie der Erzählperspektive in *Der Nazi und der Friseur*', in *Edgar Hilsenrath: Das Unerzählbare erzählen*, ed. by Kraft, pp. 135–49.
11. Peter Arnds, 'On the Awful German Fairy Tale: Breaking Taboos in Representations of Nazi Euthanasia and Holocaust in Günter Grass's *Die Blechtrommel*, Edgar Hilsenrath's *Der Nazi & der Friseur*, and Anselm Kiefer's Visual Art', *The German Quarterly*, 75, 4 (2002), 422–39 (pp. 422–23).
12. Ibid., p. 424. Arnds includes Günter Grass, Arno Schmidt, Alexander Kluge, Volker Schlöndorff, and Helma Sanders-Brahms in this artistic process of humanist reconstruction.
13. Ibid., p. 434.
14. Sontag, *Regarding the Pain of Others*, p. 37.
15. J. P. C. Van den Berg, 'Trauma in *Der Nazi und der Friseur* von Edgar Hilsenrath', *Literator*, 32, 1 (2011), 21–42 (p. 34). See also Fuchs, *A Space of Anxiety*, p. 170.
16. Bernhard F. Malkmus, *The German Pícaro and Modernity: Between Underdog and Shape-Shifter* (New York & London: Continuum, 2011), p. 133.
17. Friedrich Torberg, 'Ein Freispruch, der keiner ist', in *Edgar Hilsenrath: Das Unerzählbare erzählen*, ed. by Kraft, pp. 72–76 (p. 75).
18. The fact that Schulz's symptoms of trauma relate to moments when he is under threat fits with the wider scholarship on trauma that points to the importance of an individual's own agency and their control or perceived control of a situation as a vital factor in triggering trauma. This is the case in specific life-threatening situations, as is well illustrated by the higher losses from psychiatric causes on the western than the eastern front in the First World War. Despite the much higher fatalities on the more mobile eastern front, and the effectiveness of the trenches in limiting deaths, 'above all [...] it was the disempowering nature of artillery fire' and the men's 'subjective perceptions of helplessness' that were so psychologically damaging. See Alexander Watson, *Enduring the Great War: Combat, Morale and the Collapse in the German and British Armies, 1914–1918* (Cambridge: Cambridge University Press, 2008), pp. 28–29. An individual's agency in broader, social terms is also significant, as shown by studies that point to poverty, being a woman, and low socio-economic status as higher risk factors for developing PTSD. See Elna Yadin and Edna B. Foa, 'Cognitive Behavioral Treatments for Posttraumatic Stress Disorder', in *Understanding Trauma*, ed. by Kirmayer, Lemelson, & Barad, pp. 178–93 (p. 179).
19. Van den Berg, p. 37.
20. Malkmus, pp. 140 & 151.

21. Ibid., p. 133.
22. Bruno Bettelheim, *The Uses of Enchantment: The Meaning and Importance of Fairy Tales* (New York: Random House, 1976), p. 8.
23. Jennifer Taylor, 'Writing as Revenge: Reading Edgar Hilsenrath's *Der Nazi und der Friseur* as a Shoah Survivor's Fantasy', *History of European Ideas*, 20, 1–3 (1995), 439–44 (p. 443).
24. Fuchs, *A Space of Anxiety*, pp. 164–65.
25. See the discussion of shame as an emotion of self in Chapter 2.
26. Thomas Kühne, 'Male Bonding and Shame Culture: Hitler's Soldiers and the Moral Basis of Genocidal Warfare', in *Ordinary People as Mass Murderers: Perpetrators in Comparative Perspectives*, ed. by Olaf Jensen and Claus-Christian W. Szejnmann (Basingstoke: Palgrave Macmillan, 2008), pp. 55–77 (p. 65).
27. Ibid., p. 58.
28. Peter Kuon, 'From "Kitsch" to "Splatter": The Aesthetics of Violence', in *Writing the Holocaust Today: Critical Perspectives on Jonathan Littell's 'The Kindly Ones'*, ed. by Aurélie Barjonet and Liran Razinsky (Amsterdam & New York: Rodopi, 2012), pp. 33–45 (p. 39); Petra Rau, *Our Nazis: Representations of Fascism in Contemporary Literature and Film* (Edinburgh: Edinburgh University Press, 2013), p. 99.
29. Rau, pp. 95–100.
30. Jonathan Littell, *Les Bienveillantes* (Paris: Gallimard, 2006). The English paperback (2010) extends the page count to 975.
31. As Rau points out, there have been plenty of novels 'replete with horrific and graphic detail about murder and sex' and 'fictional serial killers come two a penny' (Rau, p. 96).
32. Edgar Hilsenrath in interview with Volker Dittrich, 26 March 2008, translated from the French by Hainer Kober, <http://www.dittrich-verlag.de/files/edgar_hilsenrath_-_jonathan_littell_21.4.2008.pdf> [accessed 17 September 2014].
33. Kuon, p. 42.
34. Jeremy D. Popkin, 'A Historian's View of *The Kindly Ones*', in *Writing the Holocaust Today*, ed. by Barjonet and Razinsky, pp. 187–200 (p. 196).
35. Ibid., p. 197.
36. Ibid., p. 198.
37. Jonathan Littell, interviewed by Jeffrey A. Trachtenberg, 'Facing the Holocaust', *Wall Street Journal*, 28 February 2009, <http://online.wsj.com/article/SB123578783301898945.html> [accessed 18 August 2013].
38. Jonathan Littell, quoted in Assaf Uni, 'The Executioner's Song', *Haaretz*, 29 May 2008, <http://www.haaretz.com/the-executioner-s-song-1.246787> [accessed 18 August 13].
39. Jonathan Littell, interviewed by Samuel Blumenfeld, *Le Monde* (*Le Monde des Livres*), 17 November 2006, <http://thekindlyones.wordpress.com/littell-interview-with-samuel-blumenfeld/> [accessed 18 August 2013].
40. Jonathan Littell in conversation with Pierre Nora, in *le débat*, 144 (2007), 25–44 (p. 29).
41. Jonathan Littell, interview with Blumenfeld.
42. Rau, p. 107.
43. Kuon, p. 43.
44. Dominick LaCapra, 'Historical and Literary Approaches to the "Final Solution": Saul Friedländer and Jonathan Littell', *History and Theory*, 50 (2011), 71–97 (p. 73).
45. Ibid., p. 75–76.
46. Julia Kristeva, 'De l'abjection à la banalité du mal', lecture given at the Centre Roland Barthes Université Paris-VII, 24 April 2007, <www.kristeva.fr/abjection.html> [accessed 17 September 2014].
47. LaCapra, 'Historical and Literary Approaches', pp. 81, 77, & 80.
48. E. R. Burroughs, *Carson of Venus*, first serialized in *Argosy*, 1938, published in 1939 by Edgar Rice Burroughs, Inc. (Project Gutenberg of Australia: <http://gutenberg.net.au/ebooks03/0300181h.html#chap9> [accessed 17 October 2013]).
49. Aeschylus, *Libation Bearers*, in *Oresteia*, trans. by Christopher Collard (Oxford: Oxford University Press, 2002), p. 76 (l. 900).
50. Aeschylus, *Eumenides*, in *Oresteia*, ed. by Collard, p. 86 (l. 34).

51. Jonathan Littell, 'Jonathan Littell, homme de l'année', *Le Figaro*, 29 December 2006, <http://www.lefigaro.fr/lefigaromagazine/2006/12/29/01006–20061229ARTMAG90304-maximilien_aue_je_pourrais_dire_que_c_est_moi.php> [accessed 18 September 2014].
52. Florence Mercier-Leca, '*Les Bienveillantes* et la tragédie grecque', in *le débat*, 144 (2007), 45–55 (p. 54).
53. Littell, interview with Blumenfeld.
54. Imre Kertész, *The Pathseeker*, trans. by Tim Wilkinson (New York: Melville House, 2008), p. 84.
55. Ibid., p. 87.
56. Imre Kertész, *Liquidation*, trans. by Tim Wilkinson (London: Vintage, 2007), p. 18.
57. Susan Sontag, 'Fascinating Fascism', in *Under the Sign of Saturn* (London: Vintage, 1980), pp. 73–105.
58. Liran Razinsky, 'Not the Witness We Wished for: Testimony in Jonathan Littell's *The Kindly Ones*', *Modern Language Quarterly*, 71, 2 (2010), 175–96 (pp. 192–93, n. 29).
59. Ibid., p. 194.
60. Ibid., p. 195.
61. Jonathan Littell, quoted in Uni, 'The Executioner's Song'.
62. Rau, p. 111.
63. See the discussion of trauma in the Introduction.
64. Raya Morag, *Waltzing with Bashir: Perpetrator Trauma and Cinema* (London & New York: I. B. Tauris, 2013), p. 16.
65. Ibid., p. 17.
66. Rau, p. 8.

CONCLUSION

When Benjamin refers to comedy as the lining of the coat of mourning, he draws our attention to its necessary role as part of a healing process. Paul Ricoeur and Dominick LaCapra both argue for the importance of the work of mourning, or 'working-through', resisting the notion that it is tantamount to a form of closure which involves turning away from the past.[1] And like Benjamin, both recognize the importance of comedy and laughter for responding to trauma and loss. Ricoeur insists upon the importance of gaiety and humour for countering *acedia*, the 'complaisance towards sadness', and LaCapra argues that the 'carnivalesque, along with the comic and the grotesque in general, is also a significant counterpart to the sublime, which helps to question it and bring it down to earth'.[2] Indeed, in 1804 Jean Paul already went as far as to describe comedy as the 'Erbfeind des Erhabenen'.[3] However, as is evident from the work involved in mourning, this is not an easy or pacifying process. Indeed, arguably the healing potential of comedy springs from its 'interpretative openness' and its disturbing demand for different perspectives, even while these encourage change.[4]

As Howard Jacobson points out, even against our wishes comedy facilitates 'the overcoming of what is deathly in us while we are still alive [...] by insisting we have another voice to speak with than the one we customarily use'.[5] Humour accepts ambivalence and paradox as unproblematic and in this respect is like psychoanalysis, which seeks to heal by accepting that we are not what we seem and that we fail to 'control ourselves and the world we live in'. For this reason comedy can trigger changes: 'over time, what enslaved us to the past loosens its grip and we can begin to see the world in a different light. It is only then that a humorous perspective can flourish'.[6] The point Alessandra Lemma makes here about time passing is important, for although comedy contributes to the process of mourning, healing, or change, it is also a sign that distance to the traumatic event is taking place. In the same way, comedy is both generated by distance, be that of time or of a different perspective, and itself also creates that distance. However, as is vividly represented by Benjamin's image of the lining of the coat of mourning, healing distance is not the distance assumed by superiority, but that of co-existence, of jostling perspectives, and the ability to hold different views concurrently. It is this role that comedy plays in most of the texts examined in this book.

In Bachmann's work, different perspectives are inherent to the narrative technique and form of her late prose. In her complex poetics, a tension between intense emotion, figured as feminine, and masculine evaluative distance is acted out in the relationship of melodrama and comedy. Comedy is vital in her critical exploration of how the perspective of the suffering victim can be represented. It exposes the prodigality of melodrama as debilitating and self-destructive, and as a representational mode that is inadequate for articulating the complexity of victimhood through its solipsistic and unmediated excesses. But Bachmann does not draw so centrally on melodrama simply to dismiss it. Melodrama remains a vital ethical resource, for it is a mode that insists upon the reality of suffering, that decries banal evil and which values a search for meaning in a world where absolutes have been replaced with contingency. Melodrama also ensures that the inevitable distance to suffering entailed in a comic perspective nevertheless remains firmly rooted both in empathy and in the suffering body. Finally, by drawing on melodrama and comedy as key narrative modes, Bachmann signals the importance of pleasure for representing suffering while refusing to sacralize trauma.

Fassbinder's films are disturbing in different ways, and comedy is part of this disturbance, not least because the troubling past pervades his films. Personal suffering is represented as a symptom of the wider economic systems of social and economic exchange that are inseparable from Nazism and its legacy. Fassbinder's comic brazenness and camp hyperbole draws attention to the way in which the Holocaust suffuses debates around representations of suffering and it offers a visual and emotional riposte to Holocaust kitsch. However, although it remains unclear how far Fassbinder indulges the comparison of German suffering with the suffering of the victims of Nazism or questions it, it is undoubtedly the case that the sheer comic overindulgence in misery disturbs melodramatic conventions that depend upon eliciting spectator identification with suffering. The often-ludicrous comedy refuses the solipsism of extreme suffering as well as the unreflected identification with those who suffer. Thus the jostling perspectives encouraged by comedy set a limit to the 'theatre of satisfaction' staged by melodrama. The spectator is explicitly invited to reflect upon her own pleasure attendant upon vicariously assuming the victim position through identification and to question the enjoyment that she derives from the representation of another's pain.

Comedy in Sebald's work both sustains and questions a melancholy approach to the 'history of destruction'. At one level comedy is used to sustain the privileged position of the melancholy narrators; their suffering insight into the decline they see around them and identification with traumatic suffering conjures up an idealized past world in which the forces of modernity, homogenization, and industrial murder had not yet occurred. Their perspective is sustained by satire and ridicule, largely of women and the masses who present a feminizing, physical threat to the male melancholic. At this level the melancholy aesthetic is a powerful means for acknowledging loss, and combines an ethical duty of care to remember the dead with a tactful narrative technique that refuses the emotional extremes of melodrama. However, the satirical comedy is interspersed with irony, points where the narrators enter the comic frame of the narrative, and where their melancholy excess tips into comedy. Here comedy functions not to sustain the melancholy perspective but to question it and the moral universe it upholds. This comedy contributes to the elements of narrative play in the prose works and the delight in narrative transformation that is not indebted to idealization or duty of care but which derives pleasure from sublimation. The tension in the texts between the different types of comedy and the ethical worlds they sustain remains unresolved.

Jirgl's text and Koepp's films both represent ways in which comedy, far from encouraging different perspectives, can be used to sustain a very particular view of the past. In Jirgl's *Die Stille*, *Schadenfreude* belongs to a sustained aesthetics of negation, the intention of which is to encourage the reader to reflect on social, political, historical, and aesthetic norms. Comedy is not used by Jirgl to exculpate Germans or to turn them into innocent victims of circumstance. Even though he depicts the extreme suffering experienced by Germans throughout the twentieth century, he exposes the extent to which German suffering is caused by other Germans and the state in its different manifestations. The victims themselves, far from being privileged or presented as a source of ethical value, are depicted as cruel, abusive, perverted, and psychologically damaged. *Schadenfreude* as the dominant form of comedy contributes to an unrelenting tone of negativity, so that although the novel is ostensibly told from the perspective of different characters, the novel remains monologic, with Jirgl's distinct orthographic system reinforcing authorial aims.

Koepp's films also address a disturbing German past by drawing on multiple voices, and Koepp gives his subjects the space to recount their memories. Many of them testify to various types of suffering, much of which is profound. Yet the traumatic past figures only at the level of this personal testimony. The comic edge to his work does not serve to irritate but to endear the subjects to the viewer, to make them more accessible and to evoke our empathy towards them. Furthermore, the subjects' personal experience is placed within the slowly changing landscape, with harmful events moved to the realm of an abstracted, *longue durée* of 'history' and hence away from questions of responsibility and agency. Thus Koepp's films address suffering at a resolutely personal level in order to be conciliatory in the present. Here comedy reinforces rather than limits definable directorial aims, forming part of a textual strategy that bolsters particular modes of identification and the values of reconciliation and restoration that are associated with them.

Klüger's comedy further explores the terrain that Koepp ventures into, namely the question of the ethical limits of comedy in documentaries or memoirs about real people. This is particularly acute in Klüger's case because whereas Koepp determinedly focuses on subjects who exemplify his values, Klüger speaks of others with biting humour and a tone that sometimes revels in being malicious. She insists that autobiography is history, and, furthermore, in her essayistic work she expresses reservations about comedy, linking it to cruelty and persecution. As a result, questions about the ethical significance of her own use of comedy can legitimately be asked. Klüger does not explicitly consider the question of whether she herself replicates the structures of humiliation that she considers present in comedy. However, it is evident that she sees her own humour as political: it belongs to her arsenal as a Jewish woman in her survival of and fight against persecution and prejudice. Yet comedy also plays an important role in her work in tempering the tone of *ressentiment*: Klüger also enjoys audiences that recognize her humour. As such, although it can be biting, Klüger's comedy is also amusing and thus encourages the reader to enjoy her wit, and to be suspended between conciliation and *ressentiment*.

The two novels written from the perspective of the perpetrator both use comedy to cast doubt on the possibility of justice, and on the notion of perpetrator trauma as a variation on a redemptive narrative. In one way the comedy of Hilsenrath's *Der Nazi und der Friseur* offers a provocative critique of nationalism, the ludicrous claims of racism, and the seduction of ideology for the weak or hard done by, be that Nazism or Zionism. He draws on grotesque cliché in order to expose the ridiculous assumptions underlying those clichés. However, although comedy is used as a form of critique, its provocation is ultimately contained by the grotesque and unrealistic comedy: the reader can enjoy the comedy as she would a discreet joke, one whose evident artifice does not fundamentally challenge her. The role of comedy in the novel is though more radical in its assault on the possibility of justice and redemption. Hilsenrath overturns conventional moral paradigms of good and evil by comically inverting the form of the fairy tale and showing how its schematic moral outcomes can justify atrocity. By having as his narrator a duplicitous picaro, he also exposes the way in which the perpetrator can use the discourse of trauma for his own exculpatory purposes.

Similarly, Littell's *The Kindly Ones* is an assault on the reader's desire for a redemptive narrative. Comedy and comic structures are used alongside descriptive excess and ennui to unmask the absurdity of Nazi racist ideology and practice. More importantly perhaps they function as part of a broader play with genre that militates against tragic or mythic representation. This is surprising given that the novel's intertexts are Aeschylus's *Oresteia* and the Oedipus myth, with a hint of Faust, but Littell uses these structuring intertexts to interrogate the possibility of justice, and with it, redemption. Justice is ostensibly offered in the fantasy of the Furies' retribution and in the physical punishment of Aue's trauma symptoms. However, comedy becomes part of the novel's exposure of the inadequacy and failure of tragedy and its rejection of tragic catharsis, including the reader's desire for a redemptive spark. This is also important in relation to the novel's treatment of trauma. In response to the universalization of trauma, whereby symptoms of trauma even in perpetrators are deemed to point to a redemptive, underlying humanity, *The Kindly Ones* points to trauma as a vehicle for Aue's moral self-fashioning and urges us to consider how trauma functions as an ethical sop to the reality that, as Aue demonstrates, justice has not been done.

In all of the works studied here, comedy is part of an attempt to address a disturbing past: a past that is disturbing because of its extremes of violence and suffering, and a past that still reverberates with and disturbs the present. Comedy refuses the solipsism of extreme suffering and also the unreflected identification with those who suffer. At the same time, comedy's play with perspective means that suffering need not be belittled or objectified. Crucially, however, in most of the works, comedy contributes to a further layer of disturbance by refusing to pacify unease. If the ongoing disturbance of the past can be understood as belonging to the work of mourning, then it is those aspects of comedy that thrive on and contribute to indeterminacy that make it significant in relation to representations of suffering. Far more than the sigh of relief that the scythe has passed over us, comedy jolts us out of one determinate point of view or state of emotion. All comedy has about it an element of incoherence or incompatibility, it contains the indeterminacy of play, and with it a strong element of unpredictability: what is amusing or funny for some is not so for others, nor does the reader or spectator always understand why she finds something comic.[7] Such unpredictability is characteristic of fiction generally, and is not unique to humour and comedy. But just as Robert C. Roberts sees amusement as particularly exemplifying the plasticity of the mind, so too comedy crystallizes the complex interaction and frequent incongruity of multiple perspectives that typify fiction. It is by remaining a playful irritant that comedy can negotiate suffering: irritating because it refuses to elevate suffering through tragic catharsis, and playful by insisting on the value of pleasure in the present, which co-exists with that suffering.

Notes to the Conclusion

1. LaCapra, *History and its Limits*, pp. 53–54; Ricoeur, pp. 69–80.
2. LaCapra, *History and its Limits*, p. 84.
3. Jean Paul, *Vorschule der Ästhetik*, p. 105.
4. Mulkay, p. 219.
5. Howard Jacobson, *Seriously Funny: From the Ridiculous to the Sublime* (London: Viking, 1997), p. 229.
6. Alessandra Lemma, *Humour on the Couch. Exploring Humour in Psychotherapy and Everyday Life* (London: Whurr, 2000), p. 175.
7. See also: Preisendanz, p. 156; and Hans Blumenberg, 'Komik in der diachronen Perspektive', in *Das Komische*, ed. by Preisendanz and Warning, pp. 408–09 (p. 408).

BIBLIOGRAPHY

Primary Literature

BACHMANN, INGEBORG, *Frankfurter Vorlesungen* (Munich: Piper, 1989)
—— *Wir müssen wahre Sätze finden: Gespräche und Interviews*, ed. by Christine Koschel and Inge von Weidenbaum (Munich & Zurich: Piper, 1991)
—— *Die Hörspiele* (Munich: Piper, 1992)
—— *Goldmann/Rottwitz-Roman*, in *'Todesarten'-Projekt*, ed. by Monika Albrecht and Dirk Göttsche, 4 vols (Munich: Piper, 1995), I
—— *Das Buch Franza*, in *'Todesarten'-Projekt*, ed. by Albrecht and Göttsche, 4 vols (Munich: Piper, 1995), II
—— *Malina*, in *'Todesarten'-Projekt*, ed. by Albrecht and Göttsche, 4 vols (Munich: Piper, 1995), III.1
—— 'Besichtigung einer alten Stadt', in *'Todesarten'-Projekt*, ed. by Albrecht and Göttsche (Munich: Piper, 1995), III.2
—— *Simultan*, in *'Todesarten'-Projekt*, ed. by Albrecht and Göttsche (Munich: Piper, 1995), IV
FASSBINDER, RAINER WERNER, 'My Position on *Garbage, the City, and Death*: A Statement', in *The Anarchy of the Imagination: Interviews, Essays, Notes*, ed. by Michael Töteberg and Leo A. Lensing, trans. by Krishna Winston (Baltimore, MD: Johns Hopkins University Press, 1992), pp. 119–20
—— *Rainer Werner Fassbinder Commemorative Collection, 1969–1972*, 2 vols (Arrow, 2007), I [on DVD]. Includes: *Liebe ist kälter als der Tod* [*Love is Colder than Death*]; *Katzelmacher*; *Götter der Pest* [*Gods of the Plague*]; *Rio das Mortes*; *Niklashauser Fart* [*The Niklashauser Journey*]; *Der amerikanische Soldat* [*The American Soldier*]; *Warnung vor einer heiligen Nutte* [*Beware of a Holy Whore*]; *Händler der vier Jahreszeiten* [*The Merchant of Four Seasons*]; *Die bitteren Tränen der Petra von Kant* [*The Bitter Tears of Petra von Kant*]
—— *Rainer Werner Fassbinder Commemorative Collection, 1973–1982*, 2 vols (Arrow, 2007), II [on DVD]. Includes: *Angst essen Seele auf* [*Ali: Fear Eats the Soul*]; *Fontane Effi Briest* [*Effi Briest*]; *Faustrecht der Freiheit* [*Fox and His Friends*]; *Mutter Küsters Fahrt zum Himmel* [*Mother Küster's Trip to Heaven*]; *Angst vor der Angst* [*Fear of Fear*]; *Satansbraten* [*Satan's Brew*]; *Chinesisches Roulette* [*Chinese Roulette*]; *Die Ehe der Maria Braun* [*The Marriage of Maria Braun*]
—— *Rainer Werner Fassbinder*, 2 vols (Artificial Eye, 2007), I [on DVD]. Includes: *Warum läuft Herr R. Amok?* [*Why Does Herr R. Run Amok?*]; *Martha*; *Lola*
—— *Rainer Werner Fassbinder*, 2 vols (Artificial Eye, 2007), II [on DVD]. Includes: *Deutschland im Herbst* [*Germany in Autumn*]; *In einem Jahr mit 13 Monden* [*In a Year of 13 Moons*]; *Die dritte Generation* [*The Third Generation*]; *Die Sehnsucht der Veronika Voss* [*Veronika Voss*]
—— *Berlin Alexanderplatz* (Second Sight, 2007) [on DVD]
—— *Whity* (Fantoma/Emi, 2003) [on DVD]
HILSENRATH, EDGAR, *Der Nazi und der Friseur* (Munich: DTV, 2010)
——interview with Volker Dittrich, 26 March 2008, <http://www.yumpu.com/de/document/view/13081912/adie-wohlgesinntena-von-jonathan-littell-dittrich-verlag> [accessed 17 August 2013]

——interview with Volker Dittrich, 26 March 2008, translated from the French by Hainer Kober, <http://www.dittrich-verlag.de/files/edgar_hilsenrath_-_jonathan_littell_21.4.2008.pdf> [accessed 17 September 2014]
JIRGL, REINHARD, *Gewitterlicht: Erzählung/Das poetische Vermögen des alphanumerischen Codes in der Prosa* (Hannover: Revonnah, 2002)
——'Schlußwort für einen "Nachlaß zu Lebzeiten"', in *Reinhard Jirgl: Genealogie des Tötens* (Munich: DTV, 2003), pp. 815–33
——'Die wilde und die gezähmte Schrift: Eine Arbeitsübersicht', *Sprache im technischen Zeitalter*, 42 (2004), 296–320
——*Die Stille* (Munich: DTV, 2009)
——*Abschied von den Feinden* (Munich: DTV, 2010)
——'"Das Gegenteil von Spiel ist nicht Ernst, sondern Wirklichkeit!"', in *Text + Kritik* 189 (2011), 80–85
KERTÉSZ, IMRE, *Fateless*, trans. by Tim Wilkinson (London: Vintage, 2006)
——*Liquidation*, trans. by Tim Wilkinson (London: Vintage, 2007)
——*The Pathseeker*, trans. by Tim Wilkinson (New York: Melville House, 2008)
——*Kaddish for an Unborn Child*, trans. by Tim Wilkinson (London: Vintage, 2010)
——*Fiasco*, trans. by Tim Wilkinson (New York: Melville House, 2011)
——*Dossier K.*, trans. by Tim Wilkinson (New York: Melville House, 2013)
KLÜGER, RUTH, *Frauen lesen anders* (Munich: DTV, 1997)
——*weiter Leben: Eine Jugend* (Munich: DTV, 1999)
——*Landscapes of Memory: A Holocaust Girlhood Remembered* (London: Bloomsbury, 2004)
——'"Siehe doch Deutschland": Martin Walsers *Tod eines Kritikers*', in *Erläuterungen und Dokumente. Ruth Klüger weiter Leben*, ed. by Sascha Feuchert (Stuttgart: Reclam, 2004), pp. 157–63
——*Gelesene Wirklichkeit: Fakten und Fiktionen in der Literatur* (Göttingen: Wallstein, 2006)
——*unterwegs verloren: Erinnerungen* (Munich: DTV, 2008)
——*Katastrophen: Über deutsche Literatur* (Göttingen: Wallstein, 2009)
KOEPP, VOLKER, *Holunderblüte* (Edition Salzgeber, 2008) [on DVD]
——*Memelland* (Edition Salzgeber, 2010) [on DVD]
——*Berlin — Stettin* (Edition Salzgeber, 2010) [on DVD]
——*Volker Koepp Kollektion* (Edition Salzgeber, 2010) [on DVD]. Includes: *Herr Zwilling und Frau Zuckermann*; *Kurische Nehrung*; *Uckermark*; *Dieses Jahr in Czernowitz*; *Pommerland*; *Schattenland*
——interview with Rainer Rother, 5 May 2006, *Schattenland* (Edition Salzgeber, 2006), 20:40 [on DVD]
LITTELL, JONATHAN, *Les Bienveillantes* (Paris: Gallimard, 2006)
——*The Kindly Ones*, trans. by Charlotte Mandell (London: Vintage, 2010)
——in conversation with Pierre Nora, *le débat*, 144 (2007), 25–44
——'Jonathan Littell, homme de l'année', *Le Figaro*, 29 December 2006, <http://www.lefigaro.fr/lefigaromagazine/2006/12/29/01006-20061229ARTMAG90304-maximilien_aue_je_pourrais_dire_que_c_est_moi.php> [accessed 18 September 2014]
——interview with Jeffrey A. Trachtenberg, 'Facing the Holocaust', *Wall Street Journal*, 28 February 2009, <http://online.wsj.com/article/SB123578783301898945.html> [accessed 18 August 2013]
——interview with Samuel Blumenfeld, *Le Monde* (*Le Monde des Livres*), 17 November 2006, <http://thekindlyones.wordpress.com/littell-interview-with-samuel-blumenfeld/> [accessed 18 August 2013]
SEBALD, W. G., *Die Ringe des Saturn* (Frankfurt a.M.: Fischer, 2007)
——*The Rings of Saturn*, trans. by Michael Hulse (London: Harvill, 1998)
——*Die Ausgewanderten* (Frankfurt, a.M.: Fischer, 2008)

―― *The Emigrants*, trans. by Michael Hulse (London: Harvill, 1997)
―― *Austerlitz* (Munich: Süddeutsche Zeitung/Bibliothek, 2008)
―― *Austerlitz*, trans. by Anthea Bell (London: Hamish Hamilton, 2001)
―― *Schwindel. Gefühle* (Frankfurt, a.M.: Fischer, 2009)
―― *Vertigo*, trans. by Michael Hulse (London: Vintage, 2002)
―― interview with Sigrid Löffler, '"Wildes Denken": Gespräch mit W. G. Sebald', in Franz Loquai, *W. G. Sebald* (Eggingen: Edition Isele, 1997), pp. 135–37
―― interview with Andrea Köhler, 'Katastrophe mit Zuschauer', *Neue Zürcher Zeitung*, 22 November 1997, p. 52
―― interview with Toby Green (1999), <http://www.amazon.co.uk/gp/feature.html?ie=UTF8&docId=21586> [accessed 13 May 2013]
―― interview with Arthur Lubow, August 2001, quoted in Deane Blackler, *Reading W. G. Sebald: Adventure and Disobedience* (Rochester, NY: Camden House, 2007), p. 91
―― interview with Maya Jaggi, 'Recovered Memories', *Guardian*, 22 September 2001, <http://www.theguardian.com/books/2001/sep/22/artsandhumanities.highereducation> [accessed 16 October 2014]
―― interview with Kenneth Baker, 'Up Against Historical Amnesia', *San Francisco Chronicle*, 235, 7 October 2001, R2
―― interview with Susan Salter Reynolds, *Los Angeles Times*, 24 October 2001, <http://articles.latimes.com/2001/oct/24/news/cl-60893/4> [accessed 28 April 2011]
―― interview with Michaël Zeeman, in *W. G. Sebald: History, Memory, Trauma*, ed. by Scott Denham and Mark McCulloh (Berlin: de Gruyter, 2006), pp. 21–29

Secondary Literature

ACHBERGER, KAREN, '"Bösartig liebevoll" den Menschen zugetan: Humor in Ingeborg Bachmanns *Todesarten* — Projekt', in *"Über die Zeit schreiben": Literatur- und Kulturwissenschaftliche Essays zu Ingeborg Bachmanns "Todesarten" — Projekt*, ed. by Monika Albrecht and Dirk Göttsche (Würzburg: Königshausen & Neumann, 1998), pp. 227–43
ADORNO, THEODOR, *Prisms*, trans. by Samuel and Shierry Weber (Cambridge, MA: MIT Press, 1983)
―― *Notes to Literature I*, trans. by Shierry Weber Nicholsen (New York: Columbia University Press, 1991)
―― *Notes to Literature II*, trans. by Shierry Weber Nicholsen (New York: Columbia University Press, 1992)
AESCHYLUS, *Oresteia*, trans. by Christopher Collard (Oxford: Oxford University Press, 2002)
AHONEN, PERTTI, *After the Expulsion: West Germany and Eastern Europe 1945–1990* (Oxford: Oxford University Press, 2003)
AGAMBEN, GIORGIO, *Remnants of Auschwitz: The Witness and the Archive*, trans. by Daniel Heller-Roazen (New York: Zone Book, 2008)
ALEXANDER, JEFFREY C., *Trauma: A Social Theory* (Cambridge: Polity, 2012)
AMÉRY, JEAN, *At the Mind's Limits: Contemplations by a Survivor on Auschwitz and its Realities*, trans. by Sidney Rosenfeld and Stella P. Rosenfeld (Bloomington: Indiana University Press, 1980)
―― *Werke. Band 2: Jenseits von Schuld und Sühne. Unmeisterliche Wanderjahre. Örtlichkeiten*, ed. by Gerhard Scheit (Stuttgart: Klett-Cotta, 2002)
ARNDS, PETER, 'On the Awful German Fairy Tale: Breaking Taboos in Representations of Nazi Euthanasia and Holocaust in Günter Grass's *Die Blechtrommel*, Edgar Hilsenrath's *Der Nazi & der Friseur*, and Anselm Kiefer's Visual Art', *The German Quarterly*, 75, 4 (2002), 422–39

ASHKENAZI, OFER, 'Ridiculous Trauma: Comic Representations of the Nazi Past in Contemporary German Visual Culture', *Cultural Critique*, 78, (2011), 88–118

ASSMANN, ALEIDA, *Der lange Schatten der Vergangenheit: Erinnerungskultur und Geschichtspolitik* (Munich: C. H. Beck, 2006)

BADIOU, BERTRAND, and OTHERS, eds, *Herzzeit: Ingeborg Bachmann — Paul Celan: Der Briefwechsel* (Frankfurt a.M.: Suhrkamp, 2008)

BAKHTIN, MIKHAIL, *Rabelais and his World*, trans. by Hélène Iswolsky (Bloomington: Indiana University Press, 1984)

BARJONET, AURÉLIE, and LIRAN RAZINSKY, eds, *Writing the Holocaust Today: Critical Perspectives on Jonathan Littell's 'The Kindly Ones'* (Amsterdam & New York: Rodopi, 2012)

BARNETT, DAVID, *Rainer Werner Fassbinder and the German Theatre* (Cambridge: Cambridge University Press, 2005)

BARTHES, ROLAND, *Writing Degree Zero*, trans. by Annette Lavers and Colin Smith (New York: Hill and Wang, 1999)

BARZILAI, MAYA, 'Melancholia as World History: W. G. Sebald's Rewriting of Hegel in *Die Ringe des Saturn*', in *W. G. Sebald and the Writing of History*, ed. by Anne Fuchs and J. J. Long (Würzburg: Königshausen & Neumann, 2007), pp. 73–89

—— 'Facing the Past and the Female Spectre in W. G. Sebald's *The Emigrants*', in *W. G. Sebald — A Critical Companion*, ed. by J. J. Long and Anne Whitehead (Edinburgh: Edinburgh University Press, 2004), pp. 203–16

BAUMAN, ZYGMUNT, *Liquid Love* (Cambridge: Polity, 2003)

BAUR, BETTINA, *Melancholie und Karneval: Zur Dramatik Cecilie Løveids* (Tübingen & Basel: Francke, 2002)

BECKER, ANDREAS, 'Zeig doch mal die Deutschen', *TAZ*, 12 (2001)

BENJAMIN, WALTER, 'The Author as Producer', in *Reflections* (New York: Schocken, 1986), p. 229

—— *Ursprung des deutschen Trauerspiels*, in *Gesammelte Schriften*, ed. by Rolf Tiedemann and Hermann Schweppenhäuser, 7 vols (Frankfurt a.M.: Suhrkamp, 1991), I.I

—— *The Origin of German Tragic Drama*, trans. by John Osborne (London: Verso, 2009)

—— *Selected Writings*, ed. by Michael W. Jennings and others, trans. by Howard Eiland and others, 4 vols (Cambridge, MA: Belknap/Harvard University Press, 1996–2003)

BERGFELDER, TIM, 'Shadowlands: The Memory of the *Ostgebiete* in Contemporary German Film and Television', in *Screening War: Perspectives on German Suffering*, ed. by Paul Cooke and Marc Silberman (Rochester, NY: Camden House, 2010), pp. 123–42

BERGSON, HENRI, *Le Rire: essai sur la signification du comique* (Paris: Quadrige, 1989)

BERNARD-DONALS, MICHAEL, and RICHARD GLEJZER, 'Introduction: Representations of the Holocaust and the End of Memory', in *Witnessing the Disaster: Essays on Representation and the Holocaust*, ed. by Michael Bernard-Donals and Richard Glejzer (Madison: University of Wisconsin Press, 2003), pp. 3–22

—— *Between Witness and Testimony: The Holocaust and the Limits of Representation* (New York: State University Press of New York, 2001)

BETTELHEIM, BRUNO, *The Uses of Enchantment: The Meaning and Importance of Fairy Tales* (New York: Random House, 1976)

BIRD, STEPHANIE, '"Er gab mir, was äußerst ungewöhnlich war, zum Abschied die Hand": Touch and Tact in W. G. Sebald's *Die Ausgewanderten* and *Austerlitz*', *Journal of European Studies*, 41, 3–4 (2011), 359–75

BLACKLER, DEANE, *Reading W. G. Sebald: Adventure and Disobedience* (Rochester, NY: Camden House, 2007)

BLANCHOT, MAURICE, *The Gaze of Orpheus and other Literary Essays*, trans. by Lydia Davis, ed. by P. Adams Sitney (Barrytown, NY: Station Hill, 1981)

BLUMENBERG, HANS, 'Komik in der diachronen Perspektive', in *Das Komische*, ed. by Wolfgang Preisendanz and Rainer Warning (Munich: Fink, 1976), pp. 408–09

BOA, ELIZABETH, 'Lost *Heimat* in Generational Novels by Reinhard Jirgl, Christoph Hein, and Angelika Overath', in *Germans as Victims in the Literary Fiction of the Berlin Republic*, ed. by Stuart Taberner and Karina Berger (Rochester, NY: Camden House, 2009), pp. 86–101

BOND, GREG, 'On the Misery of Nature and the Nature of Misery: W. G. Sebald's Landscapes', in *W. G. Sebald — A Critical Companion*, ed. by J. J. Long and Anne Whitehead (Edinburgh: Edinburgh University Press, 2004), pp. 31–44

BOS, PASCALE R., *German-Jewish Literature in the Wake of the Holocaust: Grete Weil, Ruth Klüger, and the Politics of Address* (New York: Palgrave Macmillan, 2005)

BORCHMEYER, DIETER, ed., *Melancholie und Heiterkeit* (Heidelberg: Universitätsverlag, 2006)

BOSWELL, MATTHEW, *Holocaust Impiety in Literature, Popular Music and Film* (Basingstoke: Palgrave Macmillan, 2012)

BÖTTIGER, HELMUT, 'Buchstaben-Barrikaden: Von Reinhard Jirgls Anfängen bis hin zu *Die Stille* — ein in sich stimmiger ästhetischer Kosmos', *Text + Kritik*, 189 (2011), 14–24

BOTZ, GERHARD, 'Historische Brüche und Kontinuitäten als Herausforderungen — Ingeborg Bachmann und post-katastrophische Geschichtsmentalitäten in Österriech', in *Ingeborg Bachmann: Neue Beiträge zu ihrem Werk*, ed. by Dirk Göttsche and Hubert Ohl (Würzburg: Königshausen & Neumann, 1993), pp. 199–214

—— *Gewalt in der Politik: Attentate, Zusammenstöße, Putschversuche, Unruhen in Österreich 1918–1938* (Munich: Wilhelm Fink Verlag, 1983)

BRAESE, STEPHAN, and HOLGER GEHLE, 'Von "deutschen Freunden": Ruth Klüger's *weiter leben. Eine Jugend* in der deutschen Rezeption', *Der Deutschunterricht*, 47.6 (1995), 76–87

BRATTON, JACKY, 'The Contending Discourses of Melodrama', in *Melodrama: Stage, Picture, Screen*, ed. by Jacky Bratton, Jim Cook, & Christine Gledhill (London: BFI, 1994)

BRAUN, PETER, 'Landschaften mit Geschichte: Über die Dokumentarfilme von Volker Koepp', in *Die Medien der Geschichte: Historizität und Medialität in interdisziplinärer Perspektive*, ed. by Fabio Crivellari and others, (Constance: UVK, 2004), pp. 351–77

—— 'Von Europa erzählen: Über die Konstruktion der Erinnerung in den Dokumentarfilmen von Volker Koepp', in *DDR — erinnern, vergessen: Das visuelle Gedächtnis des Dokumentarfilms*, ed. by Tobias Ebbrecht and others, (Marburg: Schüren, 2009), pp. 71–91

BROOKS, PETER, *The Melodramatic Imagination: Balzac, Henry James, Melodrama, and the Mode of Excess* (New Haven, CT: Yale University Press, 1976)

BURGOYNE, ROBERT, 'Narrative and Sexual Excess', *October*, 21, Rainer Werner Fassbinder (1982), 51–61 (p. 61)

BURKE, EDMUND, *A Philosophical Enquiry into the Origins of Our Ideas of the Sublime and Beautiful* (Basle: printed and sold by J. J. Tourneisen, 1792)

BURROUGHS, E. R., *Carson of Venus*, first serialized in *Argosy*, 1938, published in 1939 by Edgar Rice Burroughs, Inc. (Project Gutenberg of Australia: <http://gutenberg.net.au/ebooks03/0300181h.html#chap9> [accessed 17 October 2013])

CALINESCU, MATEI, *Five Faces of Modernity* (Durham, NC: Duke University Press, 1987)

CAMPBELL, JAN, *Film and Cinema Spectatorship: Melodrama and Mimesis* (Cambridge: Polity, 2005)

CANBY, VINCENT, 'Mother Kusters Goes to Heaven', *New York Times*, 7 March 1977

CARUTH, CATHY, 'Trauma and Experience: Introduction', in *Trauma: Explorations in Memory*, ed. by Cathy Caruth (Baltimore, MD: Johns Hopkins University Press, 1995), pp. 3–12

CEUPPENS, JAN, 'Realia: Konstellationen bei Benjamin, Barthes, Lacan — und Sebald', in *W. G. Sebald: Politische Archäologie und melancholische Bastelei*, ed. by Michael Niehaus and Claudia Öhlschläger (Berlin: Erich Schmidt, 2006), pp. 241–58

CHARE, NICHOLAS, and DOMINIC WILLIAMS, eds, *Representing Auschwitz at the Margins of Testimony*, ed. by (Basingstoke: Palgrave Macmillan, 2013)

CIXOUS, HÉLÈNE, *The Hélène Cixous Reader*, ed. by Susan Sellers (London: Routledge, 1994)

CLARKE, DAVID, 'Einleitung', in *Reinhard Jirgl: Perspektiven, Lesarten, Kontexte*, ed. by David Clarke and Arne De Winde (Amsterdam & New York: Rodopi, 2007), pp. 7–12

COATES, PAUL, 'Swearing and Forswearing Fidelity in Fassbinder's Berlin Alexanderplatz', in *A Companion to Rainer Werner Fassbinder*, ed. by Brigitte Peucker (Oxford: Wiley-Blackwell, 2012), pp. 398–419

COHEN-PFISTER, LAUREL, 'The Suffering of the Perpetrators: Unleashing Collective Memory in German Literature of the Twenty-First Century', *Forum of Modern Language Studies*, 41, 2 (2005), 123–35

CONTER, CLAUDE, *Literatur und Holocaust* (Bamberg: Otto-Friedrich-Universität Press, 1996)

CONYBEARE, CATHERINE, *The Laughter of Sarah: Biblical Exegesis, Feminist Theory, and the Concept of Delight* (New York: Palgrave Macmillan, 2013)

COOK, JOHN, 'Lost in Translation? A Conversation with John Cook', in *Saturn's Moons: W. G. Sebald — A Handbook*, ed. by Jo Catling and Richard Hibbitt (Oxford: Legenda, 2011), pp. 357–64

COPJEC, JOAN, *Read my Desire* (Cambridge, MA: MIT Press, 1994)

—— *Imagine There's No Woman: Ethics and Sublimation* (Cambridge, MA: MIT Press, 2002)

—— 'The Object-Gaze: Shame, *Hejab*, Cinema', *Filozofski vestnik*, 27, 2, (2006), 11–29

CORRIGAN, TIMOTHY, *New German Film: The Displaced Image* (Bloomington: Indiana University Press, 1994)

COSGROVE, MARY, *Born Under Auschwitz: Melancholy Traditions in Postwar German Literature* (Rochester, NY: Camden House, 2014)

—— 'The Anxiety of German Influence: Affiliation, Rejection, and Jewish Identity in W. G. Sebald's Work', in *German Memory Contests: The Quest for Identity in Literature, Film, and Discourse Since 1990*, ed. by Anne Fuchs and others (Rochester, NY: Camden House, 2006), pp. 229–52

CRITCHLEY, SIMON, *Very Little... Almost Nothing: Death, Philosophy, Literature* (London: Routledge, 1997)

—— *Ethics-Politics-Subjectivity: Essays on Derrida, Levinas and Contemporary French Thought* (London: Verso, 1999)

DAVIES, CHRISTIE, *The Mirth of Nations* (New Brunswick, NJ: Transaction Publishers, 2002)

DAVIES, MARTIN L., and CLAUS-CHRISTIAN W. SZEJNMANN, eds, *How the Holocaust Looks Now: International Perspectives* (Basingstoke: Palgrave Macmillan, 2007)

DELEUZE, GILLES, 'Coldness and Cruelty', in *Masochism*, trans. by Jean McNeil (New York: Zone Books, 1991)

DENNELER, IRIS, *Von Namen und Dingen: Erkundungen zur Rolle des Ich in der Literatur am Beispiel von Ingeborg Bachmann, Peter Bichsel, Max Frisch, Gottfried Keller, Heinrich von Kleist, Arthur Schnitzler, Frank Wedekind, Vladimir Nabokov und W. G. Sebald* (Würzburg: Königshausen & Neumann, 2001)

DE WINDE, ARNE, 'Das Erschaffen von "eigen-Sinn": Notate zu Reinhard Jirgls Schrift-Bildlichkeitsexperimenten', in *Reinhard Jirgl: Perspektiven, Lesarten, Kontexte*, ed. by David Clarke and Arne De Winde (Amsterdam & New York: Rodopi, 2007), pp. 111–49

—— '"Das hatte ich mal irgendwo gelesen": Überlegungen zu Reinhard Jirgls Essayismus', *Text + Kritik*, 189 (2011), 86–97

DES PRES, TERENCE 'Holocaust *Laughter?*', in *Writing the Holocaust*, ed. by Berel Lang (New York & London: Holmes & Meier, 1988), pp. 216–33

DOWDEN, STEPHEN D., *Understanding Thomas Bernhard* (Columbia: University of South Carolina Press, 1991)

DÜRRENMATT, FRIEDRICH, 'Theaterprobleme', in *Gesammelte Werke*, ed. by Franz Josef Görtz, 7 vols (Zurich: Diogenes, 1988), VII, 56–57

DUTTLINGER, CAROLIN, 'Traumatic Photographs: Remembrance and the Technical Media in *W. G. Sebald and the Writing of History*, ed. by Anne Fuchs and J. J. Long (Würzburg: Königshausen & Neumann, 2007), pp. 155–71

Dyer, Richard, 'Nice Young Men Who Sell Antiques — Gay Men in Heritage Cinema', in *Film / Literature / Heritage: A Sight and Sound Reader*, ed. by Ginette Vincendeau (London: BFI, 2001)
Eberhardt, Joachim, *'Es Gibt für mich keine Zitate': Intertexutalität im dichterischen Werk Ingeborg Bachmanns* (Tübingen: Niemeyer, 2002)
Elias, Norbert, *The Civilizing Process* (Oxford: Blackwell, 2000)
Elsaesser, Thomas, 'A Cinema of Vicious Circles', in *Fassbinder*, ed. by Tony Rayns (London: BFI, 1979), pp. 24–36
—— 'Tales of Sound and Fury: Observations on the Family Melodrama', in *Imitations of Life: A Reader on Film and Television Melodrama*, ed. by Marcia Landy (Detroit. MI: Wayne State University Press, 1991), pp. 68–91
—— *Fassbinder's Germany: History, Identity, Subject* (Amsterdam: Amsterdam University Press, 1996)
—— 'R. W. Fassbinder: Prodigal Son, Not Reconciled?', in *A Companion to Rainer Werner Fassbinder*, ed. by Brigitte Peucker (Oxford: Wiley-Blackwell, 2012), pp. 45–52
Fanon, Franz, *Black Skin, White Masks*, trans. by Charles Lam Markmann (New York: Grove Press, 1967)
Fassin, Didier, and Richard Rechtman, *The Empire of Trauma: An Inquiry into the Condition of Victimhood*, trans. by Rachel Gomme (Princeton, NJ: Princeton University Press, 2009)
Ferris, David S., *The Cambridge Introduction to Walter Benjamin* (Cambridge: Cambridge University Press, 2008)
Feuchert, Sascha, ed., *Erläuterungen und Dokumente: Ruth Klüger weiter Leben* (Stuttgart: Reclam, 2004)
Finch, Helen, *Sebald's Bachelors: Queer Resistance and the Unconforming Life* (London: Legenda, 2013)
Fink, Bruce, *The Lacanian Subject: Between Language and Jouissance* (Princeton, NJ: Princeton University Press, 1995)
Freud, Sigmund, *Der Witz und seine Beziehung zum Unbewußten*, in *Sigmund Freud. Studienausgabe. Psychologische Schriften* (Frankfurt a.M.: Fischer, 1989)
—— 'Mourning and Melancholia', in *The Standard Edition of the Complete Psychological Works of Sigmund Freud. Vol. XIV (1914–1916): On the History of the Psycho-Analytic Movement, Papers on Metapsychology and Other Works*, trans. by James Strachey (London: Hogarth Press, 1917), pp. 237–58
—— *Der Humor*, in *Sigmund Freud. Studienausgabe. Band IV: Psychologische Schriften* (Frankfurt a.M.: Fischer, 1989)
Frost, Laura, *The Problem with Pleasure: Modernism and its Discontents* (New York: Columbia University Press, 2013)
Fuchs, Anne, 'Edgar Hilsenrath's Poetics of Insignificance and the Tradition of Humour in German-Jewish Ghetto Writing', in *Ghetto Writing: Traditional and Eastern Jewry in German-Jewish Literature from Heine to Hilsenrath*, ed. by Anne Fuchs and Florian Krobb (Columbia, SC: Camden House, 1999), pp. 180–94
—— *A Space of Anxiety: Dislocation and Abjection in Modern German-Jewish Literature* (Amsterdam & Atlanta, GA: Rodopi, 1999)
—— *Die Schmerzensspuren der Geschichte: Zur Poetik der Erinnerung in W. G. Sebalds Prosa* (Cologne: Böhlau, 2004)
—— and J. J. Long, eds, *W. G. Sebald and the Writing of History* (Würzburg: Königshausen & Neumann, 2007)
Fulda, Daniel, 'Abschied von der Zentralperspektive: Der nicht nur literarische Geschichtsdiskurs im Nachwende-Deutschland als Dispositiv für Jörg Friedrichs *Brand*', in *Bombs Away! Representing the Air War over Europe and Japan*, ed. by Wilfried Wilms and

William Rasch (Amsterdam & New York: Rodopi, 2006), pp. 45- 64
GALT, ROSALIND, 'Jolie Laide: Fassbinder, Anti-Semitism, and the Jewish Image', in *A Companion to Rainer Werner Fassbinder*, ed. by Brigitte Peucker (Oxford: Wiley-Blackwell, 2012), pp. 485–501
GIDION, HEIDI, 'Im Parlando-Ton und lakonisch', in *Erläuterungen und Dokumente: Ruth Klüger weiter Leben*, ed. by Sascha Feuchert (Stuttgart: Reclam, 2004)
GILMAN, SANDER L., 'Is Life Beautiful? Can the Shoah be Funny? Some Thoughts on Recent and Older Films', *Critical Inquiry*, 26, 2 (Winter, 2000), 279–308
GLEDHILL, CHRISTINE, ed., *Home is Where the Heart Is: Studies in Melodrama and the Woman's Film* (London: BFI, 1987)
GRAF, ANDREAS, 'Mörderisches Ich: Zur Pathologie der Erzählperspektive in *Der Nazi und der Friseur*', in *Edgar Hilsenrath: Das Unerzählbare erzählen*, ed. by Thomas Kraft (Munich: Piper, 1996), pp. 135–49
GRIMM, ERK, 'Die Lebensläufe Reinhard Jirgls: Techniken der melotraumatischen Inszenierung', in *Reinhard Jirgl: Perspektiven, Lesarten, Kontexte*, ed. by David Clarke and Arne De Winde (Amsterdam & New York: Rodopi, 2007), pp. 197–226
GROSSMAN, DAVID, *Falling Out of Time*, trans. by Jessica Cohen (London: Jonathan Cape, 2014)
GÜRTLER, CHRISTA, '"Malina sieht mich so listig an, dann lacht er, ich lache auch": Ingeborg Bachmanns komische Geschichten', in *Frauen verstehen keinen Spaß*, ed. by Daniela Strigl (Vienna: Paul Zsolnay Verlag, 2002), pp. 97–105
—— 'Ironie und Komik in Ingeborg Bachmanns Erzählband Simultan', in *Klangfarben: Stimmen zu Ingeborg Bachmann*, ed. by Pierre Béhar (St. Ingbert: Röhrig Universitätsverlag, 2000), pp. 12–145
HARGENS, WANJA, *Der Müll, die Stadt und der Tod: Rainer Werner Fassbinder und ein Stück deutscher Zeitgeschichte* (Berlin: Metropol, 2010)
HAZLITT, WILLIAM, *Lectures on the English Comic Writers*, in *The Selected Writings of William Hazlitt*, ed. by Duncan Wu, 9 vols (London: Pickering and Chatto, 1998), v
HEIDELBERGER-LEONARD, IRENE, *Ruth Klüger, weiter Leben: Eine Jugend* (Munich: Oldenbourg, 1996)
HILLGRUBER, KATRIN, 'Berge, Meere, deutsche Giganten', *Frankfurter Rundschau*, 16 March 2009, <www.fr-online.de/literatur/-die-stille-berge-meere-deutsche-giganten, 1472266,3085124.html> [accessed 3 September 2012]
HIRSCH, MARIANNE, and LEO SPITZER, *Ghosts of Home: The Afterlife of Czernowitz in Jewish Memory* (Berkeley: University of California Press, 2010)
HÖLLER, HANS, ' "Das Komische, mehr als das Tragische, hat seine Noten, seine nationalen": Ingeborg Bachmanns *Malina*', in *Komik in der österreichischen Literatur*, ed. by Wendelin Schmidt-Dengler, Johann Sonnleitner, and Klaus Zeyringer (Berlin: Erich Schmidt, 1996), pp. 263–74
HOLDEN, STEPHEN, 'A Grim Fassbinder on the Marriage Bond', *New York Times*, 24 Sept 1994
HORCH, HANS OTTO, 'Grauen und Groteske. Zu Edgar Hilsenraths Romanen', in *'Wir tragen den Zettelkasten mit den Steckbriefen unserer Freunde': Ata-Band zum Symposion 'Beiträge jüdischer Autoren zur deutschen Literatur seit 1945'*, ed. by Jens Stüben and Winfried Woesler (Darmstadt: Häusser, 1994), pp. 213–26
HORSTKOTTE, SILKE, 'Photo-Text Topographies: Photography and the Representation of Space in W. G. Sebald and Monika Maron', *Poetics Today*, (Spring 2008), 49–78
HUBER, MARTIN, 'Rettich und Klavier: Zur Komik im Werk Thomas Bernhards', in *Komik in der österreichischen Literatur*, ed. by Wendelin Schmidt-Dengler, Johann Sonleitner, and Klaus Zeyringer (Berlin: Erich Schmidt Verlag, 1996), pp. 275–84
HUYSSEN, ANDREAS, *After the Great Divide: Modernism, Mass Culture, Postmodernism* (Bloomington & Indianapolis: Indiana University Press, 1986)
JACKMAN, GRAHAM, 'Introduction', *German Life and Letters*, 57, 4 (2004), 343–53

JACOBSON, HOWARD, *Seriously Funny: From the Ridiculous to the Sublime* (London: Viking, 1997)
JANKÉLÉVITCH, VLADIMIR, 'Should We Pardon Them?', trans. by Ann Hobart, *Critical Inquiry*, 22, 3 (1996), 552–72
—— *Forgiveness*, trans. by Andrew Kelley (Chicago: Chicago University Press, 2005)
JANSEN, PETER W., and WOLFRAM SCHÜTTE, eds, *Rainer Werner Fassbinder* (Frankfurt a.M.: Fischer, 1992)
JAY, MARTIN, *Refractions of Violence* (London: Routledge, 2003)
JASPERS, KARL, *Von der Wahrheit* (Munich: Piper, 1958)
JENSEN, OLAF, and CLAUS-CHRISTIAN W. SZEJNMANN, eds, *Ordinary People as Mass Murderers: Perpetrators in Comparative Perspectives* (Basingstoke: Palgrave Macmillan, 2008)
JUDT, TONY, *Postwar: A History of Europe since 1945* (London: Pimlico, 2007)
KANT, IMMANUEL, *Kritik der Urteilskraft*, ed. by Wilhelm Weischedel (Frankfurt a.M.: Suhrkamp, 1996)
KANZ, CHRISTINE, *Angst und Geschlechterdifferenzen: Ingeborg Bachmanns "Todesarten"- Projekt in Kontexten der Geenwartsliteratur* (Stuttgart: Metzler, 1999)
KIRMAYER, LAURENCE J., ROBERT LEMELSON, and MARK BARAD, 'Trauma in Context: Integrating Biological, Clinical, and Cultural Perspectives', in *Understanding Trauma: Integrating Biological, Clinical, and Cultural Perspectives*, ed. by Laurence J. Kirmayer, Robert Lemelson, and Mark Barad (Cambridge: Cambridge University Press, 2007), pp. 451–74
KLOTZ, MARCIA, 'Epistemological Ambiguity and the Fascist Text: *Jew Süss, Carl Peters*, and *Ohm Krüger*', *New German Critique*, 74 (1998), 91–124
KLÜGER, RUTH, 'Wanderer zwischen falschen Leben: Über W. G. Sebald', *Text + Kritik*, 158 (2003), 95–102
KNOPP, GUIDO, *Die Große Flucht* (Universum Film, 2004) [on DVD]
KOEPNICK, LUTZ, 'Reframing the Past: Heritage Cinema and Holocaust in the 1990s', *New German Critique*, 87 (2002), 47–82
KOSOFSKY SEDGWICK, EVE, *Touching Feeling: Affect, Pedagogy, Performativity* (Durham, NC: Duke University Press, 2003)
KRAFT, THOMAS, ed., *Edgar Hilsenrath: Das Unerzählbare erzählen* (Munich: Piper, 1996)
KREUTZER, HANS JOACHIM, 'Die Auschwitznummer nicht verdecken: Ruth Klügers Erinnerungen — eine Einladung zum Streiten', in *Erläuterungen und Dokumente: Ruth Klüger weiter Leben*, ed. by Sascha Feuchert (Stuttgart: Reclam, 2004)
KRISTEVA, JULIA, 'De l'abjection à la banalité du mal', lecture given at the Centre Roland Barthes Université Paris-VII, 24 April 2007, <www.kristeva.fr/abjection.html> [accessed 17 September 2014]
KRYLOVA, KATYA, *Walking Through History: Topography and Identity in the Works of Ingeborg Bachmann and Thomas Bernhard* (Oxford: Peter Lang, 2013)
KÜHNE, THOMAS, 'Male Bonding and Shame Culture: Hitler's Soldiers and the Moral Basis of Genocidal Warfare', in *Ordinary People as Mass Murderers: Perpetrators in Comparative Perspectives*, ed. by Olaf Jensen and Claus-Christian W. Szejnmann (Basingstoke: Palgrave Macmillan, 2008), pp. 55–77
KUON, PETER, 'From "Kitsch" to "Splatter": The Aesthetics of Violence', in *Writing the Holocaust Today: Critical Perspectives on Jonathan Littell's 'The Kindly Ones'*, ed. by Aurélie Barjonet and Liran Razinsky (Amsterdam & New York: Rodopi, 2012), pp. 33–45
KUZNIAR, ALICE A., *The Queer German Cinema* (Stanford, CA: Stanford University Press, 2000)
LACAN, JACQUES, *The Ethics of Psychoanalysis 1959–1960*, trans. by Dennis Porter (London: Routledge, 1992)
—— *Television: A Challenge to the Psychoanalytic Establishment*, ed. by Joan Copjec, trans. by Denis Hollier, Rosalind Krauss, and Annette Michelson (New York: Norton, 1990)

LACAPRA, DOMINICK, *Writing History, Writing Trauma* (Baltimore, MD: Johns Hopkins University Press, 2001)
—— 'Historical and Literary Approaches to the "Final Solution": Saul Friedländer and Jonathan Littell', *History and Theory*, 50 (2011), 71–97
—— *History and its Limits. Human, Animal, Violence* (Ithaca: Cornell UP, 2009)
LAMB-FAFFELBERGER, MARGARETE, 'In the Eyes of the Press: Provocation — Production — Prominence: A Critical Documentation of Elfirede Jelinek's Reception', in *Elfriede Jelinek: Framed by Language*, ed. by Jorun B. Johns and Katherine Arens (Riverside, CA: Ariadne Press, 1994), pp. 287–302
LANZMANN, CLAUDE, 'From the Holocaust to "Holocaust"', in *Shoah: Key Essays*, ed. by Stuart Liebman (Oxford: Oxford University Press, 2007), pp. 27–36
LEAHY, CAITRÍONA, *'Der wahre Historiker': Ingeborg Bachmann and the Problem of Witnessing History* (Würzburg: Königshausen und Neumann, 2007)
LEMMA, ALESSANDRA, *Humour on the Couch: Exploring Humour in Psychotherapy and Everyday Life* (London: Whurr, 2000)
LEVI, PRIMO, *If this is a Man and The Truce*, trans. by Stuart Woolf (London: Abacus, 1993)
—— *The Drowned and the Saved*, trans. by Raymond Rosenthal (London: Abacus, 1993)
LEVINAS, EMMANUEL, *Totality and Infinity*, trans. by Alphonso Lingis (Pittsburgh, PA: Duquesne University Press, 1969)
—— *Time and the Other*, trans. by Richard A. Cohen (Pittsburgh, PA: Duquesne University Press, 1987)
—— 'Transcendence and Height', in *Basic Philosophical Writings*, ed. by Adriaan T. Peperzak and others (Bloomington: Indiana University Press, 1996)
—— 'Philosophy and the Idea of Infinity', in *Collected Philosophical Papers*, trans. by Alphonso Lingis, (Pittsburgh, PA: Duquesne University Press, 1998), pp. 47–59
LEYS, RUTH, *Trauma: A Genealogy* (Chicago: Chicago University Press, 2000)
—— *From Guilt to Shame* (Princeton, NJ: Princeton University Press, 2007)
LIPPITT, JOHN, *Humour and Irony in Kierkegaard's Thought* (London: Macmillan, 2000)
LÖFFLER, SIGRID, 'Davongekommen', in *Erläuterungen und Dokumente: Ruth Klüger weiter leben*, ed. by Sascha Feuchert (Stuttgart: Reclam, 2004)
LONG, JONATHAN J., 'History, Narrative, and Photography in W. G. Sebald's *Die Ausgewanderten*', *Modern Language Review*, 98, 1 (2003), 118–37
—— and ANNE WHITEHEAD, eds, *W. G. Sebald — A Critical Companion*, (Edinburgh: Edinburgh University Press, 2004)
—— *W. G. Sebald: Image, Archive, Modernity* (Edinburgh: Edinburgh University Press, 2007)
LOQUAI, FRANZ, *W. G. Sebald* (Eggingen: Edition Isele, 1997)
LOSHITZY, YOSEFA, 'Forbidden Laughter? The Politics and Ethics of the Holocaust Film Comedy', in *Re-Presenting the Shoah for the 21st Century*, ed. by Ronit Lentin (New York & Oxford: Berghahn, 2004), pp. 127–37
LUCKHURST, ROGER, 'Traumaculture', *New Formations*, 50 (2003), 28–47
MACHTANS, KAROLIN, *Zwischen Wissenschaft und autobiographischem Projekt: Saul Friedländer und Ruth Klüger* (Tübingen: Niemeyer, 2009)
MALKMUS, BERNHARD F., *The German Pícaro and Modernity: Between Underdog and Shape-Shifter* (New York & London: Continuum, 2011)
MARKOLIN, CAROLINE, 'Too Late to Seek, too Early to Find?: Philosophical and Aesthetic Aspects of Contemporary Austrian Fiction', in *Shadows of the Past: Austrian Literature of the Twentieth Century*, ed. by Hans H. Schulte and Gerard Schapple (Oxford: Peter Lang, 2009), pp. 125–38
MARKOVITS, ANREI S., SEYLA BENHABIB, and MOISHE POSTONE, 'Rainer Werner Fassbinder's Garbage, the City and Death: Renewed Antagonisms in the Complex Relationship

between Jews and Germans in the Federal Republic of Germany', *New German Critique*, 38 (1986), 3–27

MENKE, TIMM, 'Reinhard Jirgls Roman *Die Unvollendeten* — Tabubruch oder späte Erinnerung?', *Glossen*, 8 (2004), <http://www2.dickinson.edu/glossen/heft20/menke.html> [accessed 14 October 2014]

MERCIER-LECA, FLORENCE, '*Les Bienveillantes* et la tragédie grecque', in *le débat*, 144 (2007), 45–55

MILLER, D. A., *Jane Austen, or The Secret of Style* (Princeton, NJ: Princeton University Press, 2003)

MOELLER, ROBERT G., *War Stories. The Search for a Usable Past in the Federal Republic of Germany* (Berkeley, CA: University of Los Angeles Press, 2001)

MÖLLER, SUSANN, 'Zur Rezeption: Philosemiten und Andere — die Verlagsstationen Edgar Hilsenraths', in *Edgar Hilsenrath: Das Unerzählbare erzählen*, ed. by Thomas Kraft (Munich: Piper, 1996), pp. 103–16

MORAG, RAYA, *Waltzing with Bashir: Perpetrator Trauma and Cinema* (London: I. B. Tauris, 2013)

MORGAN, PETER, 'The Sign of Saturn: Melancholy, Homelessness and Apocalypse in W. G. Sebald's Prose Narrative', *German Life and Letters*, 58, 1 (2005), 75–92

MUCCI, CLARA, *Beyond Individual and Collective Trauma: Intergenerational Transmission, Psychoanalytic Treatment, and the Dynamics of Forgiveness* (London: Karnac, 2013)

MULKAY, MICHAEL, *On Humor: Its Nature and Its Place in Modern Society* (Cambridge: Polity, 1988)

MÜLLER, HEINER, *Gesammelte Irrtümer: Interviews und Gespräche* (Frankfurt a.M.: Verlag der Autoren, 1986)

MULVEY, LAURA, *Fetishism and Curiosity* (London: BFI, 1996)

NATHANSON, DONALD, 'Understanding What is Hidden: Shame in Sexual Abuse', *The Psychiatric Clinics of North America*, 12, 2 (1989), 381–88

NEALE, STEVE, 'Propaganda', *Screen*, 18, 3 (1977), 9–40

—— 'Melodrama and Tears', *Screen*, 27, 6 (1986), 6–23

NIEBUHR, REINHOLD, *The Essential Reinhold Niebuhr: Selected Essays and Addresses*, ed. by Robert McAfee Brown (New Haven, CT: Yale University Press, 1987)

NIEHAUS, MICHAEL, 'Sebald's Scourges', in *W. G. Sebald and the Writing of History*, ed. by Anne Fuchs and J. J. Long (Würzburg: Königshausen & Neumann, 2007), pp. 45–57

—— 'W. G. Sebalds sentimentalische Dichtung', in *W. G. Sebald: Politische Archäologie und melancholische Bastelei*, ed. by Michael Niehaus and Claudia Öhlschläger (Berlin: Erich Schmidt, 2006), pp. 173–87

NIETZSCHE, FRIEDRICH, *Menschliches Allzumenschliches II*, 202, in *Friedrich Nietzsche Menschliches, Allzumenschliches I und II. Kritische Studienausgabe*, ed. by Giorgio Colli and Mazzino Montinari (Munich and Berlin/New York: dtv/de Gruyter, 1988)

—— *Jenseits von Gut und Böse: Zur Genealogie der Moral. Kritische Studienausgabe*, ed. by Giorgio Colli and Mazzino Montinari (Munich and Berlin/New York: DTV/de Gruyter, 1988)

NIVEN, BILL, 'The Globalization of Memory and the Rediscovery of German Suffering', in *German Literature in the Age of Globalisation*, ed. by Stuart Taberner (Birmingham: University of Birmingham Press, 2004), pp. 229–46

—— 'Implicit Equations in Constructions of German Suffering', in *A Nation of Victims?: Representations of German Wartime Suffering from 1945 to the Present*, ed. by Helmut Schmitz (Amsterdam & New York: Rodopi, 2007), pp. 105–24

—— *Representations of Flight and Expulsion in East German Prose Works* (Rochester, NY: Camden House, 2014)

NIVEN, BILL, ed., *Germans as Victims. Remembering the Past in Contemporary Germany* (Basingstoke: Palgrave Macmillan, 2006)

ORICH, ANNIKA, and FLORENTINE STRZELCZYK, '"Steppende Nazis mit Bildungsauftrag": Marketing Hitler Humor in Post-Unification Germany', in *Strategies of Humor in Post-Unification German Literature, Film and Other Media*, ed. by Jill E. Twark (Newcastle upon Tyne: Cambridge Scholars Publishing, 2011), pp. 292–329

PAUL, JEAN, *Vorschule der Ästhetik*, in *Werke*, ed. by N. Miller, 10 vols (Munich: Hanser, 1980), V

PEUCKER, BRIGITTE, ed., *A Companion to Rainer Werner Fassbinder* (Oxford: Wiley-Blackwell, 2012)

PHILLIPS, ADAM, 'What's So Funny? On Being Laughed At...', in *The Anatomy of Laughter*, ed. by Toby Garfitt and others (London: Legenda, 2005), pp. 124–30

PICK, HELLA, *Guilty Victims: Austria from the Holocaust to Haider* (London: IB Tauris, 2000)

PIPOLO, TONY, 'Bewitched by the Holy Whore', *October*, 21. Rainer Werner Fassbinder (1982), 82–114

PLATO, *Philebus* (Harmondsworth: Penguin, 1982)

POPKIN, JEREMY D., 'A Historian's View of The Kindly Ones', in *Writing the Holocaust Today: Critical Perspectives on Jonathan Littell's 'The Kindly Ones'*, ed. by Aurélie Barjonet and Liran Razinsky (Amsterdam & New York: Rodopi, 2012), pp. 187–200

PREISENDANZ, WOLFGANG, 'Zum Vorrang des Komischen bei der Darstellung von Geschichtserfahrung in deutschen Romanen unserer Zeit', in *Das Komische*, ed. by Wolfgang Preisendanz and Rainer Warning (Munich: Fink, 1976), pp. 153–64

PREISENDANZ, WOLFGANG, and RAINER WARNING, eds, *Das Komische* (Munich: Fink, 1976)

RAU, PETRA, *Our Nazis: Representations of Fascism in Contemporary Literature and Film* (Edinburgh: Edinburgh University Press, 2013)

RAZINSKY, LIRAN, 'Not the Witness We Wished for: Testimony in Jonathan Littell's *The Kindly Ones*', *Modern Language Quarterly*, 71, 2 (2010), 175–96

REICH-RANICKI, MARCEL, 'Vom Trotz getrieben, vom Stil beglaubigt. Rede auf Ruth Klüger aus Anlaß der Verleihung des Grimmelshausen-Preises', in *Erläuterungen und Dokumente: Ruth Klüger weiter Leben*, ed. by Sascha Feuchert (Stuttgart: Reclam, 2004)

REINECKE, STEFAN, 'Das Land, das einfach verrostete', *TAZ*, 28 January 2010

RESTUCCIA, FRANCES L., *Amorous Acts: Lacanian Ethics in Modernism, Film, and Queer Theory* (Stanford, CA: Stanford University Press, 2006)

RHODES, JOHN DAVID, 'Fassbinder's Work: Style, Sirk, and Queer Labor', in *A Companion to Rainer Werner Fassbinder*, ed. by Brigitte Peucker (Oxford: Wiley-Blackwell, 2012), pp. 181–203

RICHTER, URS, 'Und Sonntags Krähensuppe', *TAZ*, 3 (2001)

RICOEUR, PAUL, *Memory, History, Forgetting*, trans. by Kathleen Blamey and David Pellauer (Chicago: Chicago University Press, 2004)

ROBERTS, ROBERT C., 'Humor and the Virtues', in *Søren Kierkegaard: Critical Assessments of Leading Philosophers*, ed. by Daniel W. Conway, 4 vols (London: Routledge, 2002), IV, 293–315

ROSE, GILLIAN, 'Beginnings of the Day: Fascism and Representation', in *Modernity, Culture and 'the Jew'*, ed. by Bryan Cheyette and Laura Marcus (Cambridge: Polity, 1998), pp. 242–56

ROUSSEAU, CÉCILE, and TOBY MEASHAM, 'Postraumatic Suffering as a Source of Transformation: A Clinical Perspective', in *Understanding Trauma: Integrating Biological, Clinical, and Cultural Perspectives*, ed. by Laurence J. Kirmayer, Robert Lemelson, and Mark Barad (Cambridge: Cambridge University Press, 2007), pp. 275–93

RUPPERT, PETER, 'Fassbinder, Spectatorship, and Utopian Desire', *Cinema Journal*, 28, 2 (1989), 28–47

SANDFORD, JOHN, *The New German Cinema* (London: Eyre Methuen, 1981)

SAUTERMEISTER, GERT, 'Aufgeklärte Modernität — Postmodernes Entertainment: Edgar Hilsenraths *Der Nazi und der Friseur*', in *'Wir tragen den Zettelkasten mit den Steckbriefen* unserer Freunde': Ata-Band zum Symposion 'Beiträge jüdischer Autoren zur deutschen Literatur seit 1945', ed. by Jens Stüben and Winfried Woesler (Darmstadt: Häusser, 1994), pp. 227–42

SCHIESARI, JULIANA, *The Gendering of Melancholia: Feminism, Psychoanalysis, and the Symbolics of Loss in Renaissance Literature* (Ithaca, NY: Cornell University Press, 1992)

SCHILLER, FRIEDRICH, *Über naïve und sentimentalische Dichtung, Werke*, Nationalausgabe, *Philosophische Schriften. Erster Teil*, ed. by Benno von Wiese (Weimar: Hermann Böhlaus Nachfolger, 1962), xx

SCHMIDT-DENGLER, WENDELIN, JOHANN SONLEITNER, and KLAUS ZEYRINGER, eds, *Komik in der österreichischen Literatur* (Berlin: Erich Schmidt Verlag, 1996)

—— 'Thomas Bernhard's Poetics of Comedy', in *A Companion to the Works of Thomas Bernhard*, ed. by Matthias Konzett (Rochester, NY: Camden House, 2002), pp. 105–15

SCHMIDTKUNZ, RENATA, *Das Weiterleben der Ruth Klüger* (Falter Verlag, 2012) [on DVD]

SCHMITZ, HELMUT, *On Their Own Terms: The Legacy of National Socialism in Post-1990 German Fiction* (Birmingham: University of Birmingham Press, 2004)

——, ed., *A Nation of Victims?: Representations of German Wartime Suffering from 1945 to the Present* (Amsterdam & New York: Rodopi, 2007)

——, and ANNETTE SEIDEL-ARPACI, eds, *Narratives of Trauma: Discourses of German Wartime Suffering in National and International Perspective* (Amsterdam & New York: Rodopi, 2011)

SCHÖENBERG, ARNOLD, *Pierrot lunaire*, trans. by Andrew Porter, 1984, <http://www.da-capo.org/html/PierrotEnglish.html> [accessed 29 July 2015]

SCHOPENHAUER, ARTHUR, *Die Welt als Wille und Vorstellung II* (Zurich: Haffmans Verlag, 1991)

SCHULTE, MICHAEL, ed., *Alles von Karl Valentin* (Munich: Piper, 1978)

SCHULTE-SASSE, LINDA, 'The Jew as Other under National Socialism: Veit Harlan's *Jud Süss*', *The German Quarterly*, 61, 1 (1988), 22–49

SCHULZE, RAINER, 'Forced Migration of German Populations During and After the Second World War: History and Memory', in *The Disentanglement of Populations: Migration, Expulsion and Displacement in Post-War Europe, 1944–9*, ed. by Jessica Reinisch and Elizabeth White (New York: Palgrave Macmillan, 2011), pp. 51–70

SCHUTTE, WOLFRAM, 'Franz, Mieze, Reinhold, Death and the Devil: Rainer Werner Fassbinder's Berlin Alexanderplatz', in *Fassbinder*, ed. by Ruth McCormick (New York: Tanam Press, 1981)

SHAKESPEARE, WILLIAM, *The Merchant of Venice* (Oxford: Oxford University Press, 2010)

SHALEV, ARIEH Y., 'PTSD: A Disorder of Recovery?', in *Understanding Trauma: Integrating Biological, Clinical, and Cultural Perspectives*, ed. by Laurence J. Kirmayer, Robert Lemelson, and Mark Barad (Cambridge: Cambridge University Press, 2007), pp. 207–23

SHEPHERD, SIMON, 'Pauses of Mutual Agitation', in *Melodrama: Stage, Picture, Screen*, ed. by Jacky Bratton, Jim Cook, and Christine Gledhill (London: BFI, 1994), pp. 25–37

SHEPPARD, RICHARD, 'Dexter — Sinister: Some Observations on Decrypting the Morse Code in the Work of W. G. Sebald', *Journal of European Studies*, 35 (2005), 419–63

SILLEM, PETER, '"der du gedeihen läßt und zerstörst": Melancholie, Karneval und die zwei Gesichter des Saturn', in *Zeitsprünge: Forschungen zur Frühen Neuzeit* 5, no. 1/2 (2001)

SILVERMAN, KAJA, *Male Subjectivity at the Margins* (London: Routledge, 1992)

SINGER, BEN, *Melodrama and Modernity: Early Sensational Cinema and its Contexts* (New York: Columbia University Press, 2001)

SMELSER, NEIL J., 'Psychological Trauma and Cultural Trauma', in *Cultural Trauma and Collective Identity*, ed. by Jeffrey C. Alexander and others (Berkeley: University of California Press, 2004), pp. 31–59

SONTAG, SUSAN, 'Fascinating Fascism', in *Under the Sign of Saturn* (London: Vintage, 1980)

—— 'Notes on Camp', in *A Susan Sontag Reader* (Harmondsworth: Penguin, 1982), pp. 105–19

—— *Regarding the Pain of Others* (London: Penguin, 2004)

STEINER, GEORGE, *Language and Silence* (New York: Atheneum, 1967)

STEINLEIN, RÜDIGER, 'Das Furchtbarste lächerlich? Komik und Lachen in Texten der deutschen Holocaust-Literatur', in *Kunst und Literatur nach Auschwitz*, ed. by Manuel Köppen (Berlin: Erich Schmidt, 1993), pp. 97–106

STENBERG, PETER, 'Memories of the Holocaust: Edgar Hilsenrath and the Fiction of the Genocide', *Deutsche Vierteljahrsschrift für Literaturwissenschaft und Geistesgeschichte*, 56 (1982), 277–89

STOKER, BRAM, *Dracula* (London: Penguin, 2003)

STOLZ, DIETER, '"45 Seiten aus dickem braunem Velourspapier beklebt mit 100 Mal geronnenem Tod": Reinhard Jirgls Roman *Die Stille*', *Text + Kritik*, 189 (2011), 57–68

STÜBEN, JENS, and WINFRIED WOESLER, eds, *'Wir tragen den Zettelkasten mit den Steckbriefen unserer Freunde': Acta-Band zum Symposion 'Beiträge jüdischer Autoren zur deutschen Literatur seit 1945'* (Darmstadt: Häusser, 1994)

TABERNER, STUART, 'Literary Representations in Contemporary Literary Fiction of the Expulsions of Germans from the East in 1945', in *A Nation of Victims? Representations of German Wartime Suffering from 1945 to the Present*, ed. by Helmut Schmitz (Amsterdam: Rodopi, 2007), pp. 223–46

—— *Aging and Old-Age Style in Günter Grass, Ruth Klüger, Christa Wolf, and Martin Walser: The Mannerism of a Late Period* (Rochester, NY: Camden House, 2013)

TAYLOR, JENNIFER, 'Writing as Revenge: Reading Edgar Hilsenrath's *Der Nazi und der Friseur* as a Shoah Survivor's Fantasy', *History of European Ideas*, 20, 1–3 (1995), 439–44

THER, PHILIPP, *Deutsche und polnische Vertriebene: Gesellschaft und Vertriebenenpolitik in der SBZ/DDR und in Polen 1945–1956* (Göttingen: Vandenhoeck & Ruprecht, 1998)

TORBERG, FRIEDRICH, 'Ein Freispruch, der keiner ist', in *Edgar Hilsenrath: Das Unerzählbare erzählen*, ed. by Thomas Kraft (Munich: Piper, 1996), pp. 72–76

TWARK, JILL E., 'Introduction: Recent Trends in Post-Unification German Humor', in *Strategies of Humor in Post-Unification German Literature, Film and Other Media*, ed. by Jill E. Twark (Newcastle upon Tyne: Cambridge Scholars Publishing, 2011), pp. 1–25

UHRMEISTER, BEATE, '"It was indeed a German Hollywood Film": Fassbinder-Rezeption in den USA: Notizen zu einem produktiven Mißverständnis', *Text + Kritik*, 103 (1989), 80–85

UNI, ASSAF, 'The Executioner's Song', *Haaretz*, 29 May 2008, <http://www.haaretz.com/the-executioner-s-song-1.246787> [accessed 18 August 2013]

VAHSEN, PATRICIA, *Lesarten — Die Rezeption des Werks von Edgar Hilsenrath* (Tübingen: Niemeyer, 2008)

VAN DEN BERG, J. P. C., 'Trauma in *Der Nazi und der Friseur* von Edgar Hilsenrath', *Literator*, 32:1 (2011), 21–42

VICARI, JUSTIN, 'Fragments of Utopia: A Meditation on Fassbinder's Treatment of Anti-Semitism and the Third Reich', *Postmodern Culture*, 16, 2 (2006), 1–30

VON JAGOW, BETTINA, *Ästhetik des Mythischen: Poetologien des Erinnerns im Werk von Ingeborg Bachmann* (Cologne: Böhlau, 2003)

WALPOLE, HORACE, letter to Anne, Countess of Ossory, 16 August 1776, <http://archive.org/stream/lettersaddressed02walpuoft/lettersaddressed02walpuoft_djvu.txt> [accessed 1 September 2014]

WASSERMAN, STEVE, 'In this Distant Place: A Conversation with Steve Wasserman', in *Saturn's Moons: W. G. Sebald — A Handbook*, ed. by Jo Catling and Richard Hibbitt (Oxford: Legenda, 2011), pp. 365–76

WATSON, ALEXANDER, *Enduring the Great War: Combat, Morale and the Collapse in the German and British Armies, 1914–1918* (Cambridge: Cambridge University Press, 2008)

WATSON, WALLACE STEADMAN, *Understanding Rainer Werner Fassbinder* (Columbia: South Carolina University Press, 1996)

WEIGEL, SIGRID, *Ingeborg Bachmann: Hinterlassenschaften unter Wahrung des Briefgeheimnisses* (Vienna: Paul Zsolnay Verlag, 1999)

WEINSTEIN, VALERIE, 'Dissolving Boundaries: Assimilation and Allosemitism in E.A. Dupont's *Das alte Gesetz* (1923) and Veit Harlan's *Jud Süß* (1940)', *The German Quarterly*, 78, 4 (2005), 496–516

WELLERSHOFF, DIETER, '*Schöpferische und mechanische Ironie*', in *Das Komische*, ed. by Wolfgang Preisendanz and Rainer Warning (Munich: Fink, 1976), pp. 423–25

WELZER, HARALD, 'Schön unscharf: Über die Konjunktur der Familien- und Generationsromane,' *Mittelweg*, 36, 1 (2004), 53–64

WIESEL, ELIE, 'The Holocaust as Literary Inspiration', in Elie Wiesel, Lucy Dawidowicz, and others, *Dimensions of the Holocaust* (Evanston, IL: Northwestern University Press, 1977), pp. 4–19

—— *From the Kingdon of Memory* (New York: Summit Books, 1990)

WILLIAMS, LINDA, 'Film Bodies: Gender, Genre, and Excess', *Film Quarterly*, 44, 4 (1991), 2–13

YADIN, ELNA, and EDNA B. FOA, 'Cognitive Behavioral Treatments for Posttraumatic Stress Disorder', in *Understanding Trauma: Integrating Biological, Clinical, and Cultural Perspectives*, ed. by Laurence J. Kirmayer, Robert Lemelson, & Mark Barad (Cambridge: Cambridge University Press, 2008), pp. 178–93

ŽIŽEK, SLAVOJ, *The Plague of Fantasies* (London & New York: Verso, 1997)

—— *Did Somebody Say Totalitarianism?: Five Interventions in the (Mis)Use of a Notion* (London & New York: Verso, 2011)

ZUPANCIC, ALENKA, *The Odd One In: On Comedy* (Cambridge, MA: MIT Press, 2008)

Websites

<http://www.joebaugher.com/usaf_serials/1942_4.html> [accessed 17 October 2014]

'Nur die Alten bleiben. Auf den Spuren jüdischen Lebens in der heute ukrainischen Stadt Czernowitz', *Die Zeit*, 24 October 1997, <http://www.zeit.de/1997/44/Nur_die_Alten_bleiben> [accessed 7 November 2011]

INDEX

❖

absurdity 3, 6, 33, 91, 93, 98–99, 182, 185, 202
  reductio ad absurdum 188
abuse 35–36, 42, 59, 80, 111, 114–15, 117–21, 140, 169, 174–75, 178, 188, 201
academia 162, 182
Achberger, Karen 46
actor 80, 90. 92, 97, 130, 131, 133, 146–47, 149, 155
Adorno, Theodor W. 10–11, 22–23, 31, 44, 140, 167
Aeschylus:
  Eumenides 191
  Oresteia 180, 189, 191, 202
Afghanistan 181
Africa 181
Agamben, Giorgio 77
agency 36, 40, 137, 168, 194, 201
  moral agency 33
aggression 7, 9, 15, 43, 63, 65, 87, 115, 120, 139, 148, 151–52, 156
alienation 6, 12–13, 23, 37, 43, 64, 76, 81, 85, 96, 105, 151, 160, 181
allegory 63, 65
Allen, Woody:
  Zelig 187
Amazons 186, 194
America 13, 45–46, 50, 58, 61, 63, 67, 87, 97, 132, 148, 153, 155, 159, 169, 183–84
  Japanese Americans 148
  see also United States (US)
Améry, Jean 15–16, 20, 145, 163, 164
amusement 2, 19–20, 45, 50–51, 61–65, 66, 74–75, 80, 86–87, 91, 94, 100, 123, 126, 128, 130–32, 145, 151, 153–56, 158, 159–60, 162, 183, 192, 201, 203
animals 73, 87–88, 90, 91, 104, 115, 122–23, 131, 159
anti-Semitism 16, 79–80, 138–39, 149, 152, 154, 161–62, 172, 183, 186, 190
  and philo-Semitism 79, 170, 172
anxiety 5–7, 20, 22–23, 43, 48, 61, 65, 68, 86, 99–100, 103, 145, 169, 176, 180
appropriateness 6, 10, 21, 23, 75, 94, 99–100, 161, 170, 177, 192
appropriation 101, 195
  misappropriation 192
Arabs 61, 172, 178
Arnds, Peter 171
art 1–2, 4–6, 10–11, 19, 23, 39, 53, 63, 89, 92, 110, 126, 133–34, 140–41, 148, 192
  high art 10, 73
artifice 65–68, 72, 148–49, 202

artificiality 4, 9, 66, 180, 188
Aryanism 149, 170, 171, 183, 187
Ashkenazi, Ofer 21
Athena 191
atonement 179
atrocity 118, 140, 167, 177, 179–80, 185, 188
  see also German: atrocities
Auschwitz-Birkenau 1–3, 11, 21–23, 135, 144, 155–56, 158, 164, 167, 171. 179, 182–83, 187, 192, 195
Austria 5, 15–16, 45–46, 50, 138, 151, 155
  and the *Anschluss* 15
  Austria-Hungary 31
  Austrian Jews 159
  Austrian literature 151–52
  Austrian national identity 15
  as victim of National Socialism 15–16
authenticity 35, 37, 40, 41, 102, 136, 180
  inauthenticity 66–67, 81
author 2, 21, 23–24, 32, 36, 50–51, 73, 75, 79, 85, 95, 100, 102, 104, 110, 141, 146–48, 161, 173, 180–81, 191, 201
authority 2, 36, 42, 90, 120, 124, 146–47, 150, 151, 160, 169, 173, 175, 177, 181
autobiography 5, 144, 145–47, 151, 152, 159, 169, 180

Babi Yar 184, 187
Bachmann, Ingeborg 2, 24, 31–54, 93, 199–200
  Das dreißigste Jahr 42
  Der gute Gott von Manhattan 32
  Simultan 47, 49, 51–52
    'Drei Wege zum See' 31, 44
  Todesarten 35, 36, 44, 49, 50–51
    Das Buch Franza 31–35, 42, 44–48, 52, 54
    Goldmann/Rottwitz-Roman 34–35, 41, 46–47, 50–53
    Malina 31, 32–33, 35–39, 43–46, 49–51, 71;
      'Besichtigung einer alten Stadt' 45–46; 'Die Prinzessin von Kagran' 31, 36, 47
  Requiem für Fanny Goldmann 41, 45, 51
  Die Zikaden 42
Bakhtin, Mikhail 146
Barnett, David 59
Barthes, Roland 39
Barzilai, Maya 86
Basil of Caesarea 8
Batty Shaw, Anthony 89
Baumann, Zygmunt 78, 79
beauty 5, 39, 40, 67, 121, 132, 133, 186
Becker, Jurek 24
  Jakob der Lügner 20

Beckett, Samuel 33, 43
  Endgame 22, 31
Belgium 91
Benigni, Roberto:
  Life is Beautiful 21
Benjamin, Walter 81, 106, 199
Bergen Belsen 70, 80, 92
Bergenfelder, Tim 137
Berlin 16, 76, 89, 110, 138, 186, 187, 190
  Berlinale 128
  Berlin Wall 110
Bernard-Dorals, Michael 11
Bernhard, Thomas 20, 24, 100, 156
Bettelheim, Bruno 178
Bitburg 79
Blanchot, Maurice 39, 41
Bochum 79
body 1, 7, 10, 19, 33–34, 36, 43–45, 53–54, 60, 73, 92, 95, 112, 115, 122–23, 125, 193
  suffering 53, 59, 66, 70, 71, 73, 80, 200
  see also corpses; female: body; German: body; women: woman's body; masculinity: male body
Bohm, Hark 65
Bolshevism 133, 182
Bormann, Martin 187
Borowski, Tadeusz:
  This Way for the Gas, Ladies and Gentleman 20, 21
Bos, Pascale 156
Bosch, Hieronymous:
  The Garden of Earthly Delights 72
Bosnia 181
Böttiger, Helmut 113
Braese, Stephan 144
Bratton, Jacky 66
Braun, Helmut 169–70
Braun, Peter 133, 137
Brecht, Bertolt 43, 76
Britain 111
  British 42, 178, 184–85
  see also United Kingdom (UK)
Brooks, Mel:
  The Producers 22
Brooks, Peter 33
Browne, Thomas 89
Buchenwald 3, 167
Burgoyne, Robert 69
Burroughs, E. R.:
  Carson of Venus 183

camerawork 60–64, 75, 127, 129–34, 146, 181
campness 68, 72, 74, 200
Carstensen, Margit 65
Caruth, Cathy 13
Catholicism 133, 153
Cavani, Liliana:
  The Night Porter 193
Celan, Paul 4, 35, 161
  'Todesfuge' 161

Ceupens, Jan 104
characterisation 7–9, 22, 32, 42, 45–46, 48, 52, 62–63, 70, 73–80, 88, 91, 113–15, 118–19, 122, 127, 130, 134, 140–41, 149–50, 169–70, 178, 181–82, 186, 190–91, 193, 201
Chechnya 181
children 151–52, 153, 172
China 94, 186
Christianity 8, 72–73, 145, 163, 172
  see also Catholicism; Protestantism
Christianstadt 144, 153
Cixous, Hélène 6
cliché 37, 45, 97, 149, 170, 176, 202
Clytemnestra 190
Coates, Paul 76
Cohn-Bendit, Daniel 79
Cold War 110–11
colonialism 91
comedy 1–24
  black comedy 20, 169
  comédie humaine 134
  deadpan 62–63, 72, 95
  double act 128
  and ethics 5–15, 49–53
  situation comedy 155
  slapstick 155
comic book 124
communism 16, 133
complicity 36, 64–65, 90–91, 149, 151, 161, 168, 181, 192
concentration camp 1–4, 15, 79, 156, 158–59, 167–68, 173–74, 176, 183–84, 192
confession 173, 175, 176, 195
Congo 91
Conrad, Joseph 33
conscience 156, 174, 179
Conter, Claude 170, 173
contrition 99, 190
Copjec, Joan 66–67, 77, 104, 106
corpses 32, 34, 60, 75–76, 92, 96, 122, 152, 171, 174
Corrigan, Timothy 64
Cosgrove, Mary 23, 85–86
crime 12, 20, 34, 37, 58, 97, 163, 173–75, 177, 179, 184, 189, 191
  war crime 122, 169, 177
  see also Nazism: Nazi crimes
Critchley, Simon 18, 44, 53, 54
cruelty 14, 18, 35, 41, 53, 70, 91, 112, 114, 117–19, 134–35, 140, 148, 151, 158, 178–79, 190, 201
crying 6, 42, 54, 63, 75, 93
  see also women: woman's weepie
Cukor, George:
  The Chapman Report 43
culture 12–14, 17, 19, 21–22, 86, 101, 103, 105, 123, 138, 149–50, 153, 164, 168–69, 171, 180, 182, 192, 195
  cultural anthropology 182
  cultural criticism 5
  cultural memory 137
  cultural trauma 5, 14

mass 10, 19
multiculturalism 127, 137, 140
shame 179
victimized 20–21
visual 132
culpability 13, 15, 16, 17, 24, 168, 173, 189
   see also German: culpability
Czech Republic 111
Czechoslovakia 117

Davies, Christie 9, 10, 150
death 10, 12, 39, 40–42, 72–73, 78, 93, 120–22, 127, 144, 147, 152, 156–57, 174, 177, 179, 184, 190, 199–200
death camp, see extermination camp
Deleuze, Gilles 69–70, 78
deportation 1, 3, 116–17, 138, 168
derision 22, 86, 88, 91, 93, 158, 170
Derrida, Jacques 146
Diagnostic and Statistical Manual for Mental Disorders III (DSM-III) 13–14
Die Welt 162
diegesis 19, 60, 63, 68, 74, 123, 181
director 2, 21, 24, 43, 58, 65, 68–69, 74–76, 78, 123, 126, 130, 133, 148, 201
discourse 2, 9, 16, 17, 24, 36, 52, 73, 77, 85–86, 111, 119, 124, 127, 135, 140, 150, 173–74, 181, 195, 202
disgrace 114, 179
distance 3, 7–8, 10, 19–21, 31–32, 36–37, 48, 51, 54, 62–64, 68, 70, 85, 94, 127, 148–49, 155, 158, 160, 181, 199–200
Döblin, Alfred 72
documentary 110–12, 126, 128, 141, 180, 201
drama 31, 133, 146, 157
   family drama 67, 141
   threesome drama 41
dreams 9, 34, 36–37, 44, 67, 87, 97, 99, 187, 190
Dürrenmatt, Friedrich 18
Dyer, Richard 136

East Germany, see German: Germany: German Democratic Republic (GDR)
Eberhardt, Joachim 38–39
Egypt 34, 49
Eichmann, Adolf 183, 184, 187, 188
Electra 189
Elsaesser, Thomas 43, 59, 65–66, 70–72, 77
emotion 2–4, 8, 53–54, 59, 62, 77, 93, 115, 151, 155, 160, 163, 174–79, 199, 200
   see also identification: emotional
empathy 5, 51, 112, 117, 125–26, 138, 145, 147, 151, 200
England 96
   English 152–53
enjoyment 4, 6–10, 19, 23, 42–43, 49, 54, 60, 61, 65–67, 68, 86, 94, 103, 105, 112, 128–29, 144–45, 147, 150, 157, 162, 164, 173, 187, 192, 200–02
entertainment 19, 43, 45, 49, 67, 81, 151, 152
   entertainment industry 19, 170

Epstein, Leslie:
   King of the Jews 21
Erinyes (Furies) 179, 190, 191–92, 202
erlebte Rede 48–49, 51–52
eroticism 64, 67, 70, 89, 147, 193
   homoeroticism 102
essay 24, 31, 73, 144–48, 150–51, 201
ethics 5–15, 18–24, 31–33, 35, 37, 44, 49, 51–54, 59, 65, 77–79, 81, 85–86, 99–101, 103–06, 112, 118, 120–21, 126, 135, 141, 145, 150, 158, 163, 170, 174–75, 178, 180, 195, 200–02
   ethics of representation 5, 11, 86
   see also comedy: and ethics; morality
ethnicity 110, 127–28, 140, 148, 150, 172
   multi-ethnicity 31, 134–35, 137–38
   see also joke: ethnic
Eumenides, see Furies, the
Europe 9, 46, 127, 137, 145
   Eastern Europe 16, 92, 127, 134, 172
   Western Europe 132, 172
European Union (EU) 110–11, 127, 135, 137
Eurydice 39, 41
Everyman 71, 188
evil 11, 20, 21, 33–35, 41, 66, 67, 119, 163, 177–78, 185, 186, 200, 202
exculpation 16, 24, 173, 190, 193, 195, 201–02
execution 78, 117, 122, 165, 167–68, 190, 192–93
exile 91–93, 100, 156, 192
expulsion 16–17, 111, 117, 127, 137
   and the *Bund der Vertriebenen* 111
   and the *Vertriebenenverbände* 127
extermination camp 77, 158, 188

fact 1–2, 4, 24, 41, 94–95, 145–48, 180–82
fairy tale 37, 171, 174, 178, 202
family 113–15, 120, 126–27, 139, 153, 160, 194
Fanon, Frantz 9–10
fantasy 169, 173, 175, 180, 190, 195, 202
farce 59, 125, 150
fascism 193–95
Fassbinder, Rainer Werner 2, 24, 58–81, 123, 200
   Der amerikanische Soldat 62, 62
   Angst essen Seele auf 62, 64–65
   Angst vor der Angst 61
   Berlin Alexanderplatz 69–76
   Die bitteren Tränen der Petra von Kant 64
   Die dritte Generation 58
   Effi Briest 59
   Faustrecht der Freiheit 60, 62, 66
   Gastarbeiter 68
   Götter der Pest 58
   Der Händler der vier Jahreszeiten 58, 66
   In einem Jahr mit 13 Monden 69–70, 73–74, 80
   Katzelmacher 62, 68, 130
   Liebe ist kälter als der Tod 60
   Lola 62
   'Man's Cities and His Soul' 73
   Martha 58, 60–62, 65–66

Der Müll, die Stadt und der Tod 79
Mutter Küsters Fahrt zum Himmel 59, 66
Die Niklashauser Fart 63, 68
Rio das Mortes 58
Satansbraten 58–59
Schatten der Engel 79–80
Warnung vor einer heiligen Nutte 58, 60, 63
Warum läuft Herr R amok? 61–62
Whity 67, 76
Fassin, Didier 14
fate 167, 181, 189, 192–93
fathers 32–34, 36, 44, 48, 64, 67, 75, 114, 119, 124–25, 137–39, 140, 144, 152–54, 157, 163, 169, 171, 189, 190
  grandfathers 89–90, 127, 135, 139, 152–53, 159
  patricide 189
  stepfathers 169, 171, 174, 184, 189
Faust 188, 189, 191, 202
fear 6, 10, 19, 21, 34, 44, 47, 96, 103, 106, 117, 120, 122, 151, 159, 174–75, 176, 179, 183
female 24, 31, 34, 88, 101, 102, 133, 151
  body 19, 54, 64, 70, 88, 93, 103
  readers 162, 188
  suffering 33, 43
  see also women
femininity 5, 10, 19, 36–38, 69, 102, 103, 144, 199, 200
feminism 23, 144, 146
fiction 1–2, 4–5, 9, 20, 24, 31, 39–40, 43, 54, 65, 69, 74, 76, 78, 85–86, 89, 92–95, 99–101, 107, 115, 141, 145–50, 168–69, 180–81, 185, 191, 194–95, 203
film 2, 9, 22, 24, 43, 49, 58–81, 99, 146, 149, 155, 181, 193, 200
  action film 180
  adaptation 79–80
  film studies 43
  gangster film 70
  Heimatfilm 136
  heritage film 136
  Holocaust film 21, 144
  horror film 67, 180
  musical 70
  see also documentary; women: woman's weepie
First World War 90, 116
Flaubert, Gustave 33
Fontane, Theodor:
  Der Stechlin 139
forgiving 163, 164, 192
France 135, 139, 169, 187, 190
  French Revolution 91
Frank, Hans 187
Frankfurt 79
Fraser, George MacDonald:
  Flashman 187
Freud, Sigmund 7, 8, 10, 85, 101, 154
  and the superego 8, 102, 188
  and the unconscious 8
  and trauma 12

friendship 3, 44, 48, 52, 128, 131, 135, 186
Frost, Laura 10
Fuchs, Anne 21, 101
Führer, see Hitler, Adolf
Fulda, Daniel 17

Galt, Rosalind 79
Gehle, Holger 144
gender 24, 54, 69, 86, 161
genius 19, 86, 103, 186, 189
genocide 11, 110, 117, 119, 127, 138, 149, 168, 172, 179–80, 184, 188, 190–91
  see also Jews: and genocide
genre 6, 19, 23, 43, 112, 133, 146, 178, 182, 185, 202
German:
  atrocities 59, 138
  body 59, 80
  culpability 24, 173, 201
  culture 138, 164, 169, 171, 185
  ethnicity 110, 117, 127, 135, 140, 169, 171, 185
  and forced expulsion 16–17, 110, 117
  Germany 15, 16, 93, 110–11, 113, 118, 135, 138, 144, 155, 162, 168, 183–84
    Federal Republic of Germany (FRG) 16, 110–11, 132, 135, 169, 178; and the *Stunde Null* 171
    German Democratic Republic (GDR) 110, 113, 123, 132–33, 170; and collectivization 130, 132–33
    post-war 15, 21, 86, 152, 156, 169, 172, 178
    and the reunification 16, 22, 110–11, 113, 130; Eastern Territories 110
    and the *Wende* 110, 116, 133
    Wilhelmine 124, 129
    see also Nazism: Nazi Germany
  language 2, 22, 64, 89, 98, 127–28, 131, 133–34, 152, 154, 171
  literature 2, 50, 111, 149–50
    Romanticism 154; and *Todessehnsucht* 154
  Jews 18, 117, 128
  national identity 16, 71, 77, 110–11, 124, 134, 171, 188
  nationalism 172
    Greater Germany 110; *Volk* 188; *Volksgemeinschaft* 13, 116
  perpetrators 138–39
  readership 21, 61, 138, 147, 155–56, 160, 169–70
  responsibility 16, 138
  suffering 5, 16–18, 24, 59, 110–11, 118–19, 135, 140, 200–01
  understanding of the past 15–19, 21–22, 110–11, 135–38, 171, 201
  victimhood 16–18, 110, 118–19
ghettoization 144, 169
Gilman, Sander 21
Glejzer, Richard 11
God 46, 89, 98, 120, 161, 177, 179
Goebbels, Joseph 184

Goethe, Johann Wolfgang von 189
    Iphigenia in Tauris 191–92
    Torquato Tasso 69
Göring, Hermann 184
Goscinny, René and Albert Uderzo:
    Asterix in Gaul 124
grace 79, 114, 163–65, 167, 179, 192–93
Grass, Günter 20, 149
    Die Blechtrommel 170
Grimm, Erk 115–16
Grimm, Jacob and Wilhelm:
    Hänsel und Gretel 171
Grimmelshausen, Hans Jakob Christoffel von 149, 152
Grossmann, David:
    Falling Out of Time 53
grotesque 47, 87–88, 98, 112, 122, 169, 170, 173, 177–78, 194, 199, 202
guilt 13, 16, 21, 110, 113, 116, 119, 155, 163, 170, 172, 174–75, 177–79, 189, 195

Hague, The 96, 97, 105
Hanna, William, and Joseph Barbera:
    Tom and Jerry 73
Harlan, Veit:
    Jud Süß 150
Hazlitt, William 7
Heidegger, Martin 12
Hergé 191
Hermann, Irm 65
Heydrich, Reinhard 184, 187
Hilberg, Raul 182
Hillgruber, Katrin 115
Hilsenrath, Edgar 2, 180
    Der Nazi und der Friseur 19, 23, 168–79, 194–95, 202
    Nacht 169
Himmler, Heinrich 183–85, 187, 194
history 9, 13–14, 16–17, 19, 21–22, 36, 39–41, 45, 46, 59, 72, 75, 77, 80, 85, 90–92, 101, 110, 113, 115, 120, 133–35, 136–37, 140, 145–48, 150–51, 157, 159, 161, 167, 178–81, 185, 191, 194–95, 200–01
    ahistoricity 101
    chronicle 180
    family history 113, 115, 126
    historical fiction 147–48
    historical novel 145
    historical reportage 187
    historical trauma 14
    Historikerstreit 17
    oral history 111
Hitler, Adolf 15, 18, 22, 116, 171, 172, 173, 174, 175, 183, 184, 186, 187
Höller, Hans 32, 43–44, 53
Hollywood 67, 81, 110
Holocaust 2–3, 10–12, 15–17, 21–23, 85, 144–45, 147, 161, 169–70, 177, 180, 194, 200
    and the *Endlösung* 188
    and the *Muselmann* 22
    piety 11, 22, 167
Homer:
    The Odyssey 190
homosexuality 44, 70, 80, 119, 169, 186, 193–94
Horch, Hans Otto 170
horror 1, 2, 4, 11, 19, 46–47, 102–03, 112, 151, 176
Horstkotte, Silke 105
Höß, Rudolf 187
humanity 6, 8–9, 12--21, 33, 40, 42, 45, 52, 54, 59, 63, 65, 68, 74, 77–78, 85, 90, 95, 98, 104, 111, 114–15, 117, 119, 121, 123, 127, 133, 136, 140, 145, 149, 154, 163–64, 167–68, 171, 173–75, 177, 179, 182–83, 188, 195, 202
    dehumanization 7, 53, 100, 123
    inhumanity 42, 170
    subhuman 163, 176
humiliation 9, 36, 50–51, 65, 68, 78, 114, 116, 118, 126, 150, 158–61, 194, 201
humour 6–10, 21–22, 31, 46–47, 58–60. 64, 68–69, 71–72, 75, 84, 87, 91–94, 99–100, 103, 11, 122–24, 128, 130, 139, 141, 144–45, 148–49, 151–55, 159–62, 169–70, 177, 199, 201, 203
Hungary 2, 153, 168, 183
hyperbole 43, 46–47, 54, 66–67, 74, 81, 86, 98, 100, 103, 106, 124, 141, 151, 156–57, 159–60, 200
hysteria 102

Ian Fleming:
    James Bond 186
identification 5, 9, 13, 54, 59, 66, 69–76, 78, 85–86, 138, 144, 148, 183, 185, 200–01, 202
    emotional 2, 4, 42, 75
    see also melancholy: melancholic identification
identity 147, 168, 179, 187
    false 191
    mistaken 170, 179
    national 110–11, 127, 134–35, 178
    racial 170
    see also German: national identity; Jews: Jewish identity
ideology 7, 14, 21–22, 43, 59, 92, 118, 136, 149–50, 161, 170, 172–73, 178, 185–88, 202
implausibility 187, 189
incest 169, 188–89
incongruity 7, 8, 60–61, 65, 93–94, 97, 154, 156, 203
individuality 6–9, 12, 14, 18–20, 33, 41, 53–54, 59, 77, 86, 90–91, 98, 102, 113, 115, 117, 119–21, 127, 132–34, 136, 140, 145, 147, 163, 165, 167, 177, 182, 188–89, 192–93, 195
innocence 33–35, 96, 116, 118–19, 137, 174, 184, 201
Innsbruck 96
irony 2, 6, 48, 70, 72, 74, 75, 86, 103–04, 124, 126, 152–55, 159, 161–62, 164, 171, 184, 200
Israel 16, 79, 169, 172
    and the Knesset 79
    Israeli nationalism 173

Italy 79, 169

Jacobson, Howard 199
James, Henry 33
James, William 9
Jankélévitch, Vladimir 164
   Forgiveness 163
   'Should We Pardon Them?' 163
Jansen, Peter 58
Japanese 90, 92, 148
   Japanese Americans 148
Jasper, Karl 18, 195
Jay, Martin 6
Jelinek, Elfriede 20, 24
Jerusalem 104
Jews 1, 16, 21, 34, 45, 75–76, 79–80, 89, 99, 101, 117–18, 127, 128, 130–31, 137–38, 145, 149–52, 154–56, 162–63, 168–73, 178, 183, 185, 201
   East European 92, 172
   and genocide 117, 138, 168, 188–89
   Jewish history 161
   Jewish identity 21, 149, 154, 161–62
   Jewish jokes 149, 159
   Jewish stereotypes 170, 172
   Jewish suffering 117
   persecution of 152, 186
   representation of 79–80, 149
   as survivors 16, 139
   as victims 73, 75, 105, 150, 171, 174, 182–84, 186–87
   see also anti-Semitism; Austria: Jews; German: Jews; ghettoization
Jirgl, Reinhard 2, 110–26, 140–41, 201
   Die Stille 24, 111–26, 201
   Die Unvollendeten 117
joke 1–4, 8–10, 31, 65, 92, 94, 144, 148–49, 150, 158, 163, 173. 179, 202
   bad joke 150, 159, 169
   ethnic jokes 9, 148, 150
   Kalauer 123
   see also Jews: Jewish jokes
Joyce, James 33
justice 168, 170, 173, 175, 179, 189–91, 195, 202

Kafka, Franz 43, 96, 98
Kaliningrad 113, 131, 136, 138, 140
Kant, Immanuel 6, 7
   and the categorical imperative 188
Kanz, Christine 44
Keitel, Harvey 130, 132
Kennedy, John F. 124
Kertész, Imre 1–5, 11, 18, 165, 179, 193
   Kaddish for an Unborn Child 18
   Fateless 22, 167, 185
   Dossier K. 4, 167–68
   Fateless 1, 3, 4
   Fiasco 1, 2, 4, 167, 185

Liquidation 192
The Pathseeker 191
Kierkegaard, Søren 7
killing 1, 37, 63–64, 78, 114, 118, 120–22, 125, 137, 169, 171, 174, 176–77, 181–84, 189, 191
Kindertransport 90, 157
Kissingen 90
kitsch 10, 19, 147, 149, 164, 200
Kleist, Heinrich von:
   Penthesilea 150–51
Klüger, Ruth 2, 24, 144–65, 201
   Landscapes of Memory 153, 156, 159–60
   unterwegs verloren 153–55, 161–62, 164
   weiter leben 144, 147, 151–62, 164–65
Koch, Gertrud 80
Koepp, Volker 2, 24, 110, 111–12, 126–40, 140–41, 201
   Berlin — Stettin 126–28, 137
   Dieses Jahr in Czernowitz 130, 132, 138
   Herr Zwilling und Frau Zuckermann 128–32, 136–38
   Holunderblüte 131, 136–38
   Kurische Nehrung 133, 136, 140
   Memeland 131, 133
   Pommerland 130–31, 137
   Schattenland 131–32, 134–35, 137
   Uckermark 129–30, 132–34, 137, 139
Kohl, Helmut:
   'Gnade der späten Geburt' 79
Krankenhagen, Stefan 23
Kristeva, Julia 181
Kühne, Thomas 179
Kuon, Peter 180, 181
Kuzniar, Alice A. 65–66, 69

labour camp 135, 138
Lacan, Jacques 13, 121
LaCapra, Dominick 11, 12, 13, 15, 85–86. 100–01, 181, 199
Lanzmann, Claude 11
laughter 6–8, 43–44, 58, 61, 64–66, 68, 71. 75, 80, 126, 128, 131, 139–40, 155, 179, 199
Laurel, Stan, and Oliver Hardy 129, 139, 191
Leahy, Catríona 39
Lemma, Alessandra 199
Levi, Primo 2–3, 11, 77
Levinas, Emmanuel 12, 77
Levy, Dani:
   Mein Führer — Die wirklich wahrste Wahrheit über Adolf Hitler 22
Leys, Ruth 13
Lithuania 135, 140
Littel, Jonathan 2
   The Kindly Ones 24, 168–69, 179–95, 202
London 94
love 1, 13, 31–37, 41–42, 47–49, 59, 61–64, 67–72, 81, 86, 88–89, 92, 103–06, 114, 119, 121, 134, 136, 138–39, 150, 152, 154, 157, 163, 169, 171, 189, 193

Lowestoft 84–85, 105
Löwitsch, Klaus 80

Maier, Arnim 69
Majdanek 11
malice 8–9, 31, 114, 149, 151–52, 154, 156, 159–60, 162, 164, 201
Malkmus, Bernhard F. 177–78
Manea, Norman 138
Mann, Thomas 189
Märchen, see fairy tale
Marienbad 91
Marquardt, Fritz 133
masculinity 5–6, 19, 24, 35–36, 47, 54, 60, 69–72, 74, 86, 89, 162, 199
   castration 53
   emasculation 87, 96
   male body 70, 102
   male masochism 24, 60, 69–70
   male subjectivity 69–71, 74
   male suffering 70
   and melancholy 5, 19, 24, 86, 103, 200
masochism 24, 69–75, 78, 193
melancholy 5, 19, 23–24, 31, 58, 60, 84–85, 86, 90, 93, 98, 99–100, 101–04, 107, 126, 137, 139, 141, 200
   melancholic identification 86, 103
melodrama 5, 19, 23–24, 32–39, 54, 59–60, 66, 69, 80–81, 100, 103, 126, 137, 141, 199–200
   see also women: woman's weepie
memoir 144–46, 155–56, 164, 185, 201
memory 4, 20, 31, 86, 97, 100, 133, 136, 144, 160, 163–64, 174–75, 190, 201
   cultural 137
   and Holocaust studies 11
   memory studies 17
Mengele, Josef 135
Mephistopheles 187, 188, 189
metaphor 4, 33, 36, 100, 178, 185, 189, 192
migration 16, 89, 92, 110, 127, 133, 156, 169
Miller, D. A. 77
Miller, Glenn:
   'In the Mood' 73
mise en scène 63, 64, 72, 76, 81
misogyny 149, 162
mockery 3, 7, 9, 22, 91, 93, 149, 154, 171
   Spottlust 159, 161
modernism 10
Moers, Walter:
   Adolf, die Nazi-Sau 22
montage 115, 127
Morag, Raya 195
morality 2–11, 13–21, 23–24, 32–34, 41–43, 50–51, 53, 62, 68–69, 77–78, 85, 86, 90, 92, 99–107, 111, 117–18, 145–49, 160–64, 167, 170–73, 175, 178–80, 184, 188–89, 191, 194–95, 200, 202
   moral anxiety 6–7, 145, 163

moral response 2, 9, 21, 34
moral responsibility 6, 13, 16, 147, 195
moral value 10, 41, 59–60, 77, 101
play 188–89
see also ethics; Nietzsche, Friedrich
Moscow 186
Moscow Declaration 15
mothers 155, 156–57, 160, 169, 171, 189
   matricide 180, 184, 189, 190–91
mourning 23, 85–86, 103–04, 164, 199, 202
Mucci, Clara 12, 164
Mulkay, Michael 2
Müller, Heiner 122
Mulvey, Laura, 9
Munich 90
murder 31, 40–41, 54, 71, 119–21, 124, 138, 144, 150, 161, 167, 171–72, 174, 176, 179, 183, 186–90, 192, 194, 200
   mass murder 73–75, 167–68, 170, 174–75, 185, 192
Murnau, F. W.:
   Nosferatu 67
myth 37, 89, 147, 178, 180, 181, 185, 188, 190, 191, 202

Napoleonic Wars 91
narrative 3–5, 12, 14–18, 20, 24, 31–32, 35, 37–54, 71, 76–77, 84–107, 110–16, 118, 123, 126, 131, 135, 137, 139, 144, 146, 152, 155, 161, 168–69, 170, 173–78, 180–82, 185, 187–95, 199–200, 202
National Socialism, *see* Nazism
nationalism 127, 172–73, 184, 202
   see also German: nationalism
Nazism 15–16, 21–22, 59, 72–73, 79, 90, 116–18, 129, 133, 139, 152, 155, 169–73, 177–78, 180–83, 185–90, 193–94, 200, 202
   crimes of 18, 20, 138, 168, 171, 174, 188, 191
   legacy of 16, 21–22, 79, 110, 138, 171, 200
   ideology of 21, 180, 187–88, 182–83, 187–88, 202
   Nazi Germany 15, 110, 124, 127, 133, 136, 138–39 188
   Nazi party 16, 116, 123, 174–75, 185, 193
      Bund Deutscher Mädel 161; Hitler Youth 116; *Sturmabteilung* (SA) 174; Horst-Wessel Lied 71
   Nazi perpetrators 22, 24, 138
   racial ideology of 118, 168, 170–72
   Schutzstaffel (SS) 24, 117–18, 157, 168–69, 179, 182–85, 187, 191, 193
   Sicherheitsdienst (SD) 186, 194
   victims of 16, 117, 168, 200
Neale, Steve 150
Netherlands, the 79
New York 94, 152, 153
New York Times 59
Niebuhr, Reinhold 8
Niederlausitz 112
Niehaus, Michael 101

Nietzsche, Friedrich 163
  Zur Genealogie der Moral 145
Niven, Bill 17
nostalgia 136–37
novel 1–2, 4, 11, 23–24, 32–36, 38–41, 47, 50, 73, 111–15, 118–23, 126, 145–47, 149–50, 168–71, 173–75, 177–82, 184–95, 201–02

Oder-Neisse line 110–11, 113, 135
Oedipus 180, 189, 190, 202
Offenbach, Jacques 23, 92
onanism 19, 193
Orestes 180, 189, 190, 191–92
  see also Aeschylus: *Oresteia*
Orpheus 39
Orton, Joe 59
Oz, Amos 146. 147

pain 3, 5–7, 19, 23, 34, 41, 47, 53, 72, 77–78, 88, 93–94, 104, 112, 114, 116, 139, 157, 190, 194, 200
painting 5, 97, 105, 147
  landscape 133–34
  portraiture 134
Palestine 169, 172, 174
pastiche 72–73
patriarchy 36, 64, 69, 71
Paul, Jean 199
perpetrator 15, 138, 168–70, 173, 175–80, 190, 192–94
  perpetrator justice 165
  perpetrator suffering 2, 13–14
  see also German: perpetrators; trauma: perpetrator
persecution 110, 134, 144, 149, 169, 201
perversion 46, 69, 154, 169, 181, 193, 201
photography 5–6, 95, 102, 104–06, 113, 121, 134, 139, 149, 150
picaresque 176, 177–78, 187–88, 189, 191, 195, 202
Pick, Hella 15
Pipolo, Tony 81
pity 54, 106, 117, 145, 151
  self-pity 43, 71
Plato 10
pleasure 4–8, 10, 42–44, 58, 63, 76, 94, 97, 103–04, 112, 144, 147, 151, 154, 170, 173, 176, 194, 200–01, 203
Poland 111, 116–17, 127, 134–35, 171,177, 184
Pomerania 110, 135
Popkin, Jeremy D. 180
pornography 148, 149, 193
post-modernism 170
post-traumatic stress disorder (PTSD) 12–13
Pres, Terence des 20–21
Protestantism 133
Prussia 110, 113, 132, 135
Przemysl 116, 117
psychoanalysis 13, 77, 152, 199
punishment 175–76, 202
Pylades 189

Raab, Kurt 65
Raabe, Wilhelm:
  Der Hungerpastor 149
racism 8–9, 67, 148, 168, 172, 173, 182, 188, 202
  racial stereotypes 172, 173
Radnóti, Miklós 4
rape 16, 34, 36, 47, 115, 117, 147, 150, 169, 171, 174, 178, 192
Rau, Petra 180
Razinsky, Liran 193
Reagan, Ronald 79
realism 169, 182, 194
Rechtman, Richard 14
reconciliation 201
redemption 119, 168, 173, 175, 185, 191, 195, 202
refugees 113, 117–18, 132
Reinecke, Stefan 134
  representation of 10, 18, 20–21, 39, 144–45, 168, 169, 170, 194
repression 7, 21, 61, 63, 66, 69, 88, 111, 148, 169, 172, 175, 191
responsibility 59, 100, 111, 119, 174, 201
  see also German: responsibility
ressentiment 24, 110, 119, 145, 151, 158, 163, 164, 201
Restuccia, Frances 121
revenge 120–21, 145, 189
Rhodes, John David 76–77
Richter, Urs 136
Ricoeur, Paul 85, 146, 199
ridicule 7–8, 22, 32, 49, 50–52, 69–70, 72, 76, 87–88, 91, 101, 112, 125–26, 134, 141, 170–71, 184, 200, 202
Rimbaud, Arthur 40
Riva 94
Roberts, Robert C. 8–9, 9, 10, 61, 65, 203
Roth, Joseph 152
Rother, Rainer 134
Russia 118, 133, 135, 138, 174, 178, 184, 186–87

sadism 65, 167, 194
sadomasochism 58
Saint Paul 163
Sandford, John 58
sarcasm 2–3, 71
satire 7, 22, 44, 46, 58, 84, 86–88, 90–91, 93–94, 149–50, 170–71, 173, 183, 200
Sautermeister, Gert 19, 170
Schadenfreude 5, 111–12, 122, 126, 141, 201
Schelm, see picaresque
Schiller, Friedrich 8, 43–44, 53
Schmidtkunz, Renata:
  Das Weiterleben der Ruth Klüger 155
Schmitz, Helmuth 110
Schnitzler, Arthur 152
Schönberg, Arnold 33
  'Pierrot lunaire' 38
Schopenhauer, Arthur 7

Schulze, Rainer 16
Schütte, Wolfram 58, 72
Sebald, W. G. 2, 24, 84–107, 123, 126, 132, 200–01
   Die Ausgewanderten 87–88, 90–91, 94–95, 98–101, 105, 107
   Austerlitz 89–91, 98–99, 102, 104–05, 107
   Die Ringe des Saturn 84–89, 92, 94–97, 101–02, 104–05
   Schwindel. Gefühle 89–90, 93, 96–97, 102, 104–05
Second World War 79, 110, 116, 136–37, 148
Sedgwick, Eve 77
sentimentality 23, 117, 149
seriousness 2, 6, 8–11, 21, 32, 43, 63, 65–66, 72, 74, 76, 92, 99, 124, 126, 139, 149, 151, 157, 173
sex 8, 61–62, 67, 70–71, 79–80, 87, 95, 114, 123, 125, 169, 171, 174, 176, 179–81, 186, 194
   sexual difference 54, 69
   sexology 46
   see also homosexuality; incest
sexism 65
Shakespeare, William:
   King Lear 92
   The Merchant of Venice 163
shame 60, 76–79, 178–79
Shoah, the 11, 21
   see also Holocaust, the
Silverman, Kaja 69–77
Sirk, Douglas 43
slave labour 144, 168, 188
Snow White 155
Sontag, Susan 5, 65, 67, 68, 193
Sophocles:
   Antigone 121
   Oedipus at Colonus 189
South Africa 89
Soviet Union 138, 139, 182, 186
   and the Red Army 117, 122, 186, 190
Speer, Albert 184, 187
Spengler, Oswald:
   Der Untergang des Abendlandes 154
Spiegelman, Art:
   Maus 21
Stalin, Joseph 18, 116
Stalingrad 184, 186, 187
Steinlein, Rüdiger 20
Stenach 90
Stenberg, Peter 20
stereotype 21, 80, 87, 97, 132
   see also Jews: Jewish stereotypes; racism: racial stereotypes
Stettin, *see* Szczecin
sublimation 24, 103–04, 106–07, 154, 163–64, 201
sublime 10–12, 18, 22, 53, 185, 199
suffering 2, 5, 6, 10, 16–18, 22, 35, 36, 40, 42–43, 47, 53–54 58, 59–60, 65–66, 69, 71, 76, 78, 81, 85, 93, 99–100, 103, 110–12, 118, 120, 135, 140, 156, 164, 190, 200–03
   see also body: suffering; German: suffering; Jews: Jewish suffering

Suffolk 95
suicide 32, 34, 47, 50, 64, 69–70, 92, 99, 114, 118, 122, 157
survivors 5, 7, 16, 174–76, 179, 191–92, 201
   see also Jews: as survivors
Szczecin 110, 126, 127

Taberner, Stuart 162
tastelessness 88, 99
Terezín 102
testimony 12, 104, 136, 146–47, 181, 194, 201
Theresienstadt 117, 144, 156, 159
Third Reich, *see* Nazism: Nazi Germany
Torberg, Friedrich 177
torture 150, 156, 161, 188, 192
totalitarianism 167
tragedy 6, 18–19, 22, 24, 32–33, 42, 43, 64, 126, 133, 151, 167, 181–82, 185, 189–94, 202
   and catharsis 6, 191, 202, 203
tragicomedy 133
trauma 2, 4–6, 11–15, 17, 20–21, 23, 31, 35, 37, 39–40, 43, 49, 60, 77–78, 85, 99–100, 111, 118, 164–65, 168, 173–79, 190, 195, 199–202
   perpetrator 174, 177, 191, 195, 202
truth 6, 10–11, 14, 19, 33, 38, 40–41, 69, 77–78, 101, 130, 177, 178
Twark, Jill 21

Ukraine 184, 190
uncanny 6, 151, 153, 187
United Kingdom (UK) 169
   see also Britain
United States (US) 14, 79, 114, 119, 152, 156, 159, 169, 173

Vahsen, Patricia 170
Valentin, Karl:
   'Maskenball der Tiere' 58
Van den Berg, J. P. C. 175, 177
Vicari, Justin 79
victimhood 5, 15, 23, 32–33, 35–36, 41, 46–47, 54, 66, 78, 85, 105, 110–11, 118–19, 163, 165, 167–68, 170, 172–75, 192, 194–95, 200
   see also Austria: as victim of National Socialism; culture: victimized; German: victimhood; Jews: as victims; Nazism: victims of; women: as victims
Vienna 44–45, 151–52, 154, 161
Vietnam War 14
Vilnius 135
Vincendeau, Ginette 136
violence 6, 110–12, 120, 139–40, 150, 163, 168–69, 172, 174–77, 179, 183
Visconti, Luigi:
   The Damned 193
Voss, Hermann 188
voyeurism 5–6, 180

Vranitzky, Franz 16

Wales 97
Walser, Martin 46, 158
   Tod eines Kritikers 150
Wapnjarka-Podolsk 174
war 110–11, 116, 119, 153, 168–69, 183, 184–85
   war crimes 169, 177
   war literature 185
Warsaw 176
Watson, Wallace Steadman 58, 60, 66
Wehrmacht 16, 105, 184
Weigel, Sigrid 39, 40
Weimar 192
Wellershoff, Dieter 126
Werfel, Franz 152
West Germany, *see* German: Germany: Federal Republic of Germany (FRG)
Wiesel, Elie 11
women 16, 19, 31–32, 34–36, 41, 44–47, 49, 51, 63–65, 70–73, 84–86, 88–91, 93, 95–96, 99, 101, 118, 123, 129, 132–34, 137, 140, 144, 147, 149–50, 153, 156, 158, 161–62, 171, 174, 178, 186, 188, 200–01
   marginalization of 89
   objectification of 147
   oppression of 34
   and trauma 117–18
   woman's body 19, 64, 70, 88
   woman's weepie 19, 23, 31, 41–42
   women's suffering 19, 41, 51, 70, 93
   women's rights 90
   as victims 36, 51, 54, 70
   see also female; femininity
World War Two, *see* Second World War

Zionism 172–73, 202
Žižek, Slavoj 21, 22
Zupancic, Alenka 98
Zweig, Stefan 152

www.ingramcontent.com/pod-product-compliance
Lightning Source LLC
LaVergne TN
LVHW061250060426
835507LV00017B/1993